Constitutional Law in Kazakhstan

Constitutional Law in Kazakhstan

Second Edition

Beibit Shangirbayeva

This book was originally published as a monograph in the International Encyclopaedia of Laws/Constitutional Law.

Founding Editor: Roger Blanpain
General Editor: Frank Hendrickx
Volume Editors: André Alen & David Haljan

Wolters Kluwer

Published by:
Kluwer Law International B.V.
PO Box 316
2400 AH Alphen aan den Rijn
The Netherlands
E-mail: lrs-sales@wolterskluwer.com
Website: www.wolterskluwer.com/en/solutions/kluwerlawinternational

Sold and distributed by:
Wolters Kluwer Legal & Regulatory U.S.
7201 McKinney Circle
Frederick, MD 21704
United States of America
Email: customer.service@wolterskluwer.com

ISBN 978-94-035-4661-2

e-Book: ISBN 978-94-035-4422-9
web-PDF: ISBN 978-94-035-4852-4

The Author

Dr Beibit Shangirbayeva is an Associate Professor at L.N. Gumilyov Eurasian University (Nur-Sultan, Kazakhstan) where she teaches Law of International Treaties and European Union Law, as well as other subjects in Kazakh, English and Russian. She was a Fulbright Visiting Scholar (2020–2021) at Arizona State University (USA).

Beibit Shangirbayeva was born in Shalkar in the Aqtobe region. She graduated from the Kazakh State Law Academy with distinction (Almaty, 2000) and started her career as a lawyer in the oil and gas business sector. In 2003, she was awarded a full scholarship for postgraduate study and research at her alma mater. In 2006, Beibit Shangirbayeva successfully defended a dissertation on the participation of a state in international lawmaking and received a Candidate's Degree in Jurisprudence. In 2010, she was awarded a full scholarship for PhD research at the Sant'Anna School of Advanced Studies (Pisa, Italy). In 2013, under the supervision of Professor Andrea de Guttry, she successfully defended her PhD dissertation on the impact of the implementation of the International Covenant on Civil and Political Rights (ICCPR) on the protection of human rights.

In 2009, Dr Shangirbayeva was a guest postdoctoral researcher at the Sociology of Law Department at Lund University in Sweden. In 2012, under the supervision of Dr Siddharth Saxena, she completed a research stay at the Cambridge Central Asia Forum (University of Cambridge, United Kingdom). She received a fellowship from the Fernand Braudel IFER incoming programme within the European Union's Seventh Framework Programme for her postdoctoral research during 2015 at the Centre of Theory and Analysis of Law at the Université Paris Ouest-Nanterre La Défense in France.

Dr Shangirbayeva has extensive experience of working in various international institutions and diplomatic agencies. She has completed a traineeship at the United Nations (UN) Office of the High Commissioner for Human Rights in Geneva (Switzerland, 2011), has worked at the EU Delegation to Kazakhstan, and with the Embassies of Japan and South Africa to Kazakhstan. As a national expert in the EU Project on Enhancing Criminal Justice in Kazakhstan, Dr Shangirbayeva organized an international expert analysis of Kazakhstan's court management to improve the administration of justice.

The Author

Her research interests cover the theory of state and law, constitutional law, international public law and international relations, human rights and politics. Dr Shangirbayeva speaks Kazakh, Russian, English, Italian and French.

Dedication

This encyclopaedia is dedicated to the memories of my mother, Kadyr Omarovna, and my father, Yunis Ybrashevich.

Dedication

Table of Contents

Table of Contents

List of Abbreviations

CIS	Commonwealth of Independent States
CEDAW	Convention on the Elimination of all forms of discrimination against women of 1979
EAEU	Eurasian Economic Union
EPCA	Enhanced Partnership and Cooperation Agreement of 2015
FIC	Foreign Investors' Council
ICCPR	International Covenant on Civil and Political Rights of 1966
ICESCR	International Covenant on Economic, Social and Cultural Rights of 1966
IPA CIS	Interparliamentary Assembly of Member Nations of the Commonwealth of Independent States
Kazakh SSR	Kazakh Soviet Socialist Republic
MFA	Ministry of Foreign Affairs
MIA	Ministry of Internal Affairs
OP	Optional Protocol
UDHR	Universal Declaration of Human Rights of 1948
UN	The United Nations
UNICEF	The United Nations Children's Fund
USSR	Union of Soviet Socialist Republics

List of Abbreviations

Acknowledgements

I would like to express my sincere gratitude to all the universities where I studied, received degrees and worked for the opportunities of personal inner-growth and professional development they have afforded me. Special thanks to my research consultants and professors, Andrea de Guttry and Emanuele Sommario, Sergey Udartsev and Ghairat Sapargaliyev, Siddharth Saxena, Karsten Åström and Per Wickenberg, Håkan Hydén, Pierre Brunet and Jean-Louis Halpérin for their inspirations and insights into further research and for their tremendous support. I am grateful to my friend, Dariya Ainekova, for her generosity in sharing her knowledge and wisdom with me. The completion of this research would not have been possible without the help of Mrs Shirley Scott regarding my English in this work, and I am indeed indebted to her. I would also like to thank my family and my other friends for their support and their belief in me.

Acknowledgements

General Introduction

§1. An Outline of the Constitutional History of Kazakhstan

1. The gradual dissolution of the Union of Soviet Socialist Republics (USSR) led to the adoption of the Declaration of the Kazakh Soviet Socialist Republic (Kazakh SSR) on State Sovereignty of the Kazakh SSR on 25 October 1990, the document that kicked off the constitutional history of contemporary Kazakhstan. This document declared the intention of the country to be a sovereign party within the Union of Sovereign Republics (Article 1), a confederal entity that was supposed to replace the USSR.

2. Declaration on State Sovereignty symbolized the spiritual renaissance of the Kazakh people, was progressive in nature and transformative in substance, and determined further development of the statehood of the Republic. Referring to a prominent Kazakh scholar, Salyk Zimanov, one of the authors of the Declaration and a Chair of the Conciliation Commission created for finalization of the draft of the Declaration at the Supreme Council, the document has had a special role in the history of Kazakhstan and has realized the dreams of many generations of the Kazakh people to be an independent State. Two drafts of the Declaration on State Sovereignty (October 1990) were proposed to the Supreme Council, and every article of the drafts stirred up heated disputes at the Council.[1]

3. Recognizing the rights envisaged in the Universal Declaration of Human Rights (UDHR) and the right of people to self-determination, the Declaration proclaimed the sovereignty of the Kazakh SSR in its internal and external affairs and established the supremacy of the Constitution of the Republic on its territory (Article 8). State power was divided into three branches, where the Supreme Council of the Kazakh SSR led the legislative power, the President, the executive power, and the Supreme Court of the Kazakh SSR, judicial power (Article 7). The document prohibited the testing of nuclear weapons and the functioning of testing sites of other types of weapons (chemical, bacteriological, biological and others) on its territory.

1. Salyk Zimanov, *The Parliament of the Republic of Kazakhstan in the Difficult Years of Proclamation of Independence* 134–146 (2011).

4. The Law of the Supreme Council of the Kazakh SSR of 10 December 1991 changed the name of the Kazakh SSR into the Republic of Kazakhstan.[2] After that, on 16 December 1991, the Supreme Council immediately adopted the Constitutional Law of the Republic of Kazakhstan on State Independence of the Republic of Kazakhstan.

The Constitutional Law on State Independence, together with the Declaration, constituted the core foundation documents of the newly emerging Kazakhstan. The Constitutional Law was very resolute in spirit and established the full independence of the Republic of Kazakhstan. It proclaimed that Kazakhstan is a democratic State, based on the rule of law, with full power on its territory, and independently defines and conducts its internal and foreign policy (Article 1). According to the Constitutional Law, the Constitution and other laws of the Republic and norms of international law recognized by the country rule the territory of Kazakhstan (Article 4). The document confirmed the principle of separation of powers and established the Constitutional Court as a supreme body for the judicial protection of the Constitution of the Republic. The Constitutional Law included adherence of the country to human rights arising from the UDHR and generally recognized norms of international law. The Law established that Kazakhstan is a member of the international community and subject to international law.

5. As Academician Marat Baymakhanov (another founder of the constitutional development of Kazakhstan) noted, the constitutional framing and ensuring of the independence of the State was one of the primary tasks of state politics of that time. The unlimited political and economic sovereignty of the State which emerged should have been embodied into the whole system of the political and legal institutions.[3] According to the opinion of Academician Salyk Zimanov, the adoption of the Constitutional Law on State Independence led to international recognition of Kazakhstan as a sovereign State, and the Constitutional Law did not replace that, but simply developed and complemented the provisions of the Declaration on State Sovereignty.[4]

6. The Declaration on State Sovereignty together with Constitutional Law on State Independence underlay the first Constitution of independent Kazakhstan adopted by the Supreme Council of the Republic on 28 January 1993.[5]

The Constitution of 1993 replaced the Constitution of Kazakh SSR of 1978 and announced that Kazakhstan is a democratic, secular, and unitary state. As in previous documents, the division of state power into three branches was confirmed, and the principle of checks and balances was added in the text of a new document. This

2. Law of the Supreme Council of the Kazakh SSR of 10 Dec. 1991 on Changing the Name of the Kazakh SSR into the Republic of Kazakhstan. Available at: http://adilet.zan.kz/rus/docs/Z910003900_ (accessed 7 Dec. 2017).
3. Marat Baymakhanov, The Constitutional Reform: Searches and Finds in *Selected Works on Theory of State and Law* 356–362, 356 (2003).
4. Zimanov, *supra* n. 1, at 145-146.
5. The text of the Constitution of the Republic of Kazakhstan of 28 Jan. 1993 is available at: http://adilet.zan.kz/rus/docs/K930001000_ (accessed 5 Dec. 2017).

document established the supreme legal force and direct application of the Constitution, and the inviolability of the foundations of the constitutional system. Human rights and freedoms were defined as the highest values of the State, and the whole first chapter of the Constitution was devoted to fundamental civil and political, social, economic and cultural rights, and their guarantees. Chapter Two was about the foundations of the economy and society of the Republic. Chapter Three regulated state institutions. The Supreme Council was defined as a single legislative body which had a unicameral structure. The Supreme Council had a right to amend the Constitution and to elect the members of the Constitutional Court, the Supreme Court and the Supreme Arbitration Court, and other key officials of the Republic. The President of the Republic was defined as Head of State, who led the executive branch of power and guaranteed observance of human rights and the Constitution and other laws of the State. Along with the President, the rank of Vice-President was established, and both were elected by direct suffrage. The Cabinet of Ministers constituted the Government and this was responsible to the President. The Constitutional Court, the Supreme Court and the Supreme Arbitration Court and subordinate courts established by law represented the judicial power of the Republic and aimed to protect human rights and freedoms and to ensure justice and the supremacy of the Constitution. The Constitutional Court was responsible for the consideration of legal claims in compliance with the Constitution of laws and other acts, international treaties, and other obligations of Kazakhstan. The Office of Prosecutor had the responsibility to supervise the stringent and uniform application of laws on the entire territory of the Republic and had a right to carry out criminal prosecutions.

7. The current Constitution of Kazakhstan, adopted by a national referendum on 30 August 1995, replaced the Constitution of Kazakhstan on 28 January 1993.[6] With this new Constitution, Kazakhstan proclaimed itself as a State with a presidential system of government and so the status of the President of Kazakhstan was much strengthened. As per the Constitution, the President is defined as the highest official, who defines the internal and external politics of the State and guarantees the inviolability of the Constitution. The President shall ensure coordinated functioning of all branches of state power and the responsibility of state bodies to people. The bicameral Parliament is defined as the highest representative body of the Republic performing legislative functions. The Government, formed by the President, became responsible for the executive branch of power, and for leading the system of executive bodies. The Constitutional Council replaced the Constitutional Court and became a consultative body. Along with other competencies, the Council is responsible for the official interpretation of the Constitution. Rendering justice rests as usual on the shoulders of the judicial power, which consisted of the Supreme Court, local courts and other courts established by law. According to the Constitution, the judiciary is responsible for ensuring the implementation of the Constitution, and the courts should not apply laws which contradict the individual rights and freedoms

6. Constitution of the Republic of Kazakhstan adopted at the national referendum on 30 Aug. 1995 (last amendments were made on 23 Mar. 2019). Available at: http://adilet.zan.kz/rus/docs/K950001000_ (accessed 12 Jun. 2019).

envisaged in it. The local representative and executive bodies exercise local administration. As before, the Constitution has high legal force and direct application on the territory of the Republic. The Kazakh language is defined as the state language, and Russian can be used along with Kazakh in official state bodies.

8. In the view of the First President Nazarbayev, Kazakhstan did not come to the Constitution of 1995 out of the blue; even apart from the Constitution of 1993, 140 Decrees had been adopted and given the force of law by the President of Kazakhstan. Each article of the new Constitution had been discussed thoroughly.[7] Referring to Nazarbayev, the Constitution of 1995, adopted at a national referendum, became, in essence, the social contract that created Kazakhstan as a democratic, secular and social State, and delineated the responsibilities of citizens to observe the Constitution and the laws.[8]

A prominent scientist Ghairat Sapargaliyev, one of the drafters of the constitutional documents of Kazakhstan, mentioned that all four constitutional documents gradually recognized the principle of the division of state power into three branches.[9]

§2. Characteristics of Kazakhstan as a State

I. Constitutionalism and the Rule of Law

9. As per Article 1 of the Constitution of the Republic, Kazakhstan affirms itself as a State based on the rule of law. According to the official interpretation of Article 1(1) given by the Constitutional Council of the Republic on 21 December 2001, 'affirms itself' means that Kazakhstan intends to be such a State.[10] Article 3(4) of the Constitution establishes that the execution of state power in Kazakhstan is based on the Constitution and laws. The norms of the Constitution, of relevant laws and other normative regulatory acts, norms of international treaties and other obligations of Kazakhstan and normative decrees of the Constitutional Council and the Supreme Court of Kazakhstan constitute the current 'law of Kazakhstan' (Article 4(3)). The Constitution has the highest legal force and direct effect within the entire territory of the Republic (Article 4(4)). As per Article 34(1) of the Constitution, everyone must observe the Constitution and legislation of the Republic. Everyone shall be equal before the law and courts (Article 14(1)).

10. The President of the Republic is the symbol and guarantor of the inviolability of the Constitution (Article 40(1)). In his oath, the President swears to observe the Constitution and the laws of the Republic (Article 42(1) of the Constitution of Kazakhstan) strictly.

7. Nursultan Nazarbayev, *The Kazakhstan Way* 46, 76 (2006).
8. *Ibid., at* 51.
9. Ghairat Sapargaliyev, *Some Conceptual Ideas about the State System, and the Principle of Separation of Power into Branches*, 5, Bull. Inst. Legis. Republic of Kazakhstan, 5–17, 5 (2007).
10. Normative Resolution of the Constitutional Council of Kazakhstan of 21 Dec. 2001 No. 18 on the Official Interpretation of Art. 1(1) of the Constitution of Kazakhstan.

11. The laws and international treaties cannot be signed, ratified and entered into force if they are recognized as inconsistent with the provisions of the Constitution. Laws and other normative regulatory acts, recognized as unconstitutional, shall be annulled and shall not be applied (Article 73(1, 2) of the Constitution of Kazakhstan).

12. The judiciary is established by the Constitution of the Republic and constitutional law (Article 75(3)). One of the roles of judicial power is to ensure the performance of the Constitution, laws, other normative regulatory acts, international treaties of the Republic (Article 76(1)). A judge, while executing justice, shall be independent and obey only the Constitution and the law of the Republic (Article 77(1)).

13. On behalf of the State, the Office of the Prosecutor performs supreme supervision, within the limitations and forms established by law, over the observance of the laws on the territory of the Republic (Article 83(1) of the Constitution of Kazakhstan).

II. The Separation of Powers

14. The only source of state power in Kazakhstan is the people (Article 3(1) of the Constitution). As per the Constitution, the state power in the Republic is set up in accordance with the principle of division of power into legislative, executive and judicial branches, which interact with each other through the system of checks and balances (Article 3(4)). The President of the country ensures harmonious functioning of all branches of state power and the responsibility of state authorities to the people.

15. The President of the country is the Head of the State, the highest official, who determines the main directions of domestic and foreign policy (Article 40(1)). Upon the consent of the *Mazhilis* of the Parliament, he appoints the Prime Minister of the Republic. The President independently appoints ministers of foreign and internal affairs and minister of defence, and he dismisses members of the Government (Article 44(3)). The Government performs the executive power, leads the system of executive bodies and performs leadership over their activities (Article 64(1)). The local executive bodies are a constitutive part of the system of executive state bodies of the Republic (Article 87(1)).

16. The Parliament is the highest representative body of the Republic, which executes legislative power (Article 49(1)). The Parliament consists of two Chambers: the *Mazhilis* and the Senate (Article 50(1) Constitution).

17. Justice in the Republic is exercised only by the courts (Article 75(1) of the Constitution of Kazakhstan). The judiciary consists of the Supreme Court, local and other courts established by law (Article 75(3)). Interference with the activity of the courts in rendering justice is inadmissible and will be dealt with in accordance with the law (Article 77(2) Constitution).

III. National Sovereignty

18. In accordance with Article 2(2) of the Constitution, the sovereignty of the State extends all over the territory of the Republic. The State provides for the integrity, inviolability and inalienability of its territory.

19. The Constitutional Council of Kazakhstan provided a comprehensive official interpretation of Article 2(2) of the Constitution.[11] According to the Normative Resolution of the Council, the constitutional provisions that Kazakhstan ensures the integrity, inviolability and inalienability of its territory implies that the State develops and realizes a complex of measures of economic, political, military, legal and organizational character aimed at:

- strengthening the state immunity in economic interactions;
- the legal impossibility of unilateral cession of the territory of Kazakhstan to another State;
- prevention of seizure, annexation and division of the territory of Kazakhstan;
- prohibition of creation and operation of public associations which activities violate the integrity of Kazakhstan;
- lack of rights of local bodies to raise a question on unilateral secession and changing its legal status;
- imposing on state bodies duties to take necessary and sufficient measures for protection of sovereignty and territorial integrity of the Republic.

As stated in the Resolution, territorial integrity is a determining condition for ensuring national security. Territorial integrity is protected by the principles of International Law and the Constitution of Kazakhstan. Amendments and addendums to the Constitution of Kazakhstan on the change of the unity and territorial integrity of the Republic cannot be raised. Arbitrary change of the status of the local regions of Kazakhstan is not allowed. Using natural resources of the country cannot be done without the permission of Kazakhstan.

The Resolution of the Constitutional Council states that Kazakhstan provides to a foreign country land for placement of its diplomatic mission on condition of the lease. The Republic of Kazakhstan is designed to ensure integrity, inviolability and inalienability of its territory and in such cases, the land remains a property of Kazakhstan. The conditions of using land for placement of foreign diplomatic mission

11. Normative Resolution of the Constitutional Council of Kazakhstan of 23 Apr. 2003 No. 4 on Official Interpretation of Arts 2(2) and 6(3) of the Constitution of the Republic of Kazakhstan. Available at: https://ksrk.gov.kz/kk/solutions/kazakhstan-respublikasy-konstituciyasynyn-2-baby-2-tarmagyn-zhne-6-baby-3-tarmagyn-resmi (accessed 1 Aug. 2021).

are specified depending on relations of Kazakhstan with that foreign country and based on international agreements ratified by the Republic.

IV. Presidential System

20. According to Article 2(1) of the Constitution, the Republic of Kazakhstan has a presidential form of government. The form of the Government cannot be changed and has a permanent character (Article 91(2) of the Constitution of Kazakhstan). The full right to act on behalf of the people and the State belongs to the President of the country (Article 3(3)). The President serves as Head of State and highest official, who defines its internal and external policy and represents Kazakhstan in its internal and external affairs (Article 40(1) of the Constitution of Kazakhstan). He is directly elected by the people for a five-year term on the basis of universal, equal and direct suffrage by secret ballot (Article 41(1)). The Government is responsible to the President and the Parliament of the Republic (Article 65(2) of the Constitution of Kazakhstan). The President of Kazakhstan is the Commander-in-Chief of the Armed Forces of the Republic and appoints and replaces the highest Command of the Armed Forces (Article 44(12) of the Constitution of Kazakhstan).

V. Unitary State

21. The Constitution of Kazakhstan establishes that Kazakhstan is a unitary State, and the State ensures the integrity, inviolability and inalienability of its territory (Article 2(1, 2)). In line with Article 91(2) of the Constitution of Kazakhstan, the independence, unitarity and territorial integrity, form of governance are established by the Constitution, as well as the fundamental principles of the activities of the Republic laid down by the Founder of independent Kazakhstan, the First President of the Republic, and their status is unalterable.

22. The territory of Kazakhstan consists of fourteen administrative regions *(oblasts)* and three cities, Nur-Sultan, Almaty and Shymkent, which have national significance and special status. Nur-Sultan is the capital of the State (Article 2(3) Constitution). With the Decree of the President of Kazakhstan dated 19 June 2018, Shymkent, a southern city with a population of over one million, became the city of national importance, and the South Kazakhstan region was renamed as the Turkestan region with its centre in Turkestan city.[12]

12. Decree of the President of Kazakhstan of 19 Jun. 2018 No. 702 on Some Issues of the Administrative-Territorial Structure of the Republic of Kazakhstan. Available at: http://www.akorda.kz/ru/legal_acts/decrees/o-nekotoryh-voprosah-administrativno-territorialnogo-ustroistva-respubliki-kazahstan (accessed 9 Feb. 2019).

§3. State Territory

23. The territory of Kazakhstan stretches over 2,724,900 sq. km. Kazakhstan is the ninth-largest country and the largest landlocked country in the world. Its northern and western borders are shared with Russia, and this is considered the longest continuous land border in the world (7,591 km). In the east, Kazakhstan is a neighbour of China (1,783 km), and in the south with Kyrgyzstan (1,242 km), Uzbekistan (2,351 km), and Turkmenistan (426 km).[13]

§4. Population and Demographics

24. According to the data of the Bureau of National Statistics of the Agency for Strategic Planning and Reforms of the Republic, as of 1 July 2021, the population of Kazakhstan is 19,009.6 million.[14] The indigenous people are Kazakhs who are Muslims. According to the population census carried out in 2009, Kazakhs constitute 63.07% of the population. Other ethnicities are Russians – 23.7%, Uzbeks – 2.85%, Ukrainians – 2.08%, Uighurs – 1.4%, Tatars – 1.28%, Germans – 1.11%, others – 4.51%.[15]

25. According to the official statistics in Kazakhstan for 2019, the birth rate was 21.73 per 1,000 people; the mortality rate was 7.19 for 1,000 people; natural population growth was 14.54 per 1,000 people; as of the beginning of 2020, the median age was 31.9.[16]

---

13. General information on the Republic of Kazakhstan is available at the official website of the President of Kazakhstan: http://www.akorda.kz/en/republic_of_kazakhstan/kazakhstan (accessed 23 Dec. 2017).
14. Information is available at the official website of the Bureau of National Statistics of the Agency for Strategic Planning and Reforms of Kazakhstan: https://stat.gov.kz (accessed 1 Aug. 2021).
15. General information on the Republic of Kazakhstan is available at the official website of the President of Kazakhstan: http://www.akorda.kz/en/republic_of_kazakhstan/kazakhstan (accessed 23 Dec. 2017).
16. Information is available at the official website of the Bureau of National Statistics of the Agency for Strategic Planning and Reforms of the Republic of Kazakhstan: https://stat.gov.kz/edition/publication/collection (accessed 1 Aug. 2021).

Part I. Sources of Constitutional Law

Chapter 1. The Constitution

§1. Characteristics

26. The Constitution of Kazakhstan is the main legal document of the country, which contains the provisions establishing the statehood of the Republic, the guiding principles of its functioning and directions for further development. The Preamble to the Constitution recognizes that the statehood of the country is built on the ancestral land of the Kazakhs and that the people of Kazakhstan consider themselves as a peace-loving civil society committed to the ideals of freedom, equality and concord, also that the country wishes to have a respected place in the world community, and recognizes its high responsibility to current and future generations. As interpreted by Academician Ghairat Sapargaliyev, the Preamble to the Constitution of Kazakhstan reflects the spiritual condition of the people of Kazakhstan and plays an ideological and constituent role in the main body of the Constitution.[17]

27. The Constitution of Kazakhstan was adopted by a national referendum on 30 August 1995 and, apart from the Preamble, consists of nine chapters and ninety-eight articles. Chapter 1 contains general provisions and includes nine articles. Chapter 2 is devoted to the legal status of individuals and citizens, their rights and freedoms, and contains thirty articles. Chapter 3 regulates the status of the President of the Republic and consists of nine articles. Chapter 4 is about the status of the Parliament and comprises fifteen articles. Chapter 5 of the Constitution is on the legal status of the Government and consists of seven articles. Chapter 6 concerns the status of the Constitutional Council and contains four articles. Chapter 7 is devoted to courts and justice and comprises nine articles. Chapter 8 regulates local governance and self-governance and consists of five articles. The last chapter contains nine articles and is about final and transitional provisions.

17. *Constitution of the Republic of Kazakhstan. Scientific legal commentary.* Prepared by the Constitutional Council of Kazakhstan, 10 (Almaty, 2010).

§2. AMENDING THE CONSTITUTION

I. Outline

28. During its historical development, the acting Constitution of Kazakhstan has been amended several times. Amendments were passed on 7 October 1998, 21 May 2007, 2 February 2011, 10 March 2017, and 23 March 2019. Other than the ones on 2 February 2011 and 23 March 2019, these amended the procedures for making amendments and addenda to the Constitution.

29. The amendments to the Constitution of Kazakhstan made on 10 March 2017 are important since they have had an influence in strengthening the position of the Parliament of Kazakhstan. The Parliament has now been defined as a high representative body of the Republic exercising legislative power (Article 49(1) Constitution).

With the amendments of March 2017, for instance, the composition (structure) of the Government, apart from the Ministers of Foreign and Internal Affairs and Minister of Defence, upon consultations with the *Mazhilis* (the first Chamber of the Parliament), shall be submitted by the Prime Minister to the President. As an example, on 13 June 2019, at the Committee of Social and Cultural Development of the *Mazhilis* of the Parliament of Kazakhstan, the candidacy of Ashat Aimamgambetov was discussed for the position of Minister of Education and Science of the Republic. The head of the Chancellery of the Prime Minister presented this candidacy to the *Mazhilis*. After some questions to the candidate, the members of the *Mazhilis*'s Committee recommended Aimamgambetov for the position of Minister.[18]

The amendments to the Constitution of March 2017 allowed the Senate of the Parliament of Kazakhstan, upon a proposal of the President of Kazakhstan, to elect the Commissioner for Human Rights for the Republic of Kazakhstan for a five-year term and then release him from office (Article 55(1.1) Constitution).

The right of the Parliament at the joint sessions of its Chambers to delegate legislative powers to the President of Kazakhstan for not more than one year, which existed in subparagraph 3 of Article 53 of the Constitution of Kazakhstan, has been eliminated.

II. Procedure of Amendments

30. According to the current provisions of the Constitution, the President plays a leading role in the procedures of amending the Constitution. Article 91(1) of the Constitution envisages that the amendments and addenda to the Constitution may be brought to the national referendum upon the decision of the President himself, or

18. Aimagambetiv was then appointed as Minister of Education and Science. Available at: https://www.nur.kz/1799411-ajmagambetov-naznacen-ministrom-obrazovania-i-nauki.html (accessed 14 Jun. 2019).

a decision he makes based on the proposals of the Parliament or the Government. The President may avoid a referendum and bring the draft of the amendments for discussion before the Parliament.

31. The procedure for amending the Constitution is not simple per se. The President decides whether to amend by way of national referendum or by discussion in Parliament. The Parliament and the Government can make proposals to the President to amend the Constitution via a national referendum. Only the President has the right to take a decision to hold a nationwide referendum (Article 10 Constitutional Law on Nationwide Referendum).[19]

In the case where the President rejects the proposal of the Parliament to amend the Constitution via a national referendum, the Parliament has a right by a majority of not less than four-fifths of the total votes of the deputies of each Chamber to adopt the law amending the Constitution. In such a case, the President will sign the law or submit a draft thereof to a national referendum. The referendum will be counted as valid if half of the eligible citizens participate in it. The draft of the amendments and addenda to the Constitution will be adopted if more than half of the participating voters vote in favour of the amendments in at least two-thirds of the *oblasts* (regions), cities of the national significance, and the capital (Article 91(1) Constitution; Article 31(3) Constitutional Law on Nationwide Referendum).

In the case where the President decides to amend the Constitution via the Parliament, the latter discusses it at a joint meeting of the Chambers (Article 53 Constitution); having at least two hearings on the issues of amendments and addenda is obligatory (Article 62(6) Constitution). The votes of a majority of not less than three-quarters of the total number of deputies of each Chamber are required in order to make such amendments and addenda (Article 62(3) Constitution).

The draft of the amendments to the Constitution to be submitted to a national referendum or to be discussed by the Parliament should contain a judgment by the Constitutional Council on their compliance with the requirements of Article 91(2) of the Constitution. According to Article 91(2), the independence, the unity and the territorial integrity of Kazakhstan, the form of its governance, as well as fundamental principles of the activities of the Republic, established by the Founder of independent Kazakhstan, the First President of the Republic and his status are to remain unaltered.

§3. HIERARCHY

32. In the hierarchy of national legislation, any Law amending the Constitution takes the first position after the Constitution itself (Article 10 Law on Legal Acts).

19. Constitutional Law of the Republic of Kazakhstan of 2 Nov. 1995 No. 2592 On Nationwide Referendum. Available at: https://online.zakon.kz/Document/?doc_id=1009732#pos=0;0 (accessed 2 Feb. 2018).

Chapter 2. Treaties

§1. The Treaty-Making Power

33. Kazakhstan respects the principles and norms of international law, pursues a policy of cooperation and good-neighbour relations with other States, respects the principles of equality and non-interference in the domestic affairs of other States, the peaceful settlement of international disputes, and renounces first use of armed forces (Article 8 Constitution). The President of Kazakhstan defines the main directions of the country's domestic and foreign affairs and represents the country within the State and in its international relations (Article 40(1) Constitution). He has a right to speak on behalf of Kazakhstan and its people (Article 3(3) and Article 71(1) Constitutional Law on President of Kazakhstan).[20]

34. International treaties of Kazakhstan are part of the current Law (Article 4(1) Constitution). International treaty-making by Kazakhstan (i.e., the issues of conclusion, execution and termination of international treaties by the Republic) is specifically regulated by the Law on International Treaties of the Republic of Kazakhstan adopted in 2005.[21] The Law on International Treaties makes a distinction between interstate international treaties signed on behalf of the State, intergovernmental international treaties signed on behalf of the Government, and those international treaties made on behalf of state bodies directly responsible to the President and of central executive bodies (Article 2 Law on International Treaties).[22]

35. Since the Ministry of Foreign Affairs (MFA) of Kazakhstan is a state body responsible for the external affairs of the country, interactions with foreign States or international organizations on the issues of the conclusion, entry into force, execution, amending, suspension, or termination of international treaties are to be done via the MFA (Article 6 Law on International Treaties).

36. General Article 44(11) of the Constitution enables the President to negotiate and sign international treaties and instruments of ratification on behalf of the Republic.[23] The President has a right to undertake all actions related to the conclusion of international treaties and without presenting credentials (Article 10(1) Law on International Treaties). He also can issue credentials to negotiate and sign international (interstate) treaties of the Republic (Article 7(2) Constitutional Law on President).

---

20. Constitutional Law of 26 Dec. 1995 No. 2733 on the President of Kazakhstan. Available at: https://online.zakon.kz/document/?doc_id=1004068 (accessed 16 Jan. 2018).
21. Law of 30 May 2005 No. 54 on International Treaties. Available at: https://online.zakon.kz/Document/?doc_id=30012948#pos=102;-46 (accessed 30 Apr. 2020).
22. Issues of international lawmaking of Kazakhstan are discussed in Beibit Shangirbayeva, *The Role of State in International Law-Making*, Dissertation for the Candidate's Degree in Jurisprudence (2007).
23. *Here – interstate treaties.*

37. In accordance with Article 9(15) of Constitutional Law of 18 December 1995 on the Government of the Republic, the Government takes a decision to conduct negotiations and sign intergovernmental treaties.[24] The Prime Minister of the Republic represents the Government and signs intergovernmental treaties and agreements (Article 19(1) sub (3) Constitutional Law on Government).

38. With regard to an international treaty concluded on behalf of a central state body of Kazakhstan, heads of the central state bodies of the Government take decisions to initial an agreement, to adopt the text and sign international treaties, and authorize representatives to do such actions.

39. All international treaties to which Kazakhstan is intended to become a party and their drafts should pass review by the Ministry of Justice (Article 3(1) Law on International Treaties). The Ministry checks whether the document is in compliance with the laws of Kazakhstan or not, and defines the ways of expressing the consent to be bound by the international treaty.

40. The international treaties to which Kazakhstan is intended to become a party and the drafts of the international treaties following review by the Ministry of Justice are then subject to approval by the MFA (Article 3(2) Law on International Treaties). The MFA:

(1) gives an opinion on the compliance of the draft of the international treaty with the provisions of existing international agreements and other obligations of the Republic, and on other questions related to their conclusion, entry into force, execution, amending, suspension and termination; and
(2) determines the types of international treaties concluded by the Republic.

41. The Parliament of Kazakhstan participates in international treaty-making when it is necessary to receive the consent of the Parliament to be bound by an international treaty.[25]

Article 11 of the Law on International Treaties envisages that an international treaty should pass approval and consent of the Parliament of Kazakhstan if:

(1) it concerns the rights and freedoms of individuals and citizens;
(2) its implementation requires changing the national law or adoption of new law, or contains other provisions not found in the existing law of Kazakhstan;

---

24. Constitutional Law of 18 Dec. 1995 No. 2688 on the Government of Kazakhstan. Available at: https://online.zakon.kz/Document/?doc_id=1003973 (accessed 18 Jan. 2018).

25. On the participation of Kazakhstan in international lawmaking, *see*: Shangirbayeva Beibit, *The Problems of Development of National Legislation of Kazakhstan on Its Participation in International Lawmaking, Materials of International Scientific Conference 'National Legislation of the Republic of Kazakhstan: The Ways of Development'*, The Institute of Legislation, The Ministry of Justice of Kazakhstan, 150–153 (2008).

(3) it concerns territorial delimitation of Kazakhstan with other States, including international treaties on state borders of the Republic, as well as delineation of its exclusive economic zone and its continental shelf;
(4) it is about fundamentals of interstate relations, questions of disarmament or international arms control, ensuring international peace and security, international peace or collective security;
(5) it is related to the participation of Kazakhstan in interstate associations or international organizations which requires transferring its sovereign rights to the organization or establishing a legally binding force of the decisions of their bodies;
(6) it concerns state loans;
(7) it concerns economic or other state assistance to other countries, except humanitarian and official development assistance;
(8) the parties during negotiations agreed on the subsequent ratification of a treaty;
(9) it envisages that the consent of Parliament is necessary to express the will of a State to be bound by the treaty.

The Parliament, consecutively at the *Mazhilis* (the lower Chamber of the Parliament) and then at the Senate (the upper Chamber of the Parliament), at separate meetings, gives its consent to be bound by the treaty (Article 54(1(7)) Constitution).

42. The international treaties to which Kazakhstan is a State Party shall be published (Article 4(4) Constitution). The international treaties which come into force and those which have a provisional application only are published in the *Bulletin of international treaties of the Republic of Kazakhstan* and on the internet registry defined by the Government upon the proposal of the MFA. Such international treaties to which Parliament gave its consent to be legally bound should be published in the official publications of the Parliament upon the proposal of the MFA (Article 24 Law on International Treaties).

§2. Hierarchy

43. International treaties, ratified by the Republic (i.e., approved by Parliament), have priority over its laws (Article 4(3) Constitution). The Constitution of the Republic has the highest judicial force (Article 4(2) Constitution).

44. As per the official interpretation of Article 4(3) of the Constitution given by the Constitutional Council of the Republic in its Decision of 11 October 2000 No. 18/2, an international treaty concluded in accordance with the Constitution has primacy over *national legislation* of the Republic if approval or consent to the international treaty was given by the Parliament by adopting the relevant Law (national law uses 'ratification').[26] Article 1 of the Law on Legal Acts states that 'legislation' signifies the sum total of the normative legal acts adopted in accordance with the established procedure.[27]

45. There are also some questions regarding the hierarchy of international treaties of Kazakhstan concluded before the adoption of the Constitution of 1995. The previous Constitution of 1993 accepted that all international treaties have priority over the national law of Kazakhstan. In its Decision of 11 October 2000 No. 18/2, the Constitutional Council explained that the international treaties concluded before 30 August 1995 which did not require the approval of the Parliament remain valid and keep their supremacy over national legislation if such supremacy is envisaged in the law to be applied.

46. The hierarchy of other international treaties of Kazakhstan that do not require approval or consent of the Parliament has not been clearly defined so far. Answers will depend upon what is written in the treaty and which state body has concluded the treaty.

26. Normative Resolution of the Constitutional Council of Kazakhstan of 11 Oct. 2000 No. 18/2 on the Official Interpretation of Paragraph 3 Article 4 of the Constitution. Available at: https://online.zakon.kz/Document/?doc_id=1020290 (accessed 30 Apr. 2020).
27. Law of Kazakhstan of 12 Jul. 2021 No. 480-V ZRK on Legal Acts. Available at: https://online.zakon.kz/document/?doc_id=37312788#pos=3;-106 (accessed 1 Aug. 2021).

Chapter 3. Legislation and the Normative Legal Acts

§1. Types of Legislation and the Normative Legal Acts

I. Outline

47. According to Article 4(1) of the Constitution, the 'current laws' or 'laws in force' of Kazakhstan are the norms of the Constitution, the relevant laws, other normative legal acts, international treaties and other obligations of the Republic, as well as normative resolutions of the Constitutional Council and the Supreme Court of the Republic. So the wording 'the current laws of Kazakhstan' is interpreted by the Normative Resolution of the Constitutional Council No. 6/2 of 28 October 1996 as a system of norms contained in the normative legal acts adopted by eligible subjects (competent authorized bodies) in a prescribed manner and contained in international obligations of Kazakhstan.

In general, issues around the question of what the 'current laws' or 'laws in force' of Kazakhstan have been raised at the Constitutional Council of Kazakhstan many times. These include, among others, the Normative Resolutions of the Constitutional Council No. 6/2 of 28 October 1996, No. 3 of 6 March 1997, No. 3/4 of 31 July 1997, No. 20/2 of 29 October 1999, No. 3/2 of 31 May 2000.

48. In line with Article 62(8) of the Constitution, procedures for the drawing up, submission, discussion, enactment and publication of legislative and other normative legal acts of the Republic are regulated by a special law and by the regulations on the internal working procedures of the Parliament and its Chambers.

According to the official interpretation of the Constitutional Council given to Article 62(8) of the Constitution, the wording 'other normative legal acts' envisaged in the article imply any other normative legal acts that do not have legislative character. From the official interpretation of the article, it emerges that the special law covers other issues of lawmaking and law application activities of state bodies and officials, including procedures of drawing up and adopting legal acts that do not have normative character.[28]

49. As given in Normative Resolution of the Constitutional Council of 6 March 2013, the acts of the President are the Decrees and Orders of the President (Article 45(1) Constitution), the Orders of the Prime Minister (Article 69(1, 2) Constitution), the Decisions of the *maslikhats* and the *akim*, the Resolutions of the *akimat*, the laws of Parliament, the resolutions of Parliament and its Chambers (Article 62(1) and Article 72(1) Constitution). State bodies and officials of Kazakhstan enact normative and non-normative legal acts. But the Constitution of the Republic does

28. Normative Resolution of the Constitutional Council of Kazakhstan of 6 Mar. 2013 No. 1 on the Official Interpretation of Arts 62(8) and 83(1) of the Constitution of the Republic of Kazakhstan. Available at: https://ksrk.gov.kz/index.php/ru/solutions/np-ks-rk-ot-6032013-g-no1-ob-oficialnom-tolkovanii-norm-punkta-8-stati-62-i-punkta-1 (accessed 30 Apr. 2020).

not contain a full range of legal acts that could be adopted by state bodies and officials since it regulates only those that concern the current laws in force in Kazakhstan.

50. The Law on Legal Acts of 6 April 2016 No. 480-V is a special Law that regulates the issues of legislation, including their types, procedures of submission of their drafts, discussion, adoption, registration, entry into force, amending, termination, suspension, and their publication. The previous one was Law on Normative Legal Acts of 24 March 1998 No. 213-1.

51. The legislation of Kazakhstan can be classified depending on the state body which has adopted the normative legal act, whether that is the Parliament, the President and the Government (other executive state bodies), or local representative and executive state bodies. A special position is given to the normative acts of the Constitutional Council and the Supreme Court of the Republic.

II. The Parliamentary Normative Legal Acts

A. *Laws Amending the Constitution and the Constitutional Laws of the Republic*

52. Laws amending the Constitution and the Constitutional Laws of the Republic have a supreme position over other national legislation but stay subordinate to the Constitution of the Republic.

53. According to Article 62(4) of the Constitution and Article 1 of the Law on Legal Acts, the Constitutional Laws of the Republic are adopted on the questions mentioned in the Constitution and by a majority of not less than two-thirds of a total number of deputies of each Chamber.

According to the acting Constitution, Constitutional Laws are adopted in Kazakhstan on issues concerning:

(1) the description of state symbols, such as the national flag, the national emblem and the anthem, and the procedure for their official use (Article 9);
(2) the status of the President of the Republic (Article 41);
(3) the status of the First President of the Republic (paragraph 4 was added to Article 46 with the amendments of 21 May 2007);
(4) the status and activities of the Parliament and its deputies (Article 49(4));
(5) the elections of the Republic (Article 51(5));
(6) the competence, organization and activities of the Government (Article 64(4));
(7) organization and activities of the Constitutional Council (Article 71(6));
(8) the judiciary of Kazakhstan (Article 75(4));
(9) the special legal regime in the financial sphere, in accordance with the recent amendments of 10 March 2017 on establishing in the capital (Article 2(3-1)).

54. Apart from this list, there are also some Constitutional Laws adopted before the Constitution of 1995, such as the Constitutional Law Establishing the Independence of Kazakhstan of 16 December 1991, or the Decree of the President of Kazakhstan on the nationwide referendum of 2 November 1995. The Decree had the force of the constitutional level and later was transformed into Constitutional Law.

55. Laws amending the Constitution and the Constitutional Laws of the Republic are signed by the President (Article 35 Law on Legal Acts).

B. The Codes, Consolidated and Ordinary Laws

56. A Code is a Law which combines and systematizes the legal rules regulating the most important homogeneous social relations (Article 1 subparagraph 11 Law on Legal Acts). A Code is adopted on questions which concern the national budget, civil and civil procedural relations, marriage and family, environment, water, land, taxation, forest, customs, labour relations, execution of criminal penalties, administrative and criminal liability, penal procedure relations, health service, and issues of entrepreneurship (Article 8 Law on Legal Acts). So, in Kazakhstan, there are the Budget Code, the Civil Codes (general and special parts), the Civil Procedure Code, the Land Code, the Tax Code, the Customs Code, the Penal Code and the Penal Procedure Code, the Penitentiary Code, the Code on Health of Population and Health service, the Code on Administrative Offences, and so on.

57. According to Article 34(2) of the Law on Legal Acts, the drafts of any Codes should have at least two readings and discussions at separate meetings of each Chamber of the Parliament of Kazakhstan.

These Codes are then adopted for improving the structure of legislation, and to unite the Laws regulating comprehensive social relations in the field of state property, local governance and self-governance, education and science, civil protection, housing, control over and regulation of the financial market, transport, getting permissions and notifications, rehabilitation and bankruptcy, architecture, urban planning and construction (Article 9 Law on Legal Acts).

58. Ordinary laws regulate the most important social relations and establish the fundamental principles and norms envisaged in the Constitution of the Republic (Article 1 subparagraph 4 Law on Legal Acts).

59. The right to initiate legislation belongs to the President, deputies of the Parliament, the Government, but it can only be effected through the *Mazhilis* (Article 61(1) Constitution). The President has a right to define the priority of consideration for the draft laws, and those draft laws with the highest priority should be adopted within two months (Article 61(2) Constitution).

60. Laws are adopted at the separate sessions of the *Mazhilis* and the Senate (Article 54(1) Constitution). The *Mazhilis* discusses the draft of the Law, and after approval voted by a majority the total number of deputies, it is submitted to the Senate for discussion. The Senate should consider the draft for not more than sixty days. After approval by the Senate, also by a voted majority, the draft becomes Law and is submitted to the President for signature (Article 61(4) Constitution). The Codes and ordinary Laws are signed by the President (Article 35 of the Law on Legal Acts).

C. The Normative Resolutions of the Parliament and Its Chambers

61. According to the Law on Legal Acts, the Parliament and its Chambers adopt Normative Resolutions (Article 10(2)). The Constitutional Law on Parliament mentions that Parliament adopts the resolutions, along with the Senate and the *Mazhilis* of the Republic(e.g. the resolutions on the issues of their competencies, Article 13(1) Constitutional Law on the Parliament).[29] Hence the special Law on the Parliament does not specify that the resolutions of the Parliament and its Chambers are normative.

62. The Regulations on the Internal Working Procedure of the Parliament mention different cases when adoption of the resolution of the Parliament is possible but does not specify whether it is normative or not.

In general, the Parliament and its Chambers adopt Normative Resolutions if these concern their internal working procedures. For instance, in conformity with paragraph 132 of the Regulations of the Internal Working Procedures of the Parliament, the Regulations and the amendments to them should be adopted by Resolution of Parliament at a joint session of the two Chambers by a majority of votes of the total number of the deputies of each Chamber. The Regulation enters into force upon adoption.[30]

The Constitutional Law on Parliament says that the Regulations on its Internal Working Procedures of the Parliament and its Chambers are approved respectively by the Resolution of the Parliament, and the Resolutions of its Chambers (Article 14 Constitutional Law on Parliament). The *Mazhilis* of the Parliament on the issues of its competencies adopts these resolutions (paragraph 15 Regulations of the Internal Working Procedures of *Mazhilis*).[31]

---

29. Constitutional Law on the Parliament of the Republic of Kazakhstan and the Status of its Deputies of 16 Oct. 1995 No. 2529 (with amendments as of 2 Jun. 2020). Available at: https://online.zakon.kz/Document/?doc_id=1003961 (accessed 1 Aug. 2021).
30. Resolution of the Parliament of 20 May 1996 on the Regulation of the Internal Working Procedure of the Parliament of Kazakhstan'. Available at: https://online.zakon.kz/Document/?doc_id=1013401#pos=1;-182 (accessed 4 Feb. 2018).
31. Resolution of the *Mazhilis* of the Parliament of 8 Feb. 1996 on the Regulation of the Internal Working Procedures of the *Mazhilis* of the Parliament. Available at: http://online.zakon.kz/Document/?doc_id=1023877 (accessed 4 Feb. 2018).

III. The Normative Legal Decrees of the President of the Republic of Kazakhstan

63. In accordance with Article 45(2) of the Constitution and Article 20(1) of the Constitutional Law on the President of Kazakhstan, the President of Kazakhstan has a right to issue and adopt decrees and orders which have a binding force on the whole territory of the Republic. Only the decrees have a legislative character (Article 21(3) Constitutional Law on President).

64. Article 21 of the Constitutional Law on the President envisages that the Decrees of the President are issued on the grounds of, and for the implementation of the Constitution and the Laws of Kazakhstan. Decrees are necessary to realize the constitutional competencies of the President and to provide for the coordinated functioning of all branches of power (Article 21(2, 3) Constitutional Law on the President). The President regulates by the adoption of Decrees the issues which are not covered by the competencies of the Parliament and the Government and other state bodies. The Decrees are adopted on the strategic issues of economic and social-political development of Kazakhstan (Article 21(4) Constitutional Law on President). As an example, we could mention the Decree of the President of Kazakhstan of 5 August 2002 No. 917 on the Approval of the Regulations on the Control Committee over Fulfilment of the National Budget.[32]

IV. The Normative Legal Acts of the Government, the National Bank and the Central Executive Bodies

A. *The Normative Legal Resolutions of the Government*

65. On the issues of its competence, the Government of Kazakhstan adopts Resolutions which have binding force within the territory of the Republic. The Resolutions of the Government and the Orders of the Prime Minister should not contradict the Constitution, legislative acts, and the Decrees and Orders of the President of Kazakhstan (Article 69 of the Constitution). The Resolutions of the Government are adopted by a majority of votes of the total number of the members of the Government (Article 10(2) Constitutional Law on Government). The Resolutions of the Government are signed by the Prime Minister of the Republic (Article 35 Law on Legal Acts). For example, Resolution of the Government of Kazakhstan of 28 October 2004 No. 1120 approved Regulations of the Activities of the Ministry of Justice and its status as a state body.[33]

32. Decree of the President of Kazakhstan of 5 Aug. 2002 No. 917 on the Approval of the Regulations on the Control Committee over Fulfilment of the National Budget (with amendments as of 11 Feb. 2021). Available at: https://online.zakon.kz/Document/?doc_id=1032443 (accessed 6 Feb. 2018).
33. Regulations on the Activities of the Ministry of Justice of Kazakhstan approved by the Resolution of the Government of Kazakhstan of 28 Oct. 2004 No. 1120. Available at: http://adilet.zan.kz/rus/docs/P040001120_#z8 (accessed 5 Feb. 2018).

B. The Normative Legal Orders of the Ministers of the Republic of Kazakhstan and Other Heads of the Central State Bodies

66. The decisions of the Ministries are formulated in the Orders of the Ministers (Article 22(4) Constitutional Law on Government). The competence of the Minister and heads of other central state bodies to adopt normative decisions are usually stipulated in the Regulations (statutes) of a Ministry or central state body. For instance, the competence of the Minister of Labour and Social Protection of the Population of Kazakhstan to adopt the normative legal acts on the questions concerning labour policy in Kazakhstan is stipulated in Articles 16(3) and 22 of the Regulations on the Issues of the Ministry of Labour. The Regulations were approved by Resolution of the Government of 18 February 2017 No. 81.[34] Several ministries and state bodies can issue one common normative legal order.

C. The Normative Legal Resolutions of the Central Election Commission of the Republic of Kazakhstan

67. The Regulations on the Competence of the Central Election Commission of 11 November 1996 No. 3205 envisage that within its competence, the Central Election Commission has a right to adopt the resolutions (paragraph 6).[35]

D. The Normative Legal Resolutions of the Control Committee over Fulfilment of the National Budget

68. The Control Committee over fulfilment of the national budget of Kazakhstan has a right to adopt the normative resolutions on the issues of its competence (paragraph 6 Regulations).[36]

E. The Normative Legal Resolutions of the National Bank and Other Central State Bodies

69. On the issues of its competence, the National Bank of the Republic has a right to adopt the normative legal resolutions for the implementation of the laws of

---

34. Regulations on the Issues of the Ministry of Labour and Social Protection of the Population of Kazakhstan approved by the Resolution of the Government of 18 Feb. 2017 No. 81. Available at: http://adilet.zan.kz/rus/docs/P1700000081#z15 (accessed 30 Apr. 2020).
35. Regulations on the Competence of the Central Election Commission of the Republic of Kazakhstan approved by the Decree of the President of 11 Nov. 1996 No. 3205 (with amendments as of 10 Jul. 2021). Available at: https://online.zakon.kz/Document/?doc_id=1011251#pos=5;-106 (accessed 1 Aug. 2021).
36. Regulations on the Control Committee over Fulfilment of the National Budget approved by the Decree of the President of Kazakhstan of 5 Aug. 2002 No. 917 (with amendments as of 11 Feb. 2021). Available at: https://online.zakon.kz/Document/?doc_id=1032443 (accessed 1 Aug. 2021).

the country which have obligatory force for all financial organizations, consumers of financial services, individuals and legal entities of the Republic (Article 4 Law on National Bank).[37]

F. *The Normative Legal Orders of Heads of the Committees (or the Governmental Agencies) Within the Central State Bodies*

70. The committees or the governmental agencies within the central state bodies have a right to issue normative legal orders. For instance, the Committee on the Regulation of Natural Monopolies of the Ministry of National Economy has the right to adopt normative legal acts on the issues of its jurisdiction.[38]

V. Normative Legal Acts of Local Governance and Self-Governance Bodies

A. *Normative Legal Decisions of the* Maslikhats

71. In accordance with Article 88(1) of the Constitution of Kazakhstan, the *maslikhats* (the local representative bodies) and *the akims* (heads of the local executive bodies) adopt the decisions on the issues of their competencies that have obligatory force within the relevant administrative-territorial unit of the country.

B. *Normative Legal Resolutions of the* Akimats, *Normative Legal Decisions of the* Akims

72. The power of *the akim* to adopt normative decisions is replicated in Article 37(3) of the Law on the Local Governance and Self-Governance in the Republic of Kazakhstan.[39]

In general, the *akimats* adopt the resolutions for the realization of the Constitution of the Republic and other legislation (Article 37 Law on Local Governance and Self-Governance). The resolutions are signed by the *akims*. As per Article 27(1 sub (1-13)) of the Law on Local Governance and Self-Governance, the *akimats* of the regions (*oblast*), cities of special national importance, and the capital adopt normative legal acts which provide for the implementation of state policy at the local level. Those acts of the *akimat* have obligatory force over the whole territory of the relevant administrative-territorial unit.

---

37. Law on the National Bank of the Republic of Kazakhstan (with amendments as of 1 Jul. 2021). Available at: https://online.zakon.kz/Document/?doc_id=1003548#pos=0;0 (accessed 30 Apr. 2020).
38. Regulations on the Committee on Regulation of Natural Monopolies of the Ministry of National Economy approved by the Order of the Minister of National Economy of 29 Jul. 2019 No. 190. Available at: http://adilet.zan.kz/rus/docs/G19NT000190 (accessed 26 Sep. 2020).
39. Law on Local Government and Self-Governance of 23 Jan. 2001 No. 148. Available at: http://adilet.zan.kz/rus/docs/Z010000148_ (accessed 30 Apr. 2020).

VI. Normative Resolutions of the Constitutional Council and the Supreme Court of the Republic of Kazakhstan

73. In accordance with Article 74(3) of the Constitution, the Constitutional Council takes decisions which have obligatory force over the entire territory of the Republic. These normative resolutions are final and cannot be subject to appeal. In general, there are several kinds of decisions taken by the Council, and only Normative Resolutions are a part of the acting law of Kazakhstan (Article 32 Constitutional Law on Constitutional Council).[40]

74. The Constitutional Council of Kazakhstan adopts Normative Resolutions interpreting officially the provisions of the Constitution. Normative Resolutions are also adopted by the Council if they concern consideration for compliance with the Constitution of laws adopted by the Parliament before signing by the President; consideration of the Resolutions of the Parliament and its Chambers for their compliance with the Constitution; consideration of international treaties for their compliance with the Constitution before receiving the consent of Parliament to be bound by the treaty; review of the constitutionality of Laws and other normative legal acts upon the request of the courts, and, upon the request of the President, review of the constitutionality of Laws and other normative legal acts proposed for the protection of human rights and other values (Article 44(10-1) of the Constitution).[41] According to Article 5 of the Law on Legal Acts, the Normative Resolutions of the Constitutional Council are based only on the Constitution of the Republic, and consequently, other normative legal acts cannot contradict the Normative Resolutions of the Council.

75. The Supreme Court of Kazakhstan also adopts Normative Resolutions, as per Article 17(2(3)) of the Constitutional Law on the Judicial System and the Status of Judges of the Republic of Kazakhstan.[42] The Normative Resolutions of the Supreme Court of Kazakhstan contain an explanation of the issues within the judicial practice of the country (Article 5(3) Law on Legal Acts). The Normative Resolutions are adopted at the plenary session of the Supreme Court by at least two-thirds of the number of the Supreme Court's judges on a quorum of at least three-fourths of the total number of the Supreme Court's judges (Article 22(1(3)) Constitutional Law on Judicial System).

76. As an example of the Normative Resolutions of the Supreme Court of Kazakhstan can be mentioned that of 10 July 2008 on the application of international

40. Constitutional Law of 29 Dec. 1995 No. 2737 on the Constitutional Council (with amendments as of 22 Dec. 2017). Available at: https://online.zakon.kz/Document/?doc_id=1004022#pos=2;-97 (accessed 30 Apr. 2020).
41. Website of the Constitutional Council of Kazakhstan: http://ksrk.gov.kz/index.php/ (accessed 30 Apr. 2020).
42. Constitutional Law of 25 Dec. 2000 No. 132-II on the Judicial System and the Status of Judges (with amendments dated 21 Feb. 2019). Available at: https://online.zakon.kz/Document/?doc_id=102116 4#pos=5;-106 (accessed 30 Apr. 2020).

treaties to which Kazakhstan is a party.[43] This explains why and how to apply international treaties in court decisions and what the consequences are of non-application or incorrect application of the provisions of international treaties.

Another example is the Normative Resolution of the Supreme Court No. 1 dated 15 January 2016 on Access to Justice and the Competence of the Supreme Court in the Revision of Judicial Acts. The Supreme Court clarified the practice of the application of legislation on access to justice and the competence of the Supreme Court to revise judicial acts and to study judicial practice.[44]

§2. Hierarchy

77. Article 10 of the Law on Legal Acts establishes the following hierarchy of normative legal acts:

(1) The Constitution (the highest judicial force).
(2) The Laws amending the Constitution.
(3) The Constitutional Laws of Kazakhstan.
(4) The Codes of Kazakhstan.
(5) The consolidated and ordinary Laws of Kazakhstan.
(6) The Normative Resolutions of the Parliament of Kazakhstan and its Chambers.
(7) The Normative Legal Decrees of the President of Kazakhstan.
(8) The Normative Legal Resolutions of the Government.
(9) The Normative Legal Orders of the Ministers of Kazakhstan and other heads of the central state bodies, the Normative Legal Resolutions of the Central Election Commission of Kazakhstan, the Control Committee over Fulfilment of the National Budget, the National Bank and other central state bodies.
(10) The Normative Legal Orders of heads of the committees (or the governmental agencies) within the central state bodies.
(11) The Normative Legal Decisions of the *maslikhats*, the Normative Legal Resolutions of the *akimats*, the Normative Legal Decisions of the *akims* and the Normative Legal Resolutions of the revision commissions.

78. According to this Article, the acts (formal decisions) of the Chair of the Security Council of Kazakhstan, the Normative Resolutions of the Constitutional Council and the Supreme Court of Kazakhstan are outside the hierarchy of these normative legal acts. In accordance with Article 5(1) of Law on Legal Acts, none of the normative legal acts should contradict the normative resolutions of the Constitutional Council.

43. Normative Resolution of the Supreme Court of Kazakhstan No. 1 of 10 Jul. 2008 on the Application of International Treaty Norms. Available at: http://www.zakon.kz/117905-normativnoe-postanovlenie-verkhovnogo.html (accessed 26 Feb. 2019).

44. Normative Resolution of the Supreme Court No. 1 of 15 Jan. 2016 on Access to Justice and the Competence of the Supreme Court in the Revision of Judicial Acts'. Available at: https://online.zakon.kz/Document/?doc_id=38948636#pos=3;-70 (accessed 30 Apr. 2020).

Chapter 4. Administrative Regulations and Orders (Non-normative Legal Acts)

§1. Classification

I. Nationwide Level

A. The Decrees and the Orders of the President of Kazakhstan

79. In line with Article 45(2) of the Constitution and Article 20(1) of the Constitutional Law on the President of Kazakhstan, the President has a right to adopt Decrees and Orders which have a binding force over the whole territory of the Republic. The Decrees of the President of Kazakhstan are intended to implement the Constitution and the Laws of Kazakhstan; the Orders are adopted to implement the Decrees of the President of the Republic as well (Articles 21(1), 22(1) Constitutional Law of Kazakhstan on the President).

80. Decrees of the President of administrative nature are used, for example, to appoint (dismiss) the judges, the Ministers and the Prime Minister, the Chair of the Committee on the National Security of the Republic, the Chair of the Central Election Commission of Kazakhstan, the Chair of the Control Committee over fulfilment of the national budget, the Chair of the National Bank of Kazakhstan, etc.

81. The Orders of the President are used purely to solve administrative, operational and individual issues; they are adopted in the case of appointment and dismissal of the officials who do not have a constitutional status (Article 22(2,3) Constitutional Law of Kazakhstan on President).

82. In the case of discrepancies between the acts (legal documents) of the President of the Republic having the same legal force, the more recent should prevail unless other conditions are envisaged in the relevant act of the President (Article 24(3) Constitutional Law of Kazakhstan on President).

B. The Resolutions of the Government and the Orders of the Prime Minister

83. Article 10 of Constitutional Law on the Government of Kazakhstan regulates the issues of the legal acts of the Government. According to this, the Government adopts Resolutions of an individual character (on individual issues) as well. The Orders of the Prime Minister embraces administrative, operational and individual issues. Both documents should be adopted in line with the procedures and legal techniques envisaged in the Regulations of the internal working procedures of the Government. The Resolutions of the Government must be abolished by the Government; the Orders of the Prime Minister may be abolished by the Government and the Prime Minister.

84. Chapter 4 of Regulations of the Internal Working Procedures of the Government of Kazakhstan is devoted to the issues of the procedure of adoption of the Resolutions and the Orders of the Government.[45] In accordance with section 4.1 of Regulations, responsible state bodies prepare the drafts of the Resolutions; the drafts of the Resolutions and the Orders of the Prime Minister can be prepared by the Chancery of the Prime Minister of Kazakhstan. The Resolutions of the Government and the Orders of the Prime Minister are signed by the Prime Minister; the registration and recording are done by the Chancery of the Prime Minister of Kazakhstan. The signed Resolutions should be stamped with the seal of the Government (sections 4.7 and 4.8 Regulations).

C. *The Orders of the Ministers and Heads of the Central Executive Bodies and of the Committees (or the Governmental Agencies) Within the Central State Bodies*

85. The decisions of the Ministry are formulated in the Orders of the Minister (Article 22(4) Constitutional Law on Government). For instance, the decisions of the Ministry of Labour and Social Protection of the population of Kazakhstan are formulated in the Orders of the Minister, according to Chapter 1(7) of Regulations on Issues of the Ministry of Labour of Kazakhstan.

86. The Chair of the Control Committee over fulfilment of the national budget of Kazakhstan has the right to adopt the orders on the issues of his competence (as per paragraph 19(3) Regulations on Competence of the Control Committee over Fulfilment of the National Budget).

87. The Central Election Commission issues the decisions and other acts regarding the organization and conduct of elections (paragraph 15(37) Regulations on Competence of the Central Election Commission).

88. The committees within the ministry formulate their decisions in the Orders of the head of the committee (Article 24(5) Constitutional Law on Government). If necessary, the central executive bodies can adopt one joint order in order to solve the problems of their joint competencies (paragraph 17, Chapter 2 Regulations of Internal Working Procedures of Government).

45. Regulations of the Internal Working Procedures of the Government of the Republic of Kazakhstan approved by the Resolution of the Government of Kazakhstan of 10 Dec. 2002 No. 1300. Available at: http://adilet.zan.kz/rus/docs/P020001300_ (accessed on 30 Apr. 2020).

II. The Local Administrative-Territorial Level

A. *The Decisions of the* Maslikhat, *the Orders of the* Akims *and the Resolutions of the* Akimat

89. The *maslikhat* (a local representative body) adopts the Decisions (Article 7 of the Law on Local Governance and Self-Governance). The local representative bodies work in accordance with the internal working procedures adopted in line with Article 9 of the Law on Local Governance. So, for instance, the internal working procedure of the *maslikhat* of the *Shortandy* district envisages that the *maslikhat* adopts the Decisions by a majority of the voices of the total number of deputies of the *maslikhat* if other procedures are not stipulated by the Law (paragraph 18 Internal Working Procedures of the *Maslikhat* of *Shortandy* District).[46]

90. In accordance with Article 37 of the Law on the Local Governance and Self-Governance in the Republic of Kazakhstan, the *akim* (head of the local executive bodies) adopts the Orders of an administrative, operational and individual character as well, and the *akimat* (a local executive body) adopts the Resolutions. The *akim* signs the Resolution of the *akimat*. If necessary, three local bodies can adopt one joint Resolution of an administrative character, for instance, on the issue of renaming the main street of a city.

§2. Hierarchy

91. In general, administrative acts are adopted by all state bodies that are authorized to implement legislation. The hierarchy of the issued administrative regulations and orders depends on the hierarchy of the state body, which adopts the legal document. A legal document of non-normative character can be adopted, for instance, by the regional departments regulating issues of education, construction or taxation. The following, but a non-comprehensive hierarchy of such non-normative legal acts may be proposed:

(1) The Decrees and the Orders of the President of Kazakhstan.
(2) The Resolutions of the Government and the Orders of the Prime Minister.
(3) The Orders of the Ministers and Heads of the Central Executive Bodies, and the Orders of the Heads of the Committees (or the Governmental Agencies) within the central state bodies.
(4) The Decisions of the *maslikhat*, the Orders of the *akims* and the Resolutions of the *akimat*.

46. Internal Working Procedure of the *Maslikhat* of *Shortandy district* of 8 Jun. 2016 No. C-3/4, approved by the Decision of the *Maslikhat* of *Shortandy* district. Available at the official web site of the *Maslikhat*: http://maslihat-short-old.akmol.kz/reglament_maslixata.html#77 (accessed 30 Jul. 2019).

Chapter 5. Codification, Interpretation and Publication

§1. Codification

92. Chapter 11 of Law on Legal Acts of Kazakhstan regulates the issues of systematization and record-keeping of the normative legal acts in Kazakhstan. In accordance with Article 52 of the Law, the state bodies that adopt the normative legal act keep records and systematize such acts. They maintain the control copies of the adopted documents and make timely amendments and addenda to them.

93. The state record of the normative legal acts includes the State Registry of the Normative Legal Acts of Kazakhstan and the Standard Control Bank of the Normative Legal Acts of the Republic of Kazakhstan (Article 53(1) Law on Legal Acts). The Standard control bank of the normative legal acts is a bank of all paper and electronic copies of the normative legal acts registered in the State Registry of the Normative Legal Acts of the Republic. The National Center of Legal Information of the Ministry of Justice is responsible for the maintenance of the Standard Control Bank.[47]

94. The state bodies adopting the normative legal act should submit the paper and electronic copies of the documents to the State Registry of the Normative Legal Acts of Kazakhstan and the Standard control bank of the normative legal acts for keeping records. The control bank plays a role as a single centralized depository of electronic versions of all normative legal acts of Kazakhstan certified by the electronic signature of the body adopting the document. Its information array is updated daily in the Kazakh and Russian languages.

95. The Ministry of Justice of Kazakhstan creates a unified system of legal information and assists the central executive and other central state bodies in their search of data and enquiries (Article 53(5) Law on Legal Acts).

96. The legal acts of the *akimats* and (or) the *akims* that have a common obligatory force and concern rights, freedoms and duties of citizens should be registered by the local representation of the Ministry of Justice in accordance with the established procedure (Article 37(7) Law on Local Governance).

§2. Interpretation

97. There is a general rule in the Law of the legal acts that the content of the legal act should be clear to avoid misinterpretation (Article 24(3)). Chapter 13 Law on Legal Acts is devoted to the issues of giving clarifications to the normative legal

47. Official website of the National Center of Legal Information, *see*: http://www.rkao.kz/ru/node/4172.

acts of the Republic. So, in accordance with Article 58, in cases of revealing discrepancies and differences in understanding of the normative legal acts and contradictions in their application, there should be given an official clarification to the provisions of the normative legal acts. The official clarification is given only to get more specific information on the content of a legal norm and cannot change its meaning.

98. According to Article 58 of the Law on Legal Acts, the official interpretations do not constitute the normative legal acts, but they have an obligatory force in a case of application of the normative legal act. The official interpretations do not create the legal norms and do not fill gaps in the legislation of the Republic.

Depending on the situation, the official clarification of the provisions of the normative legal acts is carried out upon the initiative of the authorized bodies or upon the request of the individuals or the legal entities in line with the procedures established by the Administrative Procedures Code.[48]

99. The meaning of a legislative act (the term includes the Laws amending the Constitution, the Constitutional Laws of the Republic of Kazakhstan, the Codes, the consolidated and ordinary laws of the Republic, the normative Resolutions of the Parliament of Kazakhstan and its Chambers) should be interpreted in compliance with the provisions of the Constitution (Article 59(2) Law on Legal Acts).

The meaning of the subordinate legislative acts, i.e., other normative legislative acts in the hierarchy of the national legislation not mentioned above, should be interpreted in compliance with the Constitution of Kazakhstan, laws and the principles of legislative regulations (Article 59(1) Law on Legal Acts).

100. In accordance with Article 72(1(4)) of the Constitution, the Constitutional Council provides the official interpretation of the provisions of the Constitution of Kazakhstan. The right of the Parliament to provide the official interpretation of its adopted laws is not established by the Constitution. 'There is a great need for the interpretation of the current legislation. Only the Parliament can provide an authentic interpretation of the laws.'[49]

101. In conformity with Article 60(2) of the Law on Legal Acts, the official interpretation of the normative legal acts of the Government is carried out upon the instruction of the Prime Minister by the Ministry of Justice jointly with the interested state bodies. The Regulations of the internal working procedures of the Government say that the instruction to give the official interpretation to the normative legal acts of the Government can be done not only by the Prime Minister but also by the Government (paragraph 6 of the Regulations of the internal working procedures of the Government).

---

48. Administrative Procedures Code of Kazakhstan of 29 Jun. 2020 No. 350-VI ZRK. Available at: https://online.zakon.kz/document/?doc_id=35132264#pos=3;-110 (accessed 1 Aug. 2021).
49. Ghairat Sapargaliyev, *Some Conceptual Ideas about the State System, and the Principle of Separation of Power into Branches*, 5, Bull. Inst. Legis. Republic of Kazakhstan, 5–17, 5 (2007).

102. The official interpretation of the normative legal resolutions of the Central Election Commission of Kazakhstan, the Control Committee over fulfilment of the national budget, the National Bank and other central state bodies, the normative legal orders of the ministers of Kazakhstan and other heads of the central state bodies, the normative legal orders of heads of the committees within the central state bodies, the normative legal decisions of the *maslikhats*, the normative legal resolutions of the *akimats*, the normative legal decisions of the *akims* and the normative legal resolutions of the revision commissions are carried out by the relevant state bodies or the officials that adopted the document (Article 60(3) Law on Legal Acts).

103. The state bodies that carry out and implement state policies in the field can, within their competence, provide interpretations of the normative legal acts with regard to their application to any specific persons or case. Such interpretations are not legally binding and have the character of recommendations (Article 60(4) Law on Legal Acts).

104. The document which provides the official interpretation of the normative legal act should consist of its introductory, descriptive and conclusive parts (Article 61(1) of the Law on Legal Acts). The document should be published on the website of the authorized body (official) that provided the interpretation (Article 62(1) Law on Legal Acts).

§3. Publication

105. The official publication of the normative legal acts is aimed to disseminate the full text of the normative legal act in Kazakh and Russian for general knowledge, information and their correct application. Chapter 8 of the Law on Legal Acts of the Republic regulates the general issues of the official publication of the normative legal acts of Kazakhstan. According to the Constitution of the Republic, the official publication of the normative legal acts concerning human rights and duties of citizens is an obligatory condition of their application.

106. The official publication of the normative legal act in Kazakhstan means publication for general information of the full text of the normative legal act in the Kazakh and Russian languages in the standard control registry of electronic versions of the normative legal acts of the Republic, in the official, printed publications, as well as in print periodicals in cases stipulated by the Law (Article 1(30) of the Law on Legal Acts). The National Center of Legal Information of the Ministry of Justice is responsible for the electronic publication. People have free access to the database of the Standard control bank of the normative legal acts via the website *http://zan.gov.kz/client/#*.

107. The Bulletin of the Parliament, the Collection of Acts of the President and the Government of Kazakhstan, the Bulletin of the National Bank of Kazakhstan are considered the official editions in Kazakhstan (Article 37(1) Law on Legal Acts).

Some periodicals also make an official publication of the legislative acts if they receive such a right via special competition.

108. The first official publication of the normative legal acts should be done simultaneously in the Kazakh and Russian languages within thirty calendar days from the day of their entry into force.

As a general rule, the texts of any normative legal act shall be published in full. If the text of the document is too large, it may be published in several issues of a periodical publication. In such case, the day of the last issue with the final part of the document in Kazakh and Russian is considered as the day of its official publication (Article 40 Law on Legal Acts).

Any non-official publication can be done only after the official publication of the normative legal act (Article 37(6) Law on Legal Acts).

Part II. Form of Government

Chapter 1. General

§1. Introduction

109. Kazakhstan declared itself as a Republic with a presidential form of government (Article 2 Constitution). According to the Constitution, the single source of power in Kazakhstan is the people. The people exercise power directly, or through republican referenda and free elections, and delegate the exercise of their power to the state bodies as well. No one can arrogate power in Kazakhstan. Usurpation of power is prosecuted by law. The right to speak on behalf of the people and the State belongs to the President of Kazakhstan; the Parliament also has the right to do so within its constitutional competencies. The Government of the Republic and other state bodies have the right to speak on behalf of the State within their delegated competencies (Article 3 Constitution).

110. The Constitution of Kazakhstan has supreme legal force in the Republic and was adopted by the people via a referendum. State power in Kazakhstan is unified and realized on the basis of the Constitution and the law, in accordance with the principle of division of state power into three branches (legislative, executive and judicial) using a system of checks and balances (Article 3(4) Constitution).

111. For the first time in the history of Kazakhstan, the office of the President had been established on 24 April 1990 by Law on Establishing the Post of the President and Making Amendments and Addendums to the Constitution (Organic Law) of the Kazakh SSR.[50]

According to the current Constitution dated 30 August 1995, the President is the Head of State and the highest official. He ensures the coordinated functioning of all branches of state power and the responsibility of the authorities to the people (Article 40 Constitution). He is elected by universal direct suffrage of adult citizens by secret ballot, voting every five years (Article 41(1) of the Constitution). The President of Kazakhstan is the symbol of the unity of the people and of state power, the inviolability of the Constitution, and the rights and freedoms of human beings and citizens (Article 40 Constitution).

50. Alima Auanasova & Yerkesh Nurpeisov, *The Institute of Presidency – step towards the democratic changes*, Newspaper *Kazakhstanskaya Pravda* of 30 Nov. 2018.

Chapter 2. Head of State

§1. Designation

112. According to the provisions of the current Constitution, the President is elected for five years. The Constitution of Kazakhstan prescribes the following for any candidate for the presidency: citizenship of Kazakhstan by birth, not younger than 40 years of age, fluency in the state language, residence in Kazakhstan for the last fifteen years, and degrees from higher education. Additional requirements for a candidate for a president can be established by the Constitutional Law (Article 41(2) Constitution).

113. On 25 April 2019, the Normative Resolution of the Constitutional Council of Kazakhstan provided the official interpretation of Article 41(2) of the Constitution upon an appeal by the President of the Republic, Kassym-Jomart Tokayev, to clarify a residency requirement for a candidate to be President. In line with the Constitution, in order to be nominated for the position of President, a candidate needs to have been living within the territory of Kazakhstan for the last fifteen years.[51] The subsequent question for the Constitutional Council was whether the residence of a candidate abroad because of his/her diplomatic mission with overseas agencies of the Republic or with an international organization of which Kazakhstan is a Member State would be counted into 'the last fifteen years'.

The Constitutional Council came to a conclusion that the period abroad due to a person's work with the diplomatic mission or appointment to international organizations of which Kazakhstan is a Member State is counted into the length of fifteen years of residence in Kazakhstan. The members of the diplomatic mission abroad perform a state service. The Republic of Kazakhstan fulfils its foreign functions when sending its citizens abroad to work with international organizations. Kazakhstan fulfils its external functions while being a member of international organizations by sending its citizens abroad to work with the international organizations (Article 8 Constitution).

In some cases, citizens of Kazakhstan can have a leadership position within international organizations which is not due to the fact of being seconded or appointed to that position by the State. Taking into account the international mission of such officials, their long-term state and diplomatic service, their high-professional qualities and merits, such citizens are treated as the personnel of the overseas agencies of Kazakhstan. Their work within international organizations is counted as the experience of diplomatic personnel and public servants. That is in conformity with Articles 12(2) and 32-1 of the Law on the Diplomatic Service.[52]

51. Normative Resolution of the Constitutional Council of Kazakhstan of 25 Apr. 2019 on Official Interpretation of Art. 41(2) of the Constitution of the Republic of Kazakhstan. Available at: https://ksrk.gov.kz/solutions/np-ks-rk-ot-25-aprelya-2019-goda-no-4-ob-oficialnom-tolkovanii-punkta-2-stati-41 (accessed 4 Jul. 2019).

52. Law of Kazakhstan of 7 Mar. 2002 No. 299-II on the Diplomatic Service. Available: https://online.zakon.kz/Document/?doc_id=1029703 (accessed 5 May 2019).

In such circumstances, a citizen of Kazakhstan does not lose his/her citizenship and does not change his/her permanent residence, but simply lives temporarily abroad and continues to have a sustainable political and legal connection with their country. A citizen residing temporarily abroad is under the full protection of Kazakhstan and has the full rights, freedoms and duties of a citizen of Kazakhstan (Article 11(2) and Article 12(1, 3) Constitution of Kazakhstan).

According to Article 54(2) of the Constitutional Law on Elections of 28 September 1995, the Central Election Commission considers the residence facts of each candidate individually and analyses the relevant documents.[53]

Thus, the Constitutional Council concluded that according to Article 41(2) of the Constitution of Kazakhstan, a candidate for the Presidency of the Republic may be a citizen of Kazakhstan who resided permanently within the territory of Kazakhstan for the last fifteen years. In the fifteen years of residence within the territory of Kazakhstan may be included a period of stay abroad as the diplomatic personnel and equated with them, appointed (elected) to a post at international organizations, of which Kazakhstan is a Member State.

114. Regular presidential elections are carried out on the first Sunday of December and cannot coincide with general elections for the Parliament of the Republic. Early presidential elections are designated by the decision of the President and carried out in accordance with the rules and terms envisaged in the Constitutional Law of the Republic (Article 41(3, 3-1) Constitution). The candidate receiving more than 50% of votes is considered elected. If no one candidate receives the necessary percentage of votes, a second ballot is organized between those two candidates who obtained the greatest number of votes. The candidate who receives the greatest number of votes in this second ballot is deemed to have been elected (Article 41(5) Constitution).

115. The President of Kazakhstan has the right to decide to hold early presidential elections, and the elections shall be carried out within the rules and terms envisaged by the Constitutional Law on the elections (Article 41(3-1) Constitution). This provision of the Constitution was interpreted by the Constitutional Council on 24 February 2015 at the request of the Chair of the Senate of the Parliament.[54] The questions were whether the right of the President to designate early presidential elections is unconditional and whether the Constitution of the Republic envisages any conditions and restrictions on the President when he/she takes a decision on the designation of early presidential elections.

According to the opinion of the Constitutional Council of Kazakhstan, the designation of early presidential elections is within the exclusive competence of the President of the Republic. The Constitutional Council stated that the decision and

53. Constitutional Law of Kazakhstan of 28 Sep. 1995 No. 2464 on the Elections in the Republic of Kazakhstan. Available at the official website of the Ministry of Justice of Kazakhstan: http://adilet.zan.kz/rus/docs/Z950002464_#z56 (accessed 8 Mar. 2018).

54. Normative Resolution of the Constitutional Council of Kazakhstan No. 2 of 24 Feb. 2015 on Official Interpretation of Art. 41(3-1) of the Constitution of Kazakhstan. Available at: https://ksrk.gov.kz/kk/solutions/kazakhstan-respublikasy-konstituciyasynyn-41-babynyn-3-1-tarmagyn-resmi-tusindiru-turaly (accessed 1 Aug. 2021).

actions of the President, including the decisions on having early presidential elections shall be aimed at achieving the goals and values established in the Preamble and Chapter 1 of the Constitution, as well as in other provisions of the Constitution. Some of these fundamental principles of Kazakhstan include social concord and political stability, economic development for the benefit of its people, Kazakhstani patriotism, and resolving problems of national importance by democratic means, including voting at the national referendum or in the Parliament,

In the view of the Constitutional Council, the coincidence of regular presidential elections with parliamentary ones may be a reason for calling early presidential elections in the Republic.

116. The President takes office after giving the following oath to the people: 'I solemnly declare to serve the people of Kazakhstan, to follow strictly the Constitution and the Laws of the Republic of Kazakhstan, guarantee the rights and freedoms of citizens, and perform the high duties of the President of Kazakhstan in good faith' (Article 42(1) Constitution). The oath is sworn on the second Wednesday of January in a solemn ceremony in the presence of the deputies of the Parliament, members of the Constitutional Council, judges of the Supreme Court and ex-Presidents of the Republic. An official who has temporarily assumed the authority of the President in accordance with Article 48 of the Constitution swears the oath within one month after taking office (Article 42(2) Constitution).[55]

117. The powers of the President shall terminate from the moment the new elected President takes office, and also in a case of early release or dismissal of a President from the office, or of his death. All former Presidents, apart from those who were impeached, have the status of ex-Presidents (Article 42(3) Constitution).

118. One and the same person cannot be re-elected as the President of the Republic more than twice. The First President of Kazakhstan is exempted from such restriction (Article 42(5) Constitution).

§2. Legal Status

119. The legal status of the President of Kazakhstan is defined by Chapter 3 of the Constitution and the 1995 Constitutional Law on the President of Kazakhstan. Among all state bodies, regulation of the President's status in the Constitution comes first. This confirms the form of the government structure of Kazakhstan.

120. As Head of the State, the President of Kazakhstan defines the main directions of the domestic and foreign policy of the State. He is the highest official of the country and 'does not belong to any branch of power and takes a special position in the system of state powers', but 'close to the executive power'.[56] He ensures the

55. Such temporary assumption of power that took place in practice is discussed in Chapter 2 § 6 of this monograph.
56. Ghairat Sapargaliyev, *The Constitutional Law of the RoK. Academic Course* 292–293 (2002).

coordinated functioning of all branches of state power and the responsibility of the authorities to the people (Article 40 Constitution).

121. The President, his honour, and his dignity are inviolable. Encroachment upon the honour and dignity of the President of the Republic is prosecuted by law (Article 1(5) Constitutional Law on President).

122. The President is not entitled to be a deputy of a representative body, and he has no right to occupy other paid posts or to carry out entrepreneurial activities (Article 5(1) Constitutional Law on the President). The President has a lapel badge and a standard as the symbols of distinction. The President becomes by appointment a chevalier of '*Altyn Kyran*' ('Golden Eagle') (Article 6 Constitutional Law on President).

123. The Administration of the President is the state body which is responsible for ensuring the activities of the President (Article 32 Constitutional Law on President).

§3. The Powers

I. The Powers of the President in Foreign Policy of Kazakhstan

124. The powers of the President in relation to the foreign policy of Kazakhstan are elaborated in Article 7 of Constitutional Law of the Republic of Kazakhstan. The President conducts international negotiations on behalf of Kazakhstan. The President assigns credentials to negotiate, and signs international treaties of the Republic and the instruments of ratification; he takes the decision to suspend the operation of international treaties that have not been subject to ratification by the Republic. The President submits proposals to denounce international treaties concluded by the Republic. He appoints and recalls the heads of all diplomatic missions of the country. The President accepts the diplomatic service credentials and letters of recall of those accredited in Kazakhstan and other representatives of foreign states. The President alone appoints the Minister of Foreign Affairs (Article 10 subparagraph 2 Constitutional Law on President).

II. The Powers of the President in Ensuring the Defence and Security of the State

125. Article 8 of the Constitutional Law of the Republic elaborates the President's powers in ensuring defence and security of the State. According to Article 8 of Constitutional Law on the Status of the President, the President of Kazakhstan is the Supreme Commander-in-Chief of the Armed Forces of the Republic; he appoints and dismisses the top military officers of the Armed Forces of Kazakhstan.

126. In case of a serious and direct threat to the democratic institutions of Kazakhstan, where the country's independence and territorial integrity, political stability, the security of citizens, and normal functioning of the constitutional bodies of the State have been disrupted, the President, after official consultations with the Prime Minister and Chairs of the Parliament's Chambers, may take such measures as are dictated by the circumstances, including the imposition of a state of emergency over the whole territory of the Republic or only in some parts of it, and to mobilize the military. The President will immediately inform the Parliament of the Republic about his decision.

127. In case of aggression against Kazakhstan or a direct external threat to its security, the President imposes on the whole territory of the Republic or in some places martial law, announces partial or general mobilization, and informs the Parliament of Kazakhstan.

128. The President submits a proposal for consideration at the joint session of the Chambers of the Parliament on using the Armed Forces of the Republic to fulfil its international obligations in supporting peace and security.

129. The President controls the state security services. The President approves the Military Doctrine of Kazakhstan. He takes a decision on recruitment of citizens of the Republic for military service and on the dismissal of conscripts. With the consent of the Senate of the Parliament, he appoints the Chair of the Committee on National Security and dismisses him.

III. The President and the Parliament

130. The President of the Republic plays an important role in the activities of the Parliament. Such competence is envisaged in the Constitution of Kazakhstan and the Constitutional Law regulating the status of the President of Kazakhstan. So, in accordance with Article 9 of the Constitutional Law on the President, the President of Kazakhstan determines both regular and snap elections of the Parliament and its Chambers.

131. Within the observance of the rules established by Article 51(4) of the Constitution, the President appoints fifteen deputies of the Senate to ensure cultural representation and other important interests of society (Article 9 subparagraph 2 Constitutional Law on President).

132. The President convenes the first session of the Parliament no later than thirty days after publication of the results of the elections. The President takes the oath of the deputies of the Parliament given to the people of Kazakhstan. The President nominates a candidate for Chair of the Senate of the Parliament. As a rule, he opens the sessions of the Parliament.

133. In the period between the sessions of the Parliament, he may convene an extraordinary session of the Parliament either upon his own initiative or upon the proposal of the Chairs of the Chambers, or at least one-third of the total number of the deputies of the Parliament. Such a session of Parliament can discuss only the issues which were the reasons for its convocation (Article 9 subparagraph 7 Constitutional Law on the President).

134. The President signs any Law submitted by the Senate of the Parliament within one month, promulgates it, or returns the Law or its articles for rediscussion and voting. If Parliament confirms its previously adopted decision taken in line with Article 54(2(2)) of the Constitution, the President signs the Law within one month (Article 9 subparagraph 8 Constitutional Law on President).

135. The President has the right to submit the draft of amendments and addenda to the Constitution of the Republic for consideration of the Parliament. In his Presidential message, since he has the power to initiate legislation, the President submits the drafts of Laws for the consideration of the *Mazhilis*. The President has the right to define the priority of consideration of these drafts. In such cases, the prioritized draft Laws should be considered within two months (Article 9 subparagraph 10 Constitutional Law on President).

136. The President has the right to participate in any sessions of the joint sessions of the Chambers of the Parliament, or any separate meetings, and to be heard there (Article 9 subparagraph 11 Constitutional Law on President).

137. In accordance with Article 63 of the Constitution, the President may dissolve the Parliament or the *Mazhilis* of the Parliament after consultations with the Chairs of the Parliament and the Prime Minister. The Parliament or the *Mazhilis* of the Parliament cannot be dissolved during a state of emergency or martial law, during the last six months of the President's term, or within one year after the dissolution of the previous Parliament (the *Mazhilis* of the Parliament) (Article 63 Constitution).

IV. The President and the Government

138. With the consent of the *Mazhilis* of the Parliament, the President appoints the Prime Minister of the Republic and dismisses him. Upon the proposal of the Prime Minister, the President defines the structure of the Government. Upon the proposal of the Prime Minister and after consultation with the *Mazhilis* of the Parliament, the President appoints members of the Government. The President appoints the Minister of Foreign Affairs, the Ministers of Defence and Internal Affairs, and dismisses them (Article 10 Constitutional Law on the President).

139. The President takes the oath of the members of the Government. The President regularly hears reports from the Prime Minister on the main directions of the Government's activities and of important decisions taken by the Government. The

President coordinates the unified system of financing and remuneration of employees working for bodies financed by the national budget. The President coordinates the state programs. If necessary, he chairs the meetings of the Government on very important issues.

140. The President takes a decision on the resignation of the Government or any of its members if:

(1) they consider that further exercise of their functions is impossible;
(2) the *Mazhilis* or the Parliament passes a vote of censure on the Government;
(3) a member of the Government is not in agreement with the policy of the Government.

Within ten days the President accepts or rejects the resignation of the Government or any of its members. If the President rejects the resignation of the Government or any of its members, they continue to exercise their duties.

141. On his own initiative, the President can take a decision to terminate the powers of the Government or dismiss the Prime Minister or any other member of the Government (Article 10 subparagraph 12 Constitutional Law on President).

142. The President has the right to impose duties apart from those envisaged in the Constitution and the Laws of the Republic. He can also give instructions to the Government (Article 10 subparagraph 13-14 Constitutional Law on President).

V. The President and the Constitutional Council

143. With regards to the Constitutional Council, the President of Kazakhstan appoints the Chair and two members of the Council and has the right to dismiss them before their term ends (Article 11 Constitutional Law on President).

144. In accordance with Article 44(10-1)) of the Constitution, for the purposes of protection of human rights and freedoms and ensuring national security, sovereignty and the integrity of the State, the President requests the Constitutional Council to consider any Law that has been passed or any other normative legal act for their compliance with the Constitution of the Republic and requests its opinion in the case mentioned in Article 91(3) of the Constitution. Such an opinion of the Constitutional Council is necessary if amendments to the Constitution are introduced via a national referendum or by Parliament.

145. In compliance with Article 72 of the Constitution, when there are doubts regarding the correctness of holding elections of the President and deputies of the *Mazhilis* or the conduct of a national referendum, the President may request the Constitutional Council to consider the question. Before signing a Law, the President may request the Constitutional Council to consider the Law adopted by the Parliament for its compliance with the provisions of the Constitution of the Republic.

The President may ask the Constitutional Council to consider the compliance of international treaties with the Constitution before giving consent by the Parliament to be bound by the treaty. The President may ask the Constitutional Council to give an official explanation of the provisions of the Constitution.

VI. The President and the Judicial System

146. In accordance with the provisions of the Constitution and the Constitutional Law on the President of Kazakhstan, the President of the Republic, on the grounds of recommendations from the Highest Judicial Council, makes proposals to the Senate of the Parliament to elect (or dismiss) the Chair and the judges of the Supreme Court of Kazakhstan. Upon similar recommendations, the Highest Judicial Council appoints and dismisses the Chairs and the judges of the local or other courts (Article 12 Constitutional Law on President).

VII. The President and the Prosecutor's Office

147. Article 13 of the Constitutional Law on the President of the Republic regulates the power of the President with regards to the Office of the Prosecutor. The President, with the consent of the Senate, appoints the General Prosecutor for a five-year term and dismisses him. Upon a proposal by the General Prosecutor, the President appoints and dismisses the deputies of the General Prosecutor. At least once a quarter, the President receives a report from the General Prosecutor on the observance of the rule of law in the country.

VIII. The President and the Central Election Commission

148. In accordance with Article 14 of the Constitutional Law on the President, the President of the Republic appoints the Chair and two members of the Central Election Commission, and approves the regulations on the functionality and status of the Central Election Commission. He also hears from the Chair of the Election Commission regarding preparations for national referenda, elections of the deputies of the Parliament, the *maslikhats*, members of other bodies of the local government and the results of referenda and elections.

IX. The President and the National Bank

149. With the consent of the Parliament, the President appoints the Chair of the National Bank of Kazakhstan and dismisses him. Upon the proposal of the Chair of the National Bank, he appoints and dismisses the deputies of the Chair. At least once a quarter, the President hears the report of the Chair of the National Bank on the activities and functionality of the Bank (Article 15 Constitutional Law on President).

X. The President and the Control Committee over Fulfilment of the National Budget

150. The President of Kazakhstan appoints the Chair and two members of the Control Committee over the fulfilment of the national budget for terms of five years and has the right to dismiss them before the end of their term. The President approves the regulations on the status and functionality of the Committee. At least once a quarter, the President hears the report of the Chair of the Control Committee about the fulfilment of the national budget and the activities of the Committee (Article 16 Constitutional Law on President).

XI. The President and the Akims

151. With the consent of the relevant *maslikhats*, the President appoints the *akims* of the *oblasts* (regions), cities that have special national status, and the capital Nur-Sultan (Article 28 Law on Local Governance). For instance, with the Decrees of 13 and 17 June 2019, the newly elected President of Kazakhstan, Kassym-Jomart Tokayev, appointed the *akims* of the capital and cities of special national status, and the *oblasts*.[57]

152. The President cancels and suspends, wholly or partially, the acts of the *akims* of the regions, cities of the national importance and the capital. On the issues within his competence, the President gives instructions to the *akims* and hears the reports on their fulfilment. The President has the right to dismiss the *akims* at his own discretion, and also in the case when the relevant *maslikhats* have passed a vote of non-confidence by a majority of votes of the total number of the deputies (Article 17 Constitutional Law on President).

XII. The Powers of the President with Regards to Other State Bodies Directly Subordinated and Accountable to Him

153. The powers of the heads of the state bodies directly responsible and subordinate to the President of the Republic are terminated upon the assumption of office by a newly elected President. They fulfil their duties until other heads of these state bodies are appointed by the Head of State. The President of the Republic, upon recommendations of the heads of the state bodies directly responsible and subordinate to him, approves the regulations on the status, structure and total staff numbers of these bodies. The President of the Republic, upon recommendations of the heads of these state bodies, appoints and dismisses their respective deputies and the heads of the committees, if other rules are not stipulated by the President. The President

57. Decrees of the President of Kazakhstan of 13 and 17 Jun. 2019 on Appointment of the *Akims* of *Nur-Sultan*, *Almaty*, *Shymkent* and the Regions. Available at: http://www.akorda.kz/ru/legal_acts/decrees/o-naznachenii-kulginova-as-akimom-goroda-nur-sultana; http://www.akorda.kz/ru/legal_acts/decrees/ob-akimah-gorodov-almaty-shymkenta-i-oblastei (accessed 19 Jun. 2019).

forms, abolishes and reorganizes the committees within these state bodies. The President hears in accordance with the rules and within a timeframe defined by him the reports of the heads of the state bodies directly responsible and subordinate to the President about the activities of such state bodies (Article 17-1 Constitutional Law on President).

154. In accordance with Article 44 subparagraph 5 of the Constitution and by the Decree of the President dated 9 September 2020 two Agencies were created: the Agency on Strategic Planning and Reforms and the Agency for Protection and Development of Competition.[58] The functions and competencies of the Ministry of the National Economy on issues of strategic planning and state statistics were transferred to the newly established Agency on Strategic Planning and Reforms. The Committee on Statistics of the Ministry of the National Economy was transferred to the Agency on Strategic Planning and Reforms and renamed the Bureau of National Statistics. Thus, the Agency on Strategic Planning and Reforms:

(1) develops approaches to the realization of reforms, and to the drafting of the legal normative acts necessary for the fulfilment of reforms, as well as monitors and evaluates the progress of their fulfilment;
(2) coordinates the activities of state bodies and entities of *a* quasi-public *nature* in preparing the documents for the state planning system, as well as coordinates, monitors and evaluates the progress of their fulfilment;
(3) coordinates the proposals of the state bodies concerning the improvement of the public administration system;
(4) *coordinates* strategic forecasting and analysis of the development of the country and of the international situation;
(5) coordinates the activities on state statistics;
(6) coordinates the activities with regards to yearly assessment*s* of the efficiency of the central state and local executive bodies of the regions, the cities of national importance, and the capital.

The functions of the Ministry of the National Economy in the field of competition protection, limitations to the activities of monopolies and regulation of the activities of state monopoly were transferred to the Agency for Protection and Development of Competition.[59]

58. Decree of the President of Kazakhstan on Further Measures to Improve Governance of the Republic of Kazakhstan of 9 Sep. 2020 No. 407. Available at: http://www.akorda.kz/ru/legal_acts/decrees/o-merah-po-dalneishemu-sovershenstvovaniyu-sistemy-gosudarstvennogo-upravleniya-respubliki-kazakhstan-8 (accessed 25 Sep. 2020).
59. Decree of the President of Kazakhstan of 6 Oct. 2020 No. 427 on Some Questions of the Agency for Protection and Development Competition. Available at: http://www.akorda.kz/ru/legal_acts/decrees/o-nekotoryh-voprosah-agentstva-po-zashchite-i-razvitiyu-konkurencii-respubliki-kazahstan (Accessed 1 Aug. 2021). The official website of the Agency: https://www.gov.kz/memleket/entities/zk?lang=en (Accessed 1 Aug. 2021).

§4. THE SECRETARY OF STATE

155. Previously, the legal status of the Secretary of State was regulated by the Decree of the President of 10 July 2003 No. 1148 on the Status and Powers of the Secretary of State. Currently, the status of the Secretary of State of the Republic is regulated by the Decree of the President of Kazakhstan of 13 August 2007 No. 379.[60] The last amendments to the Decree lessened the scope of jurisdiction of the Secretary of State.

The Secretary of State is an official who is appointed and dismissed by the President of the Republic. The Secretary of State carries out activities under the direct supervision of and is accountable to and controlled by the Head of State (paragraphs 1–2 Decree on the Secretary of State). For the consideration of the President of Kazakhstan, the Secretary develops proposals on the main directions of internal policy for the country. On the instructions of the President, the Secretary represents the interests of the President in relation to the Parliament and its Chambers, other state bodies and public associations, and in international relations (paragraph 4 Decree on Secretary of State).

156. The Secretary of State coordinates the activities on social and humanitarian development, family and demographic policy, culture, physical education and sports. The Secretary of State also coordinates the activities of such consultative-advisory bodies to the Office of the President like the Anti-corruption Commission, the Commission on State Awards, Commission on Citizenship, the Commission of the First President of Kazakhstan State Peace Prize and Progress, the National Commission on State Symbols and Heraldry for the Government Departments, the National Commission on the Training Abroad of Skilled Workers, the Commission on Awarding the State Prize in Science and Technology (named *al-Farabi*), the Commission on Awarding the State Prize in the Field of Literature and Art, and the National Commission on Realization of Programs of Modernization of Public Consciousness. The Secretary coordinates the work of state analytical structures in the field of public development, as well as that of the Commission on Human Rights. The Secretary performs other tasks in accordance with the instructions of the President of the Republic.

157. In order to fulfil these duties, the Secretary of State has the following rights:

(1) to issue the orders;
(2) to give instructions to the central and local executive bodies on issues within his/her competence;
(3) to participate at the meetings of the Parliament and its Chambers, of the Government and other consultative-advisory bodies to the Head of State;
(4) to request and receive information, documents, and other materials from the state bodies and the officials on issues within his/her competence;

60. Decree of the President of Kazakhstan of 13 Aug. 2007 No. 379 on the Status and Powers of the Secretary of State of the Republic of Kazakhstan. Available at: https://online.zakon.kz/document/?doc_id=30119236 (accessed 30 Apr. 2020).

(5) to create interdepartmental working groups for preparation of the drafts of the President's legal acts and to solve the tasks instructed by the President.

The Administration of the President of Kazakhstan provides organizational, legal, informational, analytical and other support for the activities of the Secretary of State.

§5. ADVISORY BODIES TO THE PRESIDENT

I. General

158. According to Article 33 of the Constitutional Law on the President, the consultative-advisory bodies, the Assembly of the People of Kazakhstan, the Highest Judicial Council, and other institutions are organized to assist the President in fulfilling his constitutional powers and support his activities. The President of the Republic defines the membership of these organizations, appoints their heads, approves the regulations on the functionality of these bodies, and hears the reports of the heads on activities of the consultative-advisory bodies, the Assembly of People of Kazakhstan and other entities at the President's Office. Staff members of the advisory-consultative bodies, as well as the staff of the Assembly of the People of Kazakhstan at the President's Office, are considered as the staff of the Administration of the President, except in cases stipulated in the legislation of Kazakhstan.

II. The Administration of the President

159. The legal status of the Administration of the President is covered by the Regulations approved by the Decree of the President of 11 March 2008 No. 552.[61] In line with the Regulations, the Administration of the President is a state body that is formed by the President, directly subordinate and accountable to him. The mission of the Administration is to ensure high-quality and timely information, analytical, legal, protocol, organizational, documentation support to the activities of the President (paragraph 8 Regulations).

160. One of the main tasks of the Administration is to ensure the realization of the President's power:

– in the field of foreign policy;
– in the field of socio-economic and other areas of domestic policy;
– in the field of defence and state security;
– in the field of legal policy and legal order;
– in the field of personnel policy;

61. Regulations on the Administration of the President of Kazakhstan approved by the Decree of the President of 11 Mar. 2008 No. 552. Available at: http://www.akorda.kz/ru/executive_office/about_executive_office (accessed 13 Jun. 2019).

– with respect to the Parliament of Kazakhstan;
– with respect to the Government of Kazakhstan;
– with respect to the Constitutional Council of Kazakhstan;
– with respect to the courts and the judges;
– with respect to the Central Election Commission of Kazakhstan;
– with respect to the local representative and executive bodies, the *akims* of the regions, cities of national importance and the capital on issues of regional policy;
– with respect to state bodies, directly subordinate and accountable to the President.

161. The Administration of the President supports the activities of the State Secretary of Kazakhstan, the Assembly of the People of Kazakhstan and the consultative-advisory bodies to the President.

For instance, in the field of foreign policy, the Administration of the President:

(1) monitors, analyses and forecasts the process of world development, as well as topical problems in international relations, proposes recommendations to the President on the realization of his power in foreign policy;
(2) carries out the organization of a substantive part of international events with the participation of the President;
(3) provides interaction between the President and the state bodies of foreign countries and their officials, foreign political and public figures, international and foreign organizations;
(4) makes proposals to the President on the main directions and development of political and economic cooperation with foreign States and improving the image of Kazakhstan abroad;
(5) makes proposals to the President on implementing decisions of international organizations;
(6) makes proposals on issues of conclusion, suspension and termination of international treaties with Kazakhstan.

162. Another example of the Administration of the President is its role in the field of legal policy. According to paragraph 13 of the Regulations, in order to ensure the realization of the powers of the President in the field of legal policy and legal order, the Administration of the President submits proposals to the President on:

(1) the main directions and improvement of legal policy;
(2) improving the effectiveness of regulatory mechanisms;
(3) strengthening law and legal order;
(4) legal regulations of those issues that are not within the legislative powers of the Parliament and the competence of the Government and other state bodies.

The Administration of the President organizes the work on the preparation of strategic documents in the field of legal policy, ensuring observance of law and legal order in the country for the relevant time period.

163. The Administration of the President is composed of the Head of the Administration, the Secretary of the Security Council, deputies of the Head of the Administration, the assistants to the President, the Head of the Chancellery of the President of Kazakhstan, advisers to the President, the heads of the structural units and other personnel of the Administration.

III. The Security Council

164. Article 44(20) of the Constitution establishes the Security Council of the Republic. The institute has a historical background and roots. For the first time in the history of the Kazakh statehood, the Council was created on 21 August 1991 by the Decree of the President of the Kazakh SSR. With the Decree of the President of 17 June 1993, it was transformed to the Security Council.[62] The status of the Security Council was reconsidered by the Decree of the President of 22 November 1996 No. 3237 on the Security Council of the Republic of Kazakhstan. Later on, the Regulations on the Security Council were adopted by the Decree of the President of 20 March 1999 and replaced the previous document of 1996.[63] Nowadays, the legal position of the institution is strengthened by the Law on 5 July 2018 and the regulations approved by the Decree of the President dated 12 February 2019.[64]

165. In accordance with recent amendments, the Security Council is a constitutional body formed by the President. This state body coordinates the implementation of a unified state policy on national security and defence in order to provide internal stability and protection of the constitutional order, state independence, territorial integrity and national interests of Kazakhstan in the international arena.

166. The first President of Kazakhstan, because of his historical role and contribution to the formation of statehood of Kazakhstan, has the right to lead the Council as a Chair for life. The composition of the Security Council is formed by the President in consultation with the Chair of the Security Council. Former President of Kazakhstan Nazarbayev is the current Chair of the Council. The Council takes decisions by a majority of votes of persons participating at the meeting. The decisions of the Council and of the Chair have binding force for all state bodies, entities and officials of the Republic.

---

62. Please *see* historical information at the official website of the Office of the President of Kazakhstan: http://www.akorda.kz/ru/executive_office/presidential_councils/sovet-bezopasnosti (accessed 4 Jan. 2019).
63. Decree of the President of the Republic of Kazakhstan of 20 Mar. 1999 No. 88 on the Security Council of the Republic of Kazakhstan. Available at: https://online.zakon.kz/Document/?doc_id=101270 7#pos=0;19 (accessed 5 Mar. 2018).
64. Law of Kazakhstan of 5 Jul. 2018 on the Security Council of the Republic of Kazakhstan. Available at: https://online.zakon.kz/Document/?doc_id=38039248#pos=4;-51 (accessed 3 Jan. 2019); Decree of the President of Kazakhstan of 12 Feb. 2019 No. 838 on Some Issues of the Security Council of the Republic of Kazakhstan. Available at: http://adilet.zan.kz/rus/docs/U1900000838#z86 (accessed on 30 Apr. 2020).

167. The members of the Council are the President of Kazakhstan, the Chairs of the Senate and *Mazhilis* of the Parliament, the Prime Minister, the Head of the Administration of the President, an assistant to the President (the Secretary of the Security Council), the General Prosecutor, the Chair of the Committee of the National Security, the Head of the State Security Service, the Minister of Foreign Affairs, the Minister of Defence, and the Minister of Internal Affairs. If necessary, the President may appoint other additional members of the Security Council after consultation with the Chair of the Council (Part III Regulations).

IV. The Assembly of the People of Kazakhstan

168. The Assembly was created by the Decree of the President of Kazakhstan dated 1 March 1995. The status of the Assembly was strengthened due to the amendments made in May 2007 to the Constitution of Kazakhstan that allowed the election of nine deputies from among the members of the Assembly to the *Mazhilis* of the Parliament to represent the interests of all ethnic groups of the country. Subsequently, the Law on the Assembly of the People of Kazakhstan dated 20 October 2008 was adopted.[65]

169. The Assembly is a consultative-advisory body to the President of the Republic. The Assembly is formed by the President of Kazakhstan. The First President of Kazakhstan, Nazarbayev, leads the Assembly for life. At the local level, Assemblies exist for the mayors of the regions, cities of national importance and the capital (Article 1 Law on the Assembly).

170. The Assembly contributes to the development and implementation of state policy for ensuring public consent and national unity. The aim of the Assembly is to ensure the social harmony and national unity of the Republic on the grounds of Kazakh patriotism, the civil, spiritual and cultural commonness of the ethnic groups of Kazakhstan with a consolidating role of the Kazakh people (Article 3 of the Law on the Assembly). Thus, this institution plays an important role in the political life of the country and in promoting interethnic tolerance and peace in Kazakh society. It is also one of the tools for the interaction of state authorities with civil society and is a kind of public diplomacy.[66] Due to the Assembly, the minorities of the country are able to revive and develop their native languages, ethnic culture and traditions.

171. In line with Article 4 of the Law, six tasks are set for the Assembly:

---

65. Law of Kazakhstan of 20 Oct. 2008 on the Assembly of the Peoples of Kazakhstan. Available at: http://adilet.zan.kz/rus/docs/Z080000070_ (accessed 9 Jul. 2019).
66. Please *see* the official site of the Office of the President of Kazakhstan on the Assembly of the Peoples of Kazakhstan as of 7 Jul. 2019: http://www.akorda.kz/ru/national_projects/assambleya-naroda-kazahstana.

(1) ensuring the effective interactions of state bodies, organizations and civil society institutions in the field of interethnic relations, the creation of favourable conditions for further strengthening –public concord and national unity;
(2) strengthening the unity of the people of Kazakhstan;
(3) rendering assistance to state bodies in countering extremism and radicalism in society, and countering impairment of the rights and freedoms of individuals and citizens;
(4) participation in the development of the politico-legal culture of citizens;
(5) ensuring integration of the efforts of ethnocultural and other public associations to achieve the aims and tasks of the Assembly;
(6) the preservation and development of traditions, languages and cultures of the peoples of Kazakhstan.

172. The activities of the Assembly are based on the principles of priority of individuals' and citizens' rights and freedoms, the priority of the interests of the people and state, non-discrimination on the grounds of origin, social, official and property status, sex, race, nationality, language, religion, beliefs, place of residence or other circumstances, equality and the personal responsibility of the members of the Assembly for the activities of the Assembly and publicity (Article 5 Law on the Assembly).

173. According to Article 6 of the Law on the Assembly, its main directions include the following:

(1) assistance in development and realization of state policy for ensuring social concord and national unity;
(2) assistance in the development of Kazakh patriotism;
(3) development of the state language and other languages of the people of Kazakhstan;
(4) participation in development and realization of plans and events in the field of demography and migration;
(5) popularization of the Kazakh model of public concord and national unity in the country and abroad;
(6) realization of educational and publishing activities aimed at the strengthening of social concord and national unity;
(7) monitoring interethnic relations, including the application of state language and other languages of the people of Kazakhstan;
(8) participation in the socio-cultural expertise of draft Laws on issues of state policy regarding social concord and national unity;
(9) support of the Kazakh diaspora in foreign countries to preserve and develop their native language, culture and national traditions, and strengthen their ties with their historical homeland;
(10) development of recommendations and realization of practical measures for resolving disputes, prevention of conflict situations in the field of interethnic relations and participation in their resolution;
(11) methodical, organizational and legal assistance to ethnocultural public associations;

(12) holding seminars, conferences, as well as the organization of other events that strengthen dialogue with state bodies and public associations on issues of social concord and national unity;
(13) interactions with state bodies, organizations, civil society institutions and international organizations to strengthen social concord and national unity;
(14) assistance in the development of philanthropy, mediation concerning social concord and national unity;
(15) assistance in the development of connection of ethnic groups of Kazakhstan with their homeland;
(16) rendering other activities to strengthen social concord and national unity that do not contradict the legislation of Kazakhstan.

174. The Assembly consists of the Session, the Council, the Apparatus (the Secretariat), the Executive Office of the Assembly, the assemblies of the regions, cities of national importance and the capital, and ethnocultural associations of the Assembly (Article 8 Law on the Assembly). The Session of the Assembly is the highest governing body, which is convened by the President of the Republic at least once per year (Article 9 Law on the Assembly). The Council, a collegiate body, leads the activities of the Assembly between sessions. It is formed by the Decree of the President of Kazakhstan. The Council nominates candidates for the deputies of the *Mazhilis* of the Parliament of Kazakhstan to be elected by the Assembly and considers candidates for membership in the Assembly (Article 10 Law on the Assembly).

175. The Apparatus (the Secretariat) is the working body of the Assembly and functions within the structure of the President's Administration. The head of the Apparatus is the Chair of the Assembly. The Apparatus organizes and ensures the activities of the Chair and the Council; provides expert, analytical, information and other support; coordinates the work of state bodies, organizations and the civil society in strengthening public concord and national unity; considers important complaints on interethnic relations, and so on. (Article 11 Law on the Assembly).

The Chair of the Assembly leads the Assembly and its Council and carries out general leadership of the Assembly's activities (Article 12 Law on the Assembly). The executive body of the Assembly is a state institution established by the President of Kazakhstan. The activity of the executive body of the Assembly is regulated by its charter; the aim of the executive body is the creation of an effective system of organizational, financial, logistical and other functioning of the Assembly (Article 13-1 Law on the Assembly).

V. Other Councils and the Commissions to the President

176. The following councils function within the Office of the President of Kazakhstan:[67]

67. Please *see* the official site of the Office of the President of Kazakhstan as of 30 Apr. 2020: http://www.akorda.kz/ru/executive_office/presidential_councils.

(1) The Supreme Council for Reforms[68]
(2) The Oil and Gas Council
(3) The Security Council
(4) The Foreign Investor's Council
(5) The Council for Youth Policy
(6) The Council for Financial Stability
(7) The Council for National Fund Management
(8) The Council of National Investors
(9) The Legal Policy Council
(10) The National Council of Public Trust

177. According to the official website of the President of Kazakhstan, the following commissions assist in the activities of the Head of State of Kazakhstan:[69]

(1) Commission for Personnel Policies in Law-Enforcement Bodies
(2) The Anti-Corruption Commission
(3) The Commission on Citizenship
(4) The State Commission on Issues of Modernization of the Economy
(5) The Commission under the President on Issues of Non-proliferation of Weapons of Mass Destruction.
(6) The Commission on Amnesty
(7) The Commission for High Military Ranks and other Titles and Class Designations
(8) The Commission on State Decorations
(9) The Human Rights Commission
(10) The Commission on Determining Awardees of the '*Altyn Sapa*' First President's Prize and Winners of Kazakhstan's Best Production Republican Contest-Exhibition
(11) The Commission on Awarding the State Prize in Science and Techniques
(12) The Commission on Awarding the State Prize o in Literature and Art.
(13) The Commission on Awarding the State Prize on Peace and Progress of the President of Kazakhstan – Leader of the Nation.
(14) The National Commission on Modernization
(15) The National Commission for Women, Family and Demographic Policy
(16) The Commission of the Republic for Training of Personnel abroad
(17) The Commission of the Republic on State Symbols Heraldry of Departments and Similar Awards.
(18) The National Commission on the Realization of Programmes of Modernization of Public Consciousness.

---

68. Please *see* the official site of the Office of the President of Kazakhstan as of 2 Aug. 2021: http://www.akorda.kz/ru/legal_acts/decrees/o-vysshem-sovete-pri-prezidente-respubliki-kazahstan-po-reformam.
69. Please *see* the official site of the Office of the President of Kazakhstan as of 2 Aug. 2021: https://www.akorda.kz/ru/executive_office/presidential_commissions.

A. The Supreme Council for Reforms

178. The Supreme Council for Reforms had been created by the Decree of the President of 14 September 2020 for the purposes of the strategic planning of the country's sustainable development and deepening economic, social and political reforms.

B. The Oil and Gas Council

179. A Decree of the President of Kazakhstan dated 14 March 2012 No. 285 established the Oil and Gas Council as the consultative-advisory body to the President of Kazakhstan and approved the regulations on its status. The aim of the Council is to facilitate interdepartmental coordination for the stable and effective development of the oil and gas industry of the Republic.[70]

180. According to the regulations on its status, the main tasks of the Council are:

(1) drawing up proposals on the strategic directions of the development of the oil and gas industry of Kazakhstan;
(2) drawing up proposals on interactions with foreign partners working in the largest oil and gas fields of Kazakhstan.

181. On issues of its competence, the Council has the following rights:

(1) to submit proposals to the President for the development of strategic directions for the oil and gas industry of Kazakhstan;
(2) to form working groups to address issues within the competence of the Council;
(3) to request necessary information from state bodies and organizations on issues that fall within its competence;
(4) to involve specialists of interested state bodies, consultants in order to perform the tasks of the Council; and
(5) to carry out any other actions necessary to make effective the various activities of the Council within its competence.

182. The Council is led by the Chair who has the following functions:

(1) to carry out the general management of the Council's activities;
(2) to chair the meetings of the Council;
(3) to define the place and timing of the Council's meetings;

70. Regulations on the Oil and Gas Council of the President of Kazakhstan approved by the Decree of the President of Kazakhstan of 14 Mar. 2012 No. 285. Available at: https://adilet.zan.kz/rus/docs/U1200000285 (accessed 2 Aug. 2021).

(4) to exercise general control over the realization of the decisions of the Council; and
(5) to report to the President of Kazakhstan on the work of the Council twice per year.

The members of the Council have the right to submit proposals on the agenda and the procedures of discussion and to participate in the preparation of the materials for the Council's meetings and the drafts of its decisions. The meetings are held at least once every half year.

183. The working body of the Council is the Ministry of Energy. The Council performs these and other functions enumerated in paragraph 11 of the Regulations on the Oil and Gas Council, including:

(1) ensuring the organization of the Council's meetings and carrying out the preparation of the relevant materials for holding meetings of the Council based on the proposals of the Council's members and previously adopted decisions;
(2) drawing up the draft of the meeting's agenda on the proposals of the Council's members and previously adopted decisions;
(3) monitoring realization of the protocol decisions of the Council.

The Decisions of the Council are taken by a simple majority and have a recommendatory character.

184. The composition of the Council shall be approved by the President of Kazakhstan. The Council is composed of:

- the Prime Minister of Kazakhstan – the Chair of the Council;
- the Deputy Prime Minister – the Deputy Chair of the Council;
- the Deputy Head of the Administration of the President or assistant to the President of Kazakhstan on Social-Economic Issues – the Deputy Chair of the Council;
- the assistant to the President of Kazakhstan on the development of the real estate sector of the economy;
- the Minister of Labour and Social Protection of the Population of Kazakhstan;
- the Minister of Industry and Infrastructure Development of Kazakhstan;
- the Minister of National Economy of Kazakhstan;
- the Minister of Finance of Kazakhstan;
- the Minister of Ecology, Geology and Natural Resources of Kazakhstan;
- the Minister of Energy of Kazakhstan;
- the Minister of Justice of Kazakhstan;
- the Chair of the Board of the Sovereign Wealth Fund *Samruk-Kazyna*' JSC (if and as agreed);
- the Chair of the Board of the National Company KazMunaiGaz JSC (if and as agreed).

C. The Foreign Investors' Council

185. The Foreign Investors' Council (FIC) is one of the advisory bodies to the President of Kazakhstan.[71] It was created by the Decree of the President of Kazakhstan on 30 June 1998.[72] The Council is chaired by the President of Kazakhstan, and the Administration of the President ensures its activities. The Investment Committee of the MFA of Kazakhstan is the working body of the Council.

186. In line with the Decree of the President, the main task of the Council is the drawing up of recommendations and proposals on issues of:

(1) defining the main directions of the investment policies of Kazakhstan;
(2) improving the investment climate of Kazakhstan;
(3) improving the normative legal framework of the Republic relating to investments;
(4) assistance to foreign companies in the diversification of the economy, industrialization, the development of small and medium businesses in Kazakhstan;
(5) integration of the economy of Kazakhstan into world economic processes;
(6) strategies for the attraction of foreign investments to the economy of Kazakhstan;
(7) implementation of large investment programmes and projects of international importance of Kazakhstan.

187. The Chair of the FIC is the President of Kazakhstan. The permanent members of the Council are:

- the Prime Minister of Kazakhstan;
- the Chair of the National Bank of Kazakhstan;
- the First Deputy of the Prime Minister of Kazakhstan;
- the Deputies of the Prime Minister of Kazakhstan;
- the Deputy of the Head of the Administration of the President of Kazakhstan or Assistant to the President of Kazakhstan on social-economic issues;
- the Minister of Foreign Affairs of Kazakhstan;
- the Minister of Industry and Infrastructure Development of Kazakhstan;
- the Minister of Finance of Kazakhstan;
- the Minister of National Economy of Kazakhstan;
- the First Head of the working body of the Council.

The President of Kazakhstan may determine other officials to be brought into the composition of the Council.

71. Please *see* the official website of the Foreign Investors' Council: https://fic.kz/en (accessed 2 Aug. 2021).
72. Decree of the President of Kazakhstan of 30 Jun. 1998 on the Creation of the Council of the Foreign Investors at the President of Kazakhstan (most recent amendments of 9 Jun. 2021). Available at: https://online.zakon.kz/Document/?doc_id=1009972#pos=5;-155 (accessed 2 Aug. 2021).

188. Because the Council is aimed at having a platform for dialogue with foreign investors, it is also composed of foreign members, such as representatives of international economic and financial organizations and heads of the foreign companies or their deputies. The composition of the Council shall be approved by the President of Kazakhstan. The current foreign members of the Council are: the EBRD, Anadolu Group, Arcelor Mittal, Asian Development Bank, Baker & McKenzie, Cameco Corporation, Chevron, Citigroup EMEA, CNPC, Deloitte's, Deutsch Bank, ENI, ERG, Ernst and Young, Eurasian Development Bank, ExxonMobil, Mitsubishi Corporation, Marubeni, Shell, Total E&P Kazakhstan, and others. The heads of approximately thirty-three foreign companies and international organizations are members of the Council.

189. The main criterion for being a foreign member of the Council for international organizations is their contribution to the economy of Kazakhstan. They may be granted membership to the Council in case of their direct investment into the economy of Kazakhstan in the amount of not less than USD 500 million for investors working in the field of subsoil use, and for other investors working in other sectors of the economy, not less than USD 125 million. When considering an application for membership in the Council, the working body evaluates at least three years of investment activities in Kazakhstan, the creation of jobs with 70% occupancy by Kazakhstani workers, the experience and business reputation of the international organization, the importance of their activities for the economy and social sphere of Kazakhstan, participation in settlement of social and ecological issues within the territory of Kazakhstan, and participation in the improvement of the investment image of Kazakhstan, as well as other activities of that international organization or foreign company.

190. The Committee for the operational activities of the Council facilitates the effective implementation of the Council's tasks. With its decisions, the Committee creates the joint working groups to develop recommendations and proposals to the Council on the implementation of the protocol instructions of the Council's plenary meetings, on the improvement of investment policy and the development of the investment climate of Kazakhstan, on assistance to foreign investors relating to issues concerning the local, industrial and innovative development of Kazakhstan and operational activities of the companies that invest within the Republic, and the development of the digital economy of Kazakhstan (paragraph 29 FIC Regulations). No more than five joint working groups of the Council can be organized. The joint working groups adopt recommendations to be presented to the Council (paragraphs 30, 34 FIC Regulations).

191. The Working Group on the Labour Legislation, Human Capital Development and Engagement of Foreign Labour Force makes recommendations that ensure a constant dialogue between Kazakhstan and major foreign investors and increase investment opportunities within the Republic. It makes proposals concerning the further development of national legislation and the improvement of labour and migration safety and labour protection at the enterprises which attract an expatriate workforce. On 21 May 2019, a joint meeting of the Human Capital Working Group was held under the chairmanship of the Minister of Labour and Social Protection of Population of the Republic of Kazakhstan. The participants discussed many issues, including the implementation of the Action Plan of the Human Capital Working Group and the Roadmap partnership with investors, and the preparation for the next plenary session of the Council.[73]

192. The Investment Policy Working Group develops recommendations on issues concerning the investment policy of Kazakhstan, improvement of investment opportunities, and the tax and customs regime in the country. The Energy, Ecology, Oil and Gas Industry Working Group develops recommendations that ensure a constant dialogue between the Republic and major investors in the fields of energy, ecology, the oil and gas industry, and on matters that would increase investment opportunities in Kazakhstan's economy, ensure joint strategy and coordination of the activities of state bodies in the attraction of foreign investments, and that eliminate systemic, administrative and other obstacles.[74] The Working Group for the Preparation of Joint Events makes recommendations concerning preparations for the plenary and interim sessions of the Council and other events.

193. A plenary session of the FIC takes place at least once per year. The Chair defines the main issues, date and place of the session. Reports on the implementation of the protocol instructions of the previous plenary session are discussed at the Council's open plenary session (paragraphs 36–38 FIC Regulations) (paragraphs 36–38 FIC Regulations). According to the information from the official website of the FIC, the 32nd Plenary Session of the FIC was held on 4 July on the topic 'Human capital development'. At this session, the President, Tokayev, introduced new members of the FIC, such as Baker McKenzie International, METRO AG, Petro China Company Ltd, and regional representation of Deutsche Bank.[75]

194. The Prime Minister chairs the interim session of the Council between its plenary sessions. The interim sessions usually discuss the preliminary results of the implementation of protocol decisions of the last plenary session, the current problems of foreign investors, recommendations taken by the working groups of the Council (paragraphs 40–42 FIC Regulations).

195. The working body of the FIC in accordance with paragraph 48 of the FIC Regulations carries out the following functions:

(1) prepares and submits for consideration of the Committee recommendations on the composition of the Council and joint working groups of the Council and the Committee;

---

73. Please *see* the official site of the FIC: https://fic.kz/en/media/news/56 (accessed 2 Jul. 2019).
74. The information is available at the official website of the FIC: https://fic.kz/eng/work_groups/energy / (accessed 2 Jul. 2019).
75. *The 32nd FIC Plenary Session chaired by the President of the RoK*. Available at: https://fic.kz/en/plenary_sessions/show/48 (accessed 2 Aug. 2021).

(2) organizes and holds the plenary and interim meetings of the Council, thematic and additional meetings of the Council's Chair;
(3) coordinates the activities of the joint working groups;
(4) monitors implementation of the protocol decisions of the Council, its joint working groups and Committee.

D. The National Council of Public Trust

196. The newly elected President of Kazakhstan, Kassym-Jomart Tokayev, on 12 June 2019, created the National Council of Public Trust, in line with subparagraph 20 of Article 44 of the Constitution of Kazakhstan. The Administration of the President was instructed to conduct negotiations with the leaders of the political parties, NGOs, and representatives of civil society on how to create the Council and organize its work, within one month of that date.[76]

197. The Decree of the President of Kazakhstan of 17 July 2019 No. 63 approved the Regulations on the National Council of Public Trust.[77] The National Council of Public Trust is a consultative-advisory body to the President of Kazakhstan. Its aim is to develop recommendations on important issues of state policy based on intensive discussion with representatives of society, political parties and civil society.

198. In accordance with Chapter 2 of the Regulations, the main tasks of the National Council of Public Trust are:

(1) to conduct public expertise of the drafts of concepts, state programmes and normative legal acts;
(2) to consider significant strategic problems taking into account opinions of public and civil society;
(3) to ensure a constructive dialogue between representatives of public, political parties, NGOs and state bodies;
(4) to carry out other activities within its competence that do not contradict the legislation of the Republic.

199. The Chair of the National Council is the President of the Republic who carries out general leadership of the Council's activities, defines the place and timing of holding the meetings of the National Council, and gives instructions to the Deputy Chair, members and a secretary of the National Council.

---

76. Decree of the President of Kazakhstan of 12 Jun. 2019 on Creation of the National Council of Public Trust to the Office of the President. Available at: http://www.akorda.kz/ru/legal_acts/decrees/o-sozdanii-nacionalnogo-soveta-obshchestvennogo-doveriya-pri-prezidente-respubliki-kazahstan (accessed 16 Jun. 2019).
77. Regulations on the National Council of Public Trust approved by Decree of the President of Kazakhstan dated 17 Jul. 2019 No. 63. Available at: http://www.akorda.kz/ru/legal_acts/decrees/ob-utverzhdenii-polozheniya-i-sostava-nacionalnogo-soveta-obshchestvennogo-doveriya-pri-prezidente-respubliki-kazahstan (accessed 18 Jul. 2019).

200. The National Council is composed of prominent state and public figures, representatives of the political parties, NGOs. The Head of the President's Administration, the Commissioner for Human Rights, the Commissioner for Children's Rights, and the Commissioner for protection of entrepreneurs' rights are members of the National Council due to their official posts.

201. The members of the National Council have the following rights:

(1) to submit proposals concerning the work plan, agenda and procedure of discussion at the National Council;
(2) to participate in the preparation of the materials for the National Council's meetings and drafts of its decisions;
(3) to take part in the discussion and explanation of questions concerning social issues that are under discussion in the National Council's meeting.

202. In line with Chapter 5 of the Regulations, the working body of the National Council is a relevant structural unit of the President's Administration.

The working body of the National Council:

(1) carries out information and analytical support of the Council's activity;
(2) requests and receives from state bodies and organizations information, documents and materials necessary to fulfil its tasks;
(3) coordinates the activities of the working groups;
(4) controls the implementation of the Council's decisions;
(5) carries out other competencies necessary for ensuring the activity of the National Council.

E. The State Commission on Issues of Modernization of the Economy of Kazakhstan

203. The State Commission on Issues of Modernization of the Economy of Kazakhstan is an advisory-consultative body to the President of Kazakhstan, which was created on 13 April 2007 by decree of the President.[78] The task of the State Commission is to make recommendatory decisions on issues concerning the increase of competitiveness and efficiency of the economy of Kazakhstan. It passes recommendatory decisions on industrial-innovative development and modernization of the economy of Kazakhstan. It monitors targeted and efficient use of anti-crisis funds allocated from the National Fund of Kazakhstan and requests information, documents, and materials from the central and local executive bodies, necessary for the fulfilment of the tasks assigned. The State Commission evaluates

78. Decree of the President of Kazakhstan of 13 Apr. 2007 No. 314 on the Measures for Modernization of the Economy of the Republic of Kazakhstan. Available at: https://online.zakon.kz/Document/?doc_id=30097964#pos=15;-46; https://adilet.zan.kz/rus/docs/U070000314_/links (accessed 3 Jul. 2019).

the efficiency of measures taken by state bodies and other organizations for the promotion of competitiveness and efficiency of Kazakhstan's economy. It considers the reports of state bodies and their officials.

204. The working body of the State Commission is the Ministry of the National Economy. The tasks of the State Commission include ensuring the preparation of the meetings of the State Commission, drawing up the drafts of quarterly plans and submitting them for the approval of the Chair of the State Commission, the submission of consolidated information on the work fulfilled to the President's Administration, the collection of and presenting of materials on the agenda to the Chair of the State Commission, as well as carrying out other tasks (paragraph 10 Regulations).

205. The State Commission is composed of:

(1) The Prime Minister (Chair of the Commission).
(2) Assistant to the President (Deputy Chair).
(3) Members of the Government.
(4) Members of the Board of Directors of Samruk-Kazyna National Welfare Fund.
(5) A representative of the *Mazhilis*.

State officials who are not members of the State Commission, as well as representatives of the media, may be invited to the meetings.

206. The decisions of the State Commission are adopted by the majority of votes of the total number of its members present at the meeting and are fixed in its operating protocols. Working groups can be organized within the State Commission. The State Commission reports annually to the President of Kazakhstan on the outcomes of its work.

F. The Commission on the Issues of Non-proliferation of Weapons of Mass Destruction

207. The Decree of the President of Kazakhstan dated 11 January 2010 No. 915 established the Commission on the Issues of Non-Proliferation of Weapons of Mass Destruction. As given in the official website of the President 'the Commission serves to create an additional impetus to the activities of our country in non-proliferation and disarmament, including the elaboration of initiatives on strengthening of the world's nuclear non-proliferation regime'.[79]

79. The information is available at the official site of the Office of the President of Kazakhstan: http://www.akorda.kz/en/executive_office/presidential_commissions/commission-under-the-president-of-the-republic-of-kazakhstan-on-the-issues-of-non-proliferation-of-weapons-of-mass-destruction (accessed 3 Jul. 2019).

G. The Commission on Clemency

208. Another important Commission of the President of Kazakhstan that has advisory-consultative character is the Commission on Clemency that was established on 7 May 1996 by the Decree of the President of Kazakhstan.[80] The Decree of 1996 was replaced by one dated 5 July 2006, which approved the current Regulations on the Commission.[81] The President, at his own discretion, may pardon a convict or a person who is serving a sentence (paragraph 3 Regulations).

209. The Commission carries out preliminary consideration of materials on clemency (paragraph 6 of the Regulations). It is chaired by the President of Kazakhstan and consists of the deputy of the General Prosecutor who supervises the lawfulness of the execution of punishments and rehabilitation of citizens and the Chair of the Committee on the Penitentiary System of the Ministry of Internal Affairs (MIA) (or one of his deputies if the Chair is absent). The deputies of the Parliament and representatives of non-governmental organizations and other persons may be members of the Commission (paragraph 8 Regulations). The Chair of the Supreme Court, the Chairs of the supervisory boards of the Supreme Court, the Chairs of the National Security Committee and of the Agency for Civil Service Affairs and Anti-Corruption, the Ministers of Internal Affairs and Justice or their deputies, the Chair of the Committee of State Revenues of the Ministry of Finance may be present at the meetings and participate in discussions (paragraph 11 Regulations).

210. The working body of the Commission is the State Legal Department of the Administration of the President of Kazakhstan. It prepares the materials for consideration by the Commission and the President, carries out control over the timely realization of execution of the Decrees of the President on clemency, and summarizes the practice of application of clemency, and so on.

211. When considering a clemency issue, the Commission studies the following factors (paragraph 14 of Regulations):

(1) the nature and degree of danger of the committed crime, the personality of the convicted person, his/her behaviour and attitude to work, participation at the publicly valuable events at the detention centres, the term of punishment to be served, and any other circumstances that are important in consideration of a request for clemency;
(2) the opinions of the Chair of the Supreme Court, the General Prosecutor and Minister of Internal Affairs of Kazakhstan on appropriateness of the application of clemency to persons sentenced to the death penalty;

80. Please *see* about the Commission on Clemency at the official website of the Office of the President of Kazakhstan: http://www.akorda.kz/ru/executive_office/presidential_commissions/komissiya-po-voprosam-pomilovaniya (accessed 14 Jul. 2019).

81. Regulations on the Clemency Commission at the President of Kazakhstan approved by the Decree of the President of Kazakhstan of 5 Jul. 2006 No. 140. Available at: http://adilet.zan.kz/rus/docs/U060000140_(accessed 30 Apr. 2020).

(3) the opinions of the penitentiary administrations public associations and labour collectives (if any);
(4) the petition (if any) of the victim on clemency for the convicted person.

212. Based on the results of the consideration of the Commission's proposals to the President of Kazakhstan, the President issues decrees on clemency, which are not subject to appeal. When rejecting the request for clemency, the working body informs, in writing, the bodies executing punishment and the bodies of internal affairs to inform further the petitioner about a pardon or a person who filed independently such application (paragraph 32 Regulations).

§6. Early Termination of a Term or Dismissal of the President

213. As per Article 47 of the Constitution and Article 26 of the Constitutional Law on the President, the President of Kazakhstan may be dismissed before the end of his term by the decision of the Parliament if the President is consistently unable to carry out his duties because of a health condition. In accordance with the rules established in Article 47 of the Constitution of the Republic, the Parliament organizes a commission composed of equal numbers of the deputies of each Chamber of the Parliament and the experts in the relevant fields of medicine. The decision on early dismissal should be taken at the joint session of the Chambers of the Parliament by a majority of at least three-fourths of the total number of deputies of each Chamber. The decision should be grounded on the opinion of the commission and the opinion of the Constitutional Council on the observance of the established constitutional procedures.

214. The President bears responsibility for treason committed during the fulfilment of his duties. In accordance with Article 47 of the Constitution and Article 26 of the Constitutional Law on the President, treason is considered as a deliberate action done for the purpose of undermining and weakening the external security and sovereignty of the Republic, expressed in the form of defection during war or armed conflict, or assisting a foreign State in hostile activities against Kazakhstan.

215. The decision on accusation and investigation may be taken by the majority of the total number of deputies of the *Mazhilis* based on the initiative of not less than one-third of its deputies. Investigation of the charge is organized by the Senate, and upon the decision taken by the majority of voices of the total number of the deputies of the Senate the results of the investigation are transmitted for consideration at the joint session of the Parliament's Chambers. The final decision on the issue should be adopted on the grounds of the conclusion of the Supreme Court on the justification of the accusation and the conclusion of the Constitutional Council on the observance of the established constitutional provisions for such procedures. The final decision should be considered at the joint session of the Parliament's Chambers and adopted by a majority of not less than three-fourths of the total number of voices of the deputies of each of the Chambers of the Parliament. Failure to take a final decision within two months from the moment of bringing the charge implies a rejection of the accusation against the President. Rejection of the accusation against the President in committing treason at any stage entails ending before their term the powers of the deputies of the *Mazhilis* who initiated consideration of this issue.

216. The issue of a dismissal of the President in the midst of his term should not be raised during the period of consideration by the President of the issue on an early dissolution of Parliament or the *Mazhilis* of the Parliament (Article 47(3) Constitution and Article 26(3) Constitutional Law on the President). The issue of advance termination of the powers of the Parliament is regulated by Article 63 of the Constitution, and the President has the right to dissolve the Parliament or the *Mazhilis* of the Parliament after consultations with the Chairs of the Chambers of the Parliament and the Prime Minister.

217. The interpretation of the constitutional provisions of Article 42(3) on the early dismissal of the President of Kazakhstan from office was raised at the Constitutional Council of the Republic in its decision dated 15 February 2019 No. 1 and was made following the request submitted by the interim President of Kazakhstan.[82] The official interpretation was on the issue of whether the reasons for early termination of powers of the President contained in the article are exhaustive. In the view of the Council, from the content of the article, it is seen that the early release of the President of Kazakhstan from the office can be a consequence of circumstances of extraordinary character. Early release of the President from the office is possible when he/she cannot fulfil its powers sustainably because of illness.

The Council concluded that Article 42(3) does not contain a full range of reasons for the early release of the President of Kazakhstan from office. The Article neither contains, nor prohibits, the early release of the President from office because of his/her own choice. The Constitutional Council considers that the right of the Head of State to early release from office is an inalienable element of the presidential form of government and the constitutional status of the President of Kazakhstan. Free will also stems from human rights.

According to the Constitutional Council, the Constitution and the laws enshrine different types of early termination of the powers of state bodies and their servants. The constitutional approach of Kazakhstan on the early termination of the President's powers ensures the proper functioning of the supreme power for all the reasons specified in Article 42(3) of the Constitution, including the right to resignation.

Thus, the Constitutional Council came to the conclusion that the reasons specified in Article 42(3) of the Constitution for early termination of powers of the President are not exhaustive. From the constitutional status of the President stems his/her right for early termination of powers by his/her own will.

---

82. Normative Resolution of the Constitutional Council of Kazakhstan of 15 Feb. 2019 on Official Interpretation of Art. 42(3) of the Constitution of the Republic of Kazakhstan. Available at: https://ksrk.gov.kz/kk/solutions/kazakhstan-respublikasy-konstituciyasynyn-42-babynyn-3-tarmagyn-resmi-tusindiru-turaly (accessed 2 Aug. 2021).

218. In the case of an early termination of powers, or a dismissal of the President, or in the case of death, the powers of the President for the rest of that term are transferred to the Chair of the Senate of the Parliament. If the Chair of the Senate of the Parliament cannot assume the powers of the President, the powers are transferred to the Chair of the *Mazhilis* of the Parliament, and if the Chair of the *Mazhilis* cannot assume the powers of the President, the powers are transferred to the Prime Minister of the Republic. The official who accepted the powers of the President shall resign from the post of the Chair of the Senate, the Chair of the *Mazhilis* or as Prime Minister, as the case may be (Article 48(1) Constitution and Article 27(1) Constitutional Law on President).

The official who accepted the powers of the President has no right to initiate amendments and addendums to the Constitution (Article 48(2) Constitution and Article 27(2) Constitutional Law of President).

219. Since 20 March 2019, the President of Kazakhstan, Nursultan Nazarbayev, ceased to exercise the powers of the President of the country in line with Article 42(3) of the Constitution of Kazakhstan. He signed the relevant Decree dated 19 March 2019 and the rest of the presidential term was transmitted to the Chair of the Senate of Kazakhstan in accordance with Article 48(1) of the Constitution. The interim President, Kassym-Jomart Tokayev, took the oath at the joint session of the Chambers of the Parliament on 20 March 2019.[83]

83. Decree of the President of Kazakhstan of 19 Mar. 2019 No. 887 on Execution of the Powers of the President of the Republic of Kazakhstan. Available at: http://www.akorda.kz/ru/legal_acts/decrees/ob-ispolnenii-polnomochii-prezidenta-respubliki-kazahstan (accessed 3 Jul. 2019).

Chapter 3. The Legislature

§1. The Organ of State

I. Introduction

220. Chapter 4 of the current Constitution is devoted to the legal status of the Parliament. In the Constitution, the chapter regulating the status of the Parliament comes immediately after the chapter on the President's status. Together with the Constitution, the Constitutional Law on the Parliament of the Republic of Kazakhstan and the Status of its Deputies of 16 October 1995 provides the legislative framework. There are also *Regulations on the Internal Working Procedure of the Parliament dated 20 May 1996*, and separate *Regulations on the Internal Working Procedures of Each Chamber of the Parliament dated 8 February 1996.*

221. According to Article 49 of the current Constitution of Kazakhstan and the last amendments to it, the Parliament in Kazakhstan is the highest representative body carrying legislative power. The powers of the Parliament commence with the opening of its first session and end with the opening of the first session of the new convocation of a Parliament. The powers of the Parliament may be terminated early, before the end of its term, in accordance with the provisions of the Constitution. The organization and activities of the Parliament and the legal status of its deputies are defined by the special Constitutional Law of Kazakhstan mentioned above.

222. Kazakhstan has a bicameral parliamentary system. Previously a unicameral parliament had existed in accordance with the Constitution of 1993. As per Article 50 of the current Constitution, the Parliament of Kazakhstan now consists of two Chambers: the Senate and the *Mazhilis*. A deputy cannot be simultaneously a deputy of both Chambers. In total, there are forty-seven deputies in the Senate and 107 deputies in the *Mazhilis*. Each Chamber of the Parliament is led by a Chair. Both Chairs are elected by secret ballot from the deputies of the respective Chamber and should know the Kazakh language fluently. A candidate for the post of the Chair of the Senate is nominated by the President of Kazakhstan; the deputies of the *Mazhilis* nominate a candidate for the post of the Chair of the *Mazhilis*.

II. Categorization of the Members of Parliament

A. *Thirty-Four Elected Senators*

223. Two deputies from each region (*oblast*), from cities of special national importance, and from the capital of Kazakhstan compose the Senate of the Parliament (Article 50 Constitution). Half of the deputies of the Senate are re-elected every three years (Article 4(2) Constitutional Law on Parliament). There are fourteen regions (*oblasts*) and three cities of a special national significance, including the capital. So, there are thirty-four deputies representing the administrative regions of Kazakhstan in the Senate.

B. Fifteen Appointed Senators

224. Fifteen deputies of the Senate are appointed by the President of Kazakhstan to represent ethnocultural groups and other important needs and interests.

C. Ninety-Eight Deputies of the Mazhilis *Representing Political Parties*

225. The *Mazhilis* consists of 107 deputies elected in accordance with the rules envisaged by the Constitutional Law. Ninety-eight deputies of the *Mazhilis* are elected from party lists in one nationwide constituency in accordance with the principles of universal, equal and direct suffrage, and secret ballots. The electoral threshold is 7%.

D. Nine Deputies of the Mazhilis *Elected by the Assembly of the People of Kazakhstan*

226. Nine deputies of the *Mazhilis* are elected by the Assembly of the People of Kazakhstan (Article 4(4) Constitutional Law on Parliament).

III. Electoral System

A. General Introduction

227. Apart from constitutional provisions, the elections of the deputies of the Parliament are regulated by the special Constitutional Law of Kazakhstan on the Elections in the Republic of Kazakhstan of 28 September 1995 and the Law on Political Parties of 15 July 2002.[84]

228. A citizen of Kazakhstan who has reached 18 years of age has the right to vote and participate in the elections (universal active suffrage). Those citizens who are recognized as legally incapable by the court and those who are currently serving prison sentences have no right to participate in elections (Article 4(3) Constitutional Law on Elections). As a general rule, a deputy of the Parliament must be a person who is a citizen of Kazakhstan and has permanently resided in its territory for the last ten years (Article 51(4) Constitution).

B. Elections of the Deputies of the Mazhilis

229. A deputy of the *Mazhilis* must be a person who has reached twenty-five years of age (Article 51(4) Constitution).

84. Law of the Republic of Kazakhstan of 15 Jul. 2002 No. 344-II on the Political Parties. Available at the official website of the Ministry of Justice of Kazakhstan: https://online.zakon.kz/document/?doc_id=1032141 (accessed 2 Aug. 2021).

230. As per Article 51 of the Constitution of Kazakhstan, ninety-eight deputies of the *Mazhilis* are elected on the grounds of universal, equal and direct suffrage by secret ballot. They are directly elected by citizens (Article 6 Constitutional Law on Elections). Nine other deputies are elected by the Assembly of the People of Kazakhstan.

231. According to Article 87 of the Constitutional Law on Elections, the right to nominate a candidate as a deputy of the *Mazhilis* on the basis of a party list belongs to the political parties registered in accordance with established rules. The nomination of the candidates shall start two months before and end forty days before the elections.

232. At the Assembly of the People of Kazakhstan the right to nominate a candidate belongs to its Council. The decision of the Council is taken by a majority of votes (Article 87(4) Constitutional Law on Elections). The nomination of the candidates shall start one month before and end twenty days before the elections.

233. Regular elections shall be held no later than two months before the end of the term for deputies of the *Mazhilis* of the current session Parliament. The elections are carried out in the course of a normal ending to their constitutional term (Article 85(1) Constitutional Law on Elections).

234. Snap elections of deputies are carried out in the event of an early dissolution of the Parliament and the *Mazhilis* (Article 85(2) Constitutional Law on elections). Such snap elections of the deputies of the Parliament or the *Mazhilis* shall be held within two months from the date of early dissolution of the Parliament or the *Mazhilis* respectively.

235. In the VI Convocation of the *Mazhilis* elected in 2016, three parties, Nur Otan (eighty-four seats), People's Communists (seven seats), and the Democratic Party 'Ak Zhol' (seven seats), were represented. In the current *Mazhilis* (VII Convocation elected in January 2021) three parties Nur Otan (seventy-six seats), the Democratic Party 'Ak Zhol' (twelve seats), and the People's Communists (ten seats), are represented.

C. Elections of the Deputies of the Senate

236. Apart from the general requirements for a deputy, a deputy of the Senate must be a person who has reached thirty years of age, has received higher education, have at least five years of work experience and has been residing permanently in the territory of the respective region, a city of national importance, or the capital for not less than three years (Article 51(4) Constitution).

237. The deputies of the Senate are elected by indirect suffrage and secret vote. The regular elections of the deputies of the Senate are carried out if their constitutional term of office has ended normally. These regular elections are held no later than two months before the end of their term of office.

238. The deputies of the Senate are elected by 'electors' who are the deputies of the *maslikhats*. Each elector has one vote (Article 7 Constitutional Law on Elections). The electors are all deputies of all *maslikhats* of the *oblast* (region) and of a city of national importance (Article 25(2) Constitutional Law on Elections). The elections of deputies of the Senate are carried out at the joint sessions of the electors of the region (Article 77 Constitutional Law on Elections). The candidate who receives more than 50% of the votes of the participating electors is considered elected (Article 81(2) Constitutional Law on Elections).

239. The nomination of the candidates for a deputy is carried out at the session of the respective *maslikhats,* or by way of a prospective candidate submitting an application to the relevant election commission. The decision on the nomination of a candidate for deputy is made by a majority of votes of the total number of deputies of the respective *maslikhat* (Article 71 Constitutional Law on Elections).

240. Snap elections of the deputies of the Senate are carried out if their constitutional term of office has ended prematurely or in the case of the formation of a new administrative-territorial unit in the country, one which has not yet been represented in the Senate (Article 69 Constitutional Law on Elections).

§2. Legal Status

I. Mandate of the Member of the Parliament

241. Chapter 4 of the Constitution of Kazakhstan covers issues of the legal status and powers of the Parliament. Chapter 5 of Constitutional Law on Parliament is devoted to the legal status of the members of the Parliament, and Article 24 of Constitutional Law on Parliament concerns general issues related to the mandate of a deputy.

242. By and large, the representative character of the Parliament is stated in the Constitution, and in accordance with Article 3(3), the Parliament has the right within its constitutional powers to speak on behalf of the people of Kazakhstan. A deputy of the Parliament swears an oath to the people of Kazakhstan (Article 51(6) Constitution).

243. According to the Constitution, the deputy represents not only his voters but all voters of Kazakhstan. The deputy 'does not have an imperative mandate' and is not responsible before the voters for any promises.[85]

244. The term of a deputy of the Senate is six years; the term of a deputy of the *Mazhilis* is five years. The powers of the Parliament commence from the opening of its first session after regular elections and end with the beginning of the first sitting of the Parliament upon a new convocation. The order of convocation of the *Mazhilis* defines the order of convocation of the Parliament. The term of office of the Parliament is defined by the term of office of the deputies of the *Mazhilis* of the subsequent convocation (Article 2 Constitutional Law on Parliament).

245. In line with Article 24 of the Constitutional Law, the mandate of a deputy of the Parliament starts from the moment of his registration as a deputy at the Central Election Commission of the Republic. The deputy swears an oath to the people of Kazakhstan.

246. The powers of the Parliament and the *Mazhilis* may be terminated before the end of their term in accordance with the procedures stipulated in the Constitution of the Republic.

247. The mandate of a deputy shall be terminated in cases of resignation, death, a court order declaring disability, decease or whereabouts unknown, or in other circumstances stipulated in the Constitution or the Constitutional Law on Parliament.

248. The mandate of the deputies of the *Mazhilis* of the Parliament elected by the Assembly of the People of Kazakhstan may be ended early by the decision of the Assembly. The mandate of a deputy of the *Mazhilis* is terminated in case of resignation or expulsion from the party from which he was elected in accordance with the constitutional laws. The termination of the activities of the political party also brings about the termination of the mandate of a deputy of the *Mazhilis* who represented the party.

249. A mandate of the appointed deputies of the Senate may be terminated early upon the decision of the President of the Republic. A mandate of the deputies of the Senate of the Parliament elected at a joint meeting of the electors representing all *maslikhats* of the particular region, city of national importance or the capital of the Republic, may be terminated early upon the decision of the electors.

250. A deputy of the Parliament loses his mandate if he leaves Kazakhstan for permanent residency outside of the Republic or if he loses citizenship of Kazakhstan. The mandate of a deputy is terminated upon entry into force of a court conviction.

85. Ghairat Sapargaliyev, *The Constitutional Law of the Republic of Kazakhstan. Academic course*, 328 (2002).

251. The powers of the deputies of the *Mazhilis* and the Parliament shall be terminated on the dissolution of these bodies.

II. Incompatibilities, Immunities and Privileges

A. *Incompatibilities*

252. A deputy of the Parliament has no right to be a deputy of another representative body, or to hold other paid positions except carrying out academic, scientific or other creative activities. A deputy of the Parliament has no right to carry out entrepreneurial activities, to be a member of the governing body or the supervisory board of a commercial entity. Violation of these provisions entails the termination of the powers of a deputy upon recommendation of the Central Election Commission of the Republic (Articles 52(3) Constitution and 24(2) Constitutional Law on Parliament).

B. *Immunities*

253. During his term, a deputy of the Parliament cannot be arrested, forcibly brought before prosecuting bodies, subjected to administrative penalties imposed by a court, or convicted of a crime without the consent of the respective Chamber, except in cases of arrest when committing serious crimes (Article 52(4) Constitution and Article 32(1) Constitutional Law on Parliament).

254. The Central Election Commission is entrusted with addressing issues related to the application of the administrative measures against deputies and the termination of their powers and immunities (Article 52(6) Constitution).

255. In order to obtain the necessary consent to bring criminal proceedings against the deputy, to arrest him or detain him in custody, to subject him to a house arrest or bring him before prosecuting bodies, or apply the administrative measures to be imposed by a court, the General Prosecutor of Kazakhstan makes a proposal to the Senate or the *Mazhilis*. The respective Chamber sends the proposal to the Central Election Commission for preparation of the file to be discussed at the meeting of the respective Chamber. The proposal of the General Prosecutor and the conclusions of the Central Election Commission are to be discussed not later than two weeks after their submission to the Chamber. The respective Chamber has the right to request additional information from the General Prosecutor and the Central Election Commission. Within three working days, the Chamber should adopt a well-founded decision and afterwards send it to the General Prosecutor and head of the state body carrying out enquiry and investigation. The deputy has the right to participate in the Chamber's consideration of the issue on his immunity. The General Prosecutor carries out any observance of the legality of the investigation of the case.

256. The Central Election Commission requests the results of the case from the respective court that tried the deputy, and in case of conviction, the Commission shall submit a proposal to the respective Chamber on the termination of the deputy's mandate. (Article 32(4) Constitutional Law on Parliament).

C. *Privileges*

257. The privileges of a deputy are outlined in the Constitutional Law on Parliament. Any form of influence on a deputy and his close relatives intended to hamper him in the execution of his duties shall be dealt with in accordance with the laws of the Republic. The officials of the state bodies and public associations, of local self-government bodies and organizations who do not fulfil their duties in connection with the deputy, and who provide false information impeding the activities of the deputy shall be dealt with in accordance with the laws of Kazakhstan (Article 31 Constitutional Law on Parliament).

258. In accordance with Article 30(1) of the Constitutional Law on Parliament, a deputy receives a salary from the national budget. Those deputies who reside outside of the capital of the Republic for the period of their term shall be provided with furnished and convenient accommodation for free from the stock of public housing.

259. To support the relations of the deputies with their voters and to keep them regularly informed about the activities of the Parliament, and to fulfil the instructions of the Parliament and its Chambers and their bodies, each deputy has the right to take business trips to their constituencies at the expense of the national budget. Travel expenses of a deputy related to carrying out the instructions of the Parliament, the Chamber and their bodies shall be reimbursed by the national budget. A deputy gets transport, health-improving and sanatorium services.

260. At the end of his term of office, as well as in cases of his resignation or dissolution of the Parliament or the *Mazhilis*, a deputy gets a monthly allowance at the rate of his average monthly salary until obtaining other employment but for not more than three months.

§3. Powers

I. Legislation

261. Chapter 3 of the Constitutional Law on the Parliament regulates the legislative process in the Parliament of Kazakhstan. Legislative initiative deals with the official submission of the initial text of a draft law or of any other legislative act of the Parliament which it has to consider. Legislative initiative lies only with the *Mazhilis* of the Parliament. The deputies of the Parliament have the right to initiate a law, alongside the President and the Government of the Republic. As a general rule, draft laws are sent to the respective standing committees and may only thereafter be considered at the plenary session of the *Mazhilis* once they have the committees' opinion (Article 15 Constitutional Law on Parliament).

262. Parliament passes a Law, which is the first competence of the Parliament. As mentioned before, Laws are adopted regarding the most important social relations, establishing the basic principles and norms concerning any of the following issues (Article 16 Constitutional Law on Parliament):

(1) the legal personality of individuals and legal entities, civil rights and freedoms, obligations and responsibility of individuals and legal entities;
(2) the legal regime of property and other proprietary rights;
(3) fundamentals of organization and activities of the state bodies and local governments, state and military service;
(4) taxation, the establishment of fees and other mandatory payments;
(5) national budget;
(6) issues of judicial organization and legal proceedings;
(7) education, healthcare and social security;
(8) privatization of enterprises and their property;
(9) protection of the environment;
(10) administrative and territorial division of the Republic;
(11) defence and security of the state.

All other relations are regulated by Bylaws.

II. Supervision of and Control over the Executive

A. The Parliamentary Hearings

263. In accordance with Article 57 subparagraph 7 of the Constitution, each Chamber of the Parliament conducts its hearings independently of the other. Article 12 of the Constitutional Law on the Parliament envisages that the Chambers of the Parliament shall hold their hearings on issues within their competence. They are held by the permanent committees of the Chambers upon a decision of the Bureau of Chambers and may carry this out in open or closed sessions. Parliamentary hearings cannot be held during joint or separate sessions of the Chambers.

264. In accordance with recent amendments of June 2020 to Article 12, the parliamentary opposition has the right to initiate parliamentary hearings at least once during one session in line with the procedures prescribed by the Regulations on the Internal Working Procedures of the *Mazhilis* of the Parliament.

265. Paragraph 8 of the Regulations on the Internal Working Procedures of the Senate states that parliamentary hearings are the organizational form of the Senate's activity aimed at preliminary discussions on draft laws, obtaining comprehensive and objective information on the implementation of laws, the realization of the national and regional programmes related to the various areas of Government, ministerial and departmental competence, as well as in-depth analysis of the key issues of the internal and external policy of the State.[86] Parliamentary hearings are usually open to the media and the public. The duration of the hearing depends on the issues under discussion. The representatives of the Government and experts can be invited to attend. Recommendations on the matters in issue can then be adopted. For example, on 12 September 2017, parliamentary hearings were held at the Senate on the issues of education, and the Minister of Education was invited to discuss the current policy on schoolbooks.[87]

266. As per the Regulations on the Internal Working Procedures of the *Mazhilis*, the aim of the parliamentary hearings of the *Mazhilis* is a preliminary discussion of the most important questions falling within its competence. The reports on the hearings may be published in the Parliament gazette and in the media. The recommendations flowing from the results of the hearings are adopted by a majority of all deputies participating in the hearings. For example, on 12 May 2017, at the *Mazhilis* of the Parliament, the issues of providing the population with medicine and the development of the pharmacy industry in Kazakhstan were discussed at the parliamentary hearings.[88] The Minister of Healthcare and the Minister of Investment and Development prepared reports for these hearings.

B. The Right of Interpellation and the Right to Ask Questions

267. In accordance with Article 27 of Constitutional Law on the Parliament, at the joint and separate sessions of the Chambers of the Parliament, a deputy has the right to request formally of an official of a state body a reasoned explanation or clarification of a position on issues falling within the competence of that body and official.

268. A deputy of the Parliament has a right to submit questions to the Prime Minister and the members of the Government, the Chair of the National Bank, the Chair of the Central Election Commission, the General Prosecutor, the Chair of the Committee of the National Security, the Chair and the members of the Control Committee on Fulfilment of the National Budget. However, questions to the General Prosecutor or other heads of the state law-enforcement bodies should not concern

---

86. Regulations of the Internal Working Procedures of the Senate of the Parliament approved by the Resolution of the *Mazhilis* of the Parliament of 8 Feb. 1996. Available at: http://adilet.zan.kz/rus/docs/B960000002_ (accessed 30 Apr. 2020).
87. Kassym-Jomart Tokayev, *Hasty Experiments in the System of Education Should Not Be Conducted*. Available at the official website of the Senate of the Parliament of Kazakhstan: https://www.zakon.kz/4879721-k-tokaev-v-sisteme-obrazovaniya-nelzya.html (accessed 2 Apr. 2018).
88. *The parliamentary hearings on issues of providing the population with medicines were held at the Mazhilis*. Available at: https://pharm.reviews/stati/sobytiya/item/2071-v-kazakhstane-sostoyalis-parlamentskie-slushaniya-po-voprosam-lekarstvennogo-obespecheniya-i-razvitiya-farmotrasli (accessed 2 Aug. 2021).

pursuing criminal prosecution. Consideration of requests addressed to the Chair of the Committee on the National Security shall be held in camera at the Parliament and its Chambers.

269. A question can be submitted in writing and must be read aloud at the session of the Parliament. The officials must provide an oral or written response at that session of the Parliament. A written response should be submitted within one month and shall be announced at the session. If necessary, the Parliament or its Chambers may adopt a Resolution on the results of the interpellation, and they may be published in the media.

270. The deputies at the joint and separate sessions of the Chambers of the Parliament have the right to ask questions of the Prime Minister and the members of the Government, the Chair of the National Bank, the Chair and the members of the Central Election Commission, the General Prosecutor, the Chair of the Committee on the National Security and the Chair of the Control Committee on Fulfilment of the National Budget. The response should be given at the same session, and if necessary, may receive three extra days for additional preparation.

C. 'Government Hour' at the Mazhilis of the Parliament

271. In accordance with Regulations on Internal Working Procedures, the *Mazhilis* of the Parliament may hold a 'Government hour' on the issues within its competence in line with its plan of the work. During this Government hour, the deputies hear a report from a representative of the Government and, if necessary, hear a co-report of the relevant permanent committee. Thereafter the deputies may put questions to the representative of the Government.

D. Participation of the Parliament in Appointment, Election and Dismissal of the State Officials

272. In accordance with Article 22 of the Constitutional Law on the Parliament, the Chambers of the Parliament give consent to the President of the Republic in the appointment of state officials. The President submits a request to the *Mazhilis* for consent to be given to the appointment of the Prime Minister.

273. The President requests the Senate of the Parliament to give consent for the appointments of the Chair of the National Bank, of the General Prosecutor and of the Chair of the Committee on the National Security of the Republic. The President requests the Senate to give its consent to the election and dismissal of the Chair and judges of the Supreme Court and of the Human Rights Commissioner of the Republic. Before consideration in the Chamber, the relevant committee of the Senate discusses the profiles of the proposed candidates, and the members of the committee may put questions to the candidate.

274. The *Mazhilis* of the Parliament plays a consultative role in the appointment of members of the Government. The profiles of the candidates that are proposed by the Prime Minister are discussed in the relevant committees of the *Mazhilis*. The opinion of the committee has an advisory nature (Article 22-1 Constitutional Law on Parliament).

275. The decision on giving consent for the appointment, election and dismissal of the state official is taken by open vote and a majority of the total number of deputies of the respective Chamber. The decisions are formulated in the Resolutions of the Chamber (Article 23 Constitutional Law on Parliament).

276. The Chambers of the Parliament appoint the state officials. As per Article 23-1 of the Constitutional Law on the Parliament, each Chamber, independently of the other, appoints two members of the Constitutional Council; it also appoints two members of the Central Election Commission for a five-year term, and three members of the Control Committee on Fulfilment of the National Budget. The decision on the appointment of these state officials is adopted by a majority of the total number of the deputies of the respective Chamber of the Parliament and is formulated by a Resolution of the Chamber.

§4. The Working of Parliament

I. Working Procedures, Quorum and the Bodies of the Parliament

277. The working procedures of the Parliament and its Chambers are regulated by regulations on the internal working procedures of the whole Parliament and of each Chamber separately. So there are three sets of regulations. They concern such questions as the conditions and procedures for holding joint and separate meetings of the Senate and the *Mazhilis*, the order of forming the working bodies of the Parliament and its Chambers, organization of the activities of the Parliament and its Chambers, the working bodies, conditions and procedures for the exercise of competences by the deputies and the officials of the Parliament (Article 14 Constitutional Law on Parliament). The Regulations also cover the specifics of the organization and functioning of the organized parliamentary group representing a political party. The regulations shall be approved by normative Resolutions of the Parliament and its Chambers.

278. In accordance with Article 59 of the Constitution, the sessions of the Parliament take place in the form of both joint and separate meetings of the Chambers. The first session of the Parliament is opened by the President of the Republic and shall be convened within thirty days after the promulgation of the results of general elections. The first meeting of the Senate before the election of the Chair is chaired by the President; the first meeting of the *Mazhilis* is chaired by the Chair of the Central Election Commission (Article 6 Constitutional Law on Parliament).

279. In the period between sessions of the Parliament, the President of the Republic on his own initiative, upon a proposal of the Chairs of the Chambers or at least one-third of the total number of the deputies of the Parliament, may convene an extraordinary session of the Parliament (Article 6(6) Constitutional Law on Parliament).

280. The joint and separate meetings of the Parliament are carried out if at least two-thirds of the total number of the deputies of the Chamber are present. The President of the Republic, the Prime Minister and the members of the Government, the Chair of the National Bank, the General Prosecutor, the Chair of the Committee on the National Security, the State Secretary and the Head of the Administration of the President have the right to be present and to be heard at any meeting of the Parliament.

281. As envisaged in Article 60 of the Constitution, there should not be more than seven permanent committees in each Chamber of the Parliament. The two Chambers may organize joint commissions to resolve issues of common competencies. The permanent committees and the commissions issue Resolutions.

282. The Chambers of the Parliament are headed by the Chairs who are elected by secret ballot by a majority of votes of the total number of the deputies of the Chamber. As per Article 9 of the Constitutional Law on Parliament, the candidacy for the post of the Chair of the Senate is nominated by the President of the Republic. The candidacy for the post of the Chair of the *Mazhilis* is nominated by the deputies of the Chamber. The Chairs convene the sessions of the Parliament, exercise overall guidance over the preparation of questions for consideration by the Chamber, and sign the acts of the Chambers, propose the candidacy of two members of the Constitutional Council, two members of the Central Election Commission and three members of the Control Committee on the Fulfilment of the National Budget, and fulfil other duties assigned by the Regulations. On the issues of their competence, the Chairs of the Chambers issue orders. The Chair has a casting vote if the votes of the deputies are equally divided. The Chairs are assisted by two deputies elected upon a proposal of the Chair by a majority of votes of the total number of the deputies of the Chamber.

283. According to Article 10 of the Constitutional Law on Parliament, the coordinating bodies of the Parliament are the Bureau of the Senate and the Bureau of the *Mazhilis*. The Bureau includes the deputies of the Chairs of the Chambers and the Chairs of the permanent committees of the Chambers. The Bureau of the *Mazhilis* is also composed of heads of the organized parliamentary groups of the political parties represented in the *Mazhilis*. The Bureaus coordinate the activities of the committees and the commissions of the Chambers. The quorum of the Bureau is two-thirds of the total number of its members.

284. As mentioned in Article 11 of the Constitutional Law on Parliament, the working bodies of the Parliament are the permanent committees of the Senate and the *Mazhilis* and the joint commissions of the Chambers. The permanent committees of the Chambers are organized for carrying out law-drafting activities, preliminary consideration and preparation of the questions falling within the competence of the Chambers. The quorum of the committees and the commissions is two-thirds of the total number of its members. They adopt the Resolutions on the issues of their competencies.

285. The Parliament of the Republic may set up the consultative-advisory bodies which adopt decisions of recommendatory character.

II. Legislative Proceedings

286. The order of consideration of the draft laws and other acts at the Parliament is defined by the Parliament of Kazakhstan and its Chambers, and in certain cases stipulated in the Constitution; the order of consideration may be defined by the President of the Republic. The President in his special address (message) has the right to define which draft laws are in priority and should, therefore, be adopted within two months. The procedures of consideration of prioritized laws by the Chambers of the Parliament are prescribed by the Constitution and the Regulations of the internal working procedures of the Chambers of the Parliament (Article 17 Constitutional Law on Parliament).

287. Article 18 of the Constitutional Law on Parliament envisages the procedures for the adoption of laws.

288. The draft of ordinary law considered and approved by the majority of votes of the total number of the deputies of the *Mazhilis* shall be submitted to the Senate. At the Senate, the draft should be discussed no more than sixty days. When approved by the majority of votes of the total number of the deputies of the Senate, the draft becomes law and shall then be submitted to the President for his signature. If the draft law is rejected by the Senate, it is sent back to the *Mazhilis*. If the *Mazhilis* by a two-thirds majority of votes reaffirm the draft, it shall be submitted to the Senate for a second discussion and vote. If rejected a second time, it cannot be resubmitted during the same session.

289. The Senate of the Parliament of Kazakhstan can add amendments to the draft law and approve it by a majority of votes of the total number of the Senate. The draft with such amendments shall be sent to the *Mazhilis*. If the *Mazhilis* agrees with the amendments by the majority of votes, the draft law is adopted as law. If the *Mazhilis* by the same majority of votes does not agree with the amendments of the Senate, disagreements should be resolved via conciliation procedures.

290. The draft of the constitutional law discussed and approved by not less than two-thirds of votes of the total number of the *Mazhilis*'s deputies shall be transmitted to the Senate. At the Senate, the draft shall be discussed for no more than sixty days. Adopted by two-thirds of votes of the total number of the deputies of the

Chamber, the draft becomes a constitutional law and within ten days shall be submitted to the President for signature. Rejection of the whole draft by the *Mazhilis* or the Senate shall be done by the majority of the total number of the deputies of the Chamber. The rejected draft shall be returned to its initiator.

291. If the *Mazhilis* rejects a draft law submitted by the Government, the Prime Minister may raise a question of a motion of non-confidence in the Government at a joint session of the Parliament. If a majority of the total number of the deputies of each Chamber does not vote in favour of a motion of no confidence in the Government, the draft law submitted by the Government is considered as adopted without any vote. The Government cannot use such a right more than twice per calendar year (Article 18 Constitutional Law on Parliament).

III. President's Assent, Promulgation and Publication of Acts

292. The laws of Kazakhstan come into force only after signing by the President of the Republic. Article 19 of the Constitutional Law on the Parliament regulates the issues of submission of the laws for the signature to the President of the Republic.

293. A law passed by the Parliament shall be signed by the Chairs of each Chamber, as well as by the Prime Minister if a draft law was submitted and drawn up by the Government. It shall be submitted for signature within ten days to the President of the Republic. The President has the right to sign and promulgate the submitted law within a month, or to return the law or any part of it to the Parliament for rediscussion and re-voting.

294. According to Article 20 of the Constitutional Law on Parliament, reconsideration and a revote on the law or its articles returned by the President shall be done within one month. After receiving the opinion of the respective permanent committee of the *Mazhilis*, the returned law shall be submitted to the plenary meeting of the *Mazhilis*. If the *Mazhilis* confirms the previous decision by two-thirds of votes of the total number of the deputies, the law, with the President's objections, shall be submitted to the Senate. If the *Mazhilis* does not confirm the previous decision, the *Mazhilis* stops further consideration of the law, and the law will be considered as not adopted or adopted in the wording proposed by the President.

295. The respective permanent committee of the Senate gives its opinion on the law with the President's objections, and after that, the law shall be transmitted to the plenary meeting of the Senate. If the Senate does not confirm the previous decision on the law, the latter will be considered as not adopted or as adopted in the wording proposed by the President

296. If the Senate by a two-thirds majority of the total number of the deputies of the Chamber confirms the previous decision on the law, the President's objections will be rejected. In such a case, the law will be adopted in the wording as it was before the President's objections. The President shall sign the law within one month after its submission for his signature.

297. In regard to constitutional laws, the President's objections to them must be overcome by at least three-fourths of the votes of the total number of the deputies of each Chamber.

298. In accordance with Article 37 of the Law on Legal Acts of Kazakhstan, the adopted law should be published in such official publications as the Bulletin of the Parliament (*Vedomosti Parlamenta Respubliki Kazakhstan*). Also, the official publication of legislative acts shall be done by the periodic print media who won the competition for doing so, in compliance with the rules determined by the Government of Kazakhstan. Official publication of electronic versions is also carried out by the Standard Control Bank of the Normative Legal Acts of Kazakhstan.

299. As mentioned in a previous chapter, the first official publication of the law should be done simultaneously in the Kazakh and Russian languages within thirty calendar days after the day they come into effect. The text of the law should be published in full. The official publication of the laws which concern the human rights, freedoms and duties of citizens is an obligatory condition for their application.

300. Since the State keeps records of normative legal acts, including the Laws, the Law should be registered in the State Registry of Normative Legal Acts and the Standard Control Bank of the Normative Legal Acts of Kazakhstan (Article 53(1) Law on Legal Acts).

§5. Miscellaneous

I. Legislation Having Retroactive Effect

301. As a general rule, a Law has proactive effect, but there are some exemptions from this rule. In accordance with Article 43 of the Law on Legal Acts, a Law can have retroactive effect if such circumstances are envisaged in the Law and if the new Law excludes duties imposed on citizens or improves their condition. The Laws that impose new duties or new responsibilities on citizens, or worsen their situation, do not have retroactive effects. For wrongdoing committed before the new Law came into force, if the new Law abolishes or alleviates responsibility for that offence, it should be so applied.

Chapter 4. The Executive

§1. The Organ of State

I. General Introduction

302. Chapter 5 of the Constitution of Kazakhstan is devoted to the legal status of the Government of Kazakhstan. The status of the Government in the Constitution comes after the Regulation on the Status of the Parliament. The competence, organization and activity of the Government are elaborated in Constitutional Law of 18 December 1995 No. 2688 on the Government of the Republic of Kazakhstan. The Internal Working Procedures of the Government are settled by the Regulations approved by its Resolution of 10 December 2002 No. 1300.

II. The Way of Forming a Government

303. In accordance with Article 65 of the Constitution, the Government of Kazakhstan is formed by the President of Kazakhstan. According to Article 44 subparagraph 3 of the Constitution of Kazakhstan, after consultations with the organized parliamentary groups of the political parties represented in the *Mazhilis*, the President of the Republic submits the candidacy of the Prime Minister for approval. The *Mazhilis* of the Parliament by a majority of voices of the total number of the deputies gives consent to the President of the Republic for the appointment of the Prime Minister of the Republic (Article 56(1(2)) Constitution of the Republic). So, the President of the Republic appoints the Prime Minister of Kazakhstan, with the consent of the *Mazhilis*. The President dismisses the Prime Minister.

304. The President defines the structure of the Government. Proposals on the structure and composition of the Government are made to the President by the Prime Minister of the Republic within ten days of his appointment, in line with Article 19(1(4)) of the Constitutional Law on the Government of Kazakhstan. After consultations with the *Mazhilis* of the Parliament, the Prime Minister of the Republic submits to the President his proposals on candidacies for the appointment of the members of the Parliament, except for the candidacies of the Minister of Foreign Affairs, the Minister of Defence and the Minister of Internal Affairs. He also makes proposals to dismiss members of the Government, including those who do not agree with the policy of the Government or do not conduct it to the President (except the Ministers of Foreign Affairs, Defence and Internal Affairs). The Minister of Foreign Affairs, the Minister of Defence and the Minister of Internal Affairs are appointed by the President of the Republic independently (Article 44 subparagraph 3 Constitution).

III. Composition and Organization of the Government

305. As written in Article 3 of Constitutional Law on Government, the structure of the Government comprises the various ministries. In the current Government, there are eighteen ministries.[89] At the time of writing, the following Ministries compose the Government of Kazakhstan:

– the Ministry of Agriculture;
– the Ministry of Culture and Sport;
– the Ministry of Defence;
– the Ministry of Digital Development, Innovations and Aerospace Industry;
– the Ministry of Education and Science;
– the Ministry of Ecology, Geology and Natural Resources;
– the Ministry of Energy;
– the Ministry of Finance;
– the MFA;
– the Ministry of Healthcare;
– the MIA;
– the Ministry of Industry and Infrastructural Development;
– the Ministry of Information and Public Development;
– the Ministry of Labour and Social Protection;
– the Ministry of Justice;
– the Ministry of National Economy;
– the Ministry of Trade and Integration;
- . the Ministry of Emergency Situations.

306. According to Article 3(4) of Constitutional Law on the Government of Kazakhstan, the members of the Government of Kazakhstan are the Prime Minister of the Republic, his deputies, ministers and other officials of the Republic.

307. These proposals on the structure and composition of the Government are to be submitted to the President of the Republic by the Prime Minister within ten days of the appointment of the Prime Minister.

308. According to Article 18 of Constitutional Law on the Government, the meetings of the Government are held at least once per month. They are convened by the Prime Minister or the President of the Republic. They are chaired by the Prime Minister, in case of his absence – by his deputy. If necessary, in case of consideration of very important questions, the President of the Republic chairs the meeting. At the meeting, at least two-thirds of the members of the Government should be present. The meetings of the Government are open to the public. Upon the initiatives of the President or the Prime Minister, closed meetings can also be held. As mentioned before, there are special Regulations of the internal working procedures of the Government of Kazakhstan.

89. Please see the official website of the Government of the Republic of Kazakhstan: https://government.kz/kz/government/state (accessed 2 Aug. 2021).

§2. Legal Status

309. In accordance with Article 64 of the Constitution, the Government is responsible for the activities of the executive bodies since it exercises the executive power in the Republic and leads the system of the executive bodies. The Government is a collegiate body and in all its activities is accountable to the President and the Parliament of the Republic. The members of the Government are accountable to the Chambers of the Parliament as stipulated in the Constitution. They swear an oath to the people and the President of Kazakhstan (Article 65(3) Constitution).

310. The Government acts on the grounds and for the realization of the Constitution, of the Constitutional Law on the Government of Kazakhstan, laws and other normative legal acts of the Republic (Article 2 Constitutional Law on Government).

311. The Government shall work within the term of office of the *Mazhilis* of the Parliament and shall resign when the new *Mazhilis* is elected. The Government will continue to exercise power until approval of the new composition of the Government (Article 4 Constitutional Law on Government).

312. Article 5 of the Constitutional Law on Government regulates the issues of resignation. The Government and any of its members may inform the President if they wish to resign if they consider that further realization of their functions is not possible. Those members of the Government who do not agree with the policy of the Government also have a right to resign. The Government informs the President about his/her resignation if the *Mazhilis* of the Parliament or the Parliament expresses a vote of no confidence in cases stipulated by the Constitution of the Republic, and in such cases, the President has ten days to decide whether or not to accept the resignation. In general, acceptance by the President of the resignation of the Prime Minister signifies the termination of the powers of the whole Government. If the President rejects the resignation, he instructs the Government or its member to continue to exercise their duties.

313. Article 6 of the Constitutional Law on Government covers the issues of termination of the Government's powers upon the initiative of the President. The President on his own initiative may take a decision to terminate the powers of the Government and to dismiss any member of the Cabinet. The dismissal of the Prime Minister signifies the termination of the powers of the entire Government. The members of the Government shall be dismissed if they do not agree with the policy of the Government or do not carry it out.

314. There are certain restrictions related to the activities of a member of the Government stemming from his/her position. The members of the Government have no right to be a deputy of a representative body, to hold other paid positions except for teaching, scientific or any other creative activity, to carry out entrepreneurship, and to be a member of the governing or supervisory board of any commercial entity except for commercial entities with state participation in cases stipulated by the decisions of the Government.

§3. POWERS

I. The Overall Powers of the Executive

315. Overall, the executive branch of power in Kazakhstan is responsible for enforcement and implementation of the Constitution and the laws of the Republic, for provision of public services to people and management of state property, for the maintenance of public order and for exercising defence of the state from external threats. There are central and local state bodies in Kazakhstan exercising executive power.

316. The Government of Kazakhstan is a collegiate body. It leads the system of state bodies in a hierarchical structure. Chapter 2 of the Constitutional Law of Kazakhstan contains the main provisions regulating the powers of the Government, and Article 9 concerns a particular competence of the Government. In accordance with this, the Government of Kazakhstan is responsible for strategic forecasts and their execution. So the Government decides the main directions of the social and economic policy of the state, of its defensive capacity, security and maintenance of public order, and organizes its realization; with the concurrence of the President, the Government approves the state programs and ensures their executions, it defines the system of state planning; the Government approves policies for the social and economic development.

317. With regards to the national budget, the Government is charged with drafting and presenting it to the Parliament and for its execution and must report on this to the Parliament of the Republic. The Government creates the national budgetary commission, approves the regulations on its status and defines its composition. The Government determines the procedure for drawing up and submitting an annual report on the execution of the national budget.

318. With regards to finance and state property, the Government of Kazakhstan develops and implements the measures for strengthening the financial system of the Republic; provides for state control over the observance of legality in the formation and use of state monetary, financial and material resources; it carries out structural and investment policy; it develops state policy on pricing; establishes a nomenclature of products, goods and services for which state-regulated prices are applied. The Government organizes the management of state property, develops and realizes measures on its use, ensures protection of the right to state property.

319. Concerning the social security of its people, the Government forms a system and conditions of labour remuneration, social security of citizens, state social security and social insurance; with the concurrence of the President, it approves a unified system of financing and labour remuneration for all bodies that are financed by the national budget.

320. The Government also develops the main directions of the state policy on regional development, ensures the solution of interregional problems and issues of social and economic development in the regions. The Government is responsible for state policy on the development of science and technology, implementation of new technology, culture, education, healthcare, tourism and sport.

321. The Government is charged with developing and implementing measures to ensure the rational use and protection of natural resources and the natural environment. It ensures the realization of legal policy; develops measures to protect the rights and freedoms of citizens, ensures law and order, security and defence of the country, territorial integrity and protection of state bodies of the Republic.

322. The Government develops measures for the implementation of the foreign policy of the Republic. It takes decisions on carrying out negotiations and signing intergovernmental agreements; ensures the development of relations with foreign States, international and regional organizations; adopts measures for realization of foreign economic policy and for development of foreign trade; and carries out cooperation and interaction with international financial organizations. Article 9 of the Constitutional Law envisages that the Government performs such other functions as are established by the Constitution, laws and legal acts of the President.

II. Regulatory Powers

A. *The Resolutions of the Government and Orders of the Prime Minister Necessary for the Implementation of Laws*

323. The authority of the Government to adopt legal acts for implementation of the Constitution and the laws is outlined in Article 69 of the Constitution and Article 10 of the Constitutional Law on the Status of the Government.

324. The Government of Kazakhstan can adopt resolutions on the issues of its competence which will have obligatory force within the entire territory of the Republic (Article 69(1) Constitution). They are issued to implement the Constitution, laws, the legal acts of the President, and other normative legal acts (Article 10(1) Constitutional Law). That is why they should not contradict the Constitution, legislative acts, decrees and orders of the President, as mentioned in Article 69(3) Constitution. The resolutions have normative or individual character (Article 10(1) Constitutional Law). They are to be adopted by a majority of votes of the total number of the members of the Government; they are signed by the Prime Minister of the Republic (Article 10(2) Constitutional Law).

325. The Prime Minister of Kazakhstan adopts orders which have administrative, operational and individual character and are obligatory on the entire territory of the Republic (Article 10(3, 4) Constitutional Law).

326. The internal working procedures of the Government regulate the ways and procedure for the draft and adoption of the Government's resolutions and the Prime Minister's orders (Article 10(5) Constitutional Law).

327. The Government's resolutions are denounced by the Government. The Prime Minister's orders are denounced by the Government and the Prime Minister of the Republic (Article 10(6, 7) Constitutional Law).

If necessary, the central executive bodies may adopt joint orders on the issues of concurrent jurisdiction to be signed by their respective heads (paragraph 17 of the Regulations of the internal working procedures of the Government).

328. In accordance with section 4.2 of the Regulations of the internal working procedures of the Government, depending on the subject and if there are instructions addressed to the state bodies and their heads, the drafts of the Government's resolutions and orders shall be agreed electronically via the Government intranet portal with the interested state bodies defined by the national legislation. If a draft of the resolution (order) does not concern the appointment of officials of state bodies, creation of working groups, commissions and issues of managerial character, it must be agreed with the Ministries of Justice and Finance. In such a case, the Ministry of Justice is responsible for the legal expertise of a draft, as to whether it is in compliance with the Constitution, legislative acts, acts of the President, Government and Prime Minister. A draft of any resolution that concerns state governance and planning, social-economic and regional policy must be agreed with the Ministry of National Economy. If a draft of the resolution concerns environmental threats, it must pass the state ecological expertise of a relevant state body. If a draft covers the issues of conclusion, implementation, making amendments and termination of international treaties, it shall be agreed with the relevant state bodies, the MFA and shall pass the legal expertise of the Ministry of Justice. There is also scientific and linguistic expertise envisaged by the Regulations of the internal working procedures of the Government.

329. The registration and recording of the Government's resolutions and the Prime Minister's orders are carried out by the Chancery of the Government (paragraph 72 Regulations of the Internal Working Procedures of the Government). The resolutions of the Government are published in the Collection of Legal Acts of the President and the Government of Kazakhstan, and in electronic format by the Standard Control Bank of the Normative Legal Acts of the Republic (paragraph 120 Regulations of the Internal Working Procedures of the Government).

330. The official interpretation of the normative legal acts of the Government is given by the Ministry of Justice upon the instructions of the Government or Prime Minister (paragraph 6 Regulations of the Internal Working Procedures of the Government).

331. After the adoption of the normative resolution by the Government, the ministries and their departments, the local executive bodies should bring their normative legal acts into conformity with the adopted Government's resolution within one month and, if necessary, adopt new ones in order to implement the resolution (paragraph 75 Regulations of the Internal Working Procedures of the Government).

332. The state bodies that drew up the resolution are obliged to monitor their realization continuously and assess its efficiency (paragraph 76 Regulations of the Internal Working Procedures of the Government).

333. The Head of Chancellery exercises control over the execution of the acts of the Government, Prime Minister and his/her deputies, by way of requesting necessary information, hearings and discussions of the reports on execution, by a revision or other forms of documentary verification, carrying out monitoring and on-site checking and other means in line with the legislation (paragraph 126 Regulations of the Internal Working Procedures of the Government).

B. Regulatory Powers of the Ministers

334. In accordance with Article 22 of Constitutional Law on the Government, a ministry in Kazakhstan is a central executive body of the Republic which within the limitations stipulated by legislation carries out management of the relevant field (sphere) of state management, and cross-sector coordination. The ministry within its competence realizes strategic, regulatory, practical, control and supervisory functions. The ministry is organized, reorganized, and can be abolished, by the President of the Republic upon a proposal of the Prime Minister of Kazakhstan.

335. Within its competence, the ministry takes a decision independently if the matters do not belong to the competence of the Government. The structure of the Ministry is approved by its responsible secretary. It consists of agencies, departments and directorates. The board of the ministry is an advisory body to the ministry. The decisions of the ministry are formulated in the orders of a minister (Article 22 Constitutional Law on Government).

336. An agency is an institution within a ministry and may have its regional offices. The Head of the agency is appointed and dismissed by the head of the respected ministry. Within its competence, the agency fulfils regulatory, practical and control and supervisory functions and it also participates in the realization of the strategic functions of the central executive body. The Head of the agency issues the orders (Article 24 Constitutional Law on Government).

III. National Defence and Foreign Affairs

A. National Defence

337. Issues of national defence of Kazakhstan are covered by Constitution, the special Law of 7 January 2005 on Defence and the Armed Forces of the Republic of Kazakhstan, the Military Doctrine of Kazakhstan adopted on 29 September 2017, and the Regulations on the Status of the Ministry of Defence of the Republic of Kazakhstan approved by the Resolution of the Government of 16 August 2001.[90]

338. Apart from the Government bodies, issues of national defence are also under the jurisdiction of the President of Kazakhstan, and some roles belong to the Parliament of the Republic.

339. In accordance with Article 44 subparagraph 12 of the Constitution of Kazakhstan and the provisions of the Law on defence, the President of the Republic is the Supreme Commander-in-Chief of the Armed Forces of Kazakhstan, and he appoints and releases high command of the Armed Forces. In a case of aggression against Kazakhstan or any other direct external threat to its security, the President announces the general or partial mobilization throughout the whole territory of the Republic, or in some of its parts, and then immediately notifies the Parliament of Kazakhstan (Article 44 subparagraph 17 Constitution). The President of the Republic independently appoints and dismisses the Minister of Defence (Article 44 subparagraph 3 Constitution). So, for instance, on 7 August 2018, the President appointed Nurlan Yermekbayev as Minister of Defence of Kazakhstan.[91]

340. Article 5 of the Law on Defence of Kazakhstan enumerates the power of the President on issues of defence. The President of Kazakhstan determines the defence policy of the country; he approves the Military doctrine of Kazakhstan, as well as the concept on building and development of the Armed Forces of Kazakhstan, the concept on the military security and defence, and the Guidelines on the Use of the Armed Forces of Kazakhstan. So, the Military doctrine of Kazakhstan was approved by the Decree of the President dated 29 September 2017 No. 554. The President exercises the general leadership of the Armed Forces, other troops and military formations; conducts negotiations and signs international treaties on the issues of defence and cooperation; submits proposals for using the Armed Forces to fulfil international obligations on maintaining peace and security for consideration by the joint session of the Chambers of the Parliament; and carries out other functions in accordance with the Constitution and the Law of Kazakhstan.

341. The Parliament adopts laws on the issues of ensuring defence, passes amendments, resolves the issues related to war and peace, takes decisions on using the Armed Forces of Kazakhstan to fulfil international obligations on maintaining the peace and security, ratifies international treaties on the issues of defence and

---

90. Law of Kazakhstan of 7 Jan. 2005 No. 29-III ZRK on Defence and the Armed Forces of the Republic of Kazakhstan. Available at: https://online.zakon.kz/document/?doc_id=1052592 (accessed 2 Aug. 2021); Military Doctrine of Kazakhstan approved by the Decree of the President of 29 Sep. 2017 No. 554. Available at: http://adilet.zan.kz/rus/docs/U1700000554 (accessed 30 Apr. 2020); Regulations on the Status of the Ministry of Defence of the Republic of Kazakhstan approved by the Resolution of the Government of 16 Aug. 2001. Available at: http://adilet.zan.kz/rus/docs/P010001074_ (accessed 30 Apr. 2020).
91. Decree of the President of Nazarbayev on Appointment of Nurlan Yermekbayev as a Minister of Defence of Kazakhstan. Available at: http://www.akorda.kz/ru/legal_acts/decrees/o-naznachenii-ermekbaeva-nb-ministrom-oborony-respubliki-kazahstan (accessed 29 Aug. 2018).

military cooperation, and conducts parliamentary hearings on the issues of defence and the Armed Forces (Article 6 Law on Defence).

342. The Government plays a significant role in defence issues as enumerated in Article 7 of the Law on defence. It develops the main directions of the state's military policy, implements measures to ensure the defence capability of the Republic; leads the activities of the Ministry of Defence and other central and local executive bodies. The Government takes decisions on the creation, reorganization and liquidation of military educational institutions, organizes supply of the Armed Forces of Kazakhstan and military troops with weapons, military techniques and material-technical resources. It also defines the categories and number of citizens subject to conscription for military service. The Government, in accordance with the national legislation, defines the procedures of provision and using the land, forests, waters and other natural resources for military needs, takes a decision on holding international negotiations on the issues of military, military-technical, military-economic cooperation and signing intergovernmental agreements. The Government carries out other tasks defined by the Constitution and the national legislation and acts of the President, including other tasks enumerated in Article 7. The Government organizes the stable functioning of the military organization of the state in any kind of military-political situation.

343. The functions of the Ministry of Defence are developed in Article 22 of Law on Defence. In accordance with it, the Ministry is the central executive body which realizes state policy on issues of defence, and of military-political and military-economic management of the Armed Forces, as well as any authorized body in the field of state aviation. The Ministry develops the Military doctrine, the policies on building and development of the Armed Forces of Kazakhstan, and the policy on military security and defence. It develops and approves its own structure and that of the General Staff of the Armed Forces of Kazakhstan, etc. The Ministry organizes the activities of military intelligence for the protection of the national security of the country. The Ministry controls the expenditure of finance in the Armed Forces of Kazakhstan.

344. The Ministry of Defence carries out control over observance of the rule of law and order in the Armed Forces of Kazakhstan and provides social and legal guarantees to the military servicemen and members of their families and the civilian personnel. Within its competencies, the state body adopts the normative legal acts on issues of military service, defence and the Armed Forces, and controls their execution. Within its competence, the Ministry monitors information space on issues of military security and counteracts the sources of the threats. The state body, within its competence, controls the activities of the central and local executive bodies on issues of defence of the territory, ensures implementation of a central state policy on personnel in the Armed Forces of Kazakhstan, and approves a national inventory of the armament and military-technical equipment in the Armed Forces, other troops and military formations.

345. With regards to international relations, the Ministry of Defence of Kazakhstan carries out international military and military-technical cooperation; concludes international treaties of the Republic and interacts with central and local executive bodies on issues of observance of international treaties concerning control over weapons; and observes the execution of international treaties by the other Member States of the treaty.

346. The Ministry of Defence develops and approves the normative legal acts regulating activities related to education at the military institutions which are responsible for providing education and control over the quality of education in them. The Ministry develops and approves the rules on the basic military training, on providing training in additional educational programs, on the preparation of military-technical and other specialities, on military training of retired officers, on military internship training, etc.

347. The Ministry organizes and coordinates the scientific support of defence and is in charge of scientific research on defence and security issues, and organizes control over their quality. The Ministry organizes the realization of the projects in the field of creation of space and military technology. The Ministry of Defence carries out other tasks enumerated in Article 21 and envisaged by the national law of Kazakhstan.

348. Acting Military Doctrine of Kazakhstan No. 554 approved by the President of Kazakhstan on 29 September 2017 has defensive nature and confirms the idea underlying the Constitution of Kazakhstan of refusing to be the first to use the armed forces. In accordance with the Military Doctrine, military force can only be used in the case of exhaustion of all non-military means for the protection of the military security of the State. Kazakhstan does not consider any State as its adversary. The aim of the military policy of Kazakhstan is ensuring internal stability, preventing threats of the unleashing of war against the state, expanding participation in ensuring international security, fighting against international terrorism and extremism and maintaining constant preparedness of the state for the armed defence of Kazakhstan and its allies.

349. The Military Doctrine contains the analysis of the current situation with defence, including the main conditions and factors determining the military security of, and military threats to, Kazakhstan, and the character of contemporary military conflicts. The Doctrine covers the goal and the principles, the main directions of the military security of Kazakhstan, and the measures to provide military security of the Republic.

B. Foreign Affairs

350. The foreign policy of Kazakhstan is determined by its natural geographical factor, located in the heart of the Eurasian continent; the country has to follow a multi-vector policy. The multi-vector policy enables the country to fully realize its potential.[92]

351. The Government of Kazakhstan, fulfilling the functions of the executive power in the system of state governance, adopts the measures for conducting the foreign policy of the Republic (Article 66(5) Constitution).

352. In accordance with Article 9(15) of the Law on the Government, the Government of Kazakhstan:

(1) takes decisions on holding negotiations and signing intergovernmental agreements;
(2) ensures the development of relations with foreign States, the international and regional organizations;
(3) develops measures on implementation of foreign economic policy;
(4) takes measures for the development of foreign trade;
(5) carries out cooperation and interaction with international financial organizations.

353. The MFA is the State body responsible for leadership in the field of foreign political activity. It leads the unified system of state bodies that carry out the diplomatic service of the Republic. The legal status of the Ministry is defined by Regulations on the MFA of Kazakhstan adopted by the Resolution of the Government on 28 October 2004 No. 1118.[93]

354. The mission of the MFA of Kazakhstan is to ensure the sovereignty, security, territorial integrity and inviolability of the borders of Kazakhstan, and to ensure its political, trade, economic and other interests in relation with other states and in the international arena by diplomatic means and methods (paragraph 14 Regulations on the Ministry).

355. In accordance with the Regulations, the tasks of the Ministry are the following:

(1) the development of the concept and the main directions of the foreign policy of Kazakhstan and the submission of relevant proposals to the President and the Government of Kazakhstan;

---

92. Kassym-Jomart Tokayev, *Light and Shadow,* vol. 4, 146–247 (2017).
93. Regulations on the Ministry of Foreign Affairs of the Republic of Kazakhstan adopted by the Resolution of the Government on 28 Oct. 2004 No. 1118, available at: http://adilet.zan.kz/rus/docs/P040001118_ (accessed 30 Apr. 2020).

(2) implementation of the foreign policy of the Republic, promotion of the realization of foreign economic policy and strengthening of the international image of Kazakhstan;
(3) protection of rights and interests of the Republic, its citizens and legal entities abroad;
(4) realization by diplomatic means and methods the efforts of the Republic to ensure international peace, global and regional security;
(5) protection of the sovereignty, security, territorial integrity and inviolability of the borders of Kazakhstan, its political, trade, economic and other interests in relations with other states and in the international arena by diplomatic means and methods;
(6) development of proposals on the external political and economic strategy of Kazakhstan and realization of the international initiatives of the President for his attention;
(7) realization of diplomatic and consular relations with foreign States and international organizations;
(8) coordination of the international activity of other central state bodies of Kazakhstan in order to ensure the unified external political, economic and investment policy of the Republic in relations with foreign States and international organizations;
(9) analysis of the political and social-economic situation of the world, external and internal policy of foreign States, the activity of international organizations.

356. In order to realize its tasks and functions enumerated in the Regulations, the Ministry has the right to adopt obligatory normative legal acts within its competence, and to request and receive necessary information and materials from the state bodies and officials.

C. *Treaty-Making Powers*

357. Article 2 of Law on International Treaties of the Republic of Kazakhstan distinguishes three types of international treaties:

(1) those concluded on behalf of the State;
(2) those concluded on behalf of the Government; and
(3) those concluded on behalf of the state bodies of Kazakhstan directly subordinate and accountable to the President of the Republic, as well as the central executive bodies within their competencies as defined by the national legislation of Kazakhstan.

358. The Government of Kazakhstan, in accordance with Article 9(15) of Constitutional Law of 18 December 1995 on the Government of the Republic of Kazakhstan, takes decisions to conduct negotiations and sign intergovernmental agreements. The Prime Minister of the Republic signs intergovernmental treaties and agreements (Article 19(3) of the Constitutional Law on the Government).

359. Thus, the treaty-making capacity of the Government and the central executive bodies in Kazakhstan is legally defined. As an example of the practical implications of the Government's competence to conclude international treaties, the Agreement between the Government of Kazakhstan and the Government of the Republic of Croatia on the avoidance of double taxation and the prevention of tax evasion with regards to income taxes and the Protocol to it done in the capital of Kazakhstan in September 2017 can be mentioned. On 27 December 2018, the Senate of the Parliament adopted the Law on signing this Agreement.[94] The Agreement reflects the model put forward by the Organisation for Economic Cooperation and Development.

360. Some examples of the competence of the central state bodies of Kazakhstan in international treaty-making, including the ministries, are given below. For instance, the Ministry of Defence of Kazakhstan carries out international military and military-technical cooperation and concludes international treaties. For example, between the Ministries of Defence of Kazakhstan and China, an agreement on provision of free military assistance to Kazakhstan by China was signed and entered into force on 19 September 2015.[95] The Ministry of Healthcare of Kazakhstan, in accordance with the Rules on the Legal Status of the Ministry Approved by Decision of the Government of Kazakhstan on 17 February 2017, carries out international cooperation in the field of healthcare (paragraph 16 subparagraph 5).[96]

361. The Committee on National Security of Kazakhstan within its competencies and in line with the procedures established by the national legislation shares in the preparation of international treaties of the Republic on the provision of national security (paragraph 12 subparagraph 7).[97] This Committee has the right to conclude cooperation agreements with special services, government and special communication agencies of foreign countries, and international law-enforcement organizations in accordance with international treaties of the Republic (paragraph 13 subparagraph 16); it has the right to cooperate with research institutions and the universities of foreign countries following international agreements (paragraph 13 subparagraph 23).

362. In line with the Regulations on the Office of the General Prosecutor of Kazakhstan, one of the main functions of the Office of the General Prosecutor is participation in drawing up the drafts of international treaties of Kazakhstan and in the

94. *President of Kazakhstan signed the Law on the Avoidance of Double Taxation Between the Republic of Kazakhstan and Croatia.* Available at: https://kursiv.kz/news/politika/2019-01/prezident-kazakhstana-podpisal-zakon-ob-izbezhanii-dvoynogo-nalogooblozheniya (accessed 30 Apr. 2020).
95. Agreement between the Ministries of Defence of the Republic of Kazakhstan and China on Provision of Free Military Assistance by China to Kazakhstan, entered into force on 19 Sep. 2015. *Diplomatic courier*, 2006, No. 4.
96. Regulations on the Ministry of Healthcare of the Republic of Kazakhstan adopted by the Resolution of the Government of Kazakhstan of 17 Feb. 2017 No. 71: http://adilet.zan.kz/rus/docs/P17000000 71#z23 (accessed 10 Dec. 2018).
97. Regulations on the Committee on National Security of the Republic of Kazakhstan, approved by the Decree of the President of the Republic on 1 Apr. 1996 No. 2922. Available at: https://online.zakon.kz/Document/?doc_id=1005395#pos=4;-106 (accessed 12 Oct. 2019).

work of international, interstate and other organizations in accordance with international treaties of the Republic.[98] In accordance with the Order of the General Prosecutor of January 2018, the Department of International Cooperation of the General Prosecutor Office is responsible for international cooperation of the prosecuting bodies of the Republic with the competent bodies of foreign countries and international organizations.[99] The Department is also responsible for enhancing and improving the legal framework of Kazakhstan with foreign States on issues of crime prevention, the rule of law and public order. This includes the preparation of drafts of international treaties on extradition, legal assistance on criminal cases and other related issues (paragraph 6 Regulation on the Department of International Cooperation).

363. The MIA identifies priority areas, organizes and realizes international cooperation on issues of crime prevention, maintenance of public order and other issues within the competence of the Ministry (paragraph 16 subparagraph 22 Regulations on Status of the Ministry).[100]

364. The Ministry of Justice also contributes to the international treaty-making of the country. One of the tasks of the Ministry of Justice to realize its mission is the provision of legal support for Kazakhstan's activities in the international arena in order to protect the national interests of the country and to strengthen the authority of the Republic in the global community by various means, including by way of preparation and conclusion of international treaties of the Republic (paragraph 15 subparagraph 2 Regulations on the Ministry). One of the functions of the Ministry is establishing and maintaining international relations with the relevant organizations of foreign countries (paragraph 16 subparagraph 2 Regulations on the Ministry). The central apparatus of the Ministry of Justice in line with the national legislation prepares and organizes the conclusion of international treaties on legal assistance and legal cooperation with foreign countries (paragraph 16 subparagraph 3 Regulations on the Ministry of Justice).[101]

365. The Ministry of Justice plays an important role in giving consent to be bound by a treaty. According to the Law on International Treaties, after approval by the competent, relevant state bodies, the international treaties to which Kazakhstan

---

98. Regulations on the Office of the General Prosecutor of the Republic of Kazakhstan approved by the Decree of the President on Some Issues of Prosecutor Bodies of the Republic of Kazakhstan of 13 Oct. 2017 No. 563. Available at: http://adilet.zan.kz/rus/docs/U1700000563 (accessed 30 Apr. 2020)

99. Order of the General Prosecutor of the Republic of Kazakhstan of 8 Jan. 2018 No. 5 on Approval of the Regulation on the Department of International Cooperation of the General Prosecutor's Office of the Republic of Kazakhstan: https://www.gov.kz/memleket/entities/prokuror/documents/details/172802?lang=kk (accessed 28 Dec. 2018).

100. Regulations on issues of the MIA of the Republic of Kazakhstan, adopted by the Decree of the Government of Kazakhstan of 22 Jun. 2005 No. 607. Available at: http://adilet.zan.kz/rus/docs/P050000607_ (accessed 30 Apr. 2020).

101. Regulations of 28 Oct. 2004 No. 1120 on the Ministry of Justice of the Republic of Kazakhstan, approved by the Decree of the Government of Kazakhstan. Available at: http://adilet.zan.kz/rus/docs/P040001120_ (accessed 19 Oct. 2019)

is intended to be a party and their drafts have to be approved by the legal expertise of the Ministry of Justice. The Ministry of Justice provides a conclusion on the compliance with international treaties and their drafts to the national legislation and defines ways of expressing consent to their obligatory force (Article 3(1) Law on International Treaties).

366. The international treaties to which Kazakhstan is intended to be a party, and the drafts of the international treaties, after vetting by the expertise of the Ministry of Justice of Kazakhstan shall then be approved by the MFA of the Republic (Article 3(2) Law on International Treaties). The MFA of Kazakhstan gives its opinion on its compliance with the provisions of other international treaties and obligations of Kazakhstan, and other questions related to the entry into force and execution of the treaty. The MFA also defines the types of international treaties that should be concluded.

367. The international treaties to which Kazakhstan is intended to become a State Party and their drafts can also be required to pass scientific expertise (legal, linguistic, environmental, financial, and other expertise). In case the international treaty requires ratification (approval by the Parliament), it is obliged to pass the scientific expertise (Article 4 Law on International Treaties). The scientific expertise implies an assessment of the quality, justification, timeliness and legitimacy of participation in the international treaty or its draft.

368. The state bodies that are directly subordinated and accountable to the President of the Republic on issues of their competence shall submit to the President the proposals on signing, approval, adoption and accession to the international treaties to be concluded on behalf of Kazakhstan no later than fourteen calendar days before the date of signing. If the international treaty is to be concluded on behalf of the Government, the state bodies that are directly subordinated and accountable to the President of the Republic submit their proposals to the Government, again no later than fourteen calendar days before the date of signing (Article 5(1) Law on International Treaties).

369. On issues of their competence, the central state bodies of Kazakhstan submit their proposals to the Government of the Republic on signing, ratification, adoption of international treaties and accession to them no later than fourteen days if the international treaty should be concluded on behalf of the Government, and no later than thirty days if the international treaty should be concluded on behalf of the Republic (Article 5(2) Law on International Treaties). Before submission to the Government, such proposals should be discussed with the relevant state bodies and the MFA of the Republic.

370. Apart from other requirements, the proposals on signing the international treaty should include justification of the reasonableness of conclusion, its compliance to the national legislation and international treaties of Kazakhstan, assessment of possible political, legal, financial, economic and other consequences of the conclusion of an international treaty, and mention of the state bodies responsible for the implementation of the international treaty and other information enumerated in Article 6 of Law on International Treaties.

371. The decisions on initialling, adopting texts and signing international treaties, as well as authorizing the execution of these acts with regards to international treaties concluded on behalf of Kazakhstan are taken by the President of the country. With regard to international treaties concluded on behalf of the Government, such decisions are taken by the Government. The relevant decisions concerning international treaties concluded on behalf of the central state bodies are taken by their first heads or persons who replace them (Article 8 Law on International Treaties). The capacity to implement the aforementioned acts related to the conclusion of international treaties should be confirmed by the MFA of the Republic. The Ministry issues credentials to authorize the implementation of such acts (Article 9 Law on International Treaties).

372. For the purpose of adopting the text of a treaty between the accrediting State and the receiving State, the heads of diplomatic missions have a right to represent without full powers. In virtue of their functions, the same applies to representatives accredited by States to an international conference or to an international organization or one of its organs. For adopting the text of a treaty, they have a right to act without presenting credentials. Article 7 of the Vienna Convention on the Law of Treaties 1969 regulates these issues.[102] The national law of Kazakhstan confirms the provisions of Article 7 of the Vienna Convention concerning the issues of the status of heads of diplomatic missions and representatives authorized by the country.

373. The President of Kazakhstan has the right to fulfil all actions related to the conclusion of international treaties without presenting any credentials. For the purpose of all actions relating to the conclusion of international treaties, the Prime Minister and the Minister of Foreign Affairs shall represent the country without any additional credentials or documents. International law and the national law of Kazakhstan allow the Head of Government and Minister of Foreign Affairs wide competencies in international treaty conclusion, including the expression of consent to be bound by an international treaty.

374. In accordance with constitutional provisions and Article 11 of the Law on International Treaties, some international treaties of Kazakhstan require the approval of the Parliament before they can be given full consent. The Law uses the word 'ratification' by the Parliament. It is the second stage of the treaty-making process when a state expresses its consent to be bound by a treaty.

375. The consent of the Parliament is necessary in the following cases:

---

102. Vienna Convention on the Law of Treaties 1969, done at Vienna 1969, entered into force on 27 Jan. 1980. United Nations, Treaty Series, vol. 1155, at 331.

(1) if an international treaty concerns rights and freedoms of an individual and citizen;
(2) if the implementation of the provisions of an international treaty requires changing national legislation or the adoption of new laws, as well as establishes other rules than exist in the laws of Kazakhstan;
(3) if an international treaty concerns the territorial delimitation of the Republic with other states, including issues on state borders, delimitation of the exclusive economic zone and the continental shelf of Kazakhstan;
(4) if an international treaty concerns the principles of interstate relations, disarmament, ensuring peace and security, as well as issues of peace and collective security;
(5) if an international treaty that regulates issues of participation of Kazakhstan in interstate unions and international organizations requires the transfer of sovereign rights of Kazakhstan or establishes the legally binding force of their decisions to the country;
(6) if an international treaty concerns state loans;
(7) on the provision by Kazakhstan of economic and other assistance except for humanitarian aid and official development assistance;
(8) if the parties to an international treaty upon signing agreed on subsequent ratification;
(9) if an international treaty envisages that such approval shall be expressed by ratification.

IV. The Executive and the President

376. The President of Kazakhstan has enough power with regards to the activities of the Government of the Republic and other executive bodies. The President of the country appoints and dismisses the Prime Minister of the Republic, with the consent of the *Mazhilis* of the Parliament. Upon the recommendation of the Prime Minister and in consultation with *Mazhilis* of the Parliament, the Head of State appoints the members of the Government (Article 44(3) Constitution). The President independently appoints the Minister of Foreign Affairs, the Minister of Defence and the Minister of Internal Affairs. He can also dismiss the members of the Government. The President and the people of Kazakhstan take the oath of the members of the Government.

377. With the consent of the Senate of the Parliament, the President appoints the Chair of the National Bank, the General Prosecutor and the Chair of the Committee on National Security of Kazakhstan. He also has the right to dismiss them.

378. In accordance with Article 44(5) of the Constitution of Kazakhstan, the President of Kazakhstan organizes, abolishes and reorganizes the state bodies which are directly subordinate and accountable to him, and appoints and dismisses their heads. The President also appoints and dismisses the heads of diplomatic missions of Kazakhstan (Article 44(5) Constitution). The Head of State appoints for five years the Chair and two members of the Central Election Commission of the Republic, and the Chair and two members of the Control Committee over fulfilment of the national budget (Article 44(7) Constitution).

379. The President of Kazakhstan chairs the meetings of the Government on issues of special importance; he also has the right to cancel or suspend in whole or in part the effect of the instructions of the mayors of regions, cities of national importance and the capital (Article 44(3) Constitution).

380. In accordance with Article 57(6) of the Constitution of Kazakhstan, the President has the right to hear the reports of the members of the Government on issues of their competence upon initiation of not less than one-third of the total number of the Chamber of the Parliament. After the hearings of the report, each Chamber of the Parliament independently by a majority of not less than two-thirds of votes of the total number of the deputies has the right to adopt an address to the President to dismiss a member of the Government if he does not perform the laws of the Republic. In such cases, the President dismisses that member of the Government.

V. Powers Regarding the Parliament

381. Overall, in its own activities, the Government is responsible before the President and the Parliament of the Republic (Article 64(2) Constitution). Moreover, the Government abdicates before a newly elected *Mazhilis* of the Parliament (Article 70(1) Constitution). There are some cases when the Government plays a definite role in the activities related to the Parliament of the country.

382. In accordance with Article 59(6) of the Constitution, the joint and separate meetings of each Chamber are held openly. In some cases, the meetings can be closed to the public. The Prime Minister and members of the Government, the Chair of the National Bank and the General Prosecutor have the right to participate actively at any meeting of the Chamber of the Parliament.

383. The Government has the right of legislative initiative, which is exclusively realized in the *Mazhilis* of the Parliament, as mentioned in Article 61(1) of the Constitution and Article 13(1) of Constitutional Law on the Government of Kazakhstan. The Government issues the Resolution on submission of a draft law for consideration by the *Mazhilis*.

384. Usually, any draft law that implies cutting state revenues or increasing state expenditures can be submitted for consideration of the *Mazhilis* only if the Government of the Republic is in favour of it (Article 61(6) Constitution).

385. As elaborated in Article 61(7) of the Constitution, if the draft law submitted by the Government is rejected, the Prime Minister has the right at the joint sessions of the Chambers of the Parliament to raise a question of confidence to the

Government. Voting on this issue shall be held not earlier than forty-eight hours from the moment of raising a question of confidence. If a question of confidence does not receive a majority of votes of the total number of the deputies of each Chamber, the draft law should be accepted without voting. However, such a right of the Government cannot be used more than twice a year.

VI. Powers Regarding Judiciary

386. With regards to the powers of the Government regarding the judiciary, we shall mention the competence of the Ministry of Justice of Kazakhstan. One of the tasks of the Ministry of Justice of Kazakhstan is to set up and implement state policy and control in the field of forensic expertise (paragraph 15 subparagraph 5 Regulations on the Ministry of Justice). One of the functions of the central apparatus of the Ministry of Justice is the adoption of normative legal acts of Kazakhstan in the field of forensic expertise (paragraph 16 subparagraph 24 Regulations on the Ministry of Justice).

387. In accordance with Chapter 2 of Regulations on the Ministry of Justice, the Ministry controls the activities of the state bailiffs (executors of the judicial decisions); gives licenses to the private enforcement bailiffs, regulates and controls within its competencies the activities of the private enforcement bailiffs; licenses the forensic expertise, accepts a qualification examination and issues certificates to fulfil a certain type of forensic examination.

388. One of the other tasks of the Ministry regarding judiciary is making proposals to the Government on initiating litigation and arbitration with foreign investors, upon proposal by the competent state body (paragraph 16 subparagraph 5 Regulations on the Ministry of Justice). Upon the instruction of the Prime Minister, his deputies or the Head of the Prime Minister's Office provides legal and advisory assistance to state bodies in legal proceedings (paragraph 16 subparagraph 21 Regulations on the Ministry of Justice).

389. The executive can influence the judiciary via the functionality of the Highest Judicial Council of the Republic. The legal status and functions of the Highest Judicial Council are defined by Law on the Highest Judicial Council adopted on 4 December 2015 (Article 82(5) Constitution).[103] The Council is responsible for assisting the President of the country to form courts, guarantee the independence of judges and their immunity (Article 1(1) Law on the Highest Judicial Council). On a competitive basis, the Council selects candidates for the vacant positions of a chair, a judge of the district (equal to district) court, of the regional (equal to regional) court and judges of the Supreme Court of the Republic (Article 3(2) Law

103. Law of Kazakhstan of 4 Dec. 2015 on the Highest Judicial Council. Available at: https://www.gov.kz/memleket/entities/vss/about?lang=kk (accessed 2 Aug. 2021).

on the Highest Judicial Council). Along with other competencies, the Council organizes admission qualification examinations of persons who express a desire to work as judges (Article 3(1.8) Law on the Highest Judicial Council).

390. The Highest Judicial Council consists of a Chair and other persons appointed by the President of the Republic. The Chair of the Supreme Court, the General Prosecutor, the Minister of Justice, a head of a state body on civil service and anti-corruption affairs and the Chairs of the permanent committees of the Senate and *Mazhilis* of the Parliament are appointed by the President of Kazakhstan. Legal scholars, lawyers, foreign experts and the representatives of the community of lawyers may be appointed as members of the Council (Article 4(1) Law on the Highest Judicial Council). Members of the Council are independent and obey only the Constitution of Kazakhstan, the laws and legal acts of the President of the Republic (Article 4(8) Law on the Highest Judicial Council).

VII. Other Powers

391. Here we discuss the relations of the Government with local executive bodies. In line with Article 16(1) of Constitutional Law on the Government, the Government leads the activities of the local executive bodies of the Republic on issues of governance and controls the implementation of the laws, legal acts of the President and the Government. The Government cancels or suspends in whole or in part the decisions of the local executive bodies and can submit proposals on their abolition or suspension for consideration of the President of the Republic.

392. In line with Article 16(2) the Constitutional Law on the Government, *akims* are considered as representatives of the President and the Government of the Republic and must submit to Government proposals on issues of State governance.

§4. Miscellaneous

I. The Office of the Prime Minister (the Chancellery)

393. As envisaged in Article 25(1) of Constitutional Law on the Government of Kazakhstan, the Office of the Prime Minister provides informative, analytical, organizational and legal support for the activities of the Prime Minister and the Government of the Republic. It does not have special prerogatives but can use any information available to the state bodies and has the right to participate at the meetings of the state bodies collegiums. The Head of the Office is appointed and dismissed by the Resolution of the Government.

394. The Office of the Prime Minister is a state body coordinating the activities of state bodies and carrying out control and other functions envisaged by the legislation and the Regulations on the Office.[104] The Office prepares financial, economic, legal and other expertise on the drafts of the legal acts submitted by the Government; prepares the drafts of the Resolutions of the Government and the Orders of the Prime Minister. The Office of the Prime Minister carries out control over the realization of the acts and orders of the Head of State, acts of the Government, orders of the Prime Minister and his deputies, protocol decisions of the meetings of the Government, and informs the Prime Minister of the Republic on these issues. The Office of the Prime Minister enables interactions of the Government and the Prime Minister with the Parliament. The Office informs the Prime Minister of the actions done with regards to the inquiries of the deputies. The Chancellery ensures the interactions of the Prime Minister with mass media. The Office provides organizational support of interstate relations and international cooperation of the President, the Government, the Prime Minister and his deputies. It organizes international meetings, negotiations and conversations of the Prime Minister and his deputies, as well as their participation in international events. There are many other functions enumerated in the Regulations.

II. Transitional Powers

395. Article 48 of the Constitution of Kazakhstan regulates the transition of powers if the President of the country has early release, faces dismissal or dies. The rest of the term of the President shall be passed to the Prime Minister, only if the Chair of the Senate and the Chair of the *Mazhilis* are unable to assume the powers. The Prime Minister, once he has taken the power of the President, must relinquish the duties of the Prime Minister. A person who receives the power of the President cannot initiate making amendments to the Constitution of the Republic.

104. Regulations on the Chancellery of the Prime Minister of the Republic of Kazakhstan, approved by the Resolution of the Government of Kazakhstan of 11 Sep. 2002 No. 993. Available at: http://adilet.zan.kz/rus/docs/P020000993_; Additional information on the Chancellery of the Prime Minister can be found at the official website of the Government: https://primeminister.kz/ru/government/offices (accessed 30 Apr. 2020).

Chapter 5. The Constitutional Council of the Republic of Kazakhstan

§1. Legal Status of the Constitutional Council

396. Chapter 6 of the Constitution of Kazakhstan is devoted to the legal status and competence of the Constitutional Council of the Republic. As previously mentioned, there is the Constitutional Law on the Constitutional Council of the Republic of Kazakhstan of 29 December 1995 No. 2737 that elaborates the constitutional provisions for the Council. On organizational issues and rules of procedure not covered by the Constitution and the Constitutional Law, the Constitutional Council adopts Regulations on its internal procedures (Article 9 Constitutional Law on the Constitutional Council).

397. According to Article 1 of the Constitutional Law on the Constitutional Council, the Council is the state body that provides for the supremacy of the Constitution over the entire territory of the Republic. In exercising its powers, the Council is independent of other state bodies, officials and citizens, obeys only the Constitution of the Republic and cannot make conclusions based on political and other reasons. The Council exercises its powers in accordance with the Constitution of Kazakhstan and the Constitutional Law on the Constitutional Council and should refrain from an examination of other questions which fall within the competence of the courts and other state bodies.

§2. Composition and Status of the Chair and the Members of the Council

398. Article 71 of the Constitution of Kazakhstan and the Constitutional Law provisions (Articles 2, 3 and 5, and Chapter 2) cover issues of composition, appointment and the term, and immunity of the members of the Constitutional Council of the Republic. The Constitutional Council of Kazakhstan consists of seven members. With the exception of the former Presidents of the Republic who are lifetime members of the Council, the term of the members lasts six years. The Chair of the Council is appointed by the President of the country. Two other members of the Council are also appointed by the President, two members – by the *Mazhilis*, two members – by the Senate of the Parliament of Kazakhstan. Half of the members of the Constitutional Council are renewed every three years. Any citizen of Kazakhstan, not younger than thirty years, who has been residing on the territory of Kazakhstan, who has a degree in jurisprudence and work experience as a lawyer for not less than five years, can be a member of the Council.

399. The Chair and the members of the Constitutional Council cannot be a member of the Parliament, or governing bodies or steering committee of a commercial organization, or carry out any paid position, entrepreneurial activity, except for teaching, scientific activity, any other creative activity. During the term of the post, the Chair and the members of the Constitutional Council cannot be arrested and taken into custody or subjected to administrative penalties imposed by a court or to criminal sanctions without consent of the Parliament, except for cases of being apprehended on the scene of a crime or committing grave crimes.

§3. JURISDICTION OF THE CONSTITUTIONAL COUNCIL

400. In conformity with Article 72 of the Constitution of Kazakhstan, upon requests of the President of Kazakhstan, the Chairs of the Senate and the *Mazhilis*, not less than one-fifth of the total number of the members of the Parliament and the Prime Minister, the Constitutional Council shall:

(1) in cases of dispute decide any issue of the correctness of holding the elections for the President of Kazakhstan, the members of the Parliament, and a national referendum;
(2) consider the laws adopted by the Parliament on their compliance with the Constitution of Kazakhstan before they are signed by the President;
(3) consider the resolutions adopted by the Parliament and its Chambers on their compliance with the Constitution of Kazakhstan;
(4) consider international treaties of the Republic before their ratification on their compliance with the Constitution of Kazakhstan;
(5) give an official interpretation to the provisions of the Constitution;
(6) give an opinion in cases stipulated in Article 47(1-2) of the Constitution of Kazakhstan:
   (a) when the decision of the Parliament of Kazakhstan on the early release of the President in case of his constant inability to exercise his duties due to health conditions is raised at the joint meeting of the Chambers of the Parliament and supported by a majority of at least three-quarters of the total number of deputies of each Chamber. Such a decision shall be based on the conclusion of the Constitutional Council on the observance of all constitutional procedures and as well as on the conclusion of the commission composed of equal numbers of the members of both Chambers and the medical specialists of the relevant field,
   (b) the Constitutional Council of the Republic gives its opinion on the observance of all constitutional procedures in cases when the Parliament raises the question of the responsibility of the President of Kazakhstan for treason.
(7) consider requests of the President of Kazakhstan in cases stipulated by Article 44(10-1) of the Constitution:
   (a) when the President of the country in order to protect the rights and freedoms of individuals and citizens and as well as to ensure the national security, sovereignty and integrity of the state submits a request to the Constitutional Council to consider the issue on compliance of the legal act entered into force with the Constitution of the Republic;
   (b) when the President of the country with the same aforementioned reason asks the Constitutional Council to consider the compliance of the proposed changes and amendments to the Constitution of Kazakhstan to the

requirements of the Constitution regarding statehood of the Republic (its independence and sovereignty, integrity, form of governance, the fundamental principles of Kazakhstan established by the First President) before they are put to referendum or given for consideration of the Parliament (Article 91(2, 3) of the Constitution).

(8) consider the request of the courts to recognize the normative legal act as unconstitutional because it constrains human rights and freedoms. This competence is stipulated in Article 78 of the Constitution of Kazakhstan, and the author of this writing analysed it in the Chapter regarding the Judiciary in the paragraph concerning judicial review in Kazakhstan.

§4. Constitutional Proceedings

401. Chapter 4 of the Constitutional Law on the status of the Constitutional Council is devoted to constitutional proceedings. The participants of the constitutional proceedings are the officials and state bodies that requested initiation of the proceedings. They are the President of the Republic, the Chairs of the Senate and *Mazhilis* of the Parliament, and not less than one-fifth of the total number of the members of the Parliament, the Prime Minister, courts of the Republic, state bodies and the officials whose legal acts are under consideration (Article 20 Constitutional Law).

402. In accordance with Article 21 of the Constitutional Law on the Constitutional Council, the participants of the constitutional proceedings have the following rights:

(1) the right to familiarize themselves with the materials of the proceedings, to make copies;
(2) the right to present the evidence, participate in their examination and to prove the circumstances to which they are referring;
(3) the right to express to the Constitutional Council their own arguments and opinions on all issues arising during the proceedings;
(4) the right to file petitions and express opinion on these petitions;
(5) the right to give, either orally or in writing their explanations to the Constitutional Council.

403. A participant who initiated the constitutional proceedings has the right before the beginning of the Council's meeting, at which the final decision is going to be taken, to change the grounds of the request (petition), to enlarge or lessen the volume of the request or to resile from it. A participant, whose acts became the reason for the constitutional proceedings, has the right to admit claims fully or partially, or object to them.

404. Participants of the constitutional proceedings are obliged:

(1) to use their rights in good faith; submission of deliberately false information or failure to submit the documents requested by the Constitutional Council, the materials and other information is regarded as disrespect to the Constitutional Council and entails responsibility under the law;
(2) to respect the Constitution of the Republic and the Constitutional Council, the requirements and procedures of the Constitutional Council;
(3) to obey the instructions of the presiding chair to observe the order of the meeting.

405. Article 22 of the Constitutional Law is about the form and content of the request that is going to be submitted to the Constitutional Council of the Republic. The request to the Council shall be submitted in writing. It shall contain the name of the Constitutional Council, the name, address and other necessary data about a petitioner, the name, address and other information about a representative of the petitioner and its competencies, the draft of amendments to the Constitution of the Republic in cases where the Council is requested to give an opinion on their compliance with the Constitution of Kazakhstan according to Article 91(3) of the Constitution, the essence of the request, other facts and circumstances that are reasons for it, the provisions of the Constitution and the Constitutional Law that ensure the right to appeal to the Constitutional Council, the list of enclosed documents, and other relevant information enumerated in Article 22 of the Law depending on the subject of the procedure. And in case the Council is requested to give an opinion on the correctness of holding elections of the President and the members of the Parliament, or national referendum, information must be given concerning the name, location and addresses of the state bodies, officials who signed or adopted the acts related to the elections. The request should be signed.

406. The Constitutional Council considers a request within one month. In case of the urgency of an issue, this term may be shortened up to ten days upon the President's request (Article 24 Constitutional Law of the Constitutional Council).

407. In line with Article 25 of the Constitutional Law of the Constitutional Council, the meeting of the Council should be held within three days upon receiving a request, and the Council must accept it for consideration or return it. The Council shall return it in cases where if:

(1) the form and substance of the request does not correspond to the requirements of the Constitutional Law on the Council, or has been submitted by an inappropriate party;
(2) the subject matter of the request does not fall within the competence of the Constitutional Council;
(3) the constitutionality of the act had been already considered by the Council, and there is a decision of the Council that has legal force;
(4) the issue of the request has not been resolved in the Constitution;
(5) the act that is contested has been abolished or lost its legal force.

408. Article 26 of the Constitutional Law on the Constitutional Council regulates the procedures of examination of the request admitted for consideration by the Council. The Chair by its order designates a member of the Constitutional Council – a rapporteur – who is obliged to prepare materials for the meeting of the Council. A member of the Council:

(1) determines the participants of the proceedings and explains to them their rights and duties;
(2) has the right to request documents and other information necessary for consideration of a case;
(3) if necessary, he/she questions the relevant officials, involves scientists, practitioners and experts as the specialists on the issue, and arranges for the conduct of inspections, examinations and expertise;
(4) not later than two days before starting the meeting of the Council ensures the delivery of the copies of the materials of the case to the members of the Constitutional Council;
(5) prepares the draft of the decision of the Constitutional Council;
(6) and conducts any other actions to ensure due consideration of the case.

409. After completion of all preparatory work, the Chair of the Constitutional Council defines the date when the issue will be considered and adopts the relevant order with the date of the Council's meeting.

410. Article 27 of the Constitutional Law on the Council provides for holding the meeting of the Council for the consideration of the request. The Chair checks a quorum and opens the meeting, reads aloud issues that are going to be considered, gives the floor to the designated member of the Council, asks the participants whether they have petitions, and announces the opening of the consideration on the merits of the issue to be considered. Consideration of the request starts with a speech from a rapporteur who outlines the essence of the issue, the reasons and grounds for consideration, and the content of the materials in the case. The members of the Council have the right to ask him clarifying questions. The parties to the request, representatives of the state bodies and the officials (their representatives), whose formal acts and actions are being checked for their constitutionality, as well as observance by them of the constitutional procedures, if necessary, or of their own will or upon the request of the Constitutional Council may participate at the meeting of the Constitutional Council. If necessary, listened explanations and speeches from the participants of the constitutional proceedings, experts, specialists and other invited people may be heard. If the question is sufficiently clarified, the Chair announces the opening of the consultation procedure of the Constitutional Council's members to draw up a final decision. Disclosure of the judgments delivered during the meeting, the course and results of voting are prohibited. The course of the meeting of the Council shall be recorded in the minutes. The language of the proceedings shall be Kazakh or Russian. If necessary, interpretation shall be provided.

411. Article 30 of the Constitutional Law covers issues of termination of the constitutional proceedings. Termination of the constitutional proceeding may happen at any time, before the adoption of a final decision, in cases:

(1) if a party who lodged a request withdraws it;
(2) if the act that is being checked for constitutionality has been abolished or lost its legal force;
(3) if the submitted request does not fall within the competence of the Constitutional Council.

If the Council adopted a decision to terminate consideration of the case, the party who submitted a request has no right next time to apply for consideration on the same grounds.

§5. Decisions of the Constitutional Council

412. Chapter 5 of the Constitutional Law is devoted to the decisions that are adopted by the Constitutional Council. In accordance with Articles 31 and 32, there are final and other decisions. The decisions of the Council can be in the form of resolutions, including normative ones which are part of the acting law of Kazakhstan, concluding findings and addresses. The Council adopts the decisions collegiately, and no one has the right to abstain from voting. The Council has the right to adopt additional decisions if there is a need to interpret the decision of the Council or to correct it.

413. Article 36 of the Constitutional Law on the Constitutional Council regulates issues of revision of the decision of the Constitutional Council. The decision of the Council can be revised on the initiative of the President or on the initiative of the Council if the rule of the Constitution that was the grounds for taking the decision has been changed; if new substantial circumstances have been revealed concerning the subject matter of a dispute. If there are needs to protect the rights and freedoms of individuals and citizens, ensure national security, sovereignty and integrity of a state the decision of the Constitutional Council can be subject to review upon the initiative of the President. The Council adopts any resolution on the revision of the decision and cancels the previous one.

414. According to Article 38 of the Constitutional Law, the final decision of the Constitutional Council enters into force from the day of adoption, and is binding on the entire territory of the Republic, final and cannot be appealed. In consequence of the decisions adopted by the Constitutional Council that enumerated in Article 39 of the Constitutional Law:

(1) the laws and international treaties considered not to be compliant with the Constitution shall not be signed, ratified or entered into force. The recognition

of laws that do conform to the Constitution resumes the time period for signing. The recognition of international treaties as conforming to the Constitution resumes the process of their ratification;

(2) changes and amendments to the Constitution of the Republic, recognized as not meeting the requirements established by Article 91(2) of the Constitution of Kazakhstan regarding its statehood (the independence of the Republic and its sovereignty, integrity, form of governance, the fundamental principles of Kazakhstan established by the First President), cannot be submitted to a national referendum or to the Parliament of the Republic;

(3) laws and other legal acts recognized as unconstitutional, as well as infringing the rights and freedoms of individuals and citizens envisaged in the Constitution, lose their legal force, cannot be applied and shall be abolished. The decision of the courts and other law-enforcement bodies, taken on the grounds of such a law or other legal act, shall not be enforceable;

(4) the elections of the President of the Republic, recognized as not conforming to the Constitution by the decision of the Central Election Commission at the respective polling stations (administrative-territorial units), shall be declared invalid. The recognition of the elections of the President as conforming to the Constitution entails the registration of the elected President of the Republic;

(5) the elections of the members of the Senate and the *Mazhilis* of the Parliament, recognized as unconstitutional, by the decision of the Central Election Commission in the respective administrative-territorial units and electoral districts shall be declared invalid. The recognition of the election of the members of the Senate and the *Mazhilis* of the Parliament corresponding to the Constitution entails the registration of the elected members;

(6) the results of the national referendum recognized as not conforming to the Constitution are deemed invalid by the decision of the Central Election Commission of the respective polling stations (administrative-territorial units). Recognition of the referendum held that it meets the requirements of the Constitution and entails the resumption of summing up the results of the referendum;

(7) in line with Article 47(1, 2) of the Constitution, the concluding opinion about non-compliance of the established constitutional procedures given to the Parliament for making the decision on early release from office or the final decision on dismissal of the President of the Republic leads to the termination of consideration of the issue. The concluding opinion on the observance of the established constitutional procedures entails the continuation of the consideration of the issue on the early release of the President of Kazakhstan, or dismissal of the President from office, respectively.

415. The state bodies and the officials should inform the Constitutional Council about the measures taken to enforce decisions of the Council within a defined deadline. The recommendations and proposals of the Council on improving the legislation shall be considered by the respective state bodies and the officials, and the Council should be informed about decisions taken within the deadline established by the Council (Article 40 Constitutional Law on the Constitutional Council).

416. The final decisions of the Constitutional Council shall be sent to the respective parties (or their representatives) who submitted the issue for consideration. In all cases, the final decisions of the Council are sent to the President, the Chambers of the Parliament, the Supreme Court, the Office of the General Prosecutor, and the Ministry of Justice of the Republic. The final decisions are published in Kazakh and Russian languages in the official nationwide printing sources. Other decisions, if necessary, are published and sent to the respected state bodies and the officials in cases stipulated in the internal regulations of the Constitutional Council (Article 41 Constitutional Law on the Constitutional Council).

Chapter 6. The Judiciary

§1. Organization of the Judiciary

I. General Introduction

A. *Judicial Organization: The Supreme Court, Local Courts and Specialized Courts*

417. According to constitutional provisions, the judicial system in Kazakhstan shall be established by the Constitution and by Constitutional law. Chapter 7 (Articles 75–82) of the Constitution of Kazakhstan is devoted to the courts and the rendering of justice. The special Constitutional Law of Kazakhstan 25 December 2000 No. 132-II on the Judicial System and the Status of Judges of the Republic of Kazakhstan elaborates these constitutional provisions.[105] Judicial proceedings are regulated by the Civil Procedure Code of the Republic of Kazakhstan adopted on 31 October 2015,[106] by the Penal Procedure Code of the Republic of Kazakhstan adopted 4 July 2014,[107] by the Code on Administrative Offences of 5 July 2014[108] and the Administrative Procedures Code of 29 June 2020.[109]

418. In accordance with Article 76 of the Constitution, judicial power shall be exercised on behalf of Kazakhstan, and its purpose is to protect the rights, freedoms and legal interests of citizens and entities, to ensure observance of the Constitution, laws, other normative legal acts, and international treaties of the Republic. The judicial power shall be extended to all cases and litigation arising from the Constitution, other normative legal acts, and international treaties of Kazakhstan. The court decisions, sentences and other judgments of the courts have an obligatory force within the entire territory of the Republic.

419. Justice in Kazakhstan shall be rendered only by the courts. The judicial power shall be exercised through civil, criminal and other established forms of proceedings. In certain cases, stipulated by law, criminal proceedings shall be carried out with the participation of jurymen. The establishment of special and extraordinary courts at any time is prohibited (Article 75 Constitution).

420. The court system comprises the Supreme Court of the Republic, along with local and other courts established by the Constitution and the Constitutional Law

105. Constitutional Law of Kazakhstan of 25 Dec. 200 No. 132-II on the Judicial System and the Status of Judges of the Republic of Kazakhstan. Available at: https://online.zakon.kz/Document/?doc_id=1021164 (accessed 2 Aug. 2021).
106. Civil Procedure Code of Kazakhstan of 31 Oct. 2015 of 377-V ZRK, available at: http://adilet.zan.kz/rus/docs/K1500000377 (accessed 6 Jan. 2019).
107. Penal Procedure Code of Kazakhstan of 4 Jul. 2014 No. 231-V ZRK, available at: http://adilet.zan.kz/rus/docs/K1400000231 (accessed 7 Jan. 2019).
108. Code of Kazakhstan of 5 Jul. 2014 No. 235-V on Administrative Offences, available at: https://online.zakon.kz/Document/?doc_id=31577399#pos=5;-250 (accessed 10 Jan. 2019).
109. *Supra* n. 48.

on the judicial system. The local courts are regional *(oblastnoy)* courts and courts with a similar status (Nur-Sultan City Court and courts of the cities of the national importance), and district *(rayonnyi)* courts and courts of similar status (city courts and interdistrict courts). There could be other courts, including specialized ones like military, financial, economic, administrative, juvenile courts and so on. Specialized courts have the status of regional or district level courts (Article 3 Constitutional Law on the Judicial System).

421. In line with Articles 6 and 10 of the Constitutional Law on the judicial system, district courts, regional courts and courts with similar status can be formed, reorganized, renamed and abolished by the President of Kazakhstan upon the proposal of the Chair of the Supreme Court in agreement with the Highest Judicial Council.

422. The President may separate one district court into several administrative-territorial units or may merge several district courts into one administrative-territorial unit. The total number of judges of district and regional courts is approved by the President upon the proposal of the Chair of the Supreme Court in agreement with the Highest Judicial Council.

423. District and regional courts consider cases under their jurisdiction (Articles 8 and 12 Constitutional Law on the Judicial System). In addition, regional courts study the judicial practice and consider issues of observance of law by regional judges, and perform other functions (Article 12 Constitutional Law on the Judicial System). District and regional courts are composed of the Chair and judges. There are the following bodies in the regional court: plenary and extended plenary assemblies, the presidium of the plenary assembly, a judicial chamber for civil cases and a judicial chamber for criminal cases (Article 11(3) Constitutional Law on the Judicial System). The Council on interactions with judges is created as a consultative-advisory body to the regional courts of Kazakhstan to assess the moral quality of candidates for the position of a judge (Article 11(6) Constitutional Law on the Judicial System).

424. Specialized courts are formed by the President of Kazakhstan and can have the status of a regional or district court. Specialized courts are military, financial, economic, administrative, juvenile and other courts. For instance, specialized inter-district economic courts consider civil cases of economic character as enumerated in Article 27(1) of the Civil Procedure Code. Military courts consider civil cases involving appeals by military servicemen of the Armed and other forces, or citizens doing military training towards the actions of the bodies of military administration. Military courts consider civil cases also if one of the parties is a military serviceman or a unit of military administration (Article 27(2) Civil Procedure Code). In Kazakhstan, there are also specialized administrative district courts and courts with a similar status that consider cases of administrative offences in accordance with the Code on Administrative Offences dated 5 July 2014. Administrative cases stemming from relations stipulated by the Administrative Procedures Code of 29 June 2020 are regulated by the Code itself.

425. The specialized interdistrict juvenile courts consider cases related to children when, for instance, it is necessary to determine a place of residence of the child, to regulate issues of communication with parents, to deprive (restrict) or restore parental rights, adopt a child, to define paternity, or to collect alimony for the child, etc. In accordance with Article 307 of the Penal Procedure Code of the Republic of Kazakhstan, the specialized interdistrict juvenile courts consider criminal offences covered by Article 106 (Intentional infliction of grievous harm to health), Article 107 (Intentional infliction of moderate harm to health), Article 132 (Involvement of a minor to commit criminal offences), Article 133 (Involvement of a minor to commit antisocial actions), and other articles of the Penal Code of the Republic.[110] In accordance with Article 684 of the Code on Administrative Offences, cases of hooliganism committed by a minor (Article 435), deliberately false call of special forces like fire service, ambulance, police, emergency perpetrated by a minor (Article 438(3)) and other offences committed by minors are within the scope of consideration of the specialized interdistrict juvenile courts.

426. The Supreme Court of Kazakhstan is the highest judicial body on civil, criminal and other cases and considers judicial cases and materials under its jurisdiction, and provides explanations on issues concerning judicial practice through the adoption of normative decisions. The Supreme Court studies judicial practice and, following the results of consolidation, examines issues of observance of the law in rendering justice by courts of the Republic (Article 17(2) Constitutional Law on the Judicial System). Such a function helps to harmonize case law in the country. The Supreme Court adopts normative resolutions and resolutions; it carries out other competencies envisaged by law.

427. The Supreme Court of Kazakhstan is composed of a Chair and judges. There are the following bodies in the Supreme Court: plenary and enlarged plenary assembly, a judicial chamber for civil cases, a judicial chamber for criminal cases and a judicial chamber for administrative cases (Article 18(3) Constitutional Law on the Judicial System). There is also a scientific-consultative council, an international council and a printing body at the Supreme Court. The Academy of Justice as an education and training centre functions at the Supreme Court.

428. The court of the Astana International Financial Centre (AIFC, financial hub) has a special status, which is not included in the judicial system of the country (Article 3(5) Constitutional Law on the Judicial System).

B. The Court of First Instance, Appellate Court and Cassation

429. Article 8 of the Constitutional Law on the judicial system says that the district court is a Court of First Instance. This is also repeated in the Penal Procedure

110. Penal Code of Kazakhstan of 3 Jul. 2014 No. 226-V ZRK. Available at: http://adilet.zan.kz/rus/docs/K1400000226#z583 (accessed 2 Aug. 2021).

Code of Kazakhstan in Article 306. A Court of First Instance is authorized to examine a case directly, to study evidence, to define the full circumstance of the case at court hearings, and to adopt a judicial decision or judgment accordingly. A judicial decision of a Court of First Instance can be appealed in the cassation or appellate court.

430. Part 2 of the Civil Procedure Code of Kazakhstan regulates the judicial proceedings of civil cases at a Court of First Instance. The Court of First Instance considers a civil case on its merits. In accordance with Article 223(1) of the Civil Procedure Code of Kazakhstan, this court (of a first instance that considers the case on its merits) adopts a judicial decision. To adopt a judicial decision, a Court of First Instance examines the evidence, determines whether circumstances important for the case have been identified, which law should be applicable to this case and whether a legal claim needs to be satisfied (Article 225(1) Civil Procedure Code of Kazakhstan). Overall, a full judicial trial in the classical sense takes place at the Court of First Instance. In general, the Court of First Instance in civil cases can adopt orders and make judicial decisions, rulings and resolutions (Article 21(1) Civil Procedure Code of Kazakhstan).

431. Part 3 of the Civil Procedure Code of Kazakhstan is devoted to judicial proceedings. There are appellate and cassation instances in the judicial system of Kazakhstan. Appeal proceedings of civil cases are regulated by Chapters 52–53 of the Civil Procedure Code; cassation proceedings by Chapter 54 of the Code. According to Article 21(1) of the Civil Procedure Code, the appellate and cassation courts adopt rulings and resolutions.

432. An *appellate* instance in civil cases verifies presented factual circumstances, the application and interpretation of the substantial legal norms, and observation of the procedural legal norms in consideration of the case (Article 412 Civil Procedure Code). In accordance with Article 424 of the Civil Procedure Code, the appellate court has the right to leave the previous decision as it was; to change a decision of a Court of First Instance; to cancel the judicial decision of a Court of First Instance and adopt a new one; to cancel a judicial decision in full or in part and to terminate the proceedings, or leave an appeal without consideration in the circumstances envisaged in the Civil Procedure Code, etc.

433. An appellate judicial chamber for civil cases of the regional court or court with similar status can revise a case or reconsider the judicial decisions of the courts of first instance that have not been carried out (Articles 401(1) Civil Procedure Code of Kazakhstan). The Penal Procedure Code of Kazakhstan in Article 310(1) clearly envisages that the regional court or one with similar status shall function as an appellate instance. Appellate instances consider appeals, or the petition of a prosecutor to sentences and resolutions of the district court or a court of similar status, of specialized interdistrict juvenile courts and also specialized interdistrict courts on criminal cases which have not been put into effect.

434. Appeals on investment issues considered by the Nur-Sultan City Court as a Court of First Instance can be reconsidered by the specialized judicial chambers of the Supreme Court of Kazakhstan by three judges (Article 402 of the Civil Procedure Code of Kazakhstan). An appeal should be submitted through the court that made the judicial decision and within a month of its so doing (Article 403 Civil Procedure Code of Kazakhstan).

435. Reasons for overturning or changing of the judicial decision by the appellate instance can be: a wrong clarification of circumstances important for the case; failure to prove evidence for important circumstances; inconsistency of findings of the Court of First Instance on the circumstances of the case; violation or incorrect application of material and procedural norms; and if there is no protocol of the court session or of a procedural separation action that is obligatory according to the Civil Procedure Code (Article 427).

436. Chapter 45 of the Code of Kazakhstan on Administrative Offences regulates issues concerning the reconsideration of courts' resolutions by an appellate instance. The resolutions that did not enter into effect can be appealed to a higher judicial body by the interested parties mentioned in certain articles of the Code or reconsidered on the grounds of the prosecutor's request (Article 830(1) of the Code on Administrative Offences). An appeal or prosecutor's request to reconsider a court's resolutions that have not taken effect should be sent to the Court that adopted the resolution. Then, as a general rule, the Court should send all the materials of the case to a higher appellate instance within three days from the date of receipt of a request (Article 831(1) Code on Administrative Offences). If the appeal concerns reconsideration of a case that imposes an administrative arrest, it should be sent to a higher court on the day of receipt (Article 831(4) Code on Administrative Offences). As a general rule, the prosecutor's request for appeal can be submitted ten days from the day of the handing over or receipt of the court's resolution (Article 832(1) Code on Administrative Offences).

437. The *cassation* court checks the legality of judicial decisions that have entered into force and been adopted by the courts of first instances and the appeal courts. The cassation court takes into account the materials given in the case within the arguments of a petition and protest. As mentioned in Article 444(4) of the Penal Procedure Code of Kazakhstan resolutions of the appellate instance can be reconsidered by a cassation court.

438. In accordance with Article 451(2(5)) Civil Procedure Code, the cassation court can cancel the rulings and judicial decision of a Court of First Instance, rulings and resolutions of an appellate court, or send the case for reconsideration by the appellate instance, or send the case to a Court of First Instance if it was not considered by the appellate court or was not considered on its merits.

439. According to Article 17(1) of the Constitutional Law on the Judicial System of Kazakhstan, the Supreme Court functions as a cassation instance as well. In line with Article 434(1) of the Civil Procedure Code, the Supreme Court of Kazakhstan can reconsider in cassation the judicial decisions of the local and other courts that have taken effect in cases of observance of appellate procedure. The reasons for such reconsideration of a case should be significant violations of substantive and procedural law that resulted in the making of unlawful judicial decisions (Article 438(5) Civil Procedure Code).

440. In some other circumstances, including cases when local and other courts' judicial decisions were not taken effect, and the appellate procedure on them was not properly observed, upon a proposal of the Chair of the Supreme Court and a protest of the General Prosecutor of Kazakhstan, the case can be reconsidered under cassation (Article 434(3) Civil Procedure Code). The reasons for it can be cases:

(1) where enforcement of the judicial resolution may result in grave consequences to the life or health of the people or to the economy and security of the Republic;
(2) if the adopted resolution violates the rights and legitimate interests of an indefinite number of people or other public interests;
(3) if the adopted resolution violates the uniformity of interpretation and application of legal norms by courts.

The Chair of the Supreme Court and the General Prosecutor on their own initiative, or upon the request of interested parties, has a right to challenge the judicial decisions (Article 435 Civil Procedure Code).

441. With regards to criminal cases, Article 484 of the Penal Procedure Code says that the Supreme Court considers cases upon petitions to first-instance courts' sentences and resolutions that entered into force after their consideration by an appellate instance, upon prosecutor's protests, as well as to the sentences and resolutions of the appellate instance. In line with Article 313(1) of the Penal Procedure Code, the Supreme Court of Kazakhstan as the highest judicial instance considers in its chambers:

(1) petitions on reconsideration of the sentences, resolutions of a Court of First Instance after their consideration by the appellate instance, also the sentences and resolutions of the appellate instance;
(2) requests of the Chair of the Supreme Court, protests of the General Prosecutor to the sentences and resolutions of a Court of First Instance regardless of their review by the appellate instance, or the sentences and resolutions of the appellate instance.

442. Request for reconsideration of judicial decision on the civil case of the appellate instance that has entered into force can be made within six months of the judicial decision coming into effect (Article 436(1) Civil Procedure Code).

443. With regards to criminal cases, the filing of a cassation petition with the request to reconsider a conviction sentence on the grounds of the innocence of a convicted person, or on the grounds of the need to apply the law alleviating or improving conditions for a convicted person, does not have a time limitation. The lodging of a cassation appeal can be done anytime (Article 487(1) Penal Procedure Code). The filing of a cassation petition with the request to reconsider an acquittal that was effected or to apply for a more severe punishment or other provisions that aggravate conditions of a convicted person, or the resolution of a court to discontinue a case should be done within one year of such verdicts (Article 487(2) Penal Procedure Code).

444. Chapter 46 of the Code on Administrative offences covers issues on consideration at cassation instance of relevant cases. In accordance with Article 848 of the Code on Administrative Offences, in a case of the administrative offence, a quest for cassation revision can be made by the Chair of the Supreme Court, the Chair of the Judicial Chamber of the Supreme Court of Kazakhstan, by the General Prosecutor, his deputies, prosecutors of the regions and prosecutors of a similar level. The request should be fulfilled by the court no later than seven days from the date of receipt and can be done either in writing or electronically.

II. Constitutional and Legal Status of the Members of the Judiciary; Judicial Independence

A. *The Independence of the Judiciary*

1. Life Appointment

445. The constitutional and legal Status of the Members of the Judiciary is regulated by Chapter 7 'The Judges and Justice' of the Constitution and Part III 'The Status of Judges' of the Constitutional Law on the Judicial System, and by provisions of some other laws of the Republic.

446. In line with Article 23 of the Constitutional Law on the Judicial System, the judges of all courts of the Republic have a single status and differ only in their competencies. A judge is an official of the state who is empowered by the procedures established by the Constitution and the Constitutional Law to exercise justice on a permanent basis, and who holds judicial power.

447. The national legislation of Kazakhstan, including the Constitution and Constitutional Law on the judicial system, proclaims the independence of the judiciary and the judges; the judge's independence is protected by the Constitution and law (Article 25(1) Constitutional Law on the Judicial System). So, in accordance with Article 77 of the Constitution of Kazakhstan, the judge is independent while rendering justice, and obeys only the Constitution and the Law of Kazakhstan. Any interference with the activity of a judge in rendering justice is considered inadmissible and shall be prosecuted by law. A judge is not accountable in any specific case. The secret of the deliberations room should be ensured in all cases without exception (Article 25(2) Constitutional Law on the Judicial System).

448. The Constitutional law in Article 26 enumerates the following guarantees for the independence of judges:

(1) the procedures of rendering justice that are envisaged in Law;
(2) liability for interference into the activities of a judge in rendering justice, and for contempt for court and judges;
(3) immunity of a judge;
(4) the procedures of election and appointment to the post, termination and suspension of the powers of a judge, the right of a judge to resign envisaged by the Constitution, Constitutional Law on the judicial system, the Law of Kazakhstan on the Highest Judicial Council;
(5) granting at the expense of a state material support and social security to judges corresponding to their status, and as well as a prohibition on their deterioration;
(6) judges, members of their families, and their property are under state protection. The bodies of internal affairs are obliged to take timely and comprehensive measures to provide for the security of judges and members of their family, and the safety of their property, if the bodies of internal affairs receive such a request from a judge. The harm inflicted to a judge and his property because of his professional activity should be reimbursed at the expense of the national budget.

449. According to Article 79(1) of the Constitution of Kazakhstan, a court of Kazakhstan consists of permanent judges with lifetime appointments. *Who can be a judge in the Republic of Kazakhstan?* As per Article 79(3) of the Constitution of Kazakhstan, requirements for a judge of the courts of the Republic shall be defined by the Constitutional Law. They are envisaged in Article 29 of the Constitutional Law on the Judicial System of Kazakhstan. There are age and other main requirements to a judge depending on the level of a court.

450. As a general rule, a candidate for the position of a judge of a district court should be a citizen of Kazakhstan who has reached the age of thirty, has higher legal education, high moral standards, impeccable reputation and not less than five years of experience in the legal profession. A candidate for the position of a judge of a district court should also pass a qualification exam, medical check-up, polygraph examination and should successfully accomplish paid training at court and receive a positive recommendation of the plenary session upon the results of training. There are other details regarding a qualification exam.

451. Apart from the aforementioned requirements, a candidate for the position of a judge of a regional court should have fifteen years of experience in the legal profession, including five years as a judge. He needs to receive a recommendation from the plenary session of the relevant regional court.

452. In addition to these, a candidate for the position of a judge of the Supreme Court should have overall not less than twenty years of experience in the legal profession. He/she should have ten years of experience as a judge, including five years of experience as a judge of a regional court. He/she also needs to receive a positive recommendation from the plenary session of the Supreme Court. A candidate for the position of a Chair of the Supreme Court does not need to have judicial experience, accomplishment of training or the positive recommendation of a plenary session of the Supreme Court.

453. Participants in competition for the position of a chair and judge of a district court, or as judges of the regional court, must receive concluding opinions on the ability to cooperate with courts from the Council on interactions with courts and from a plenary meeting of the Supreme Court or regional court respectively. A concluding opinion has an advisory character. Participants in competition for a position of a judge of the Supreme Court should also receive a concluding opinion from the Council on the ability to cooperate with courts, which is also advisory in character (Article 29(3-1) Constitutional Law on the Judicial System).

454. What is the role of the Highest Judicial Council in the appointment of judges? The Highest Judicial Council has an important role in the appointment of judges, as was mentioned in Chapter 4 concerning the Executive ('Powers Regarding Judiciary') of this writing. So, the Highest Judicial Council of Kazakhstan as a state institution was created to ensure the constitutional powers of the President of Kazakhstan in the formation of courts and to ensure guarantees of the independence of judges and their inviolability (Article 1(1) Law on the Highest Judicial Council).

455. The Highest Judicial Council selects candidates on a competitive basis for any vacant position of a chair and a judge of a district court (or court of similar status), a judge of a regional court (or court of similar status), and for a vacant position of a judge of the Supreme Court. Upon the results of this competition, the Council recommends the appointment of chosen candidates for the vacant position of a chair and judge of a district court (court similar to district one), a chair of a judicial chamber and a judge of a regional court (court similar to regional one) to the President of the Republic. Again, upon the results of the competition, the Council recommends a particular nominee's candidature for a position of a judge of the Supreme Court to the President, which he will place before the Senate of the Parliament (Article 3 paragraph 1 subparagraph 2 Law on the Highest Judicial Council).

456. Following proposals from a Chair of the Supreme Court, the Council considers candidatures for vacant positions of chairs of regional courts and chairs of the judicial chambers of the Supreme Court. Then the Council recommends their chosen candidates to the President of Kazakhstan. The Highest Judicial Council also considers a candidature for a vacant position of the Chair of the Supreme Court and recommends it to the President of the Republic. He will then submit the proposal to the Senate of the Parliament (Article 3 paragraph 1 subparagraphs 3–4 Law on the Highest Judicial Council). The Council considers issues of termination of powers of the Chair, chairs of judicial chambers and judges of the Supreme Court, and chairs of judicial chambers and judges of local courts and other courts (Article 3 paragraph 1 subparagraphs 5 Law on the Highest Judicial Council). Jointly with the Supreme Court, the Highest Judicial Council forms the personnel reserve for the positions of the chair of the district court, the chair of the regional court and the chairs of their judicial chambers, a judge and the chairs of the judicial chambers of the Supreme Court (Article 3 paragraph 1 subparagraph 16 Law on the Highest Judicial Council).

457. Article 82 of the Constitution regulates the main issues of the appointment of judges in Kazakhstan. So, the Chair and judges of the Supreme Court of Kazakhstan are elected by the Senate upon the proposal of the President of the Republic based on a recommendation from the Highest Judicial Council. The Chairs and judges of local and other courts are appointed by the President of the Republic upon the recommendation of the Highest Judicial Council of Kazakhstan. The procedure of appointment of the Chairs of the Judicial Chambers is regulated by the Constitutional Law of Kazakhstan.

2. Immunity of Judges

458. The immunity of judges is covered by Article 79(1) of the Constitution and Articles 24, 27 of the Constitutional Law of Kazakhstan on the judicial system. The competence of a judge can only be terminated or suspended on grounds established by the law (Article 79(1) of the Constitution, Article 24(2) Constitutional Law on the judicial system). Except in the case of being apprehended on the scene of a crime or committing grave crimes, a judge cannot be arrested and taken into custody, subjected to administrative penalties imposed by a court or subjected to criminal sanctions without the consent of the President of Kazakhstan based on a conclusion report of the Highest Judicial Council of the Republic (Article 79(1) Constitution and Article 27 Constitutional Law). Stripping immunity from the General Prosecutor, Chair or judges of the Supreme Court of Kazakhstan would require an exceptional act of the Senate of the Parliament of Kazakhstan that is mentioned in Article 55 paragraph 3 of the Constitution of Kazakhstan.

3. Financial Independence from the Executive

459. The financing of courts and provision of judges with housing is done at the expense of the national budget and should provide the possibility of the full and independent exercise of justice (Article 80 Constitution, Article 25(4) Constitutional Law on the Judicial System).

4. Conflicts of Interest

460. A judge cannot carry out non-judicial functions and duties other than envisaged by law. He cannot be a member of state bodies working on anti-corruption issues or issues on the observance of law and legal order. The post of a judge is not compatible with membership in Parliament or having any paid position, entrepreneurial activity, or membership of the executive board or steering committee of a commercial enterprise, subject to teaching, scientific or other creative activity (Article 79(4) Constitution).

461. While rendering justice, a judge is obliged to observe judicial ethics and avoid everything that could discredit the authority or dignity of a judge, or could raise doubts as to his honesty, fairness, objectivity and impartiality. A judge should observe the secrecy of the judges' conference. He/she should resist all kinds of corruption and attempts at unlawful interference into activities involved in rendering justice. A judge cannot be a member of a political party or a professional union, nor support any political party (Article 28 Constitutional Law on the Judicial System).

III. Judicial Proceedings

462. The main principles of the judicial proceedings of Kazakhstan that are common and applicable to all the courts and judges of the Republic are enumerated in Article 77(3) of the Constitution of Kazakhstan. There are also other principles relating to judicial proceedings that are elaborated in the Codes on Civil and Penal Procedures, and on Administrative Offences.

463. According to the Constitution of Kazakhstan, in the application of the law, a judge should be guided by the following principles:

(1) a person shall be considered innocent of a crime unless his guilt is recognized by the sentence of a court that has been entered into force;
(2) no one may be subject twice to criminal or administrative liability for one and the same offence;
(3) no person without his consent shall be changed a court's jurisdiction to consider a case established by law;
(4) everyone has the right to be heard at court;
(5) the laws establishing or intensifying liability, imposing new duties to the citizens or aggravating their position, do not have retroactive effect. If after an offence has been committed a new law abolishes or reduces responsibility, the new law shall be applied;
(6) the accused person is not obliged to prove his innocence;
(7) no one shall be compelled to give testimony against himself, his/her spouse or close relatives. Clergy are not obliged to testify against those who have confided to them in confession;
(8) any doubts as to a person's guilt shall be interpreted in favour of the accused;
(9) evidence obtained unlawfully have no legal force. No one can be sentenced on the grounds of his/her own plea of guilty;
(10) penal law cannot be applied by analogy.

464. The ordinary litigation procedure of a civil case at a Court of First Instance can be taken here as an example to describe a pure classical judicial proceeding at a trial. In general, according to the Civil Procedure Code of Kazakhstan, there are the following proceedings at a Court of First Instance:

(1) simplified (expedited) proceedings;
(2) ordinary litigation proceedings;
(3) special litigation proceedings;
(4) special proceedings;
(5) proceedings on the restoration of lost judicial or enforcement proceedings;
(6) proceedings on consideration of a request to return a child or realization of a right of access to a child on the grounds of an international agreement by Kazakhstan.

465. Chapter 18 of the Civil Procedure Code of Kazakhstan is devoted to ordinary litigation proceedings. As a general rule, consideration of a civil case by the court should take up to two months from the date of completion of case preparations for trial (Article 183(2) Civil Procedure Code). Depending on the subject under consideration, and taking into account reasonableness and sufficiency, that term can be shorter. The court hearing is presided over by a Chair; he/she needs to ensure due observance of procedural sequences and actions, and of the procedural rights and duties of those participating in the trial. A Chair should take necessary measures to ensure proper order at a court hearing (Article 185 Civil Procedure Code).

466. The court, when considering and resolving the case, is obliged to examine directly the evidence in the case. The court is obliged to hear arguments and evidence from both parties, and from other participants in the case, the testimony of witnesses, and the opinions of the relevant experts, state bodies and local government. The Court is obliged to familiarize itself with the documents in the case, to examine material evidence, to listen to audio recordings and to watch video, film, photo materials and to familiarize itself with the means for converting information. If necessary, the court shall listen to the consultations and explanations of a specialist. The trial is conducted orally. Hearing the explanations of the parties, other persons participating in litigation, the testimony of witnesses, and expert, state body and local government opinions may be carried out through video conference (Article 186 Civil Procedure Code).

467. The presiding judge opens the court hearing and reads aloud the case to be considered, as well as authorizing the use of audio and video recordings of the court hearing. Persons participating in the trial and present in the courtroom are obliged to behave appropriately and keep order in the courtroom. The presiding judge informs an interpreter of his rights and duties and of criminal liability for knowingly providing false interpretation. Witnesses to be heard should be excluded from the courtroom. The Chair presents the composition of the court, the prosecutor, expert, specialist, the clerk of the court, and explains to persons participating in the case their right to move for recusal. The Chair explains the rights and duties of the parties, including their right to settle the dispute by mediation, agreement on a participatory procedure, arbitration, settlement of a dispute by the court of the Astana

International Financial Centre or in any other way established by law and the legal consequences thereof (Articles 189–194 Civil Procedure Code).

468. Persons participating in the case are obliged to notify the court in advance about any reasons for their non-attendance at the hearing and present the relevant evidence for such. In the circumstances established by law, the court has the right to consider the case *in absentia* only in the case of recognition that participants were duly informed about the time and place of consideration of the case. The parties have the right to request in writing that the court consider the case in their absence (Article 196 Civil Procedure Code). Adjournment of a trial may occur only if the court considers that a hearing is not possible because of the absence of one of the persons participating at the trial, or if there is the need to present additional evidence in line with the requirements of the Code, or if a counterclaim has been filed, and so on. (Article 198 Civil Procedure Code).

469. The court explains to any experts and specialists their rights and duties, including criminal responsibility for knowingly giving a false opinion (Article 200 Civil Procedure Code).

470. The beginning of consideration of a case on its merits starts with the questions from a presiding judge as to whether the plaintiff supports his claims, or whether the defendant admits the claims of a plaintiff, or whether the parties wish to come to an amicable agreement or to transfer a dispute to arbitration or the court of the Astana International Financial Centre, or to resolve a dispute by mediation or participative procedure or any other means established by law (Article 201 Civil Procedure Code).

471. The court hears explanations from persons participating in the case (plaintiff and defendant, their representatives and third parties) and defines the order of examination of evidence. The court warns a witness about criminal responsibility for refusal to testify and for a false affidavit. Every witness gives testimony separately, and he/she can use written materials when giving testimony. A judge has a right to ask questions at any time of questioning and can organize the confrontation of witnesses. Interrogation of a witness who has not reached fourteen years of age and, at the discretion of the court, interrogation of a witness between the ages of fourteen and sixteen is performed with the participation of a teacher and legal representatives. Testimonies of witnesses are read aloud at the court hearing, after which participants of the case have the right to give explanations for them (Articles 202–207 Civil Procedure Code).

472. The documents and protocols of physical inspections shall be read aloud at the court hearing and presented to persons participating in a case, to their representatives, and if necessary, to the experts, specialists and witnesses. In order to protect privacy, the disclosure and examination of personal correspondence and telegraph messages at open court hearings can be done only with the consent of those citizens to whom this correspondence and the messages belong. The physical evidence is examined by the court and presented to persons participating in the case, and, if necessary, to the experts, specialists and witnesses, and the relevant protocols should be read aloud at the court session, and persons participating in a case may give their explanations. Any document and physical evidence difficult to present or deliver to the courtroom can be inspected on-site, and the results of on-site inspection shall be described in the protocol and attached to the case (Articles 208–211 Civil Procedure Code).

473. The reproduction of sound recording and the demonstration of video recording, photo and film materials and their examination should be done at the court session or in any other place where there is special equipment. This should be reflected in the protocol of the court hearing, mentioning the distinctive features and time of demonstration. After that, the court hears any explanation of the persons participating in the case and their representatives. The court may involve a specialist and assign an expert (Article 212 Civil Procedure Code).

474. An expert opinion shall be read aloud at the court session. Questions can be asked of an expert to clarify their opinion. The court has the right to ask questions of an expert at any time during consideration of the case. If necessary, the court can assign additional or repeated expertise (Article 213 Civil Procedure Code). In cases that do not require special studies, a specialist can give an opinion orally or in writing; questions may be asked of a specialist at the court hearing. State bodies and local governance can be requested to present their opinions (conclusions) (Articles 214–215 Civil Procedure Code).

475. After examination of all the evidence, a judge asks participants of the case and their representatives whether they have any supplementary information to add. If there is nothing to add, a judge announces the end of a case examination and proceeds to the judicial debates (Article 216 Civil Procedure Code).

476. The judicial debates consist of speeches from the persons participating in a case and their representatives. Participants in these judicial debates have no right to refer to evidence that has not been examined and considered by the court. A plaintiff and his representative take the floor first, followed by the defendant and his representative. A third party who has a separate claim on the subject of a dispute and his representative in the judicial process that has been started takes the floor after the plaintiff and defendant and their representatives altogether. A prosecutor, representatives of state bodies and bodies of local governance, legal entities and citizens who applied to the court to protect their rights, freedoms and legal interests of others take the floor last in the judicial debates (Article 217 Civil Procedure Code). After all the speeches of the participants of the judicial debates, the participants may address with a remark. The right of the last remark always belongs to the defendant and his representative (Article 218 Civil Procedure Code).

477. A prosecutor who is not a party to the case can participate in one, on the grounds enumerated in the Code of Civil Procedure, to express a concluding opinion on its merits on the whole after the judicial debates, which shall be attached to the materials of the case (Article 219 Civil Procedure Code).

478. If the court recognizes that there is the need to explore additional circumstances necessary for a correct resolution of the case or to examine further evidence, the court announces resumption of the merits of the case during or after the judicial debates. This shall be indicated in the protocol of the court hearing (Article 220 Civil Procedure Code).

479. After the debates, the court leaves the courtroom for adjudication. After adopting and signing the decision, the judge reads aloud a full decision or its resolution part. Then the presiding judge explains the legal grounds and consequences of the adoption of the decision, the procedure and deadlines for appealing the decision and announces the date when the decision will be prepared in a final form, and the participants can receive copies. After these actions, the presiding judge announces the close of the court hearings (Articles 221–222 Civil Procedure Code).

IV. Disciplinary Liability of Judges

480. Chapter 2 of the Constitutional Law on Judicial System covers issues concerning the disciplinary liability of judges. So, in accordance with Article 39 of the Constitutional Law, a judge can be subject to disciplinary liability if he/she commits a disciplinary offence. The disciplinary offence is a guilty action (or inaction) done while on duty or in off-duty time that results in a violation of the provisions of the Constitutional law on the judicial system and (or) the Code on Judicial Ethics, and that, therefore, undermine the judicial authority or damage the reputation of a judge.

481. According to the Regulations on Judicial Jury approved by the Decree of the President of Kazakhstan dated 26 June 2001 No. 643, a judge may be subjected to disciplinary liability only on the grounds stipulated by the Constitutional Law on Judicial System and Status of Judges (paragraph 15).[111]

In line with Article 39 of the Constitutional Law on the Judiciary, a judge can be subjected to disciplinary liability in the following cases:

(1) a gross violation of the due course of law during consideration of a case;
(2) a discreditable act contrary to judicial ethics.

111. Please *see* more about Judicial Jury in the Regulations on Judicial Jury Approved by the Decree of the President of Kazakhstan of 26 Jun. 2001 No. 643. Available at: http://adilet.zan.kz/rus/docs/U010000643_ (accessed 18 Jul. 2019).

The chairs of the courts and judicial chambers may also be subject to disciplinary liability for improper performance of their official duties as stipulated in the Constitutional law.

482. In line with Article 40 of the Constitutional Law on the Judiciary, the following types of penalties can be applied to a judge:

(1) reproof;
(2) reprimand;
(3) dismissal from the office of a chair of the court or chair of the judicial chamber for improper performance of duty;
(4) dismissal from the office of a judge on the grounds envisaged by the Constitutional Law on the Judiciary.

483. Disciplinary proceedings against a judge must be initiated not later than three months after the day of detection of the misdemeanour, except for initiating disciplinary proceedings upon the complaints of individuals not later than one year after the date of committing the offence. Disciplinary proceedings on the grounds of complaints of individuals may be initiated not later than six months from the day of submission. A disciplinary case must be considered during the two months after the day of initiation (Article 42 Constitutional Law on the Judiciary).

484. There are two chambers in the Judicial Jury: a qualification commission and a disciplinary commission. In line with Article 44 of the Constitutional Law, the qualification commission of the Judicial Jury after due consideration of materials on the evaluation of qualification of actual judges takes one of the following decisions:

(1) to recognize a judge's qualification as relevant to the position occupied;
(2) to recommend for appointment to the posts of a judge of a higher instance, chairs of the court or its chamber;
(3) to recommend a person for inclusion on the list of the candidates' pool for a higher position (to a higher judicial instance);
(4) to transfer to another court, or to another specialization;
(5) to reject as non-qualifying to the position held because of professional unsuitability;
(6) to withhold a recommendation for appointment to the post of a judge of a higher instance, of a chair of the court or a chair of the judicial chamber.

485. The decision of the Judicial Jury on recognition of a judge as non-qualified to the position held because of professional unsuitability shall be a reason for submission by the Chair of the Supreme Court of a proposal for dismissal from the post to the Highest Judicial Council.

486. Upon consideration of the disciplinary case by the Judicial Jury, one of the following decisions is taken:

(1) imposition of a disciplinary penalty; or
(2) termination of the disciplinary proceedings.

487. The decision of the Judicial Jury is the reason for consideration by the Highest Judicial Council of the question to dismiss the chair, a chair of the judicial chamber or a judge from their posts. A judge may appeal against the decision of the Judicial Jury to the Highest Judicial Council.

488. If within one year since the day of imposition of a penalty, a judge is not subjected to any new disciplinary penalty, he is considered as if he has not been subjected to any penalty. After six months from the date of imposition of a disciplinary sanction, in cases of impeccable behaviour and conscientious attitude to the duties, such a judge will be exempted from any further disciplinary penalty (Article 45 Constitutional law on the Judiciary).

§2. JUDICIAL REVIEW

489. According to Article 78 of the Constitution of Kazakhstan, the judges have no right to apply laws and other normative legal acts that infringe the rights and freedoms of an individual and citizen. If a court finds that the law or any other normative legal act that should be applied infringes the rights and freedoms of an individual, the court is obliged to suspend legal proceedings in the matter and address the Constitutional Council to consider the issue of the constitutionality of this normative legal act.

490. Article 23(3) of the Constitutional Law on the Constitutional Council says that judicial proceedings on the case shall be suspended in case of appeal to the Council. In line with Article 24 of the Constitutional Law on the Constitutional Council, as a general rule, the Council considers an appeal (address) during the month following receipt of the request. The Council organizes a special meeting (session) to consider the request; disclosure of opinions expressed during that discussion is prohibited.

491. One recent request received by the Constitutional Council was from the Karaganda Regional Court on the constitutionality of Article 27(5) of the Law of Kazakhstan on Court Enforcement Proceedings and the Status of the Law-Enforcement Officials. The Constitutional Council adopted the Normative Resolution on 3 July 2018.[112] The substance of the request (appeal) was that the state law-enforcement bodies of the Karaganda region refused to carry out decisions of

112. Normative Resolution of the Constitutional Council of the Republic of Kazakhstan of 3 Jul. 2018 No. 5 Review for the Constitutionality of paragraph 5 of Article 27 of the Law on Court Enforcement Proceedings and the Status of the Law-Enforcement Officials upon a Request of the Karaganda Regional Court. Available at the official website of the Constitutional Council of Kazakhstan: https://ksrk.gov.kz/kk/solutions/kr-konstituciyalyk-kenesinin-karagandy-oblystyk-sotynyn-usynysy-boyynsha-atkarushylyk (accessed 16 Jan. 2019).

private enforcement officials on forcibly bringing a debtor, despite the express authorization by the court. The request of the court of the Karaganda region was based on the case that was considered by court No. 2 of the *Kazybek byi* district of Karaganda city upon a claim of a private enforcement official. The district court decided that refusal of the state law-enforcement bodies to carry out the decision of the private enforcement official was not legal. This decision was appealed by the Department of the Internal Affairs of the Karaganda region to a higher judicial instance. Examining the case, the Karaganda regional court considered that Article 27(5) of the Law of the Republic of Kazakhstan on Court Enforcement Proceedings and the Status of the Law-Enforcement Officials infringed the constitutional rights and freedoms of individuals and citizens and were contrary to Article 39(1,3) of the Constitution of Kazakhstan.

492. The Constitutional Council decided that Article 27(5) of the Law of Republic of Kazakhstan on Court Enforcement Proceedings and the Status of the Law-Enforcement Officials did not contradict the provisions of the Constitution, but the Council enumerated substantive gaps in the national legislation on issues of mechanisms of forced appearance to court. As mentioned in the Resolution, the absence of due legal mechanism can result in violations of human rights and freedoms. The Constitutional Council recommended that the Government of Kazakhstan fully regulate issues of forced appearance to court, clarify the functions and liability of state bodies in law-enforcement proceedings, and initiate the adoption of amendments to the Law on Court Enforcement Proceedings and the Status of the Law-Enforcement Officials of 2 April 2010. Here, in this example, we can see the influence of the judiciary on the legislative and executive branches of power in Kazakhstan.

§3. The Prosecutor's Office

493. Article 83 of the Constitution of Kazakhstan covers the constitutional status of the Prosecutor's Office of the Republic. The Prosecutor's Office, on behalf of the state and within the limits and forms established by law, carries out supervision over the observance of the law on the territory of Kazakhstan; represents the interests of the state and initiates criminal prosecution on its behalf. The Prosecutor's Office is a centralized system with a lower level Prosecutor's office subordinate to a higher level and to the Office of the General Prosecutor. It exercises its authority independent of other state bodies, state officials, and is accountable only to the President of the Republic.

494. The General Prosecutor of Kazakhstan, during his/her term of office, cannot be arrested, or subject to detention, nor can measures of administrative penalties be imposed by any court; nor can he/she be subject to criminal proceedings without the consent of the Senate of the Parliament of Kazakhstan, except where caught at the scene of a crime or when committing grave crimes. The term of office of the General Prosecutor of the Republic is five years.

495. As mentioned in the Constitution, the jurisdiction, organization and operating procedures of the Prosecutor's Office shall be regulated by law. The Law of Kazakhstan on the Prosecutor's Office was adopted on 30 June 2017.[113] In line with Article 5, within the legal limits and procedures established by the law, the Prosecutor's Office exercises supreme supervision over the legality of:

(1) the activities of the state, local representative and executive bodies, local governance bodies and their officials, other entities regardless of their form of ownership, and the actions and decisions taken;
(2) judicial decisions that taken effect;
(3) enforcement proceedings of court decisions and proceedings on cases of administrative offences;
(4) activities of the law enforcement and special state bodies in the fields of pretrial investigation, operational investigative and counterintelligence activities, pursuance of criminal punishment and other measures of state coercion, observance of international treaties of the Republic;
(5) state legal statistics and special recordings;
(6) other directions defined by law.

496. With regards to the executive bodies, in conformity with Article 10 of the Law on the Prosecutor's Office, for instance, oversees compliance with the Constitution and with laws and legal acts of the President of Kazakhstan of the following:

(1) the formal acts and decisions of the Government, other state, local representative and executive bodies, local governance bodies and their officials with some exceptions;
(2) the formal acts and decisions of other entities regardless of their form of ownership if these formal acts and decisions concern indefinite numbers of people or have a public character.

497. The Prosecutor's Office has no right to protest against legislative acts, or other acts of the President of Kazakhstan, the Administration of the President of Kazakhstan, the Constitutional Council, normative resolutions of the Supreme Court, acts of the Highest Judicial Council, the Control Committee over fulfilment of the national budget (as a result of inspections), or normative acts of a technical character (Article 24 Law on the Prosecutor's Office).

498. With regards to the judicial branch of power, the Prosecutor's Office supervises the legality of court decisions whether criminal, civil or administrative. The prosecutor (within limits established by law) has the right to request from the court the criminal, civil, administrative cases and cases on administrative offences on which the decisions have been made, as well as to request the materials related to enforcement of judicial sentences, and to study the legality of adopted acts. If there

113. Law of Kazakhstan of 30 Jun. 2017 No. 81-VI ZRK on the Prosecutor's Office. Available at: https://online.zakon.kz/Document/?doc_id=31690116#pos=70;-58 (accessed 2 Aug. 2021).

are sufficient reasons, the prosecutor has the right to protest. The prosecutor considers petitions to protest against judicial acts that entered into force and performs other functions envisaged by law (Article 13 Law on the Prosecutor's Office).

499. With regards to the general lawmaking powers in line with Article 37 of the Law under consideration, the General Prosecutor within his competence adopts normative legal acts on issues concerning:

(1) the application of the provisions of the criminal procedural legislation and legislation on criminal intelligence;
(2) state legal statistics and special recordings;
(3) the formation, access, use, storage, protection and destruction of information from the system of information exchange of law enforcement, special state and other bodies;
(4) the procedure of conducting appointments by the officials of the prosecutor's office with individuals and representatives of the legal entities;
(5) the procedure for admission to the higher education institution at the Prosecutor's Office;
(6) the procedure of conducting interdepartmental scientific research in law-enforcement issues, their coordination and monitoring; and
(7) other normative legal acts, in accordance with legislation.

500. With regards to participation in international lawmaking, the Office of the General Prosecutor represents the Prosecutor's Office in the field of international cooperation, develops the drafts of international treaties on criminal procedural issues, as well as coordinates the preparation of drafts of international treaties initiated by other state bodies related to the activities of the Prosecutor's Office (Article 38(2(7)) Law on the Prosecutor's Office).

Chapter 7. Consultative-Advisory Bodies to the Parliament and Government of Kazakhstan

§1. Consultative-Advisory Bodies to the Parliament of Kazakhstan

501. In accordance with Article 11-1 of Constitutional Law of Kazakhstan on the Parliament of the Republic of Kazakhstan and the Status of its Deputies, the consultative-advisory bodies can be created at the Parliament and its Chambers in order to adopt proposals on issues that fall within the competence of the Parliament and its Chambers. The decisions of these consultative-advisory bodies have recommendatory character; their procedures are regulated by the internal regulations of the Parliament of Kazakhstan and its Chambers. Their working bodies are part of the apparatus of the Chambers of the Parliament.

502. As given in Chapter 10-1 of the Senate's Regulations of the internal working procedures, the Senate of the Parliament can create consultative-advisory bodies and the Apparatus of the Senate is their working body.

503. At the *Mazhilis* of the Parliament, consultative-advisory bodies can be created in accordance with Chapter 8(132-1) of the *Mazhilis*'s regulations of internal working procedures, in order to develop proposals on issues that fall within the competence of the *Mazhilis*. Their decisions have an advisory character. The *Mazhilis* creates, reorganizes and abolishes such advisory bodies. The Bureau of the *Mazhilis* defines their composition, appoints their senior officials and approves the regulations for them; it also at quarterly intervals hears the reports of senior officials on their activities. They are part of the apparatus of the *Mazhilis* of the Parliament. The representatives of such consultative-advisory bodies can be involved in the working groups which draw up draft laws (Chapter 3(29) Internal Regulations of the *Mazhilis*).

504. There is also the Public Chamber at the *Mazhilis* of Kazakhstan. Its status, competence and organization are covered by the Regulations adopted on 20 November 2007.[114] The main tasks of the Public Chamber are to examine draft laws, to make the recommendations and proposals on their development, and to forecast possible consequences in case of the adoption and implementation of such laws; also to consider and evaluate proposals on improving the current legislation that is in the process of being submitted to the *Mazhilis* of the Parliament (Article 2(4) Regulations on the Public Chamber). The main functions of the Public Chamber are to give advice in developing the draft laws that are being submitted by the members of the *Mazhilis* in the exercise of its legislative initiative; to study and summarize the lawmaking experience of the parliaments of the foreign countries; to hold, and

114. Regulations of 20 Nov. 2007 No. 72-IV on the Public Chamber at the *Mazhilis* of Kazakhstan. Available at: https://online.zakon.kz/document/?doc_id=30155883#pos=0;2 (accessed 21 Jan. 2019).

participate in, round tables, seminars, hearings, conferences and other events which have a bearing on the problems of the legislative activities (Article 2(5) Regulations on the Public Chamber).

505. Within its competencies, the Public Chamber defines the list of draft laws to be considered by the Chamber. It has the right to request and receive necessary information on the relevant draft laws from the structural units of the *Mazhilis*; to assign its own representatives for participation in meetings of the working groups of the *Mazhilis*; and to involve experts of the scientific and state bodies, non-governmental organizations and the public associations, etc. (Article 3(6) Regulations on the Public Chamber).

506. In practical terms, the Public Chamber has been involved in discussions of many important draft laws, including the one on religious activities and religious organizations. That meeting was held in September 2011 at the L.N. Gumilyov Eurasian National University. Another example was when the Public Chamber was involved in the discussion of the question on the criminal responsibility of certain legal entities in June 2011.

§2. The Consultative-Advisory Bodies to the Government of Kazakhstan

507. In accordance with Article 26 of Constitutional Law of Kazakhstan of 18 December 1995 No. 2688 on the Government of the Republic of Kazakhstan, the commissions, councils and other consultative-advisory bodies can be created by the Government of Kazakhstan to develop proposals on issues that fall within the competence of the Government. The Prime Minister, his deputies, and members of the Government lead such bodies. The decisions of these consultative-advisory bodies have advisory character.

508. There is the Prime Minister's Order of 29 September 2016 No. 90-p on Some Issues of the Consultative-Advisory Bodies at the Government of Kazakhstan.[115] In line with this Order, there are the following consultative-advisory bodies:

(1) the Council on the Competitiveness at the Government;
(2) the Council for Improvement of the Investment Climate;
(3) the Consultative Council on Taxation Issues;
(4) the Commission on Counteraction to the Shadow Economy in the Republic of Kazakhstan;
(5) the Commission on the Industrial Development of the Republic of Kazakhstan;
(6) the Interdepartmental Commission for the Prevention of Offences;

115. Order of the Prime Minister of Kazakhstan of 29 Sep. 2016 No. 90-p on Some Issues of the Consultative-Advisory Bodies at the Government of Kazakhstan. Available at the official website of the Government: https://primeminister.kz/ru/orders/29092016-90 (accessed 30 Apr. 2020).

(7) the Interdepartmental Commission on the Use of Water Resources from the Irtysh Cascade of Water Reservoirs.

509. There are many other Councils. For instance, there is the Council on Economic Policy at the Ministry of National Economy.[116] It considers proposals on the main directions of the social-economic development of the country, on defining strategy and the measures for its realization, and those mechanisms that provide for the sustainable development of the economy. The aim of the Council is to develop proposals and recommendations on the main directions of social-economic development for both mid and long terms. The Chair of the Council is the Prime Minister of the Republic. The Council is composed of the First Deputy of the Prime Minister, the Vice-Minister of National Economy, the Deputies of the Prime Minister, the Ministers of National Economy, Industry and Infrastructural Development, Labour and Social Protection, Finance, Trade and Integration, the Chair of the National Bank, the Chair of the Agency for the regulation and development of the financial market (if and as agreed), the Chair of the Agency for Strategic Planning and Reforms (if and as agreed), the Deputy Head of the President's Administration or the Assistant of the President on social-economic issues (if and as agreed), the Head of the Chancellery of the Prime Minister, the Board Chair of the Sovereign Wealth Fund the 'Samruk-Kazyna' JSC and the National Managing Holding 'Baiterek' JSC (if and as agreed) and the Chair of the Presidium or the Chair of the National Chamber of Entrepreneurs 'Atameken' (if and as agreed).

510. With the Order of the Prime Minister of the Government of Kazakhstan No. 11-p on 19 February 2016, the Interdepartmental Commission on Issues of the Legislative Drafting Activities was established.[117] It is composed of many officials, such as the Minister of Justice (the Chair of the Commission), the Deputy of the Minister of Justice (the Deputy Chair), the Director of the Department on the legislation of the Ministry of Justice (Secretary of the Commission), a Member of the Senate of the Parliament (if and as agreed), and a Member of the *Mazhilis* of the Parliament (if and as agreed), the Head of the Unit on the legal expertise of the Senate's Apparatus (if and as agreed), the First Deputy of the General Prosecutor (if and as agreed), the First Deputy Chair of the Agency of Kazakhstan for Financial Monitoring (if and as agreed), the Deputy Chair of the Committee on the National Security, the Deputy Head of the State Guard Service of Kazakhstan (as and if agreed), the Deputy of the Minister of Internal Affairs, the Deputy of the Minister of Defence, Vice-Minister for Emergencies, Vice-Minister of Healthcare, Vice-Minister of Labour and Social Protection, Vice-Minister of Culture and Sport, the Deputy Chair for Civil Service Affairs (if and as agreed), the Deputy Chair for Anti-corruption Agency (if and as agreed), Vice-Minister of Finance, Vice-Minister of

116. Order of the Prime Minister of Kazakhstan of 3 May 2016 No. 33-p on Creation of the Council on Economic Policy. Available at: http://adilet.zan.kz/rus/docs/R1600000033 (accessed 2 Aug. 2021).
117. Order of the Prime Minister of the Government of Kazakhstan of 19 Feb. 2016 No. 11-p on Organization of the Interdepartmental Commission on Legislative Drafting Activities. Available at: http://adilet.zan.kz/rus/docs/R1600000011 (accessed 2 Aug. 2021).

Education and Science, Vice-Minister of Agriculture, Vice-Minister of National Economy, the Deputy Chair of the National Bank, a member of the Governing Board of the Board of the Commercial lawyers 'Kazakhstan Bar Association', lawyer of the Public Fund 'Legal Media Center' (if and as agreed), Senior partner of the Center for Strategic Initiatives LLP (if and as agreed), and others.

511. The Commission has many important tasks, including the following ones:

(1) to provide an analysis of the legislative drafting activities of the Government and other authorized state bodies of Kazakhstan;
(2) to draw up recommendations on the current plan for drafting the legislative activities of the Government of Kazakhstan, and a conceptual plan of legislative work, taking into account the instructions and the yearly address by the President of Kazakhstan, normative resolutions and yearly addresses of the Constitutional Council of Kazakhstan, yearly and special reports of the Commission on human rights at the President of Kazakhstan, report of the Authorized Representative on human rights, state programmes and programmes approved by the Government of Kazakhstan, the plans of events to realize these, also decisions of the Government, results of the legal monitoring of the normative legal acts, the laws, relevant to the Budgetary Code, decisions of the Prime Minister, and the opinion of the Budgetary Commission on proposals to increase or reduce the revenues of national or local budgets;
(3) to submit proposals on priority directions of the legislative drafting activities to the Government; and
(4) to prepare proposals to regulate disagreements between state bodies that might have occurred during the process of developing and passing bills by the Government and the Parliament, etc.

The Order of the Prime Minister of the Government envisages many other important tasks. Overall, there are twelve tasks mentioned in the Order.

512. In the Government of Kazakhstan, there is also a Commission on cooperation with international organizations. This Commission was created by Order of the Prime Minister of Kazakhstan of 16 August 2017 No. 112-p to develop proposals on the cooperation of state bodies of Kazakhstan with international organizations and to consider issues on the accession of the Republic to the international organizations, on leaving or participating in them, and of the accession of Kazakhstan to the international treaties.[118] The working body of the Commission is the MFA of Kazakhstan. The meeting of the Commission takes place not less than twice per year.

118. *The meeting of the Commission on cooperation with international organizations has been held in Nur-Sultan.* Available at: https://avesta-news.kz/zasedanie-komissii-po-sotrudnichestvu-kazahstana-s-mezhdunarodnymi-organizatsiyami-proshlo-v-nur-sultane/ (accessed 30 Apr. 2020).

Part III. The Local Governance Level

Chapter 1. The Local Governance Level

§1. General Outline

513. Chapter 8 of the Constitution of Kazakhstan is devoted to the local state governance and self-governance in the country. The competence of the *maslikhats*, procedures of their organization and their activities, and the legal status of their deputies are regulated by the special Law of the Republic. Law of Kazakhstan on the Local State Governance and Self-Governance in the Republic of Kazakhstan of 23 January 2001 regulates issues of local governance in the country.[119] In accordance with Article 85 of the Constitution, the local state government is realized by the local representative and executive bodies that are responsible for the state of affairs within the respective territory.

514. In line with Article 3 of Law on the Local Governance, the economic and financial grounds of the local state governance and local self-governance consist of:

(1) the local budget;
(2) property allotted to the communal legal entities;
(3) other property that is in communal ownership in accordance with the national legislation.

515. The main requirements of the *maslikhats* and *akimats* are established in Article 4 of the Law on Local Governance. In their activities the *maslikhats* and *akimats* are obliged:

(1) to prevent the taking of decisions not corresponding to the main directions of domestic and external policy of the country;
(2) to observe the interests of the Republic in ensuring national security;
(3) to follow the established national standards in socially significant fields of activities;
(4) to ensure respect for human rights and for the legitimate interests of citizens.

119. Law of Kazakhstan of 23 Jan. 2001 No. 148-II on the Local State Governance and Self-Governance in the Republic of Kazakhstan. Available at: https://online.zakon.kz/Document/?doc_id=1021546#pos=3;-106 (accessed 2 Aug. 2021).

516. The *maslikhats* and *akimats* shall not make decisions that impede the formation of a single labour market, or that impede capital, finance, and the free movement of goods and services within the territory of the Republic. The plans for the development of territories adopted by the *maslikhats* and *akimats* shall comply with the strategic development plans of the Republic.

§2. *The Maslikhats* as the Local Representative Bodies: Their Creation, Competence and Organization of Their Work

I. Creation of the *Maslikhats*

517. According to Article 86 of the Constitution of Kazakhstan, the local representative bodies are the *maslikhats.* They express the will of the population of the respective administrative-territorial unit and, in line with the common state interests, define the measures necessary for the realization of and control over their fulfilment. Creation of the *maslikhats* is also regulated by Article 5, Chapter 2 of the Law on the Local Governance. The *maslikhats* are elected by the population via universal, equal and direct suffrage by secret ballot for a five-year term. A deputy of the *maslikhat* can be a citizen of Kazakhstan who has reached 20 years of age. A citizen of Kazakhstan can be a deputy of only one *maslikhat.*

518. In accordance with Article 9 of the Constitutional Law on the elections, the deputies of the *maslikhats* are elected from the party lists presented by the political parties, the territorial constituency. The numbers of the deputies of the relevant *maslikhats* shall be defined by the Central Election Commission: at the regional level (*oblast* level), cities of national importance and the capital – around fifty deputies; at the city *maslikhat* – around thirty; at the district level – around twenty deputies. The *maslikhat* shall be considered eligible to start its work if at least three-quarters of the total number of the deputies determined by the Central Election Commission have been elected. The elections of the deputies are regulated by the legislation of Kazakhstan on the elections. The competence of the *maslikhat* starts from the moment of opening of its first session and ends with the start of the first session of the *maslikhat* of the new convocation (Article 5 Law on the Local Governance).

519. The powers of the *maslikhat* shall be terminated early by the President of the Republic after consultations with the Prime Minister and the Chairs of the Chambers of the Parliament, as well as in a case when the relevant *maslikhat* takes a decision on a voluntary dissolution. The powers of the *maslikhat* shall be terminated upon expiration of its term (Article 23 Law on the Local Governance). In case of liquidation of the administrative-territorial unit, the relevant *maslikhat* will also be liquidated.

II. The Competences of the *Maslikhats*

520. The jurisdiction of the *maslikhats* shall include (Article 86 Constitution):

(1) approval of the plans and the economic and social development programmes of the territory, approval of the local budget and the reports on their fulfilment;
(2) solving of the problems that fall within the competence of the local administrative-territorial structure;
(3) consideration of the reports of the heads of the local executive bodies on issues that fall within the competence of the *maslikhats*;
(4) creation of the permanent commissions and other working bodies of the *maslikhat*, hearing reports on their activities, sorting out other questions related to the organization of the *maslikhat's* work;
(5) performance of other competencies to ensure the rights and legitimate interests of citizens in line with the legislation of the Republic.

521. Article 6 of the Law on the Local Governance elaborates the constitutional provisions. So, the *maslikhat*:

(1) approves the plans, economic and social development programmes of the relevant territory, local budget and the reports on their fulfilment, including approval of the budget programmes that are being implemented by the *akims* of a district in a city;
(2) approves the scheme of the administrative-territorial unit's governance on the proposal of the *akim* that is grounded on the basic structures of the local state governance approved by the Government, if other conditions are not stipulated by the laws of Kazakhstan;
(3) takes decisions on issues related to local administrative-territorial governance;
(4) approves the rules related to the heating season, the protection of green spaces, the organization of public services and amenities;
(5) gives consent on the personnel of the relevant *akimat* upon the proposal of the *akim*;
(6) considers the reports of heads of executive bodies and submits to the relevant bodies requests on bringing to justice the officials of the state bodies as well as entities for non-fulfilment of the *maslikhat's* decisions;
(7) in line with the legislative act of the Republic on the elections, elects the members of the territorial and precinct election commissions by secret ballot or open voting;
(8) controls the fulfilment of the local budget and development programmes;
(9) considers the yearly report on the implementation of the budget of the revision commissions of the regions, cities of national importance, the capital;
(10) makes proposals to the revision commissions of the regions, cities of national and the capital to include the objects of the state revision and financial control in the working plan of the revision commissions;
(11) creation of permanent commissions and other bodies of the *maslikhat*, hearing their reports, sorting out other problems related to the workflow management of the *maslikhat*;
(12) approves upon the proposal of the *akims* the personnel of the consultative-advisory bodies to the *akimats* on issues of interdepartmental character;

(13) confers and approves the rules of conferment of the title 'Honorary Citizen of the region (a city, a district)', develops and approves the rules and regulations on awarding a Certificate of Honour of the region (city, district);
(14) fulfils the realization of issues related to the use of land in accordance with the land laws of the country;
(15) assists in the performance by citizens and entities of the provisions of the Constitution of Kazakhstan, the laws, the acts of the President and the Government, normative legislative acts of the central and local state bodies, etc.

The Article enumerates other competencies of the *maslikhat.*

522. The *maslikhats* of the regions, cities of national importance and the capital, consider issues on the giving of consent to the construction of nuclear plants and facilities in the territory of the relevant administrative-territorial unit (Article 6(6) Law on the Local Governance).

523. As given in Article 88 of the Constitution of the Republic and in Article 7 of the Law on the Local Governance of Kazakhstan, the *maslikhats* adopt the decisions on issues that fall within their competencies which have binding force within the territory of the respective administrative-territorial unit. The drafts of the *maslikhat's* decisions that envisage reduction of the local budget or increase of the local budget expenses may be submitted for consideration only if there is an affirmative opinion of the *akim.* The decisions of the *maslikhat* adopted within its competence that concern human rights, freedoms and duties shall be published officially in accordance with the national legislation and have binding force within the relevant territory. The procedure for adoption of the *maslikhats*' decisions that concern human rights, freedoms and duties shall be in line with the provisions of the Law on Legal Acts of Kazakhstan. The decisions of the *maslikhats* that are not in conformity with the Constitution and the legislation of Kazakhstan may be cancelled by the *maslikhat* itself or via the judicial procedures.

III. Organization of the Work of the *Maslikhats*

524. Article 8 of the Law on the Local Governance of Kazakhstan regulates issues of the organization of the work of the *maslikhats.* The *maslikhat* carries out its powers at its sessions, via permanent commissions and other bodies, as well as via deputies and a secretary in accordance with the procedures established by the legislation of Kazakhstan. At least once a year, the *maslikhats* give reports before the population on the activities carried out. The deputies of the *maslikhats* are responsible for the population in accordance with the laws of Kazakhstan. The main form of the *maslikhats'* activity is a session where issues within their competence are discussed. The *maslikhat's* session is eligible where at least two-thirds of the total number of the *maslikhat's* deputies are present.

525. The maslikhat:

(1) elects and dismisses a secretary of the *maslikhat* and hears his reports;
(2) forms the permanent commissions and other bodies of the *maslikhat*, elects their chairs and dismisses them from office, hears their reports about the work done;
(3) determines the expenses required to ensure the activity of the *maslikhat*;
(4) approves the structure of the *maslikhat's* apparatus and defines the expenses for its maintenance as well as for material and technical support depending on the number of staff and funding established by the legislation of Kazakhstan. The limit for the number of staff of civil servants of the *maslikhat's* apparatus is determined by the number of deputies of the relevant *maslikhat*;
(5) approves the internal procedural rules of the *maslikhat*;
(6) considers the requests of the deputies and makes decisions on them;
(7) takes other decisions on the organization of its work.

526. The procedures for carrying out the *maslikhat's* sessions, the meeting of its bodies, submission and consideration of issues, formation and election of the *maslikhat's* bodies, hearing the reports on their activities before the population, consideration of the deputies' requests, the competence and organization of the activities of the deputies' associations at the *maslikhat*, the procedures of voting, organization of the *maslikhat's* apparatus, and other procedural and organizational issues shall be defined by the internal procedural rules of the *maslikhat* approved at its session (Article 9 Law on the Local Governance).

527. Article 10 of the Law on the Local Governance regulates the procedures for the convocation of the *maslikhat's* session. The first session of the newly elected *maslikhat* shall be convened by a chair of the relevant territorial election commission not later than thirty days from the day of registration of the *maslikhat's* deputies and if there are present at least three-quarters of the deputies' numbers specified for this *maslikhat.* The regular session of the *maslikhat* is convened at least four times a year and conducted by a secretary of the *maslikhats*. Not later than ten days before the start of the session, the secretary of the *maslikhat* informs the deputies, population and the *akim* about the timing and venue of the *maslikhat's* regular session and the issues that are going to be discussed.

528. Referring to Article 11 of the Law on the Local Governance, the session of the *maslikhat* is conducted in the form of plenary meetings of *the maslikhat.* The decisions are adopted by a majority of votes of the total number of the *maslikhat's* deputies. The duration of the session is determined by the *maslikhat.* As a rule, the sessions conducted by the *maslikhat* are open to the public. Having closed sessions is allowed by a decision of the *maslikhat* based on a proposal of a secretary of the *maslikhat's* session or upon a proposal of one-third of the deputies that are present at the *maslikhat's* session. The decision on conducting a closed session shall be approved by votes of a majority of the total number of the deputies present at the session. Upon an invitation of a secretary of the *maslikhat* heads of the local executive bodies, heads and other officials of organizations located within the territory of the relevant administrative-territorial unit are obliged to come to the *maslikhat's* session to present information on matters related to the competence of the *maslikhat*.

529. The *maslikhat* shall form the permanent commissions which shall be not more than seven. The list and personnel of the permanent commissions are determined by the *maslikhat*. A chair and the members of the permanent commissions are elected among the deputies of the respective *maslikhat*. The permanent commissions are responsible before the *maslikhats* and report on their activities at least once a year (Article 12 Law on the Local Governance).

530. The permanent commissions on their own initiative and on the decisions of *the maslikhats* can conduct public hearings. Public hearings are held to discuss the most important and socially significant issues at the extended meetings of these commissions with the participation of the deputies, representatives of the executive bodies, the local self-governance bodies, organizations, the media and citizens (Article 13 Law on the Local Governance).

531. Article 14 of Law on the Local Governance covers the functions and powers of the permanent commissions of the *maslikhat*. The permanent commissions of the *maslikhats* have the following rights:

(1) to submit proposals to the *maslikhat*, a secretary of the *maslikhat* for inclusion on the session's agenda, as well as proposals for any other issues that are under consideration of the *maslikhat's* session;
(2) to give opinions on issues of their competence and submitted for the consideration of the *maslikhat's* session;
(3) to present at the *maslikhats'* sessions reports and co-reports on issues related to their competence;
(4) within their competence to submit proposals to the *maslikhat* for hearing the reports of heads of the local executive bodies at the session of the *maslikhat*;
(5) to involve in the work of the commissions' other deputies, representatives of the state bodies, organizations, other bodies of the local self-governance and citizens.

532. The *akimats*, officials of the territorial subdivisions of the central state bodies, executive bodies financed by the local budget, and officials of the organizations are obliged in accordance with the rules to present to the permanent commissions' necessary information on issues of their competence.

533. The permanent commissions adopt resolutions on issues within their competence. The resolutions of the permanent commissions are adopted by a majority of votes of the total number of the members of the commission. The quorum of the permanent commission's meeting is a presence of more than half of the total number of the deputies of that permanent commission (Articles 14–15 Law on the Local Governance).

534. The chair or the secretary of the *maslikhat* has the right to organize temporary commissions on issues within the competence of this *maslikhat.* The temporary commissions adopt findings. The *maslikhat* defines the composition, tasks, term of office of the temporary commission at the time of its formation (Article 17 Law on the Local Governance).

535. As envisaged in Article 19 of the Law on the Local Governance, a secretary of the *maslikhat* is an official who is elected by open or secret ballot by a majority of votes of the total number of the members of the *maslikhat*. He shall be elected for the period of the term of the *maslikhat.* A secretary has no right to be a member of the permanent commissions of the *maslikhat.* He/she carries out the following functions:

(1) organizes the preparation of the *maslikhat's* session and of issues submitted for its consideration, ensures the drawing up of the protocol, and signs the decisions, other documents adopted or approved at the *maslikhat's* session;
(2) takes decisions on convocation of the *maslikhat's* session;
(3) conducts the meetings of the *maslikhat's* session, ensures observance of the internal working procedural rules;
(4) assists the deputies in the realization of their competencies, provides them with the necessary information, considers issues related to letting them free from the execution of their main duties in order to participate at the *maslikhat's* session, assists in the work of the permanent commissions, other bodies, and constituencies;
(5) controls consideration of the deputies' requests and appeals;
(6) manages the activities of the *maslikhat's* apparatus, appoints and dismisses its officers;
(7) regularly provides the *maslikhat* with information concerning the requests of the electorate and measures taken concerning them;
(8) organizes the interaction of *the maslikhat* with other bodies of the local governance;
(9) organizes the verification of the authenticity of the collected signatures of the *maslikhat's* deputies who initiated the issue of expressing a vote of nonconfidence in accordance with Article 24(1) of the Law;
(10) adopts orders on issues of its competence;
(11) coordinates the activities of the permanent commissions and other bodies of the *maslikhat*, and deputies' groups;
(12) represents the *maslikhat* in its relations with state bodies, organizations, local self-governance bodies and public associations;
(13) ensures publication of the *maslikhat's* decisions, defines the control measures over their execution;
(14) carries out other functions as stipulated by the Law, legislation of the Republic, the internal working procedure and the decisions of the *maslikhat.*

536. A secretary of the regional *maslikhat,* city of national importance, or the capital submits for consideration of the respective *maslikhat* the candidates for appointment to the post of a chair of the revisions commission of the region, city of national importance, or the capital, as well as preparing the proposal on his/her dismissal.

537. Article 21-2 of the Law on the Local Governance regulates the work of different deputies' unions in the *maslikhat.* The deputies of the *maslikhat* have the right to form the organized groups of the political parties, other public associations and deputies' groups. A secretary cannot be a member of the deputies' associations. A faction is an organized deputies' group representing political parties or any other public association that is registered in line with the procedures established by law. A faction is created to express the interests of the respective political party or any other public association in the *maslikhat* and should consist of at least three deputies. A deputy has the right to be a member of only one organized parliamentary group (caucus). A deputy group is a union of deputies that is created to fulfil their powers and to do joint work in the constituency. There should be at least five deputies in a deputy group. Factions and the deputies' groups are registered at the *maslikhat's* session and only for informational purposes.

IV. The Status of a Deputy of the *Maslikhat*

538. According to Article 20 of the Law on the Local Governance, a deputy of the *maslikhat* expresses the will of the population of the respective administrative-territorial unit taking into account nationwide interests. The powers of a deputy start from the moment of his/her registration as a deputy of the *maslikhat* of the respective territorial election commission and terminate from the moment of the end of the *maslikhat's* powers.

539. The powers of a deputy of the *maslikhat* end early in the following cases:

(1) if he/she is elected or appointed to a position which is incompatible with the performance of the deputy's duties according to the national legislation of Kazakhstan;
(2) because of the entry into force of a court's decision on recognition of a deputy as incapable or partially incapacitated;
(3) because of termination of the powers of the *maslikhat*;
(4) because of resignation or expulsion from the political party or termination of the activities of a political party which he/she represents;
(5) because of the death of a deputy, entry into force of a court's decision on recognition of a deputy as a missing person or a court decision declaring him/her dead;
(6) because of termination of his/her Kazakhstani citizenship;
(7) because of the entry into force of a court's sentence against a deputy for committing a crime or a deliberate criminal offence;
(8) because of departure to a permanent residence outside the respective administrative-territorial unit;
(9) because of his/her personal request to resign;

(10) because of systematic non-fulfilment by a deputy of his/her duties, including absence without reasonable excuse more than three times in a row at the plenary meetings of the *maslikhat's* session or meeting of the *maslikhat's* bodies to which he/she is elected;
(11) because of the appointment of a deputy to the post of a chair of the revision commission or a member of the revision commission of the region, a city of national importance, the capital.

540. The decision on early termination of the deputy's powers shall be taken upon the proposal of the respective administrative election commission at the *maslikhat's* session by a majority of the total number of the deputies present at the session. In a case of resignation or expulsion from the political party or termination of the activities of a political party which a deputy represented, the respective administrative election commission takes a decision affirming the loss of powers by a deputy and informs the relevant *maslikhat* about it.

541. Article 21 of Law on the Local Governance envisages the rights, duties and responsibility of a deputy of the *maslikhat.* So, a deputy of the *maslikhat* has the following and other rights enumerated in Article 21:

(1) to elect and to be elected as a secretary of the *maslikhat's* session, a chair or a member of the permanent commission, and to other bodies of the *maslikhat*;
(2) to propose issues for consideration at the *maslikhat's* session and its permanent and other bodies, to participate in their consideration and decision-making;
(3) to conduct meetings and conventions with the electorate of his/her district, as well as with other bodies of the local self-governance and organizations;
(4) to make proposals for hearing at the session the officials of the local executive and organizations located within the territory of the respective *maslikhat* on issues within its competence;
(5) to take part in the meetings of the respective *akimat*;
(6) to get acquainted with the verbatim report and the protocols of the *maslikhat's* session and its bodies;
(7) to form deputies' associations like factions or deputies' groups.

A deputy carries out other actions envisaged by Article 21 of the Law, by the legislation and the internal working procedural rules.

542. A deputy of the *maslikhat* has the following and other duties elaborated in Article 21(2) of the Law:

(1) to participate in the work of the *maslikhat* and its body to which he/she is elected;
(2) to maintain communication with the electorate of his/her district constantly, at least once a year, and to inform them about the work of the *maslikhat*, the activities of its permanent commissions and other bodies, and the fulfilment of the *maslikhat's* decisions, and to inform the electorate about the progress of

his/her own activities as well; to participate in the organization and control over fulfilment of the *maslikhat's* decisions;

(3) to consider the complaints of the electorate that he/she receives, to conduct personal meetings with the citizens;
(4) to reside in the respective administrative-territorial unit, etc.

543. The protection of the rights, honour and dignity of each deputy of the *maslikhat* is guaranteed. On issues related to his/her functional activities, a deputy has the right to freely visit the state bodies, public associations and the state organizations located within the territory of the respective *maslikhat* if the activities of these organizations do not concern state secrets. Heads and other officials of the state bodies, public associations and state organizations are obliged to admit deputies of the *maslikhat* and provide them with the necessary assistance in the exercise of their powers.

544. A deputy of the *maslikhat* bears censure and can be coerced to bring a public apology for non-fulfilment and (or) improper fulfilment of his/her duties, as well as for violation of the deputy ethics determined by the internal procedural rules of the *maslikhat*. Such forms of penalties are discussed at the *maslikhat's* session and shall be imposed if a majority of the deputies present at the meeting vote in favour. The imposition of the penalties is implemented by the territorial election commission along with their publication in the media of the respective administrative territory. A deputy cannot take responsibility twice for the same offence.

V. Powers Regarding the *Akim*

545. Article 23-1 of the Law on the local governance regulates the procedures of giving consent by a *maslikhat* for the appointment of the *akims*. So, a person who appoints the *akim* asks the *maslikhat* to give consent for the appointment of a candidate. Consideration of a proposal to give consent is realized at a regular or extraordinary session of the *maslikhat*. A candidate must be present at the *maslikhat's* extraordinary session. The deputies have the right to ask a nominated candidate questions and discuss his candidature. Voting takes place after discussion. The nominated candidate should receive a majority of votes of the total number of the *maslikhat's* deputies.

546. The nomination of a candidate by a person who appoints the *akim* can be done three times. If the *maslikhat* refuses its consent more than three times, the President of Kazakhstan has the right to terminate the powers of the relevant *maslikhat* early after consultations with the Prime Minister and Chairs of the Chambers of the Parliament. If the giving consent of the *maslikhat* concerns the *akim* of a district (a city of a regional level), the *akim* of the regions informs the President of Kazakhstan in writing and raises a question on early termination of powers of the relevant *maslikhat*. In such cases, the President of Kazakhstan or higher *akim* appoints an acting *akim* for a temporary period until the new *akim* has been appointed with the consent of the newly elected *maslikhat* in accordance with the established rules.

547. Another way to influence the executive branch of power at the local level is through an expression of a vote of no confidence in the *akim* by the *maslikhat.* In accordance with Article 24 of the Law on the Local Governance, a question of a vote of no confidence in the *akim* could be raised on the initiative of at least one-fifth of the total number of the *maslikhat's* deputies. In this case, the *maslikhat* by a majority of votes of the total number of its deputies has the right to express a vote of no confidence in the *akim* and raise a question on his removal from office before the President of Kazakhstan or the higher *akim* respectively. The reasons for consideration of a question on the expression of a no-confidence vote are non-approval twice by the *maslikhat* of the reports on the implementation of the plans, the economic and social development programmes of the territory, and the local budget, and initiation by a meeting of the local community of the issue of dismissal of the *akim* of a city of district importance, of a village, settlement and rural county. Initiation of a question of the expression of a no-confidence vote is realized by collecting signatures that should be done within ten working days from the day of the written request of the deputies who initiated the process. The *maslikhat's* session on consideration of a vote of no confidence in the *akim* shall be carried out within one month from the date of registration of the protocol on the authenticity of the collected signatures of the deputies who initiated the process. The session of the *maslikhat* adopts the decision on the issue. If the *maslikhat* adopts a decision to express a vote of no confidence in the *akim,* it should inform the President or the higher *akim* immediately.

548. From the day of receiving the *maslikhat's* decision on an expression of no confidence in the *akim*, the President of Kazakhstan or the higher *akim* within ten days considers the issue of the termination of *the akim's* powers or instructs the *akim* to continue to carry out his functions. If the President of the Republic or the higher *akim* rejects a no-confidence vote, the deputies of the *maslikhat* by a majority of votes have the right to resubmit a no-confidence vote after six months. In such cases, the President of Kazakhstan or senior *akim* dismisses the *akim.*

VI. Powers Regarding the Senate of the Parliament of Kazakhstan

549. As was discussed in previous chapters and in accordance with Article 7(1) of Law of Kazakhstan on the Elections, the deputies of the *maslikhats* participate in the election of the members of the Senate of the Parliament of Kazakhstan.

550. In accordance with Article 24(5) of the Constitutional Law on the Parliament, the powers of the deputies of the Senate elected by the electors at their joint meeting (deputies of the *maslikhats*), may be terminated early by a decision of the electors.

551. These provisions are elaborated in Article 24-1 of the Law on the Local Governance. The decision on the initiation of a question on the termination of the powers of a member of the Senate is made by the *maslikhat* of the region, city of national importance or the capital. The respective election commission and a member of the Senate should be informed about it within three days. Initiation by a decision of electors of a question on the termination of powers of a member of the Senate should be supported by not less than 25% of votes of the total number of the electors that represent all the *maslikhats* of the region, city of national importance and the capital, but not less than 25% of electors' votes of one *maslikhat.*

552. The election commission of the region, a city of national importance, and the capital after checking the authenticity of the collected signatures takes a decision on putting to vote the question about the termination of powers of a member of the Senate. The joint meeting of the electors on voting regarding the termination of the powers of a member of the Senate should be carried out within one month from the adoption by the election commission of a decision on raising a question on termination of powers. The electors' joint meeting's quorum is the presence of at least two-thirds of the electors who represent all *maslikhats* of the region, city of national importance and the capital. The voting is regarded as held if two-thirds of the total number of present electors participated in it. The results of the voting shall be established by the Central Election Commission no later than seven days from the day when voting was held. The powers of the member of the Senate are regarded as terminated if more than 50% of the electors present at the meeting vote in favour of the termination.

§3. THE *AKIMS* AND *AKIMATS* AS THE LOCAL EXECUTIVE BODIES: THE FORMATION AND COMPOSITION, COMPETENCE AND ORGANIZATION OF THEIR ACTIVITIES

I. General

553. Article 87 of the Constitution regulates the legal status of the local administrative bodies. So, the local administrative bodies are a part of the unified system of the executive bodies; they shall ensure implementation of the common state policy of the executive power in concurrence with the interests and the development needs of the respective territory.

554. The jurisdiction of the local executive bodies shall include according to Article 87(2) of the Constitution :

(1) working out the plans, economic and social development programmes of the territory, the local budget and ensuring their implementation;
(2) management of the communal property;
(3) appointment and removal from office of the heads of the local executive bodies, solving other issues related to the organization of the work of the local executive bodies;

(4) performance of other competencies for the interests of the local state government imposed by the national legislation of the Republic.

555. The local executive body is led by the *akim* of the respective administrative-territorial unit, who is a representative of the President and the Government of the Republic. As given in Article 88 of the Constitution, the *akims* adopt the decisions and orders that have binding force on the territory of the respective administrative-territorial unit. The decisions and orders of the *akims* may be cancelled by the President, the Government or higher *akim*, as well as via judicial procedure.

II. The *Akimats* of a Region (*Oblast*), a City of National Importance and the Capital

A. *Formation and Composition*

556. Article 26 of the Law on the Local Governance regulates issues of formation and composition of the *akimats* of the region, a city of national importance and the capital. The *akimats* of the region, a city of national importance and the capital, belong to the unified system of the executive bodies of Kazakhstan and ensure the carrying out of the nationwide politics of the executive power in combination with the interests and the development needs of the respective territory. The *akimat* of the region, a city of national importance and the capital, is led by the *akim*. The *akimat* of the region, a city of national importance and the capital, is a collegial body, formed by the *akim* and consists of the deputies of the *akim*, the head of the *akim's* apparatus, and the first heads of the executive bodies financed by the local budget. The personnel of the *akimat* are approved by the decision of the *maslikhat's* session of the region, a city of national importance and the capital. Heads of the territorial subdivisions of the central state bodies can take part in the work of the *akimat* of the region, a city of national importance and the capital in a consultative capacity.

B. *The Competence*

557. Article 27 of the Law on the Local Governance covers the scope of competence of the *akimats* of the region, a city of national importance and the capital. So, the *akimat* of the region, a city of national importance and the capital in accordance with the national legislation of Kazakhstan carries out many functions, including the following:

(1) carries out regulatory, implementing and control functions to ensure the resolution of the tasks of the local level of the respective administrative-territorial unit;
(2) submits the draft of the regional budget, the budget of a city of national importance and the capital to the respective *maslikhat* in accordance with the budget legislation of Kazakhstan;

(3) submits to the respective *maslikhat* and the revision commission of the region, a city of national importance and the capital the yearly report on the realization of the budget plan;
(4) adopts resolutions about the realization of decisions on the budget issues of the regional *maslikhat* and *maslikhats* of a city of national importance and the capital for the respective financial year;
(5) forms the budget commission of the region, a city of national importance and the capital, and approves the regulations on it and defines its composition;
(6) concludes agreements in the field of energy-saving and increasing the energy efficiency of the respective territory and realizes information activities on these issues;
(7) ensures implementation of the state policy on energy-saving and increasing energy efficiency;
(8) ensures implementation of the nationwide politics of the executive power in combination with the interests and the development needs of the respective territory;
(9) develops and approves the socio-economic development forecast, presents it for approval of the respective *maslikhat* and ensures its realization;
(10) adopts the normative legal acts that ensure the resolution of tasks of local significance and the realization of state policy within the respective territory;
(11) carries out control and observance over the activities of individuals and legal entities within the respective territory defined by the law of Kazakhstan;
(12) develops rules regulating the migration process in the regions, cities of national importance and the capital in accordance with model rules approved by the Government of Kazakhstan;
(13) manages the communal properties of the region, city of national importance and the capital and takes measures for their protection;
(14) assists citizens and legal entities to fulfil the provisions of the Constitution, the laws, the acts of the President and the Government, the normative legal acts of the central and local state bodies of Kazakhstan;
(15) creates conditions for the development of entrepreneurship and investment climate within the territory of the region, city of national importance and the capital;
(16) ensures realization of trade policy;
(17) carries out the organization of the exhibition and fair activities;
(18) ensures the rational and effective functioning of the agricultural sector;
(19) in accordance with the layout scheme of production forces of Kazakhstan develops the scheme for the district planning of the region, general plans for building development within the regional centre, a city of national importance, and the capital and submits them for consideration of the *maslikhat*;
(20) acts as a customer in the construction, reconstruction and repair of the communal property's objects and social and cultural objects of the region, a city of national importance, and the capital, gives permission for building public utilities and constructions;
(21) develops plans for the administrative districts, general construction development plans for the regional centres, cities of national importance, and the capital and submits them for consideration of the *maslikhat*;

(22) organizes the construction and exploitation of water pipes, sewage treatment plants, heating and electrical services that belong to the communal property, and other objects of transport and of the engineering infrastructure of the city of national importance and the capital;
(23) carries out regulation of land and water issues in accordance with the land legislation ;
(24) within its competence organizes the state environmental expertise of the objects of the second category, gives permissions to the users of natural resources to cause certain emissions for the objects of certain categories, conducts environmental protection measures and management of natural resources;
(25) ensures the construction, rational exploitation and maintenance of roads of regional importance;
(26) ensures compliance with national standards;
(27) organizes the protection of public order and security in the region, a city of national importance and the capital;
(28) organizes the transportation of passengers in accordance with the legislation of Kazakhstan in the field of transport;
(29) ensures the realization by the citizens of the right to free education;
(30) coordinates the realization of social assistance to vulnerable groups of the population;
(31) within its competence conducts state policy on employment issues by holding relevant activities;
(32) organizes activities for the protection of historical and cultural heritage, assists in the development of historical, national and cultural traditions and customs of the population, and for the development of sport;
(33) coordinates the work of the district *akimats*, the *akims* of the city's districts on issues that fall within their competence, including the creation of legal and organizational conditions for the formation and development of local self-governance;
(34) in accordance with Kazakhstan's legislation submits for consideration the relevant *maslikhat* proposals for making decisions to borrow;
(35) creates advisory-consultative bodies on issues of interdepartmental character involving the representatives of the National Chamber of Entrepreneurs to discuss questions concerning the interests of private business entities according to the legislation of Kazakhstan;
(36) creates state institutions and enterprises, sets the limits for the number of personnel of the executive bodies financed by the budget of the region, a city of national importance, the capital in accordance with the limits and standards approved by the Government of Kazakhstan. The number of personnel of the internal affairs bodies financed by the local budget is determined in accordance with national legislation;
(37) in accordance with national legislation on permissions and notifications, carries out licensing, the licensing procedures, receiving notifications;
(38) develops and submits for approval of the *maslikhat* the draft of the rules on awarding the title 'Honorary Citizen of the Region (city, district)';

(39) forms a list of goods, works and services that are produced within the territory of the region, a city of national importance and the capital, and of their producers;
(40) organizes activities for the prevention of terrorism, as well as the minimization and (or) liquidation of the consequences of terrorism in the region, a city of national importance and the capital through the work of the anti-terrorism commissions;
(41) carries out the transfer of dwellings from communal property to the private ownership of citizens under the conditions envisaged by the legislative acts of the Republic and in accordance with the procedures determined by the Government of Kazakhstan;
(42) develops and submits for approval of the *maslikhat* the rules for preparation and managing of the heating season;
(43) creates entities to provide assistance in line with the Law of Kazakhstan on Prevention of Domestic Violence;
(44) monitors the emergence of social tensions and the risks of labour disputes;
(45) creates the infrastructure for individuals to carry out sporting activities at the place of their residence and places of mass recreation;
(46) provides the champions and winners of the Olympic, Paralympic and Deaflympics Games with housing in accordance with the Law of Kazakhstan on Physical Training and Sport;
(47) coordinates the investment programme (drafts) in the activities of the natural monopoly holder that provides the respective territory of the administrative-territorial unit with services that included in the local list of the State register of natural monopolies' holders;
(48) develops and submits for the approval of the *maslikhat* the rules for maintenance and protection of green spaces. The *akimats* of the regions, the capital, city of Shymkent develop and submit to a *maslikhat* the rules for landscaping the cities' and towns' territories and their protection created on the basis of model rules approved by the authorized bodies for architecture, urban planning and construction;
(49) approves the utility services' consumption norms of gas supply, electricity, water supply, wastewater and heating for those consumers who do not have metering devices;
(50) the *akimats* of the region, city of national importance and the capital discuss the draft of the regional (*oblastnoy*) budget, the budget of a city of national importance and the capital at the meeting of the public council established in accordance with the Law of Kazakhstan on Public Councils. The mentioned *akimats* discuss the yearly report on the realization of the regional budget, the budget of a city of national importance, the capital at the meeting of the public council, etc.

The akimat of the region, a city of national importance and the capital, carries out other functions established by the national legislation for the interests of the local state governance. The mentioned *akimats* bear responsibility for the realization of its functions before the *maslikhat* of the region, a city of national importance, the capital, respectively.

C. *The* Akim *of a Region (*Oblast*), a City of National Importance, the Capital: The Procedure of Appointment and Dismissal, the Issue of His Competence*

558. The procedure of appointment and dismissal of the *akim* of the region, a city of national importance, the capital are given in Article 87(3–4) of the Constitution and in Article 28 of the Law on the Local Governance.

559. The *akims* of a region, city of national importance and the capital are appointed by the President of the Republic with the consent of the *maslikhats* of a region, city of national importance and the capital, respectively. The *akim* of a region, city of national importance and the capital is dismissed by the President of the country (Article 28 Law on the Local Governance). The *akims* of other administrative-territorial units are appointed and elected to the post, as well as are dismissed from the post in accordance with the procedures defined by the Law (Article 87(4) Constitution of Kazakhstan).

560. On the initiative of not less than one-fifth of the total number of the *maslikhats*' deputies, a question about a vote of no confidence in the *akim* may be raised. In this case, the *maslikhat* by a majority of votes of the total number of the deputies has the right to express no confidence in the *akim* and raise a question before the President of the Republic and senior *akim* about his dismissal from office. The powers of the *akim* of a region, city of national importance and the capital are terminated when a newly elected President of the Republic assumes office (Article 87(5) Constitution of Kazakhstan).

561. Article 29 of the Law on the Local Governance elaborates the competence of the *akim* of a region, a city of national importance and the capital. Article 29 sets out many functions, including the following, where the *akim*:

(1) represents the interests of the region, a city of national importance, the capital in all relations with state bodies, entities and citizens;
(2) carries out implementation, regulatory and control functions that ensure the resolution of the tasks of the local level within the territory of the relevant administrative-territorial unit;
(3) ensures the realization of a state policy of the executive power in compliance with the interests and the development needs of the respective territory;
(4) has the right to submit to the heads of the central executive bodies a proposal on the activities of the central state body's local subdivision regarding the realization by them of the laws, the President's and the Government's acts, acts of the *akims* and *akimat* of the region. If the local subdivision of the central state body does not eliminate deficiencies in the implementation of the laws, the President's and the Government's acts, the *akim* of the region has the right to submit his relevant concluding opinion for the attention of the President and the Government of Kazakhstan;
(5) submits to the President of the Republic proposals for awarding state awards, conferring honorary and other titles to relevant persons;
(6) appoints and dismisses such officials as:

(a) the deputies of the *akim* of a region, a city of national importance, the capital in consultation with the authorized higher state bodies within the number limits determined by the Government of Kazakhstan;
(b) heads of the executive bodies financed by the budget of a region, a city of national importance, capital, except for those officials who have the right to wear uniform clothing in accordance with the legislation of Kazakhstan and are given military or other special ranks, as well as first heads of the bodies in charge of education, located in the districts (towns of the regional importance);

(7) coordinates a candidacy for the post of head of the police department of the region, city of national importance, and the capital;
(8) takes decisions on the application of disciplinary measures to the heads of the executive bodies financed by the budget of a region, a city of the national importance, the capital, as well as to the *akims* of the districts (towns of the regional importance, a district in the city of national importance, a district in the capital) in accordance with the national legislation of Kazakhstan;
(9) coordinates the work of the *akimats* and *akims* of a district level (towns of regional importance, a district in the city of national importance, a district in the capital);
(10) interacts with the bodies of the local self-governance via the district *akims* (towns of the regional importance, a district in the city of the national importance, a district in the capital);
(11) submits for approval of the relevant *maslikhat* the management schemes of the administrative-territorial unit based on the basic structures of the local governance approved by the Government of Kazakhstan;
(12) proposes the personnel composition of the consultative-advisory bodies on interdepartmental issues for the approval of the *maslikhat*;
(13) within its competence, organizes and ensures the performance of the legislation on defence and the Armed Forces of the Republic on issues related to military duties and service, mobilization training and mobilization itself, and civil protection;
(14) participates in signing contracts on privatization, lease, sale of enterprises, fields and other objects of the state property, as well as participating in control over their execution on a par with authorized state bodies of the Republic;
(15) carries out control over the activities of the subordinate *akims*, etc.

562. The *akim* of a region, a city of national importance and the capital of the relevant administrative-territorial unit puts tasks before the local police services on crime prevention, to provide public order and traffic security in the territory of the relevant administrative-territorial unit and hears the relevant reports of the heads of the local police department not less than once a year. The *akim* of a region, a city of national importance and the capital, carries out other functions in accordance with the national legislation and has the right to delegate his functions to the subordinate *akim*. He/she is responsible before the President and the Government of Kazakhstan.

III. The *Akimats* of the Districts (of a Town of Regional Importance)

A. *The Formation and Composition of the District* Akimat *(of a Town of Regional Importance)*

563. According to Article 30 of the Law on the Local Governance, the *akimat* of a district (a town of regional importance) is a part of the unified system of the executive bodies of the Republic that ensures the conducting of the nationwide politics of the executive power in coherence with the interests and development needs of the respective territory. The *akimat* of a district (a town of regional importance) is led by the *akim* of a district (a town of regional importance)*;* it is a collegial body and is composed of the deputies of the *akim*, the head of the administrative office (apparatus), and first heads of the respective executive bodies. The *akimat* has its own internal procedural rules that regulate the procedure for preparing and conducting the meetings and decision-making. Standard internal rules are approved by the Government of Kazakhstan. The personnel of the *akimat* is agreed with the district's *maslikhat*. Heads of the territorial subdivisions of the central state bodies may take part in the work of *the akimat* in a consultative capacity.

B. *The Competence of the District* Akimat *(a Town of Regional Importance)*

564. The competence of the district's *akimat* (a town of regional importance) is described in Article 31 of Law on Local Governance; it has many functions, including the following:

(1) ensures realization of the district's budget (a town of regional importance);
(2) presents a yearly report on the fulfilment of the district's budget (a town of regional importance) to the respective *maslikhat* and audit commission of the region;
(3) adopts a resolution on the realization of the *maslikhat's* decision (a town of regional importance) on the budget for the relevant financial year;
(4) creates the budget commission of the district (a town of regional importance), approves regulation for it and defines its composition; the National Chamber of Entrepreneurs are involved in the work of the commission if issues of consideration concern the interests of private enterprises in accordance with the legislation of Kazakhstan;
(5) approves the regional financial plan of a district (a town of regional importance) for the first quarter of the relevant financial year in cases envisaged by the budget legislation of the Republic;
(6) develops and submits for the approval of the *maslikhat* the development programme of a district (a town of regional importance), ensures its fulfilment;
(7) ensures inclusion of activities on energy-saving and increasing efficiency into the development programme of a district (a town of regional importance), as well as implements information activity on these issues;
(8) ensures carrying out state policy on energy-saving and increasing efficiency;
(9) manages the communal property of a district (a town of regional importance) in accordance with the appropriate legislative acts and takes measures for its protection;

(10) registers the civil status of individuals and includes information about such registration into the State database of individuals in a way prescribed by the legislation;
(11) promotes performance by citizens and entities in accordance with the provisions of the Constitution, the laws, the acts of the President and the Government of Kazakhstan, the normative legal acts of the central and local state bodies;
(12) creates conditions for the development of the entrepreneurship and investment climate in a district (a town of regional importance);
(13) arranges for exhibitions;
(14) ensures the rational and effective functioning of the agricultural sector;
(15) develops master plans for the settlements and villages on the territory of a district (a town of regional importance) and submits them to a district *maslikhat* (a town of regional importance) for approval; also acts as an ordering customer of construction, reconstruction and repair services for the communal objects of a district (a town of regional importance) and the objects with a social-cultural purpose, and gives permission for construction of public utilities and facilities;
(16) organizes the construction and use of plumbing, wastewater treatment facility, heating and electric networks and other means of transport and engineering in a district (a town of regional importance);
(17) ensures organization of events for military registration, recruitment and civil defence;
(18) organizes the passenger transport in accordance with the transport legislation of Kazakhstan;
(19) regulates land issues in accordance with the land legislation;
(20) organizes the construction, use and maintenance of the district roads (towns of regional importance);
(21) organizes the construction of communal housing and its distribution;
(22) carries out activities aimed at maintaining the seismic resistance of residential buildings located in earthquake-prone regions;
(23) provides certain categories of citizens with housing in accordance with the legislative acts of the Republic;
(24) resolves issues related to the social protection of the population, especially mothers and children, and provides socially vulnerable groups with targeted assistance, coordinates the charitable assistance for them, and assists in staffing rural health organizations;
(25) ensures organization and realization of penal-enforcement activities in accordance with the Penitentiary Code of the Republic;
(26) makes proposals for declaring natural and other sites of ecological, historical, cultural and scientific value, located within their district, as protected monuments of nature, history and culture;
(27) organizes consultative-advisory bodies on issues of interdepartmental character, involving the representatives of the National Chamber of Entrepreneurs to discuss any questions that concern the interests of private business entities according to the national legislation;

(28) within its competence provides electronic services with information systems in accordance with the legislation of Kazakhstan on information system development;
(29) carries out promotes the creation of councils at the local self-governance level and develops appropriate regulations for them;
(30) implements the right of citizens to free primary, basic secondary and general secondary education;
(31) creates state institutions and enterprises in a way established by the legislation of Kazakhstan, sets the limits for the number of the personnel of the executive bodies financed by the budget of a district (a town of regional importance) within the number determined by the Government of Kazakhstan;
(32) carries out licensing in cases and in a way established by the legislation of Kazakhstan on permissions and notifications;
(33) organizes activities on the prevention of terrorism, as well as minimization and/or elimination of terrorism in the territory of a district (a town of regional importance) via anti-terrorist commissions;
(34) participates in the prevention of emergency situations of social character, as well as in the minimization and/or elimination of their consequences within the territory of a district (a town of regional importance);
(35) develops the rules for the provision of social assistance, defining the range and lists of categories of people, who need assistance in accordance with the rules approved by the Government;
(36) promotes sport;
(37) creates organizations to deliver assistance in accordance with the Law of Kazakhstan on Prevention of Domestic Violence;
(38) monitors social tensions and the risks of any labour disputes that arise;
(39) creates an infrastructure for the practice of sport for individuals at their places of residence and of mass recreation;
(40) provides champions and winners of the Olympic, Paralympic and Deaflympics Games with housing in accordance with the Law of Kazakhstan on Physical Culture and Sport, etc.

565. The *akimat* of a district conducts discussions of the draft of a district's budget (of a town of regional importance) at the meeting of the public council created in accordance with the Law of Kazakhstan on Public Councils. The *akimat* of a district conducts a discussion on the yearly financial report of a district's budget (or of a town of regional importance) at the meeting of the public council. The *akimat* of a district (a town of regional importance) carries out other functions imposed by the legislation of Kazakhstan for the interests of the local governance. The *akimat* of a district (a town of regional importance) is responsible for the district *maslikhat* (a town of regional importance).

C. *Procedure of Appointment and Dismissal, Termination of Powers of the* Akim *of a Town of Regional Importance or of a District of the Region (Rayon* Oblasti*), a Town of Regional Importance, or of a District in a City of National Importance*

566. Article 32 of the Law on the Local Governance regulates the procedure of appointment and dismissal, or termination of powers of the *akims* of a town of regional importance and of a district of the region *(rayon oblasti)*, or of a district in a town of regional importance, or of a district in a city of national importance. So, the *akim* of a town of regional importance and the *akim* of a district of the region are appointed, respectively, with the consent of their *maslikhats* in a way established by the Law. They terminate their powers and are dismissed by the *akim* of the region. The *akim* of a district in a town of regional importance is appointed with the consent of the *maslikhat* of that town in a way established by the Law. He terminates powers or is dismissed from the post by the *akim* of a town of regional importance. The *akim* of a district in a city of national importance or of the capital is appointed by the *akims* of those cities of national importance and the capital with the consent of their *maslikhats* in a way established by the Law. He terminates powers or is released from the post by the *akim* of the city of national importance. The *akim* of a town of regional importance and of a district of the region, of a district in the town of regional importance, and of a district in the city of national importance and the capital can also be relieved of his post by the President upon his discretion.

D. *The Competence of the* Akim *of a District (of a Town of Regional Importance)*

567. The competence of the *akim* of a district (of a town of regional importance) is given in Article 33 of Law on the Local Governance. In accordance with the legislation, the *akim* fulfils many functions and among them the following:

(1) he/she represents the interests of the respective administrative unit in relation to state bodies, entities and citizens;
(2) has the right to submit a proposal to the *akim* of the region on the activities of the local subdivisions of the central state bodies concerning their fulfilment of the provisions of the Constitution, the laws, the legal acts of the President and the Government;
(3) submits to the *akim* of the region a proposal on state awards, on conferring honorary titles and other titles; submits to a district *maslikhat* proposals on conferring the title 'Honorary Citizen of the District';
(4) appoints and dismisses from their posts the following officials:
    (a) deputies of the district's *akim* (of a town of regional importance); the maximum number of deputies is defined by the Government of Kazakhstan;

   (b) the staff of the *akim's* office, and heads of the executive bodies financed by the district budget (of a town of regional importance), except for first heads of state bodies in charge of education at district (town of regional importance) levels.
- (5) takes measures to protect the rights and freedoms of citizens;
- (6) interacts with the local governance bodies;
- (7) defines an executive body financed by the relevant local budget as an authorized body to register the non-professional mediators;
- (8) supports and provides social and cultural institutions with material and technical support;
- (9) assists in the collection of taxes and other compulsory payments to the budget;
- (10) submits for the approval of the relevant *maslikhat* the management scheme of the administrative-territorial unit based on the basic structures of the local governance that approved by the Government of Kazakhstan;
- (11) presents the personnel of the consultative-advisory bodies on issues of interdepartmental character for approval of the *maslikhat*;
- (12) within its competence, organizes and ensures implementation of the legislation of Kazakhstan on military duties and services, mobilization training and civil protection, registration of civilian status;
- (13) coordinates the work of subordinate *akims* on issues of his competence, including issues on creation of legal, organizational conditions for formation and development of the local self-governance;
- (14) controls over the activities of subordinate *akims*, etc.

568. The *akim* of a district (of a town of regional importance) of the relevant administrative-territorial unit puts tasks before the local police services on crime prevention, to provide public order and traffic security in the territory and not less than once a year hears the relevant reports of the heads of the local police service. The *akim* of a district (of a town of regional importance) carries out other functions imposed by the legislation. He/she has the right to delegate some of his powers to his subordinate *akims*. On issues of his competence and the competence of the *akimat* of a district (a town of regional importance), the *akim* is responsible to the President, the Government of Kazakhstan and to the *akim* of the region.

E. The Competence of the Akim *of a District in a Town (*Rayona v. Gorode*), of a Town of District Importance (*Gorod Rayonnogo Znacheniya*), a Settlement, a Village, a Rural County*

569. In accordance with Article 34 of the Law on Local Governance, the *akimats* at the level of a district within a city of national importance (the capital), a town of district importance, a settlement, a village, a rural county do not exist. As envisaged in Article 35 of the Law, the *akim* of a district in a town, of a town of district importance, a settlement, a village, a rural county is an official of the relevant district (town) *akimat* of the respective administrative-territorial unit and acts on behalf of that unit without power of attorney in relations with state bodies, entities and citizens. In accordance with the legislation of Kazakhstan, he has the following and other functions enumerated in Article 35(1):

(1) he considers the appeals and complaints of citizens, and takes measures to protect their rights and freedoms;
(2) assists in the collection of taxes and other compulsory payments to the state budget;
(3) promotes performance by citizens and entities of the provisions of the Constitution, the laws, the acts of the President and the Government of Kazakhstan, the normative legal acts of the central and local state bodies;
(4) regulates the land relations, within his competence;
(5) ensures the preservation of the communal housing fund of a town of district importance, a settlement, a village, a rural county; ensures the construction, reconstruction, repairing and maintenance of highways in the towns of district importance, settlements, villages, rural counties;
(6) assists in the organization of peasant or private farms and in the development of entrepreneurship;
(7) within his competence, organizes and ensures implementation of the national legislation on military duties and services, mobilization training and civil protection;
(8) the *akim* of a district, or a town of district importance, organizes the registration of civil status and acts in accordance with the procedures established by the legislation of Kazakhstan;
(9) the *akim* of a settlement, a village, a rural county where there are no judicial bodies organizes committing notary acts and registration civilian status in accordance with the procedures established by the legislation of Kazakhstan;
(10) the *akim* of a settlement, a village, a rural county where there are no employment agencies registers unemployed people in accordance with the procedures established by the legislation of Kazakhstan;
(11) organizes work on the protection of historical and cultural heritage;
(12) identifies people with low income, submits to the senior bodies the proposals on employment and rendering social assistance, organizes taking care of single elderly and disabled citizens at home, coordinates charitable assistance to them;
(13) organizes assistance to the disabled people;
(14) organizes the public welfare works, the internships for youth and social workplaces;
(15) assists in the development of the local social infrastructure;
(16) organizes the work of public transport;
(17) interacts with the bodies of the local self-governance;
(18) participates at the sessions of the *maslikhat* of a town, a district (of a town of regional importance) when approval or clarification of the local budget is needed;
(19) ensures the activities of cultural institutions other than for those located in a town of national importance, the capital, or towns of regional importance;

(20) as far as is within his competence, organizes the water supply of the inhabited locality and regulates water use issues;
(21) organizes the works on improvement of the living environment, illumination, landscape gardening and sanitation of the inhabited locality;
(22) deals with the registration of non-professional mediators;
(23) creates a public infrastructure for individuals to take part in sporting activities at their place of residence and in places of mass recreation;
(24) the *akim* of a settlement, a village, and a rural county has the right to make proposals to a district executive body on the organization of transport connections with a district centre, etc.

570. The *akim* of a district in a town, of a town of district importance, a settlement, a village, a rural county is responsible for the realization of these and other functions enumerated in Article 35 of the Law on Local Governance to senior *akim*, *akim* of a district (town of regional importance), of a city of national importance, of the capital.

F. The Procedure of Election and Dismissal of the Akim *of a Town of District Importance, of a Village, of a Settlement, of a Rural County*

571. With the amendments of 24 May 2021 to Constitutional Law on the Elections, an *akim* of a town of district importance, of a village, settlement and rural became officials elected by the population directly. Such a step is considered a new stage in the political modernization of the country. In comparison with the senior *akims*, as envisaged in Article 36 of the Law on the Local Governance, the *akim* of a town of district importance, of a village, settlement and rural county is elected for four years among candidates over the age of twenty-five by the population of a relevant administrative-territorial unit on the basis of universal, equal and direct suffrage by secret ballot. The same person cannot be elected as an *akim* of the same town of district importance, of a village, settlement and rural county more than twice in a row.

572. Chapter 13-1 of the Constitutional Law on the Elections in the Republic of Kazakhstan regulates the issues of holding elections for the positions of an *akim* of a town of district importance, village, settlement and rural county.

573. Nomination of a candidate for an *akim* of a town of district importance, village, settlement and rural county can be carried out among the members of the political parties registered in conformity with applicable rules, or by the citizens as a way of self-nomination of a candidate who submitted an application to the relevant constituency to run for a position of an *akim* of district importance, village, settlement and rural county, as well as an *akim* of a district (a town of regional importance), if less than two candidates have been nominated by the end of the day of a nomination period. A political party has the right to nominate only one candidate in one constituency (Article 113-3 Law on the Elections).

574. In the case of self-nomination, a candidate must be supported by at least 1% of the whole electorate of the relevant constituency eligible to vote. Voters' support is identified by their signatures (Article 113-4 Law on the Elections).

575. The Precinct election commission draws up a voting protocol upon the results of voting which is immediately delivered to a district (town) election commission (Article 113-8 Law on the Elections).

576. The election results are defined at the meeting of a district (town) election commission on the ground of protocols of the precinct election commission no later than three days after the election. A protocol shall be signed by a chair and members of a district (town) election commission. A candidate who receives the largest number of votes is considered elected (Article 113-10 Law on the Elections).

577. The relevant district (town) election commission on the ground of protocols of precinct election commissions within seven days from the date of conducting elections registers the elected *akims* of district importance, village, settlement and rural county (Article 113-11 Law on the Elections).

IV. Local Self-Governance in Kazakhstan

578. In accordance with Article 89 of the Constitution, local self-governance provides an opportunity for the local people to solve local issues independently. Within the constitutional provisions, local self-governance is realized by the people directly, as well as through *maslikhats* and other local bodies which cover the territories most densely populated. Realization of state functions may be delegated to these local self-governance bodies in accordance with relevant Law. The organization and activities of local self-governance in Kazakhstan are regulated by Law. The autonomy of these bodies is guaranteed, within their competencies established by Law. A new Concept on the Development of Local Self-Governance in Kazakhstan till 2025 was approved by the Decree of the President of the Republic No. 639 dated 18 August 2021.

579. Some constitutional provisions are detailed in the Law on local governance. As given in Article 2-1 of Law, local self-governance shall be exercised within the limits of a region, a district, a town, a district in the town, a rural county, a settlement and a village which is not a part of a rural county. The *akims* of a region, a district, a town, a district in the town, a rural county, a settlement and a village, which is not a part of a rural county, alongside with the functions of state administration carry out the functions of the local self-governance bodies, alongside their other functions. The forms of activities of the local community are the local gathering and local assembly.

580. Chapter 3-1 of Law on Local Governance is devoted to the participation of citizens in local self-governance. In accordance with Article 39-2 of the Law, the members of the local community have the following rights:

(1) to realize local self-governance directly, as well as through elected bodies of the local self-governance, regardless of origin, social, official and property status, gender, race, nationality, language, religion, belief, membership in political parties and public associations;
(2) to elect and to be elected to the bodies of local self-governance in the way envisaged by the legislation of Kazakhstan on elections;
(3) to appeal in person, to submit both individual or collective appeals to the local self-governance bodies;
(4) to realize other rights envisaged by the Law and other legislative acts.

Restrictions of rights of the local community for participation at the local self-governance are not allowed, except in cases envisaged by the legislative act, which may be appealed in a court.

581. The members of the local community have the following duties:

(1) to observe the Constitution and the national legislation;
(2) to promote strengthening the unity of people of Kazakhstan, interethnic and interfaith harmony in the country;
(3) to respect the state and other languages, the traditions and customs of Kazakhstan's peoples, and contribute to their development.

582. Article 39-3 of Law on the Local Governance regulates the local gathering and assembly. The local gathering takes place as deemed necessary on the most important questions of the local level, such as:

(1) defining the priority tasks of the local community and the timing of their realization;
(2) defining for four years the composition of participants of the local community gathering up to twenty-five people;
(3) submission of proposals to their respective *maslikhats* on local issues;
(4) hearing and discussion of the *akim's* reports on issues of realization of functions of the local self-governance;
(5) hearing and discussion of the *akims*' yearly reports of a town of district importance, a village, a settlement, a rural county on the results of realization of the Pasture Management Plan and their use;
(6) hearing and discussion of the *maslikhat's* reports on the work done by the *maslikhat* of a district (town of regional importance), activities of its permanent commissions;
(7) other questions of local level defined by the local gathering.

583. The local gathering can be convened by the *akims* of a town of district importance, a village, a settlement, and a rural county independently or it can be convened on the initiative of at least 10% of the members of the local gathering who reside in this territory, and who have the right to participate in it. Initiators should sign a request on convening the gathering, mentioning their full name and a place of residence. The request shall be submitted to the *akim* of the respective district (town of regional importance). Holding the local gathering is allowed only if the local community receives an affirmative decision from the *akim* of the respective district (or town of regional importance) (Article 39-3(5) Law on Local Governance).

584. According to Article 39-3(3) of Law on Local Governance, the local assembly is gathered to discuss current issues at the local level, such as:

(1) discussion and consideration of the drafts of the programme documents and development programme of local society;
(2) approval of the budget's draft and the report on its fulfilment;
(3) approval of the decisions of the relevant *akim's* office of district importance, a village, a settlement, a rural county on the management of the communal property;
(4) formation of a commission of the local community among the members of the local community assembly to monitor the realization of the local budget;
(5) hearing and discussion of the report on the monitoring of budget realization of a town of district importance, a village, a settlement, a rural county;
(6) approval of the alienation of the communal property;
(7) discussion of important questions of the local community, and drafts of the normative legal acts that concern the rights and freedoms of citizens, etc.;
(8) approval of a candidate presented by the *akim* of a district (a town of regional importance) for the position of the *akim* of a town of district importance, a village, a settlement, a rural county, for further nomination in a case stipulated by Article 113-3 of the Constitutional Law on the Elections;
(9) initiation of a question on removal from the post of an *akim* of district importance, a village, a settlement, a rural county;
(10) making proposals on the appointment of heads of state institutions and organizations financed by the local budget and located in the relevant territories;
(11) consideration of other daily problems.

585. Once in six months, the members of the local assembly carry out a monitoring of realization of the respective local budget. The monitoring is carried out in order to collect, systematize, analyse and summarize information on the realization of approved budget indicators of the respective territory. The report of the monitoring shall be discussed at the meeting of the local assembly. The latter adopts any recommendations on an effective realization of the budget (Article 39-3(4) Law on Local Governance).

586. The local assembly can be called by the *akims* of a town of district importance, a village, a settlement and rural county, independently or upon initiation of at least 10% of the members of the local assembly delegated by the members of the local gatherings (Article 39-3(7) Law on Local Governance).

587. The decision of the local gathering or local assembly is considered adopted if half of the participants of the meeting vote in favour of it. The decisions adopted at the local gathering or local assembly shall be considered by the *akim* of a town of district importance, a village, a settlement, a rural county. The bodies of the local governance and self-governance, the officials within their competencies ensure the realization of the decisions adopted at the local gathering or local assembly. The public should be informed about the decisions of the local gathering or local assembly via the media or other tools (Article 39-3(11–14) Law on Local Governance).

§4. The Status of Nur-Sultan as the Capital of Kazakhstan

588. In the 1990s, driven by geopolitical factors, the First President Nazarbayev pushed hard to move the capital of Kazakhstan from the south of the country to the north.[120] Paying tribute to the input of the First President of Kazakhstan and Leader of the Nation, Nursultan Nazarbayev for the development of statehood of the country, the capital of Kazakhstan was renamed from Astana to Nur-Sultan city with the amendments to the Constitution of Kazakhstan dated 23 March 2019. The construction of the capital is considered a triumph of the President of Kazakhstan.[121]

589. The status of the capital of Kazakhstan is regulated by the Law adopted on 21 July 2007.[122] According to Article 1(2) of the Law, the capital is the political and administrative centre of the state, where the President's Residence '*Aqorda*', the Parliament, the Government, the Supreme Court and other central state bodies of the Republic are located. Other central state bodies in accordance with the legislation of Kazakhstan can be located beyond the capital. The original text of the Constitution, the standards of the National flag and the National emblem of Kazakhstan are preserved at the Residence of the President of Kazakhstan '*Aqorda*'.

590. In accordance with Article 7 of the Law on the capital of Kazakhstan, the local governance bodies of the capital shall:

(1) create conditions to ensure that the city performs its functions as the political, administrative, cultural and economic centre of Kazakhstan;
(2) increase the competitive capacity of the capital among other world capitals, in creating a city of sustainable development;
(3) develop the capital as a centre of international relations;
(4) create conditions for the realization of the activities of the President of Kazakhstan, the Parliament, the Government, the Supreme Court's, and other central state bodies of the Republic, as well as the diplomatic representations of foreign states;
(5) create conditions for the organization and holding of national and international events; and
(6) realize other functions envisaged by the national legislation.

---

120. Nursultan Nazarbayev, *Era of Independence* 119–124 (2017).
121. Kassym-Jomart Tokayev, *He Makes History. Essays of Kazakhstani Diplomat.* 185–190 (2018).
122. Law of 21 Jul. 2007 on a Status of the Capital of the Republic of Kazakhstan. Available at: http://online.zakon.kz/Document/?doc_id=30114244 (accessed 3 Aug. 2021).

591. The powers of the capital's *maslikhat* are elaborated in Article 8 of the relevant Law. Along with the powers established by the national legislation, the *maslikhat* of the capital within its competencies has the following functions:

(1) to establish international relations with the local representative bodies of other countries in accordance with the legislation of the Republic;
(2) to approve:
  (a) the plans for the capital's economic and social development, the budget of the capital and the reports on its performance;
  (b) thc rules regulating the migration processes to the territory of the capital;
  (c) the amount and procedures of rendering social assistance to certain categories of people in need;
  (d) the urban development schemes in the capital's territory in order to realize a master plan for the capital; and
  (e) the urban development regulations of Nur-Sultan.
(3) to coordinate the drafts of agreements on any land alienation or other real estate to enable the seizure of land for the needs of the state.

592. Article 9 of the Law covers the competencies of the local executive body of the capital. Alongside the powers established by the national legislation, the local executive body of the capital fulfils the following and other functions, enumerated in the Article:

(1) approves a list of communal property that is not assigned to communal legal entities, possess, use and dispose of state-owned shares in joint-stock companies, and share participation in the limited liability partnerships registered in the territory of the capital, except for legal entities that are classified as national property;
(2) owns, uses and disposes of the communal property of Nur-Sultan city;
(3) issues resolutions that regulate the privatization of the communal property of Nur-Sultan city;
(4) participates in the development of state architectural, city-planning and construction policy within the territory of the capital and its suburban area;
(5) coordinates the activity of the parties on the realization of a master plan of development and construction in the capital, on the realization of the complex scheme of the urban plan for the suburban area (a draft of a district planning);
(6) organizes the development of a master plan draft and building-up the territory of the capital and suburban area;
(7) prepares the materials for preliminary conclusions of the council on the urban development of the capital;
(8) oversees the term of designing, construction and operational commissioning of the objects of reconstruction;
(9) develops the amount and procedures of social assistance to certain categories of citizens in need;
(10) coordinates labour issues, and ensures realization of the employment policy in the capital;

(11) promotes international cooperation on issues of the development of the capital;
(12) creates conditions for holding national and international events in the capital in a way established by the national legislation;
(13) defines the legal entity that will, with the full participation of the State, assist in the social-economic development of Nur-Sultan city, including the development of business tourism, as well as preparing the capital for international exhibition;
(14) coordinates operations for the effective functioning of heating, energy, water and gas supply, sewage and drainage, for the provision of public amenities, public roads, all kinds of metropolitan transport and communications, gardening, city cleaning, as well as engineering, exploitation and repairing the housing stock;
(15) coordinates the activities of medical organizations that provide medical service on the territory of the capital;
(16) realizes development policy and the workings of internal trade and domestic services, etc.

The Article enumerates many other competencies of the local executive body of the capital.

§5. The Status of the Cities of National Importance

I. The Status of Almaty as a City of National Importance

593. The status of Almaty, the former capital of Kazakhstan, is regulated by the Law of the Republic of Kazakhstan of 1 July 1998 No. 258-1 on Special Status of *Almaty* City and other normative legal acts.[123] The special status given to Almaty as a city of national importance is due to its scientific, cultural, historical, financial and industrial role in the development of Kazakhstan.

594. In accordance with Article 3 of the Law on *Almaty*, the local representative body of the city has the following rights:

(1) to adopt plans for the economic and social development of the territory, the local budget and the report on their implementation;
(2) to determine the amount and procedure of levying fines for administrative offences committed in the territory of Almaty;
(3) to approve the list of historical and cultural monuments of local importance, upon the proposal of the state territorial bodies and the public bodies on the protection of the monuments, agreed with the state bodies of the Republic on protection and the use of objects of historical and cultural heritage;

123. Law of the Republic of Kazakhstan of 1 Jul. 1998 No. 258-1 on Special Status of *Almaty* City. Available at: http://online.zakon.kz/Document/?doc_id=1009786#pos=14;-245 (accessed 30 Apr. 2020).

(4) to establish international relations with the local representative bodies of other countries within the limits and procedures defined by the legislation of Kazakhstan;
(5) to take decisions on the relevance and conditions for attracting loans by the local executive body in accordance with the budget legislation of Kazakhstan;
(6) to approve the rules regulating migration processes to the territory of Almaty;
(7) to approve the city management scheme upon the proposal of the executive body;
(8) to define the procedures for improvement and sanitation and hygiene throughout the city's territory;
(9) to establish the titles and define the procedure and conditions of conferring the title 'Honourable Citizen of *Almaty* city';
(10) to coordinate the drafts of the agreements on the alienation of a land plot or any other real estate because of the seizure of a land plot for the state's needs, etc.

The Article enumerates other competencies of the local representative body of the capital.

595. The competencies of the local executive body of *Almaty* are given in Article 4 of the Law. So, the executive body of *Almaty*:

(1) possesses, uses and disposes of the communal property of Almaty;
(2) approves the list of communal property, where they are not assigned to the communal legal entities; possesses, uses and disposes of, the state shares of joint-stock companies, and shares participation in the limited liability partnerships registered on the territory of Almaty, except for legal entities that are classified as national property;
(3) makes any decision on the privatization of communal property in accordance with the procedures established by Article 10 of the Law of the Republic on state property;
(4) ensures the ecological security of the population, and restoration of the disturbed natural ecological systems within the city territory;
(5) creates necessary conditions for holding national and international events in the city in accordance with the procedures established by the legislation of Kazakhstan;
(6) determines the traffic patterns of transit highway transport in Almaty;
(7) develops and approves the rules concerning paid parking spaces;
(8) organizes such paid parking spaces;
(9) carries out the licensing of activities according to the list determined by the Government;
(10) ensures the realization and monitoring of a master plan for the development of Almaty;
(11) submits for approval to the local representative body the management plan of Almaty in accordance with the standard structure of the state local governance;

(12) carries out compulsory alienation of a property by the State in the way established by Land Code of Kazakhstan and the Law on state property; and
(13) develops the rules regulating migration processes on the territory of Almaty in accordance with the standard rules on migration processes in the regions, cities of regional importance and the capital approved by the Government of Kazakhstan, etc.

The Article enumerates other competencies of the local executive body of Almaty.

II. The Status of Shymkent as a City of National Importance

596. On 19 June 2018, the President of Kazakhstan signed Decree on Some Issues of the Administrative-Territorial Structure of the Republic of Kazakhstan.[124] In accordance with the Decree, Shymkent city located in South Kazakhstan is now regarded as a city of national importance. Referring to the Law on the administrative-territorial structure of the Republic, a city of national importance is an inhabited locality which has special state significance or with a population of over one million.[125] Shymkent is expected to be a technology and intellectual resource centre of the Central Asia region, and as such will attract investments.

597. The administrative centre of the South Kazakhstan region was transferred from Shymkent to Turkestan city. The South Kazakhstan region was renamed the Turkestan region, the 17th region in the country. The Government was instructed to approve the plan of all organizational arrangements, together with the Supreme Court and other state bodies directly subordinate and responsible to the President of Kazakhstan. The commission on organizing and holding competitions on the preparation of a general plan for the development of Turkestan as a cultural and spiritual centre of the Turkic world was created. The central state bodies and the local state bodies of Shymkent and the Turkestan region were instructed to take measures for the smooth and effective functioning of their respective state bodies and organizations. The President's Administration took the realization of the Decree under its control.

---

124. Decree of the President of Kazakhstan of 19 Jun. 2018 on Some Issues of Administrative-Territorial Structure of the Republic of Kazakhstan. Available at: http://www.akorda.kz/ru/legal_acts/decrees/o-nekotoryh-voprosah-administrativno-territorialnogo-ustroistva-respubliki-kazahstan (3 Feb. 2019).

125. Law of Kazakhstan of 8 Dec. 1993 No. 2572-XII on the Administrative-Territorial Structure of the Republic of Kazakhstan. Available at: https://online.zakon.kz/Document/?doc_id=1007265 (accessed 3 Feb. 2019).

Part IV. Citizenship and the Administration of Justice

Chapter 1. Citizenship of Kazakhstan

§1. Constitutional Provisions Concerning Citizenship

598. Chapter 2 of the Constitution of Kazakhstan 'Individual and citizen' contains provisions that regulate some issues relating to citizenship of Kazakhstan. In accordance with Article 10, citizenship of Kazakhstan is acquired and terminated in accordance with the Law. So, the details relating to citizenship of the Republic are regulated by the Law of 20 December 1991 on the Citizenship of the Republic of Kazakhstan.[126] According to Article 10 of the Constitution, citizenship of Kazakhstan shall be indivisible and equal regardless of the grounds of its acquisition. A citizen of Kazakhstan cannot be deprived of citizenship and the right to change his/her citizenship or be expelled from the country. Deprivation of citizenship is allowed only on the grounds of having committed terrorist crimes, as well as having caused other grievous harm to the vital interests of the Republic, and only via a court decision. A citizen of Kazakhstan cannot hold simultaneously foreign citizenship with the Kazakh one.

599. The Republic shall guarantee its citizens protection and patronage beyond its boundaries. A citizen of Kazakhstan cannot be extradited to a foreign State if otherwise is not established by the international treaties of the Republic (Article 11 Constitution). In line with Article 12(3) of the Constitution of Kazakhstan, by virtue of citizenship, a citizen of the Republic shall have rights and bear duties.

126. Law of Kazakhstan of 20 Dec. 1991 No. 1017-XII on Citizenship of the Republic of Kazakhstan. Available at: https://online.zakon.kz/Document/?doc_id=1000816 (accessed 3 Aug. 2021).

§2. Provisions of the Law on Citizenship of the Republic of Kazakhstan

I. Obtaining Citizenship of Kazakhstan

600. Citizenship of Kazakhstan is acquired and terminated in accordance with the relevant law. As stipulated in Article 1 of the Law on Citizenship, in Kazakhstan, every human being has the right to citizenship. In line with Article 3 of the Law on Citizenship, the citizens of the Republic of Kazakhstan are those persons who:

(1) reside permanently on the Republic on the day of the entry into force of this Law;
(2) were born in the territory of Kazakhstan and do not hold foreign citizenship;
(3) acquired citizenship of Kazakhstan in accordance with this Law.

601. Kazakhstan is represented by its state bodies and officials and is responsible for the citizens of the Republic, and a citizen of Kazakhstan is responsible before the country. Citizens of Kazakhstan enjoy the full range of civil, political, economic and social rights and freedoms proclaimed and guaranteed by the Constitution and the laws of the Republic.

602. Article 10 of Law on Citizenship of the Republic of Kazakhstan enumerates the grounds for obtaining citizenship of the Republic. Citizenship of Kazakhstan can be obtained:

(1) by virtue of birth;
(2) as a result of conferment of citizenship of Kazakhstan;
(3) on the grounds and procedures envisaged in international agreements of the Republic;
(4) other grounds established by the Law on citizenship.

603. Regardless of the place of birth, a child both of whose parents at the time of his/her birth were the citizens of Kazakhstan is a citizen of the country (Article 11 Law on Citizenship). A child both of whose parents at the time of his/her birth were foreign citizens is not a citizen of the Republic, regardless of the place of birth (Article 11-1 Law on Citizenship).

604. Article 12 regulates the circumstances where the parents of a child have different citizenship. If one of the parents has citizenship of Kazakhstan, a child is considered a citizen of Kazakhstan if he/she is born in the territory of Kazakhstan. If a child born outside the Republic and the parents or one of them at that time had a permanent residence in the territory of Kazakhstan, he can claim citizenship of the country.

605. In a case where parents hold different citizenship and where one of them at the time of the birth of a child holds the citizenship of Kazakhstan, and both parents at that time had permanent residence outside of the Republic, citizenship of a child born outside of Kazakhstan shall be defined through the written agreement of parents.

606. In a case where one of the parents of a child holds the citizenship of Kazakhstan and another parent is without any citizenship, or his/her citizenship is unknown, a child shall be considered as a citizen of Kazakhstan regardless of the place of birth.

607. A child who resides in the territory of Kazakhstan and both of his/her parents are unknown shall be considered as a citizen of Kazakhstan (Article 13 Law on Citizenship).

608. A child, who is born in the territory of Kazakhstan to persons without citizenship, but having permanent residence in the territory of the Republic, shall be considered as a citizen of Kazakhstan (Article 14 Law on Citizenship).

609. With regards to conferment of citizenship of the Republic, foreigners and persons without citizenship permanently residing in the territory of Kazakhstan may be granted citizenship of Kazakhstan in accordance with the Law. The President of Kazakhstan takes decisions on granting citizenship of the Republic (Article 15 Law on Citizenship).

610. The conditions for granting citizenship are enumerated in Article 16 of the Law. Citizenship of Kazakhstan is granted if:

(1) a person (applicant) has resided legally and permanently in the territory of Kazakhstan for not less than five years or has been married to a citizen of Kazakhstan for not less than three years. This condition does not concern minors, legally incapable persons and persons who have special merits for Kazakhstan or obtain professions or meet the requirements of the list established by the Government, and members of their families;
(2) citizens of former Soviet Republics who arrived in Kazakhstan for permanent residence and have close relatives who are citizens of the Republic, including a child (an adopted child), spouse, one of the parents (adoptive parents), sister, brother, grandfather or grandmother regardless of the length of their stay in Kazakhstan. Issues of citizenship of military personnel on military service and deployed in the territory of Kazakhstan shall be determined by international agreements of the Republic.

611. Certain categories of people can receive citizenship in simplified procedures, and Article 16-1 of the Law enumerates the conditions of conferment. They are:

(1) returnees of the Kazakh ethnicity (*qandasy*) who reside permanently and legally reside in the territory of Kazakhstan regardless of their length of stay;

(2) rehabilitated victims of mass political repressions as well as their descendants deprived of or have lost their citizenship and legally permanently residing in the territory regardless of their length of stay;
(3) ethnic Kazakhs receiving education at the higher educational institute of Kazakhstan.

612. The processing period of the request for citizenship in a simplified manner should not exceed more than three months from the date of application.

613. Article 17 of the Law enumerates the grounds for refusal of the obtaining of citizenship and the restoration of citizenship of Kazakhstan. So, a request on the obtaining and the restoration of citizenship may be declined if a person:

(1) has committed a crime against humanity according to international law, and deliberately opposes the sovereignty and independence of Kazakhstan;
(2) calls for the violation of unity and integrity of the territory of the Republic;
(3) carries out illegal activities that are detrimental to national security and the health of the population;
(4) incites interethnic, inter-confessional and religious enmity, counteracting the functioning of the state language of Kazakhstan;
(5) belongs to terrorist and extremist organizations and is convicted of terrorist activity;
(6) is on the international wanted list, is serving a sentence on the grounds of a court verdict or his/her actions are considered by the court as a dangerous relapse;
(7) is a citizen of another state;
(8) submitted false information in his/her request for citizenship or without reasonable excuse did not submit the necessary documents within the time frame established by the national legislation of the Republic;
(9) has criminal history on record for committing an intentional crime in the territory of Kazakhstan and beyond its boundaries recognized as such by the legislation of Kazakhstan;
(10) committed an offence in the economic area within five years before the submission of a request for citizenship or for the restoration of citizenship of Kazakhstan;
(11) repeatedly within five years prior to the submission of a request for citizenship or restoration of citizenship violated the legislation of Kazakhstan on migration;
(12) lost citizenship of Kazakhstan on the grounds of the provisions (1), (2) and (5) of Article 21 of the Law on Citizenship within five years prior to submission of a request for citizenship of the Republic or restoration of citizenship of Kazakhstan;
(13) was deprived of citizenship of Kazakhstan on the grounds of Article 20-1 of the Law.

614. As mentioned in Article 18 of the Law on Citizenship, upon the request of a person, citizenship may be restored in line with the requirements of the national legislation of Kazakhstan.

II. Termination of Citizenship of Kazakhstan

615. Loss of citizenship of Kazakhstan is regulated by Chapter 3 of the Law on citizenship. In accordance with Article 19 of the Law, there are the following grounds for termination of citizenship:

(1) renunciation of citizenship of the Republic;
(2) loss of citizenship of the Republic;
(3) deprivation of citizenship of the Republic.

616. In line with Article 20 of the Law, renunciation of citizenship of Kazakhstan can be brought on the grounds of the request of a person in a manner prescribed by Law. A person may be refused renunciation if he/she has unfulfilled obligations before the Republic or property liabilities which concern essential interests of citizens and enterprises, institutions and organizations, public associations located in the territory of Kazakhstan. Renunciation of citizenship is not allowed if a suspected person acknowledged the qualification of the committed offence, or is serving a sentence on the grounds of a court decision that has entered into force, or if renunciation of citizenship of Kazakhstan contradicts the national interests of the Republic.

617. Deprivation of citizenship of Kazakhstan is regulated by Article 20-1 of the Law. It is used only on the grounds of a court decision relating to the committing of terrorist crimes, as well as crimes envisaged in the relevant articles of the Special Part of the Penal Code that caused grave harm to the vital interests of Kazakhstan.

618. Article 21 of the Law enumerates the grounds for loss of Kazakhstani citizenship, it can be lost if:

(1) a person joined the military service, security service, police, justice authorities or other state bodies and administration of another state, apart from cases envisaged in the international treaties of Kazakhstan;
(2) citizenship of Kazakhstan had been acquired on the grounds of deliberately false information or false documents;
(3) the grounds are stipulated by the international treaties of Kazakhstan;
(4) a person had acquired citizenship of another state;
(5) marriage with a citizen of the Republic that had been the grounds for acquiring citizenship of Kazakhstan was recognized as invalid by a court;
(6) a child adopted by foreigners expressed the will to abandon his/her citizenship of Kazakhstan;
(7) a person has participated or is participating in foreign armed conflicts, extremist and (or) terrorist activities in the territory of a foreign State.

619. A citizen of Kazakhstan who received foreign citizenship must inform the internal affairs bodies or foreign institutions of Kazakhstan about his/her acquisition of foreign citizenship and hand over his/her passport and (or) an identification card of Kazakhstan within thirty calendar days from the day of obtaining such citizenship. Failure to inform shall entail responsibility in accordance with the laws of the Republic.

Chapter 2. Fundamental Rights and Liberties

§1. General

I. Definition

620. The respect for fundamental rights and liberties characterizes good governance and sustainable development of a country, prevents corruption in the government and determines its accountability before the people, conditions access to information and creates a stable ground for democratic discussions. Non-respect for fundamental rights and liberties signifies a lack of political freedom, which leads to social and economic insecurity. According to Sen (2011) 'economic and social deprivation can lead to bad health and premature mortality; the denial of basic health care and education can sustain economic poverty'.[127] Moreover, insecurity may cause internal interethnic and inter-confessional conflicts. The support of internal peace is of particular importance for any country, especially for the country, which has more than 140 nationalities and is rich in natural resources. Peace inside Kazakhstan is a crucial element of Central Asian stability.

621. Fundamental rights are natural rights that are inherent to individuals by virtue of their birth irrespective of gender, race and colour, religion, language, social status and ethnicity. Fundamental rights ensure non-discrimination and the individual's physical and mental integrity, protect against unlawful interference and guarantee the democratic participation of individuals in civil society.

622. The preamble to the Constitution of Kazakhstan establishes that the Republic adheres to the ideals of liberty, equality and consent. Kazakhstan considers that its highest values are an individual, his life, rights and freedoms (Article 1(1) Constitution). Chapter 2 of the Constitution is devoted to the legal status of an individual and citizen.[128]

623. Article 12 of the Constitution of Kazakhstan envisages that Kazakhstan recognizes and guarantees the rights and freedoms of an individual in accordance with the Constitution. Human rights and freedoms shall belong to everyone by virtue of birth, be recognized as absolute and inalienable, and define content and application of laws and other normative legal acts (Article 12(2)). Exercise of rights and freedoms of an individual and citizen must not infringe the rights and freedoms of other persons, encroach on the constitutional system and public morals (Article 12(5)). Understanding of the provisions of Article 12 paragraph 2 of with regards to

---

127. Amartya Sen, 'Normative evaluation and legal analogues'. Public lecture at the School of Law of Washington University in St. Louis, at a conference on Norms and the Law, on 31 Mar. 2011, available at: https://www.cambridge.org/core/books/norms-and-the-law/AD942F5BFA60095DC909DFF7211207EC (accessed 20 Mar. 2019).
128. On Kazakhstan's practice on the implementation of civil and political rights, *see*: Beibit Shangirbayeva, 'The Impact of the Implementation of the International Covenant on Civil and Political Rights on Protection of Human Rights in Kazakhstan', PhD dissertation (Pisa, Sant'Anna School of Advanced Studies, July 2013).

human rights is given in the Decision of the Constitutional Council on the official interpretation of 28 October 1996 No. 6/2. Human rights and freedoms mentioned in Article 12 paragraph 2 are those which are recognized and guaranteed by the State in accordance with the Constitution. Recognition that human rights are absolute means that they cover all individuals residing in Kazakhstan regardless of their citizenship. The inalienability of human rights means that individuals cannot be deprived of their rights and freedoms except in cases envisaged by the Constitution and the laws adopted on its ground.[129]

624. The Constitution recognizes legal personality and right to judicial protection, equality and non-discrimination, right to life, liberty of a person, freedom from torture and other cruel, inhuman or degrading treatment or punishment, right to privacy and protection of dignity, freedom of expression and information, freedom of movement, freedom of conscience, freedom of association and peaceful assembly. The Constitution of Kazakhstan envisages freedom of labour and right to rest, protection of a dwelling place, property rights and freedom of entrepreneurship, protection of family, children and disabled parents. The Republic guarantees minimum wage and pension, right to protect health, free secondary education, right to participate in state governance, right to elect and be elected, and others.

625. The Constitution of Kazakhstan had been drafted taking into account rights and freedoms given in the UDHR, the International Covenant on Civil and Political Rights (ICCPR) and the International Covenant on Social, Economic and Cultural Rights (ICESCR).

II. Sources

626. Contemporary understanding of fundamental rights contained in many world constitutions stems from the ideas and concepts of the classical Western philosophers, such as Locke, Rousseau, Montesquieu, and Voltaire, which are 'well accepted in Western political culture'.[130] These philosophers are well studied by Kazakh academia and influenced a lot on the founders of the Kazakh constitutionalism and drafters of the Constitution of Kazakhstan.

627. Kazakhstan is a State Party to almost all core international instruments for the protection of human rights. Chronologically, Kazakhstan became a State Party to the following core international human rights documents and their protocols:

(1) The Convention on the Rights of the Child (on 12 August 1994).

---

129. Normative Resolution of the Constitutional Council of Kazakhstan of 28 Oct. 1996 No. 6/2 on Official Interpretation of Article 4 paragraph 1 and Article 12 paragraph 2 of the Constitution of the Republic of Kazakhstan. Available at https://ksrk.gov.kz/kk/solutions/kazakhstan-respublikasy-konstituciyasynyn-4-babynyn-1-tarmagyna-zhne-12-babynyn-2 (accessed 3 Aug. 2021).

130. Beth A. Simmons. *Mobilizing for Human Rights: International Law in Domestic Politics* 159 (2009).

(2) The Convention against Torture and Other Cruel Inhuman or Degrading Treatment or Punishment (on 26 August 1998).
(3) The CEDAW (on 26 August 1998).
(4) The International Convention on the Elimination of All Forms of Racial Discrimination (on 26 August 1998).
(5) The Convention on the Prevention and Punishment of the Crime of Genocide (on 26 August 1998).
(6) The Convention on the Political Rights of Women (on 28 March 2000).
(7) The Convention on the Nationality of Married Women, 1957 (on 28 March 2000).
(8) The OP to the Convention on the Rights of the Child on the Sale of Children, Child Prostitution and Child Pornography (on 24 August 2001).
(9) The OP to the CEDAW (on 24 August 2001).
(10) The OP to the Convention on the Rights of the Child on the Involvement of Children in Armed Conflict (on 10 April 2003).
(11) The OP to the Convention against Torture and Other Cruel, Inhuman or Degrading Treatment and Punishment (on 22 October 2008).
(12) The ICCPR (on 24 January 2006).
(13) The ICESCR (on 24 January 2006).
(14) The Convention for the Protection of All Persons from Enforced Disappearance (on 27 February 2009).
(15) The OP I to the ICCPR (on 30 June 2009).
(16) The Convention on the Rights of Persons with Disabilities (on 21 April 2015).

On 23 September 2010, Kazakhstan signed the OP to the ICESCR of 2008, but not ratified yet. On 11 December 2008, Kazakhstan signed the OP to the Convention on the Rights of Persons with Disabilities of 2006, but not ratified yet. The Second OP to the ICCPR, aiming at the abolition of the death penalty of 1989, has been signed, but not ratified by the Republic, and in fact, the country follows the international standard and has an unlimited moratorium on the death penalty that was introduced by the first President of the Republic in 2003. The country is not a State Party to the International Convention on the Protection of the Rights of All Migrant Workers and Members of their Families of 1990 and the OP to the Convention on the Rights of the Child on a Communications Procedure of 2011.[131]

III. Historical Outline

628. Priority of human rights and freedoms was recognized in the preamble of the first Constitution of Kazakhstan of 1993. Equality of all citizens as fundamentals of Kazakhstan's constitutionality was established in the opening articles. An individual, his life, freedom and inalienable rights were considered as the highest values of the Republic. The Constitution of 1993 established a clear separation of powers into legislative, executive and judicial branches.

131. United Nations Treaty Collection: https://treaties.un.org/Pages/Treaties.aspx?id=4&subid=A (accessed 3 Aug. 2021).

629. Chapter 2 of the Constitution of 1993 was devoted to the legal status of a citizen, his rights, freedoms and duties. The Constitution guaranteed equality of rights and freedoms and non-discrimination, established priority of international legal acts on human rights and freedoms recognized by Kazakhstan over the laws of the Republic. In accordance with Article 7 of the Constitution of 1993, Kazakhstan had the right to provide asylum to foreign citizens and stateless who had become victims of human rights violations. The Constitution of 1993 guaranteed the right to life as the natural and inalienable right of every person, inviolability of honour and dignity; freedom of expression and opinion; right to seek and disseminate information by legal means; freedom of consciousness and religion; freedom of movement and right to choose a place of residence.

630. The Constitution of Kazakhstan of 1993 established political rights and freedoms, including the right to participate in state affairs, freedom of assembly and demonstrations, the right to create public associations, etc. Section 5 of the Constitution of 1993 was devoted to a range of economic and social rights. This included the right to property, the right to work and freedom to conclude labour agreements, the prohibition of forced work, the right for a strike, the right to rest and leisure, the right to housing, protection of health and provision of free medical assistance, the right to education, the right for social security in old age, the right to favourable environment for life and health, freedom of artistic, scientific and technical creativity, etc.

631. Section 6 of the Constitution of 1993 was devoted to the main duties of individuals and citizens, such as to obey the Constitution and the laws of the Republic, to respect honour and dignity of others, to respect state symbols, to pay legally established taxes and fees, to protect the Republic and perform military service. The Constitution of 1993 protected inviolability of private life of a citizen and housing, the right to self-defence, judicial protection of all rights and freedoms envisaged in the Constitution and the laws, equality before the law and court, the presumption of innocence, the right to qualified legal service and protection, prohibited torture, ill-treatment and double jeopardy, etc.

IV. General Rules

A. *Those Entitled to Rights and Liberties*

632. The Constitution of Kazakhstan of 1995 guarantees human rights and freedoms which belong by virtue of birth. Foreigners and persons without citizenship enjoy rights and freedoms, bear responsibility like citizens of the Republic if other things are not established by the Constitution, laws and international treaties (Article 12(4)).

B. Conditions for Restrictions on Rights and Liberties

633. As a general rule, the exercise of rights and freedoms by an individual and citizen should not violate the rights and freedoms of other persons, infringe the constitutional system and public morals (Article 12(5) Constitution).

634. Article 39 of the Constitution enumerates conditions for restrictions on rights and freedoms. The rights and freedoms of an individual and citizen can be restricted only by laws and to the extent necessary for the protection of the constitutional system, rights and freedoms of an individual, health and morals of the population. Any actions that break interethnic and inter-confessional consent shall be considered unconstitutional. Any form of restriction to the rights and freedoms of the citizens on political grounds shall not be allowed. In accordance with Article 39 paragraph 3 of the Constitution, the rights envisaged in the following articles of the Constitution shall not be restricted:

(1) Article 11: A citizen of Kazakhstan shall not be extradited unless otherwise established by international treaties of the Republic. The Republic guarantees its citizens protection and patronage outside its territory.
(2) Article 13: Everyone has the right to recognition of his legal personality and protection of his rights and freedoms by all not-contradicting the law means, including self-defence. Everyone shall have the right to judicial protection of his rights and freedoms. Everyone has the right to qualified legal assistance. In cases given by law, legal assistance shall be provided for free.
(3) Article 14: All are equal before the law and court. No one shall be subjected to any kind of discrimination on the grounds of origin, social, official or wealth status, sex, race, ethnicity, language, religious belief, opinion, place of residence or any other circumstances.
(4) Article 15: Everyone has the right to life. No one shall have the right to arbitrarily deprive the life of another person. The death penalty shall be established by law as an exceptional punishment for terrorist crimes which have resulted in death casualties, and also for especially grave crimes, committed in wartime while granting a sentenced person the right to appeal for pardon.
(5) Article 16(1): Everyone has the right to personal freedom.
(6) Article 17: A person's dignity shall be inviolable. No one shall be subject to torture, violence, other cruel or degrading treatment and punishment.
(7) Article 19: Everyone shall have the right to determine and indicate or not to indicate his ethnicity, party and religious affiliation. Everyone has the right to use his mother tongue and culture, to freely choose the language of communication, bringing up, education and creativity.
(8) Article 22: Everyone has the right to freedom of conscience. The manifestation of this right must not limit the universal and civil rights and obligations to the State.
(9) Article 26(2): Property, including the right of inheritance, shall be guaranteed by law.

635. Restrictions on rights and freedoms mentioned in the Constitution depend on the type of rights. The use of the right of citizens to peacefully and without arms assemble, hold meetings, rallies and demonstrations, street processions and pickets can be restricted by law in the interests of state security, public order, and the protection of the health, rights and freedoms of other persons (Article 32 Constitution).

C. *Remedies for Violations of Rights and Liberties under the Constitution of Kazakhstan*

636. In line with Article 13 of the Constitution, everyone has the right to recognition of his legal personality and protection of his rights and freedoms by all not-contradicting the law means, including self-defence. Everyone shall have the right to judicial protection of his rights and freedoms. Everyone has the right to qualified legal assistance. In cases given by law, legal assistance shall be provided for free.

D. *Remedies for Violations of Rights and Liberties under International Conventions*

637. As a State Party to the core international human rights treaties, Kazakhstan recognized remedies that are used in case of violations of human rights and freedoms established under International Conventions. Kazakhstan ratified the ICCPR of 1966, which became effective for the country on 24 January 2006, and the Optional Protocol I to ICCPR of 1966, which became effective for the country since 30 of June 2009.[132] The competence of the Human Rights Committee under the OP I enables the Committee to receive and consider the individual communications of persons who are subjects of the jurisdiction of a State Party. The Committee adopts general comments, which interpret and clarify the civil and political standards envisaged in the ICCPR. So, the overall jurisprudence of the Committee is very useful in implementing the ICCPR at the country level. To date, the Committee has examined forty-one cases versus Kazakhstan.[133]

638. In 2011, the authorities of Kazakhstan were asked by the Committee not to extradite *Arshidin Israil* to China before examination of his case and formulation of the Committee's views.[134] These are interim measures that exist under OP I and are

132. International Covenant on Civil and Political Rights, adopted and opened for signature, ratification and accession by General Assembly resolution 2200A (XXI) of 16 Dec. 1966, entered into force on 23 Mar. 1976, in accordance with Art. 49. Available at: https://www.ohchr.org/en/professionalinterest/pages/ccpr.aspx (accessed 14 Feb. 2019).

133. On the acceptance of individual complaints procedures for Kazakhstan, *see*: https://tbinternet.ohchr.org/_layouts/15/TreatyBodyExternal/Countries.aspx?CountryCode=KAZ&Lang=EN (accessed 3 Aug. 2021).

134. Human Rights Committee. Communication No. 2024/2011 *Arshidin Israil v. Kazakhstan.* Views adopted by the Committee at its 103rd session, 17 Oct.–4 Nov. 2011. CCPR/C/103/D/2024/2011, available at: https://tbinternet.ohchr.org/_layouts/15/treatybodyexternal/Download.aspx?symbolno=CCPR%2fC%2f103%2fD%2f2024%2f2011&Lang=en (accessed 3 Aug. 2021).

used by the Committee before taking its final decision on the case in order to avoid irreparable harm to the victim. In the case of *Bahytzhan Toregozhina,* leader of a non-governmental organization, claims were made on violations of freedom of expression and public assembly, liberty of a person.[135] *Andrey Sviridov*, the human rights activist and journalist, submitted his complaint in February 2012, where he claimed a violation of Article 19 (freedom of expression) of the ICCPR.[136] The complaint of a citizen of Mali *Idrissa Traore* was sent to the Committee in February 2012.[137] He claimed violations of freedom of movement (Article 12 ICCPR) and the right to privacy (Article 17 ICCPR).

639. Individuals of Kazakhstan use remedies under other international legal instruments. To date, the Committee created under Article 22 of the International Convention Against Torture and other Cruel Inhuman or Degrading Treatment or Punishment has considered twelve individual complaints versus Kazakhstan. Kazakhstan recognizes the competence of the Committee on the elimination of discrimination against women created under the Optional Protocol to the Convention on the elimination of all forms of discrimination against women. In 2015, the Committee considered the complaint of *Anna Belousova* on sexual harassment in the workplace submitted in 2012.[138] Kazakhstan on 29 May 2008 recognized the competence of the Committee of elimination of racial discrimination within its jurisdiction to receive and consider communications from or on behalf of individuals versus Kazakhstan. To date, the Committee has not considered any complaint so far.

E. Rules Having Precedence When Differences Between Domestic and International Provisions Exist

640. In international law, the national State has the right to define the place of an international treaty in the hierarchy of national legal acts. Many decisions of the Constitutional Council of Kazakhstan, clarifying the status of the international treaties of the Republic, and the recent amendments to the Constitution of Kazakhstan of March 2017 prove the idea that the practice of the country with regards to the international treaties has been developing.

135. Human Rights Committee. Communication No. 2137/2012 *Bahytzhan Toregozhina* v. Kazakhstan. Views adopted by the Committee at its 112th session, 7–31 Oct. 2014 is available at: https://tbinternet.ohchr.org/_layouts/15/treatybodyexternal/Download.aspx?symbolno=CCPR%2fC%2f126%2fD%2f2416%2f2014&Lang=en (accessed 3 Aug. 2021).
136. Human Rights Committee. Communication No. 2158/2012 *Andrey Sviridov v. Kazakhstan*. Views adopted by the Committee at its 120th session, 3–28 Jul. 2017. CCPR/C/120/D/2158/2012, available at: http://ccprcentre.org/files/decisions/G1725864.pdf (accessed 28 Mar. 2019).
137. Human Rights Committee. Communication No. 2140/2012 *Idrissa Traore v. Kazakhstan*. Views adopted by the Committee at its 119th session, 6–29 Mar. 2017. CCPR/C/119/D/2140/2012, available at: http://ccprcentre.org/files/decisions/2140_2012_I_T__v__Kazakhstan.pdf (accessed 28 Mar. 2019).
138. Committee on the Elimination of Discrimination Against Women. Communication No. 45/2012. Views adopted by the Committee at its 61st session, 6–24 Jul. 2015. CEDAW/C/61/D/45/2012, available at: https://tbinternet.ohchr.org/_layouts/treatybodyexternal/Download.aspx?symbolno=CEDAW%2fC%2f61%2fD%2f45%2f2012&Lang=en (accessed 28 Mar. 2019).

641. The place of the international human rights treaty of Kazakhstan depends on the historical period of the conclusion of the treaty: before or after the adoption of the Constitution of 1995. Such conclusion stems from the Official interpretation of paragraph 3 of Article 4 of the Constitution done by the Constitutional Council on 11 October 2000. So, in line with the Decision of the Council, the international treaties that did not imply ratification by the Parliament as a condition of entering into force and concluded before the adoption of the Constitution of 1995 were considered as acting and preserve their priority before national legislation of the Republic, if such priority is directly established by laws governing relevant fields of legal relations.

642. According to Article 4(2) of the Constitution, the Constitution of Kazakhstan has the highest juridical force on its entire territory. After recent amendments of March 2017, paragraph 3 of Article 4 of the Constitution says: 'The international treaties ratified by the Republic shall have priority over its laws. The procedure and conditions of operation of international treaties on the territory of the Republic of Kazakhstan to which Kazakhstan is a party shall be determined by the legislation of the Republic.'

643. Paragraph 3 of Article 4 of the Constitution was interpreted by the Decisions of the Constitutional Council of the Republic of 11 October 2000 No. 18/2 and No. 2 of 18 May 2006.[139] Analysis of the Decision of 11 October 2000 No. 18/2 reveals that the concluded international treaty of Kazakhstan has precedence over its domestic legislation if the international treaty passed the approval of the Parliament to be bound by the treaty. In accordance with Article 1 subparagraph 16 of the Law on the Legal Acts of 6 April 2016 No. 480-V, 'legislation is the sum total of the domestic normative legal acts, passed in conformity with the established procedures'. Thereby, the provisions of the international human rights treaties that were ratified by the Republic after entering into force the Constitution of Kazakhstan of 1995 have precedence over domestic legislation, but not over the provisions of the Constitution.

644. In Kazakhstan, the official publication of the international treaty that concerns human rights, freedoms and duties is a compulsory condition of their application (Article 4(4) Constitution).

139. Normative Resolution of the Constitutional Council of the Republic of Kazakhstan of 18 May 2006 No. 2 on Official Interpretation of subparagraph 7 of Article 54 of the Constitution of the Republic of Kazakhstan available at: https://ksrk.gov.kz/kk/solutions/kazakhstan-respublikasy-konstituciyasynyn-54-babynyn-7-tarmakshasyn-resmi-tusindiru-turaly has been abolished by Normative Resolution of the Constitutional Council of 24 Sep. 2008 .

V. Equality

A. *Freedom and Equality*

645. Freedom of a human being implies the condition when one is free from unlawful interference of the State and coercion from the State, and, having free movement of the physical body, he/she is able to choose own behaviour and freely react to injustice. The Constitution of Kazakhstan recognizes liberty of person (Article 16), freedom of expression and information (Article 20), freedom of movement (Article 21), freedom of conscience (Article 22), freedom of association (Article 23), free choice of occupation and profession (Article 24), freedom of assembly (Article 32), etc.

646. The principle of equality of all persons before the law implies that state officials in enforcing human rights provisions must 'refrain from arbitrary conduct in the execution of their duties'.[140] Equal protection before the law requires that the State refrains from adopting laws discriminating against persons on different grounds. Discrimination on any ground is prohibited by the UN Charter (Article 1(3)), UDHR (Article 2), ICESCR and by a number of other international documents.

B. *Protection of Equality and Non-discrimination in Kazakhstan*

647. Equality implies that all persons are entitled without any discrimination to the equal protection of the law. In this respect, the law shall prohibit any discrimination and must guarantee to all persons equal and effective protection against discrimination on any ground, such as race, colour, sex, language, religion, political or other opinions, national or social origin, property, birth or other statuses.

648. Article 14 of the Constitution proclaims that all are equal before the law and court. No one shall be subjected to any kind of discrimination on the grounds of origin, social, official and wealth status, sex, race, ethnicity, language, religious belief, opinion, place of residence or any other circumstances.

649. These constitutional principles are elaborated in the Codes of Kazakhstan. Thus, the Civil Procedure Code contains Article 13 affirming the equality of everyone before the law and the courts, and stating that no one should be discriminated against. According to Article 21 of the Penal Procedure Code, justice in Kazakhstan is based on the principle of equality of everyone before the law and the court, and no one should be subject to discrimination. Moreover, the Penal Code contains punishments for violations of the equality of citizens, including those on the basis of sex in Article 145. As has been seen, the Constitution and the Codes contain the principles of equality before the law and prohibition of discrimination.

---

140. Scott N. Carlson & Gregory Gisvold, *Practical Guide to the International Covenant on Civil and Political Rights* 157 (2003).

650. One of the new steps after the ratification of the ICCPR was the adoption in 2009 of Law on State Guarantees for Equal Rights and Equal Opportunities for Men and Women.[141] The adopted Law prohibits gender discrimination and promotes gender equality. Men and women are guaranteed equal enjoyment of civil, political, economic, social, cultural and other rights. According to the Law, different treatments to protect motherhood, childhood and fatherhood cannot be considered discriminatory (Article 4).

§2. Civil and Political Rights

I. Sources

651. In international human rights law, civil rights 'guarantee the liberal freedom of the individual "from the State" and political rights guarantee the democratic freedom of access "to the State"'.[142] The Constitution of Kazakhstan envisages certain civil and political rights. Kazakhstan is a State Party to the ICCPR and the OP I to it. Another source is the Convention Against Torture and other Cruel, Inhuman or Degrading Treatment or Punishment that became effective for the country on 26 August 1998.[143] Kazakhstan as a Party to the Vienna Convention on the Law of Treaties 1969 is required to follow the principle *pacta sunt servanda*, which stipulates that 'every treaty in force is binding upon the parties to it and must be performed in good faith' (Article 26).[144]

652. The ICCPR codifies minimum universal standards on civil and political rights for countries with different political, social and legal cultures. As stipulated in the ICCPR, a State Party undertakes to ensure to all individuals within its territory and subject to its jurisdiction the rights recognized in the Covenant and to adopt laws or other measures to give effect to these rights. The ICCPR requires each State Party to ensure an effective remedy to any person whose rights or freedoms recognized in the Covenant are violated (Article 2).

653. Ratification of the ICCPR brought to making amendments to the Constitution of the Republic. So, after the amendments, the Constitution allows the arrest and detainment of persons only with the sanction of a court (Article 16(2)). Prior to these amendments, the legal prosecutor alongside a court had the right to sanction

141. Law of Kazakhstan of 8 Dec. 2009 on State Guarantees for Equal Rights and Equal Opportunities for Men and Women', available at: https://online.zakon.kz/Document/?doc_id=30526983#pos=2;-245 (accessed 3 Aug. 2021).
142. Manfred Nowak, *UN Covenant on Civil and Political Rights. CCPR Commentary* XX (2nd edn, 2005).
143. Convention against Torture and Other Cruel, Inhuman or Degrading Treatment or Punishment, Adopted and Opened for Signature, Ratification and Accession by the General Assembly Resolution 39/46 of 10 Dec. 1984, entered into force on 26 Jun. 1987, in accordance with Art. 27(1), available at: http://www2.ohchr.org/english/law/cat.htm; https://treaties.un.org/pages/ViewDetails.aspx?src=IND&mtdsg_no=IV-9&chapter=4&lang=en (accessed 29 Mar. 2019).
144. Vienna Convention on the Law of Treaties 1969, done at Vienna 1969, entered into force on 27 Jan. 1980. United Nations, Treaty Series, vol. 1155, at 331.

arrest and detention. The changes to the constitutional provisions were implemented to follow the provisions of Article 9(3) of the ICCPR. Other amendments were made to the provisions of the Constitution regarding the right to life. The death penalty is now applicable only to a limited number of crimes, such as terrorist crimes, which have resulted in death casualties, and especially grave crimes, committed in wartime (Article 15). Changes to the Penal Code of Kazakhstan concerning the definition of torture specified that instigation, consent or acquiescence in torture by public officials also constitutes the act of torture (Article 141-1 Penal Code of Kazakhstan of 16 July 1997, Article 146 of the current Penal Code). In January 2011, Kazakhstan introduced a new provision to Article 532(1.5) of the Penal Procedure Code of 1997 acting that time. The provision prohibited extradition of a person to another country where there are substantial grounds for believing that he would be in danger of being subjected to torture and other cruel, inhuman or degrading treatment or punishment. Currently, the new Penal Procedure Code of 2014 reflected the principle of *non-refoulement* in Article 590(1.7).

II. Individual Integrity, Liberty and Security

A. The Right to Life and Individual Integrity

654. The right to life is fundamental, inherent, basic to all human rights and supreme in nature, which is non-derogable. The issues of the right to give life, and the protection of life before birth, i.e., where life begins and ends, are not clear in the international legal system. Protection of life after birth consists of three components. The authorities may not intentionally kill; they must protect individual lives against attacks by others and must create conditions for the protection of life, as well as environmental, health and housing conditions favourable to the protection of life.[145]

655. In international practice, the right to life is interpreted in a wide sense and also implies the prohibition of arbitrary deprivation of life, including that by the state security forces. The national law must control and limit the circumstances of deprivation of life by state authorities. In the use of firearms, the public authorities should observe the principle of proportionality between defence and attack. Authorities should adopt effective measures to prevent the disappearance of individuals, which often leads to the arbitrary deprivation of life.

656. International treaty bodies recommend the abolition of the death penalty and the limitation of its application to the most serious crimes. Anyone sentenced to death shall have the right to seek pardon or commutation of the sentence. Amnesty,

145. Bertrand Mathieu, *The Right to Life in European Constitutional and International Case-Law* 44, 95 (Council of Europe publishing, Apr. 2006).

pardon or commutation of the sentence of death may be granted in all cases. According to the international requirements, a sentence of death shall not be imposed for crimes committed by persons below 18 years of age and shall not be carried out on pregnant women.

657. According to the interpretation of the Human Rights Committee, the right to life implies also reducing infant mortality and increasing life expectancy, elimination of malnutrition and epidemics, as well as creation.

658. The Committee considers that the prevention of war, acts of genocide and other acts of mass violence causing arbitrary loss of life, guarantees and safeguards the right to life.[146] The prevention of wars is the supreme duty of the States.[147] The treaty body raised concern on increasing weapons of mass destruction, and expressed the opinion that 'the production, testing, possession, deployment and use of nuclear weapons should be prohibited and recognized as crimes against humanity'.[148] States should take urgent steps to get rid of such weapons.

659. The right to life in the practice of Kazakhstan is recognized by national legislation and is guaranteed from birth onwards. According to Article 15 of the Kazakhstani Constitution, all shall have the right to life; no one shall have the right to arbitrarily deprive life of another person. The right not to be deprived of life is also covered by the Penal Code of the Republic, which contains many articles prohibiting causing the death of anyone. It criminalizes homicide and its different types, such as the murder of a newborn baby by its mother, murder in the heat of passion and in the cases of self-defence, causing death by negligence, abetment to suicide and other means, as well as prohibiting genocide, production and proliferation of weapons of mass destruction, planning, preparation, initiation or waging of a war of aggression. All these actions bear criminal punishments.

660. The death penalty in Kazakhstan can only be carried out for the most serious crimes.[149] According to the Constitution of Kazakhstan, 'the death penalty shall be established by law as an exceptional punishment for terrorist crimes which have

146. UN Human Rights Committee (HRC), CCPR General Comment No. 6: Article 6 (Right to Life), 30 Apr. 1982, available at: https://www.refworld.org/docid/45388400a.html (accessed 1 Apr. 2019).
147. UN Human Rights Committee (HRC), CCPR General Comment No. 14: Article 6 (Right to Life) Nuclear Weapons and the Right to Life, 9 Nov. 1984, available at: https://www.refworld.org/docid/453883f911.html (accessed 1 Apr. 2019).
148. *Ibid.*
149. The explanation of the most serious crimes is given in Normative Resolution of the Constitutional Council of 30 Jan. 2003 No. 10 on Official Interpretation of paragraph 4 of Article 52, paragraph 5 of Article 71, paragraph 2 of Article 79, paragraph 3 of Article 83 and paragraph 2 of Article 15 of the Constitution of the Republic of Kazakhstan, available at: https://ksrk.gov.kz/index.php/kk/solutions/kazakhstan-respublikasy-konstituciyasynyn-52-baby-4-tarmagyn-71-baby-5-tarmagyn-79-baby-2 (accessed 3 Aug. 2021).

resulted in death casualties, and also for especially grave crimes, committed in wartime while granting a sentenced person the right to appeal for pardon'. These amendments were made by Law of 21 May 2007 No. 254-111 Amending the Constitution of Kazakhstan.

661. On 23 September 2020 Kazakhstan signed the Second Optional Protocol to the ICCPR, Aiming at the Abolition of the death penalty of 15 December 1989.[150] The signing was done by Kazakhstan's Permanent Representative to the UN Kairat Umarov. According to the commentary on the question published by the MFA of Kazakhstan, in the course of ratification, the country has the right to make reservations.[151]

662. The death penalty is regulated by the Penal Code, the Penitentiary Code and by the Penal Procedure Code. For instance, they are Articles 52, 402, 631, 656 of the Penal Procedure Code, Article 47 of the Penal Code, and Part V of the Penitentiary Code. Shooting has been established for the execution of the death penalty.

663. The national legislation of Kazakhstan grants a sentenced person the right to appeal for pardon. According to Article 47(5) of the Penal Code of Kazakhstan, the death penalty may be replaced by life imprisonment or imprisonment for a certain period of time.

664. A convicted person has a right to a petition for pardon to the Commission on Clemency under the President. The Commission was established by the Decree of the President on 7 May 1996. Currently, its activity is regulated by the Regulations approved by the Decree of the President of 5 July 2006 No. 140.[152] The decision on clemency is taken by the President; the Commission is an advisory body to the President and reviews the materials of the case. The Commission takes into consideration the level of gravity of the crime, the personality and behaviour of the convicted, the family conditions, the opinions of official bodies of the penitentiary system and labour collective, opinions of the Chair of the Supreme Court, the General Prosecutor and the MIA, and other factors and circumstances. It studies other relevant circumstances and factors. The Commission has a right to commute the death penalty to life imprisonment or imprisonment for a certain period of time, to commute life imprisonment to imprisonment for a certain period of time, to release

---

150. Second Optional Protocol to the ICCPR, Aiming at the Abolition of the Death Penalty, Adopted by General Assembly Resolution 44/1281 of 15 Dec. 1989, entered into force on 11 Jul. 1991. Available at: https://treaties.un.org/Pages/ViewDetails.aspx?src=TREATY&mtdsg_no=IV-12&chapter=4&clang=_en (accessed on 3 Oct. 2020).
151. Commentary of the Press Service of the MFA on Kazakhstan's Accession to the Second Optional Protocol to the ICCPR of 26 Sep. 2020. Available at: https://www.gov.kz/memleket/entities/mfa/press/news/details/kommentariy-press-sluzhby-mid-rk-o-prisoedinenii-kazahstana-ko-vtoromu-fakultativnomu-protokolu-k-mezhdunarodnomu-paktu-o-grazhdanskih-i-politicheskih-pravah?lang=ru (accessed on 3 Oct. 2020).
152. Decree of the President of Kazakhstan of 5 Jul. 2006 No. 140 on the Commission on Clemency at the President of Kazakhstan. Available at: https://adilet.zan.kz/rus/docs/U060000140_(accessed 3 Aug. 2021).

the prisoner or reduce the period of sentence, replace imposed sentence with more lenient punishment, release from additional punishment, or withdraw the conviction.

665. The international standards prohibit the imposition of the death penalty on persons below 18 years of age and to pregnant women. Kazakhstan's national law goes further, and prohibits the imposition of the death penalty on women, on persons below 18 years of age, and on men who at the time of adjudication have attained 63 years of age and over (Article 47 Penal Code). On 20 July 2009, amendments to the Penal Code of the Republic changed the penalty for certain crimes from capital punishment to life imprisonment.

666. The President of the country has a right to impose a moratorium on the execution of the death penalty (Article 47(3) Penal Code). The moratorium on the death penalty until its full abolition came into force on 1 January 2004, by the Decree of the President.[153] By the time of the adoption of the Decree on the moratorium on the execution of the death penalty, 500 sentences had been executed.[154] The Inter-agency Commission was established by the Resolution on 19 July 2006 to work on the examination of questions related to the abolition of the death penalty.[155]

667. Kazakhstan, a State located at the juncture of different civilizations, plays a significant role in guaranteeing regional and global security. The country made a significant contribution to the non-proliferation of weapons of mass destruction. Kazakhstan's closing of the Semipalatinsk nuclear polygon was the first example in the world history of such a voluntary closure and was a decision of exceptional importance for the whole world community.

668. In the area of treaty lawmaking, Kazakhstan has signed such treaties as Nuclear Non-Proliferation Treaty, Treaty for the Complete Prohibition and Total Destruction of Nuclear Weapons, the Hague Code of Conduct Against Ballistic Missile Proliferation, the Krakow Initiative Aimed at the Detection and Prevention of Illegal Circulation of Weapons of Mass Destruction and the Supply of their Sources, etc. Over a period of nine years, a Treaty on the Creation of a Zone Free from Nuclear Weapons in Central Asia has been drafted with UN cooperation. At the Second Summit Conference on Interaction and Confidence Building Measures in Asia, the Member States also supported the promotion of the initiative to sign this treaty. According to it, the production and purchase of nuclear weapons on the territories

153. Decree of the President of Kazakhstan of 17 Dec. 2003 No. 1251 on Introducing the Moratorium for the Capital Punishment. Available at: http://adilet.zan.kz/rus/docs/U030001251_(accessed 1 Apr. 2019).
154. Kanat Seydgaparov, *Modernizaziya ugolovnogo processa: pervye rezultaty/Modernisation of the penal proceedings: the first results.* Newspaper 'Kazakhstanskaya Pravda' of 27 Sep. 2018.
155. Regulations on Creation of the Commission for Studying the Abolition of the Death Penalty in the Republic of Kazakhstan, Approved by the Resolution of the Government of Kazakhstan of 19 Jul. 2006 No. 687. Available at: https://tengrinews.kz/zakon/pravitelstvo_respubliki_kazahstan_premer_ministr_rk/sudoppoizvodstvo/id-P060000687_/ (accessed 1 Apr. 2019). Ceased in force.

of State Parties are prohibited; the exception is the use of nuclear energy for peaceful purposes. Thus, the Treaty on Creation of the Zone Free from Nuclear Weapons in Central Asia was signed on 8 September 2006 in Semipalatinsk between Kazakhstan, Kyrgyzstan, Uzbekistan, Tajikistan and Turkmenistan. Today, Kazakhstan cooperates with the International Atomic Energy Agency, and carries out its nuclear activity under the control of this organization, as a member of the Multilateral Organization Disarmament Conference.

669. On 3 July 2019, the Law on Ratification on the Treaty Prohibiting Nuclear Weapons had been signed by the President of Kazakhstan Kassym-Jomart Tokayev.[156]

B. The Right to Liberty and Security of Person

670. As explained by Manfred Nowak, liberty of person relates to liberty of bodily movement and freedom from 'the forceful detention of a person at a certain, narrowly bounded location'.[157] The jurisprudence of the Human Rights Committee elaborates an understanding of the arbitrariness of deprivation of liberty and says that the grounds and procedures for detention should be established by law, not by the administrative act. The right to liberty also implies that the arrested person should be informed about the reason for arrest, the court should control the legality of the arrest, and the victims should receive compensation for wrongful arrest. In the case of *Van Alphen v. the Netherlands*, Communication No. 305/1988 (18 August 1990),[158] the Human Rights Committee explained that the term 'arbitrariness' includes 'elements of inappropriateness, injustice and lack of predictability' and the detention should be not only lawful but also reasonable and necessary. This idea was repeated in *A. v. Australia.*[159] Preventive detention of suspected terrorists and prolonged detention of persons without proper justification, enforced disappearance and incommunicado detention are considered arbitrary detention according to the jurisprudence of the Committee.[160]

671. The Constitution of Kazakhstan guarantees the right to personal freedom. Arrest and detention shall be allowed only in cases stipulated in law with the right to appeal of an arrested person (Article 16 Constitution). According to Article 14 of the Penal Procedure Code, the grounds and procedure of arrest of the person are

156. *Head of State signed the Law on Ratification of the Treaty Prohibiting the Nuclear Weapons*. Available at: http://www.akorda.kz/ru/legal_acts/laws/glavoi-gosudarstva-podpisan-zakon-respubliki-kazahstan-o-ratifikacii-dogovora-o-zapreshchenii-yadernogo-oruzhiya (accessed 4 Jul. 2019).
157. Nowak, *supra* n. 142, at 212.
158. *Hugo van Alphen v. The Netherlands*, Communication No. 305/1988, U.N. Doc. CCPR/C/39/D/305/1988 (1990), available at: https://www.refworld.org/cases,HRC,525414304.html (accessed 1 Apr. 2019).
159. *A. v. Australia, Communication No 560/1993: Australia. 04/30/1997. CCPR/C/59/D/560/1993. (Jurisprudence)*, para. 7.6, available at: http://hrlibrary.umn.edu/undocs/html/vws560.html (accessed 1 Apr. 2019).
160. Nowak, *supra* n. 142, at 226–227.

regulated by the Code. The court and prosecuting authorities, head of administration of the detention place, of the medical organization are obliged to release immediately illegally detained and arrested persons, or those unlawfully placed in medical institutes, and persons held in custody for more than the period limited by law or judgment (Article 14(4) Penal Procedure Code). The procedural actions violating the inviolability of the person can be only in accordance with the rules of the Code (Article 14(6)).

672. In line with the Penal Procedure Code of Kazakhstan, the arrested person should be immediately informed about the reasons for arrest and the charges against him (Article 14(3)).

673. According to Kazakhstan law, the authorities are not permitted to detain a person for more than forty-eight hours without the sanction of the court. It is substantial progress in the development of the national human rights law of Kazakhstan. The Human Rights Committee, in its jurisprudence, expressed displeasure that detention of seventy-two hours before bringing to a judge is too long in some countries.[161]

674. Before the amendments to the Constitution of Kazakhstan of 21 May 2007, the prosecutor was also allowed to give permission for arrest. After the amendments to the Constitution, arrest and detention are allowed only with the sanction of a court. The Code repeats the provisions of the Constitution concerning the competence of the court to authorize the arrest. In addition, only a court has a right to place a person without his/her will under forensic psychiatric examination. Only a court can authorize (i.e., approve the decision of the investigator or prosecutor) arrest and house arrest, and extend their periods (Article 53(2(5)). As a general rule, detention as a measure of restraint can be applied with court sanction to crimes with the punishment of imprisonment for more than five years if other less severe measures of restrictions cannot be applied (Article 147 Penal Procedure Code).

675. Article 148 of the Penal Procedure Code regulates sanctioning by the judge the approval of detention. In taking the decision to approve detention, the judge should examine the materials of the case that are important in defining the measure and check justifiability of suspicion in committing a crime. The explanatory Resolution of the Supreme Court of Kazakhstan of 10 July 2008 on the Application of

161. The case of Uzbekistan, *see*: Human Rights Committee, *Concluding Observations: Uzbekistan*, 26 Apr. 2001, CCPR/CO/71/UZB, para. 12, available at: https://www.refworld.org/docid/3be121224 .html (accessed on 1 Apr. 2019); Human Rights Committee, *Concluding Observations: Uzbekistan*, 20 Jul. 2015, para. 15, available at: http://ccprcentre.org/country/uzbekistan (accessed 1 Apr. 201 9). Please *see also* case of Ukraine: Human Rights Committee, *Concluding Observations: Ukraine*, 12 Nov. 2001, CCPR/CO/73/UKR, para. 17, available at: https://tbinternet.ohchr.org/_layouts/ treatybodyexternal/Download.aspx?symbolno=CCPR%2FCO%2F73%2FUKR&Lang=ru (accessed 1 Apr. 2019).

International Treaties' Norms of the Republic of Kazakhstan confirmed that in cases of authorization of arrest, the decision should be based on the justifiability and legality of the measure of restraint.[162]

676. The person acquitted by the court, as well as the suspect, the accused and the defendant towards whom the criminal case had been terminated, shall have the right to rehabilitation and compensation. Chapter 4 of the Penal Procedure Code regulates such issues. The harm caused by unlawful detention should be fully compensated by the national budget (Article 38(1)).

III. Intellectual Freedoms

A. *Freedom of Expression*

677. The right to freedom of expression is very important for the development of the individual as a liberal human being wished to realize his/her potential, skills and express him/herself. Freedom of expression helps the public to weigh the actions of the authorities and to express the views how far the actions of the authorities are transparent and accountable. This freedom is essential for the enjoyment of other civil and political rights and the promotion of human rights in general. For instance, the freedom of expression is vital for 'the valid exercise of electoral rights and democratic participation guaranteed under article 25'.[163]

678. In international human rights law freedom of expression is envisaged in Article 19 of the ICCPR and this right belongs to everyone and 'shall include freedom to seek, receive and impart information and ideas of all kinds, regardless of frontiers, either orally, in writing or in print, in the form of art, or through any other media of his choice'.

679. There is General Comment No. 34 adopted by the Human Rights Committee in 2011 in its 102nd session.[164] They accumulate jurisprudence of the Committee and serve as guidelines in the interpretation of freedom of expression in the international human rights system. According to General Comment No. 34, freedom of expression is realized via 'political discourse, commentary on one's own and on public affairs, canvassing, discussion of human rights, journalism, cultural and artistic expression, teaching and religious discourse', commercial advertising using spoken, written and sign languages. The information may be disseminated through

162. Normative Resolution of the Supreme Court of Kazakhstan of 10 Jul. 2008 No. 1 on the Application of International Treaties' Norms of the Republic of Kazakhstan. Available at: http://www.zakon.kz/117905-normativnoe-postanovlenie-verkhovnogo.html (accessed 26 Feb. 2019).

163. Alex Conte & Richard Burchill, *Defining Civil and Political Rights. The Jurisprudence of the United Nations Human Rights Committee,* 85 (2nd edn, 2009).

164. UN Human Rights Committee, General Comment No. 34: Article 19 (Freedom of opinion and expression), 12 Sep. 2011, CCPR/C/GC/34, available at: http://www2.ohchr.org/english/bodies/hrc/docs/gc34.pdf (accessed on 2 Apr. 2019).

books, newspapers, pamphlets, posters, banners, dress and legal submissions in audiovisual forms, electronic and internet-based (paragraphs 11–12 General Comment No. 34).

680. Freedom of expression implies the independence of the media that provides free dissemination of information and discussion on public and political matters, playing a significant role in the exchange of information, the development of pluralism and democratic society.

681. This freedom also implies the right of access to information (records, source and the date of production) held by public bodies (governmental authorities and other bodies with public functions). With regard to the issues on protection of privacy, according to the General Comment, the right of access to information implies that every individual should have the right to know and be sure 'in intelligible form, whether, and if so, what personal data is stored in automatic data files, and for what purposes', 'which public authorities or private individuals or bodies control or may control his or her files', and rectify his or her records (paragraph 18 General Comment No. 34).

682. There could be restrictions to freedom of expression, that should be established by law, reasonable and justified to safeguard the reputation of others and protect national security and public order. The limitations must be proportional to possible negative danger.

683. According to Article 20 of the Constitution, Kazakhstan guarantees freedom of speech and creativity. Censorship is prohibited. Everyone has a right to receive freely and disseminate information by any means not prohibited by law. The list of information constituting state secrets of the Republic shall be determined by Law. Propaganda concerning or agitation for the forcible change of the constitutional system, violation of the integrity of the Republic, undermining of state security, and advocating war, social, or racial, national, religious and clannish superiority, as well as the cult of cruelty and violence shall not be allowed. As given in Article 18(3) of the Constitution of Kazakhstan, state bodies, public associations, officials, and the mass media must provide every citizen with the possibility of obtaining access to documents, decisions and other sources of information concerning his rights and interests.

684. As given in the official interpretation of the Constitutional Council of 18 May 2015 No. 3 of Article 20 of the Constitution, the realization of the right of access to information and its dissemination shall be within the limits and procedures established by the laws, and to the extent necessary for the protection of the constitutional and public order, rights and freedoms of a human being, the health and morality of the population.[165] As given in the Resolution of the Constitutional Council, a legislator, while adopting the laws, is obliged to take into account the

165. Normative Resolutions of the Constitutional Council of the Republic of Kazakhstan of 18 May 2015 No. 3 on the Official Interpretation of paragraph 1 of Article 27 of the Constitution of the

limitations to the rights and freedoms of individuals and citizens permissible by the Constitution without distorting the essence of their constitutional rights and freedoms and without imposing restrictions which are not in conformity with constitutional goals. Such legal reasoning of the Constitutional Council is in line with the provisions of international legal acts.

685. The Constitutional Council stated that a number of its Resolutions (No. 2 of 27 February 2008, No. 1 of 11 February 2009, No. 5 of 7 December 2011, No. 2 of 11 June 2014, and others) confirmed that the laws restricting the constitutional rights and freedoms of individuals and citizens should comply with the requirements of legal certainty and predictability of consequences in order to be able to distinguish legal actions from illegal and to exclude arbitrary interpretation of the provisions of law. Semantic ambiguity distorts the content of a legal norm causing the impossibility of its clear understanding, and this, in accordance with Article 7 of the Constitution, may exclude the application of such norm in its practice. As the Constitutional Council mentioned, legal clarity, certainty and predictability of consequences stem from Article 14 of the Constitution of Kazakhstan that envisages equality of everyone before the law and court.

686. Because of other reasons and the lack of clarity of some provisions concerning limitations of rights and freedoms, the Constitutional Council of Kazakhstan with the Resolution of 18 May 2015 No. 3 recognized the Laws on the Protection of Children's Health and Development from Harmful Information and on Introducing Amendments and Addenda to Some Legislative acts of the Republic of Kazakhstan on the Issues Concerning the Protection of Children's Health and Development from Harmful Information of 19 February 2015 as being unconstitutional.

687. In 2015, Kazakhstan adopted the Law on Access to Information.[166] Such Law has never existed before in Kazakhstan. Article 4 of the Law establishes such principles as lawfulness, openness and transparency of the activities of owners of information, truthfulness and completeness of information, up-to-dateness and timeliness, equality in access to information, non-disclosure of state secrets and other privities protected by law, personal and family privacy, respect for the rights and legal interests of individuals and legal entities as the main principles in ensuring access to information. Illegal restrictions to access to information can be appealed according to the requirements of the laws of Kazakhstan (Article 18(1) Law on Access to Information).

688. According to Article 7 of Law on Access to Information, the user of information has the rights:

Republic of Kazakhstan and Review for the Compliance of the Law of Kazakhstan on the Protection of Children's Health and Development from Harmful Information to the Constitution of the Republic. Available at: https://ksrk.gov.kz/kk/solutions/kr-konstituciyasynyn-27-babynyn-1-tarmagyn-resmi-tusindiru-zhne-balalardy-densaulygyna (accessed 3 Aug. 2021).

166. Law of the Republic of Kazakhstan of 16 Nov. 2015 No. 401-V ZRK on Access to Information. Available at: https://online.zakon.kz/Document/?doc_id=39415981 (accessed 3 Aug. 2021).

(1) to receive and disseminate information by any legal means;
(2) to request information;
(3) to verify the accuracy and completeness of received information;
(4) to withdraw the request;
(5) not to justify the need for information;
(6) to appeal illegal restrictions to access to information, actions (inactions) of officials;
(7) to demand in a manner established by law compensation to material and moral damages caused by a violation of his/her right of access to information.

689. According to Article 9 of Law on Access to Information, an owner of the information has the following duties:

(1) to ensure access to information;
(2) within its authority to ensure organizational, technical and other conditions necessary to provide access to information;
(3) to provide true and complete information;
(4) to ensure that provided information contains sufficient information about an official enough for verification;
(5) to ensure observance of deadlines for the provision of information that are established by law;
(6) to keep records, summarize and analyse information;
(7) to create necessary conditions when providing information to disabled people;
(8) to provide smooth operation of internet resources that contain information;
(9) to ensure training for officials and employees in the field of access to information;
(10) to conduct internal control over the quality and timing of provision of information;
(11) to observe the national legislation on state secrets and other secrets protected by law;
(12) to place information on internet resources that are open for the public;
(13) to carry out other duties envisaged by the Law on information and legislation of the Republic.

B. Freedom of Assembly and of Association

690. Freedom of assembly is strongly related to freedom of expression and freedom of association. This freedom implies only peaceful assembly, i.e., assembly without violence. The assembly can be broken up by state authorities only if it is the last way to protect public safety and order. According to the international human rights standards, the State is obliged to protect the peacefulness of assembly from interference and 'prevent a peaceful assembly from leading to riots due to provocation or use of force by security forces or by private parties (individual extremists, counter-demonstrators or "agents provocateurs"'.[167]

691. Freedom of assembly has specific restrictions, which make its scope of protection narrow in comparison with other related rights. The restrictions to the enjoyment of this freedom must not be necessarily established by law and may be imposed by administrative authorities. The restrictions must be necessary for a democratic society and are intended:

(1) to protect national security in cases of serious political or military threat to the entire nation;
(2) to provide public safety (e.g., physical safety and the lives of demonstrators or passers-by, the safety of businesses and their property);
(3) to maintain public order;
(4) to protect public health or morals (i.e., the assembly may be prohibited in a sacred or natural-conservation area);
(5) to protect the rights and freedoms of others (i.e., protection of the private property of others, or the rights of passers-by in public places).

692. Article 32 of the Constitution of Kazakhstan guarantees that citizens of the Republic shall have the right to peacefully and without arms assemble, hold meetings, rallies and demonstrations, street processions and pickets. As we see from the wording of the Constitution, freedom of assembly concerns the realization of democratic values.

693. Article 32 of the Constitution asserts that the use of this right may be restricted by law in the interests of state security, public order, and the protection of the health, rights and freedoms of other persons. As we see from the wording of the Constitution, limitations of this right may be prescribed by law. The restrictions to freedom of assembly enumerated in the Constitution are in conformity with the ICCPR standards. Moreover, Kazakhstan's Constitution has stricter requirements for the legal basis of imposition of limitations than the ICCPR. Additional rules regulating the procedures and order of conducting a gathering (demonstrations) can be adopted by the local state office (Article 10).

694. The provisions of the Constitution are elaborated in the ordinary legislative acts. The first generation of legislation of Kazakhstan on the issue was the Law of Kazakhstan of 17 March 1995 on the Procedures for Organizing and Conducting Peaceful Assemblies, meetings, Rallies, Pickets and Demonstrations in Kazakhstan.[168] In the Law on assembly, the understanding of assembly included hunger

167. Nowak, *supra* n. 142, at 487.
168. Law of Kazakhstan of 17 Mar. 1995 No. 2126 on the Procedures for Organizing and Conducting Peaceful Assemblies, Meetings, Rallies, Pickets and Demonstrations in the Republic of Kazakhstan. Available at: http://adilet.zan.kz/rus/docs/U950002126_ (accessed 3 Apr. 2019). Ceased in force.

strikes in public areas, pickets, construction of *yurts* (Kazakh national houses), tents and other facilities and picketing as well (Article 1).

695. According to that Law, the freedom of assembly in Kazakhstan was based on obtaining permission from relevant state bodies (offices). To organize an assembly, Article 2 of the law required the submission of an application to local state bodies (offices), requesting them to permit the holding of an assembly. The application should have been submitted ten days before the planned date of assembly. The statement requesting permission should have contained detailed information about the event and its organizers. Five days before the planned date was required for the local state bodies (offices) to give their response. The local authorities had the right to offer another place and time for assembly, if it was necessary, to protect the rights and freedoms of others, or for public safety and other reasons.

696. The Law of 1995 was replaced by the Law on the Procedure for Organizing and Conducting Peaceful Assemblies.[169] The Law is based on the principle of notification to local state bodies on conducting peaceful assembly. According to the Law, peaceful assembly means a public event that is peaceful, non-violent and unarmed, which does not create a threat to the interests of state security, public order, health protection, the protection of morality of the population, the rights and freedoms of others held in the form of an assembly, protest and demonstration, rally and pickets by the citizens.

697. According to Article 2(2), the right to peaceful assembly cannot be restricted. Restrictions must be done only for the purposes of state security, public order, protection of health, human rights and freedoms of others. As given in Article 5(3) of the Law, the organizers of the assembly must refrain from inciting violations of the Constitution, laws and other normative acts of Kazakhstan, mass riots, incitements to social, racial, national, religious, class and tribal hatred, publicly call for the seizure of power, violent change of the constitutional system of Kazakhstan.

698. As given in Article 10(1) of the Law, in order to organize a peaceful assembly should be submitted a notification to the local executive body in writing or electronically five days before the planned date of assembly. Such notification should be registered by the local executive body. Notification should contain full information about an assembly and its organizers. According to Article 11(1), the local executive body should consider it within three days.

699. Freedom of association refers to civil (protecting from State and third party's arbitrary interference) and political rights (entails the guarantee to participate in public affairs through unions). Freedom of association, as interpreted by Manfred

---

169. Law of Kazakhstan of 25 May 2020 No. 333-VI RK on the Procedures for Organizing and Conducting Peaceful Assemblies. Available at: https://online.zakon.kz/document/?doc_id=36271780#pos=334;-59 (3 Aug. 2021).

Nowak, is 'a right of the individual to found an association with like-minded persons or to join an existing association'.[170] The associations can be varied, and unite different kinds of interests like scientific, religious, political, social, commercial and other characteristics. The creation, and being a member of the association, must be free-willed and no one must be forced to be a part of the association. Everyone has a right to choose whether to belong to the organization and be able to leave the association whenever he/she wants. According to international human rights standards, the State is obliged to provide legal provision for it, and to prevent the violation of its rights by third parties.

700. Kazakhstan is a party to the ILO Convention No. 87 on freedom of association and protection of the right to organize of 1948, and the Republic guarantees freedom of association in the Constitution. According to Article 23 of the Constitution of Kazakhstan, citizens shall have the right to the freedom of forming associations. The activities of public associations shall be regulated by law. The Constitution recognizes the ideological and political diversity and the equality of all public associations. Illegal interference of the State in the affairs of public associations and of public associations in the affairs of the State, imposing the functions of state institutions on public associations shall not be permitted (Article 5(1, 2)).

701. These constitutional provisions are elaborated in the legislative acts. The Civil Code of the Republic in Chapter 7 establishes the basic legislative framework for the activities of the associations. It recognizes along with other associations, public (Article 106 Civil Code) and religious associations (Article 109 Civil Code), and associations of entrepreneurs (Article 110 Civil Code).[171] Public associations are the political parties, trade and other unions of citizens, created voluntarily to achieve common purposes, not contrary to law.

702. The special Law regulates the creation and activities of the public associations in Kazakhstan.[172] The preamble to the Law declares that the right to freedom of associations is under the protection of the State. The State provides for the observance of the rights and legal interests of public associations (Article 4 Law on Public Associations). The Law demands the registration of the public association. As per Article 10, the functionality of public associations needs authorization by state offices. To be registered there should be a certain number of people who initiates the creation of the association.

703. Since the gaining of independence, there have been many NGOs (national and international) working in Kazakhstan. With reference to national legislation, NGO means non-commercial organization (excluding political parties, professional

170. Nowak, *supra* n. 142, at 498.

171. Civil Code of the Republic of Kazakhstan (General Part) adopted on 27 Dec. 1994. Available at: https://online.zakon.kz/document/?doc_id=1006061 (accessed 5 Apr. 2019).

172. Law of Kazakhstan of 31 May 1996 No. 3 on Public Associations. Available at: http://adilet.zan.kz/rus/docs/Z960000003_ (accessed 5 Apr. 2019).

unions and religious organizations) created voluntarily by individuals and/or by non-governmental legal persons to achieve certain goals in accordance with the national legislation.[173]

704. The Government of Kazakhstan has, since 2003, once every two years held a national Civic forum to discuss the problems of civil society. Since 2005, the Government has been financing different projects and programmes to solve social problems through NGOs. These projects cover education, science, sport, the health of citizens, ecology, gender problems and other important issues. The 9th Civic Forum 'Society and a State: 30 years of Partnership and Development "*Birgemiz*"' was held in November 2020.[174]

705. Limitations in exercising the freedom of association. According to international human rights standards, the imitations of the freedom under consideration must be prescribed by law and which are necessary in a democratic society in the interests of national security or public safety, public order (*ordre public*), the protection of public health or morals or the protection of the rights and freedoms of others. To maintain public order, the government may require associations to notify authorities about their formation or may require official registration with the authorities or obtaining other permission. Special restrictions on members of the armed forces and of the police are allowed, and they must be clearly prescribed by law.

706. The creation and activity of public associations pursuing the goals, or promoting actions toward a violent change of the constitutional system, in violation of the integrity of the Republic, undermining the security of the State, inciting social, racial, national, religious, class and tribal enmity, as well as the creation of not envisaged by the legislation of paramilitary unit, shall be prohibited (Article 5(3) Constitution).

707. Because the creation of political parties within the state bodies is prohibited by Article 5 of the Constitution of the Republic, the military, employees of national security or law-enforcement bodies, and judges must abstain from membership in political parties, trade unions, and actions in support of any political party (Article 23(2) Constitution and Article 11 Law on Public Associations). Civilians working in law-enforcement agencies do have a right to freedom of association (in accordance with ILO Convention No. 87 on Freedom of Association and Protection of the Right to Organize of 1948).

708. All public associations in Kazakhstan must be registered with the authorities. The Law on public associations prohibits the creation and activity of extremist and illegal paramilitary associations. The establishment of paramilitary forces with

173. Law of 12 Apr. 2005 No. 36 on State Social Purchasing, Grants and Awards for Non-Governmental Organizations in the Republic of Kazakhstan. Available at: http://adilet.zan.kz/rus/docs/Z0500000 36_ (accessed 5 Apr. 2019).
174. *Birgemiz* – in Kazakh language means together.

a militarized structure, anthems, flags, special terms of internal discipline and control, and with weapons, is prohibited (Article 5 Law on Public Associations). The creation and activity of public associations which threaten the health and morals of citizens are also prohibited.

709. The activity of public associations may be suspended on the grounds of a court decision. In the case of failure to eliminate the violations, or of repeated violations, activity may be terminated (Article 23 Law on Public Associations).

710. As has been shown, most of the legislative standards of Kazakhstan on the freedom of association comply with international human rights standards, including the ICCPR requirements.

C. The Right to Address Petitions

711. As given in Article 13 of the Constitution, everyone has the right to protect his/her rights and freedom by all means that are not in contradiction with the law, including self-defence; everyone has the right to the judicial protection of his/her rights and freedom. In line with Article 33(1) of the Constitution, citizens of Kazakhstan have the right to appeal personally, as well as to address individual or collective appeals to the state bodies and the bodies of local self-governance.

712. There was special Law in Kazakhstan that regulated issues of consideration of appeals (or petitions) of individuals and legal entities dated 12 January 2007.[175] Administrative Procedures Code of 29 June 2020 No. 350-VI ZRK replaced the previously adopted Law, and it represents the second generation of the legislation on the issue. Code regulates relations concerning the implementation of the internal administrative procedures of state bodies, administrative procedures, as well as administrative proceedings (Article 3(1)).

713. According to Article 90 of Administrative Procedures Code, individuals and representatives of the legal entities have the right to have a personal appointment with heads of state bodies and discuss their concerns and issues. Heads of state bodies, bodies of local self-governance and their deputies should conduct receive individuals and representatives of legal entities at least once a month according to the schedule approved.

714. A complaint (or petition) is considered by an official alone, and in cases stipulated by the legislation, or by a decision of an administrative body – collegially. As a general rule, an official whose administrative acts (issued document), administrative action (inaction) is being appealed shall not be admitted to consideration of the complaint (Article 97 Administrative Procedures Code).

175. Law of Kazakhstan of 12 Jan. 2007 No. 221-III 3RK on the Procedures of Consideration of Appeals of Individuals and Legal Entities. Available at: https://online.zakon.kz/document/?doc_id=30086115 (accessed 5 Apr. 2019). Ceased in force.

715. The body considering complaint is obliged to take measures for a comprehensive, complete and objective investigation of the factual circumstances which are important for the correct consideration of the complaint. In line with Article 99 of the Code, the time period for consideration of a complaint is twenty days.

716. According to Article 100(1) of the Administrative Procedures Code, upon the consideration of a complaint, the body that considered a complaint (petition) take one of the following decisions:

(1) on cancellation of an administrative act (document);
(2) on cancellation of an administrative act (document) and adoption of a new one;
(3) on fulfilment of an administrative action;
(4) rejection of complaint;
(5) filing of an administrative case to an administrative body, an official whose administrative act (document) or action (inaction) is being considered for carrying out an administrative procedure indicating violations occurred and proposals for their elimination;
(6) dismissal of the complaint without consideration.

IV. The Right to Respect for Private and Family Life

A. *The Right to Respect for Private Life*

717. The right to respect for private life reflects Western philosophy and 'the core of the liberal concept of freedom' that establishes the right to privacy and protects the individual's freedom from external interference.[176] According to international human rights standards, the right to respect for private life implies the adoption of legislative, administrative and judicial measures by state authorities to prevent injustice and arbitrary interference with privacy. Any interference should be reasonable and proportionate to the justifying purposes.[177]

718. According to international human rights standards, this right implies that authorities take all measures to provide for the secrecy of correspondence and telecommunications, 'including efficient supervisory mechanisms'.[178] The jurisprudence of the Human Rights Committee on the issue says that surveillance, interceptions of communication, wire-tapping and recording of conversations should be prohibited; the authorities are required to guarantee and protect the integrity and confidentiality of correspondence, without interceptions and being read. Interference for the purposes of administration of criminal justice, prevention of

---

176. Nowak, *supra* n. 142, at 377.
177. Nowak, *supra* n. 142, at 383.
178. Nowak, *supra* n. 142, at 401.

crime (state surveillance measures) is permissible on the grounds of the enabling decision of authorities empowered by law and must comply with the principle of proportionality.[179]

719. In line with international human rights requirements, personal information (its gathering and holding, processing and using) in electronic devices should be protected by law, and individuals have the right to know what personal information concerning him/her is kept by the authorities.

720. According to Article 18 of the Constitution of Kazakhstan, everyone has the right to privacy, personal and family secrets, protection of honour and dignity. Everyone has the right to the confidentiality of personal deposits and savings, correspondence, telephone conversations, postal, telegraph and other messages. The limitations of this right shall be permitted only in the cases and in the manner directly established by law. State bodies, public associations, officials and the mass media have a duty to provide an opportunity for every citizen to see the documents, decisions and sources of information concerning his rights and interests.

721. Article 25 of the Constitution establishes the inviolability of the home. Deprivation of the home shall not be permitted unless otherwise stipulated by a court decision. Penetration into housing, its inspection and search shall be permitted only in such circumstances, and according to the procedure stipulated by law.

722. Article 16 of the Penal Procedure Code of Kazakhstan guarantees the privacy and confidentiality of correspondence, telephone conversations, postal, telegraph and other messages. Limitations of this right shall be permitted in the cases and in the manner stipulated by law. Special provisions of the Penal Procedure Code regulate the questions of interference with personal life for the purposes of administration of justice. Inspection of the home shall be done only with the consent and presence of the adult living there or with the sanction of the investigating judge (Article 220(13) Penal Procedure Code). In accordance with Article 246 of the Penal Procedure Code, a tacit control over letters, telegrams, radiograms, parcels and other mailings could be established if there are sufficient grounds to believe that they contain information, documents and other objects important for the investigation of a case. Investigator compiles the relevant resolution justifying the necessity of control.

723. The inviolability of private life, the secrecy of correspondence, phone conversations, postal, telegraph and other messages and others are the principles of civil process in Kazakhstan. The limitations of these principles shall be only in the cases and in the manner stipulated by law (Article 10 Civil Procedure Code). Another principle of civil process in Kazakhstan is respect for the honour, dignity and commercial goodwill of the persons participating in the case. Decisions and actions humiliating the dignity of the person participating in the process are prohibited.

179. Nowak, *supra* n. 142, at 402.

Moral damage caused by illegal actions of state bodies and officials during civil procedure shall be compensated in accordance with the law (Article 9 Civil Procedure Code).

724. Chapter 3 Article 115(3) of the Civil Code of Kazakhstan protects the personal non-property rights of individuals as well. The protection can be afforded by the court and in the manner stipulated by law (Article 141 Civil Code). Article 143 regulates the protection of personal honour, dignity and reputation. If the information discrediting the honour, dignity and reputation of citizens or organizations is published in the mass media, the same media must refute publicly. Citizens have the right to claim compensation for moral harm.

725. Article 144 protects the citizens' rights to secrecy of private life, including the confidentiality of correspondence, phone conversations, diaries, notes, adoption, birth, medical and attorney secrets, bank deposits. Disclosure of privacy is possible only in cases stipulated by legislative acts. The publishing of diaries, notes and other documents is permitted only with the consent of the author. Article 146 guarantees the inviolability of the home. No one can enter into a house without the consent of the owner, except in the cases stipulated by legislative acts.

726. Penal Code contains a number of articles prohibiting unlawful interference in private life (Articles 147–149). Article 147 criminalizes violation of privacy and laws of Kazakhstan on personal data and their protection. Article 148 prohibits unlawful violation of the secrecy of correspondence, telephone conversations, postal, telegraph or other communications.

727. In the Committee's view, home is considered as a place of residence usually occupied. Interference with the home is arbitrary when it happens without the consent of the person concerned.[180] A search of the home is allowed only to obtain necessary evidence; search of the body should be with respect to the dignity of the person who is being searched. Article 17 of the Penal Procedure Code guarantees the inviolability of the home. Penetration into housing against the will of persons who lives there, its inspection and search shall be permitted only in the cases and in the manner stipulated by law. Article 149 of the Penal Code criminalizes the violation of the inviolability of the home.

B. The Right to Respect of Family Life

728. In line with international human rights standards, it is incumbent on the State to protect family and home from arbitrary or unlawful interference. Arbitrary deprivations of liberty and expulsion of aliens, mandatory separation of children from their family and the prohibition of divorce all represent interference with the family.[181]

---

180. Nowak, *supra* n. 142, at 400.
181. Nowak, *supra* n. 142, at 393–399.

729. As previously said, Article 18 of the Constitution guarantees the right of everyone to family secrets. According to paragraph 1 of Article 27 of the Constitution, marriage and family, motherhood, fatherhood and childhood shall be under the protection of the State. The same provision is replicated in the Code of Kazakhstan on Marriage and Family.[182] The Code on Marriage (Matrimony) and Family and national legislation regulating the matters of marriage and family is based on many principles, including the inadmissibility of arbitrary interference in family affairs.

730. Article 53 of the Code on Marriage protects privacy, personal and family secrets. So, privacy, personal and family secrets are under the protection of the law. The officials who carry out registration of the acts of civil status, as well as other persons, who are informed about private life, are obliged to keep personal and family secrets. Disclosure of information on personal and family life entails responsibility established by the laws of the Republic.

C. The Rights of the Child

731. According to the jurisprudence of the Human Rights Committee and international state practice, minors receive greater protection than adults, and special measures are required to be adopted for the protection of children by their family, society and the State.[183] Special measures imply economic, social and cultural ones and should be aimed at reducing infant mortality, eradicating malnutrition, protecting children from violence, inhuman treatment, exploitation and trafficking, developing the personality of children through education, supporting housing, recreation and medical care.[184] The protection of a child includes preventing unlawful interference from both its own authorities and from private parties.[185]

732. Protection of child's rights implies their non-discrimination on the grounds of origin, religion, race, property, language, etc. Children should not be discriminated against on the grounds of birth, so children born out of wedlock and children born in marriage have equal rights. Parents and family bear primary responsibility for the child's protection and development. In ensuring the protection of the child, the social institutions and the State assist the family.

733. According to Article 24(2) of the ICCPR, every child has the right to be registered immediately after birth and to have a name (family name and first name). This promotes the recognition of the legal personality, reduces the ill-treatment of children and abuse of their rights.

---

182. Code of Kazakhstan of 26 Dec. 2011, No. 518-IV on Marriage (Matrimony) and Family. Available at: https://online.zakon.kz/document/?doc_id=31102748#pos=459;-47 (accessed 3 Aug. 2021).
183. General Comment No. 17: Article 24 (Rights of the child), adopted in the 35th session (1989). Available at: https://www.refworld.org/docid/45139b464.html,%20p.%20144-146 (accessed 8 Apr. 2019).
184. General Comment No. 17, 1989; Nowak, *supra* n. 142, at 547.
185. Nowak, *supra* n. 142, at 546.

734. Kazakhstan has been a Party to the Convention on the Rights of the Child since 12 August 1994 (ratified by Kazakhstan eleven years before the ratification of the ICCPR).[186] The rights of children in Kazakhstan are regulated by many legislative acts, including the Code on Marriage and the special Law of the Republic on the Children's Rights of 8 August 2002.[187]

735. According to Article 27(1) of the Constitution of Kazakhstan and Article 2(1) of the Code on Marriage, childhood is under the protection of the State. Care of children and their upbringing is a natural right and responsibility of parents. Children of full age able to work are obliged to care for disabled parents.

736. The Constitutional Council provided the official interpretation of Article 27(1) of the Constitution upon the request of the Chair of the Senate of the Republic.[188] As the Constitutional Council stated, the provisions that a family, marriage, motherhood, fatherhood and childhood are under the protection of state are the fundamental constitutional values of the Republic which stem from the highest aims and basic principles formulated in the Constitution of Kazakhstan. They ensure intergenerational continuity, conditions for the preservation and development of the people of Kazakhstan, who are the bearers of sovereignty and the only source of state power. Human rights are the basic factors in the drawing up, development, enactment of laws and other normative legal acts. Such constitutional provisions provide the social-economic, political-legal basis for state protection of childhood and further regulation in special legislation.

737. The children, because of their age, enjoy special protection. The State imposes a duty to create the necessary conditions for the full and harmonious development of minors and the protection of their rights, freedoms, and their legal interests from unlawful encroachments and the impact of various adverse factors, including information that infringes their health and development.

738. The Constitutional Council of Kazakhstan considered that to ensure duties on the protection of childhood stemming from Article 27(1) of the Constitution; the State has the right to adopt laws that put restrictions. The State imposes additional obligations on persons that bear responsibility for protecting the life and health of minors to create conditions that ensure their full-fledged physical, moral, spiritual and mental development.

739. Article 1(2) of Law on Children's Rights considers as a child any person below the age of 18. The national law establishes the equality of children. Article 4

186. Convention on the Rights of the Child, adopted and opened for signature, ratification and accession by General Assembly Resolution 44/25 of 20 Nov. 1989, entered into force on 2 Sep. 1990, in accordance with Article 49. Available at: https://treaties.un.org/Pages/ViewDetails.aspx?src=IND&mtdsg_no=IV-11&chapter=4&lang=en (accessed 8 Apr. 2019).

187. Law of Kazakhstan of 8 Aug. 2002 No. 345-II on the Children's Rights of the Republic of Kazakhstan. Available at: https://online.zakon.kz/document/?doc_id=1032460 (accessed 3 Aug. 2021).

188. Normative Resolutions of the Constitutional Council of Kazakhstan of 18 May 2015 No. 3, *supra* n. 165.

of the Law states that all children have equal rights, regardless of race or national origin, social or property status, sex, language, education, religion, place of residence, health conditions and other circumstances concerning the child, his parents and other legal representatives. Children born within a marriage and children born out of wedlock enjoy equal and full protection.

740. In the Law on the Children's Rights of Kazakhstan, the state policy towards the protection of children's rights is seen as primary. The State is obligated to create relevant bodies for the protection of children's rights and interests, to promote the physical, intellectual, spiritual and moral development of children, to protect children from harmful information, etc. (Article 6 Law on the Children's Rights). The authorities of Kazakhstan realize this through:

(1) the adoption of legislative acts protecting the rights of children;
(2) state support of a family to ensure comprehensive education of children, protection their rights, their preparation for a full-fledged life;
(3) establishing and respecting minimum social welfare standards aimed at improving rights and legal interests of children;
(4) making the authorities, individual citizens liable for the violation of the rights and interests of a child and for the infliction of harm;
(5) financially supporting public associations and other organizations carrying out the protection of a child's rights and legal interests.

741. The State takes certain responsibilities to fulfil children's rights. The child has a right to an adequate standard of living for his full physical and mental, moral and spiritual development, and the State takes responsibility for creating the social and economic conditions for this, providing minimum payment for children's welfare (Article 12 Law on the Children's Rights). As per Article 10, the State is obligated to protect a child from cruel treatment or involvement in criminal activity. It has a duty to create conditions in which the mother can give birth to a healthy child, and guarantees to some extent the provision of free medical care of the child's health (Article 8). In assigning punishment, the state officials must take into account the living conditions and upbringing of the child, his/her level of mental development and other features of personality, as well as the influence of adults on his/her upbringing (Article 48). The death penalty must not be carried out where the persons who committed the crime were under 18 years of age (Article 47(2) Penal Code of Kazakhstan).

742. Law on the Children's Rights enumerates the basic rights and duties of the child as the right to health protection (Article 8), the right to a name (first, middle and last) and the right to nationality and citizenship (Article 9), the right to life, liberty, inviolability of dignity and privacy (Article 10), the right to freedom of expression and consciousness, access to information (Article 11), the right to public assistance (Article 17), and the right of the child to rest and leisure (Article 19).

743. Article 13 of the Law on the Children's Rights protects the property rights of the child. The state guarantees the right of the child to housing (Article 14). Every child has the right to education and is guaranteed free primary and secondary education (Article 15). The child has the right to freedom of labour, and the involvement of the child in heavy physical work or work under harmful conditions is prohibited (Article 16). Every child has a right to live and grow up in a family (Article 21).

744. The whole of Chapter 25 of the Code on Marriage of Kazakhstan regulates the state registration of the birth of the child. Many other chapters of the Code on Marriage of Kazakhstan are related to children, including Chapter 10 of the Code that envisages the rights of a child and Chapter 11 that establishes the rights and duties of parents. Article 68(1) of the Code establishes the equality of the rights and duties of parents regarding the children. Dissolution of a marriage between the parents (spouses) shall not interrupt or terminate the relationships between parents and children (Article 14). If during the divorce, parents could not come to an agreement regarding the residence of a minor child, or their decision is against the interests of the child, a judge has the duty to decide with which of the parents and where the child will live, who will pay the alimony to the child and how much that should be, and other related issues to protect the interests of the child (Article 22). If the parents living separately have disagreements about the place of residence of the child, the mediator or the judge will decide the case in the interests of the child and take into account his/her opinion. The judge evaluates and takes into consideration the child's affection to one of the parents, to brothers and sisters, the age of the child, the moral and other qualities of the parents, relations between the parents and the child, and the ability of the parent to create necessary conditions for the development and the education of the child (Article 73).

Overall, the full enjoyment of the child's rights is highly conditioned by economic, social and cultural rights generally.

V. Due Process Rights

745. Due process rights are based on 'liberal principles of the separation of powers and the independence of the judiciary vis-à-vis the executive'.[189] Due process rights consist of equality before the courts and tribunals and the right to a fair and public hearing by a competent, independent and impartial tribunal established by law. Equal access to a court implies that everyone has a right to turn to the court without discrimination, and the authorities should organize it. The State must 'refrain from creating obstacles for persons who wish to initiate court proceedings', must not impose excessive court fees and cost of burdens; the organization of separate courts for various races, sexes, religious societies is prohibited.[190]

746. The national law of Kazakhstan recognizes the principle of equal access to a court. Thus, Article 14 of the Constitution stipulates the equality of everyone before the law and court and prohibits discrimination for reasons of origin, social,

189. Nowak, *supra* n. 142, at 306.
190. Nowak, *supra* n. 142, at 311–312, 309.

property status, occupation, sex, race, nationality, language, and attitude towards religion, convictions, place of residence or any other circumstances. Article 21 of the Penal Procedure Code establishes that justice is carried out on the principle of equality of all before law and court and demands that no one shall be a subject of discrimination in criminal proceedings. Equality of individuals and legal persons before the court in a civil proceeding is provided by the Civil Procedure Code in Article 13, which also guarantees against discrimination on the basis of origin, sex, race, nationality, language, religion and other circumstances. The establishment of special and extraordinary courts shall not be allowed (Article 75 Constitution).

747. In Kazakhstan, the administration of justice is regulated by the Constitutional Law on the judicial system and status of judges of 25 December 2000 and, according to it, no one shall be deprived of the right to hearings by a competent, independent and impartial court. A competent, independent and impartial judiciary demands regulation on the qualifications of judges, their appointment and removal, structural independence of court from the executive branch and the legislative, neutral position of judge in a specific case. According to the Penal Procedure Code and other main legislative acts, the judge shall be independent in rendering justice. Judges should obey the rules of the Constitution and Law of Kazakhstan; any interference in the activity of the court is prohibited, and judges are responsible for upholding this.

748. The right to a fair hearing includes such minimum standards in criminal charges as equality of arms between parties, attendance at hearings, the ability to hear from and examine witnesses and etc. The realization of the right to a fair hearing is essential to the effective guarantee of all other human rights.[191] Fair hearings entail 'the absence of any direct or indirect influence, the pressure of intimidation or intrusion from whatever side and for whatever motive'.[192]

749. The adherence to a fair hearing is formalized in the Constitution. So, the justice shall be executed independently, and any interference in the activity of the court shall be inadmissible (Article 77(1–2) Constitution).

750. Public hearings are historically a part of the Kazakh steppe and nomadic culture.[193] According to contemporary Kazakhstani law, a court hearing must be transparent and open to the public. As a general norm, according to Article 29 of the Penal Procedure Code, criminal proceedings are open to the public. Limitations can be for the reasons of protection of national secrets, the interest of the private

191. Olivier De Schutter, *International Human Rights Law. Cases, Materials, Commentary* 553 (2010).
192. Alex Conte & Richard Burchill, *supra* n. 163, at 171.
193. Beibit Shangirbayeva, *Customary Law of Kazakhs and the Institute of Biys. Their Role in Implementation of the Right to a Fair Trial in Contemporary Kazakhstan.* Amanach 'Via Evrasia', Eurasia Center of Sofia University (Bulgaria), 2017. Available at: http://www.viaevrasia.com/documents/37.%20BEIBIT%20SHANGIRBAYEVA,%20VIA%20EVRASIA,%202016,%205.pdf (accessed on 30 Apr. 2020).

lives on the basis of the motivated decision of the court if trial concerns the criminal case of minors, sex offences and others. Limitations can also be for the reason of security of victims, witnesses and other participants of the case and members of their family and close relatives. Claims to the actions and decisions of officials who render the criminal persecution are examined in a closed trial.

751. The Supreme Court of Kazakhstan issued the Regulatory Decision No. 25 on 6 December 2002 which explains the law on the publicity of criminal proceedings.[194] The courts are obliged to follow the rule of the publicity of criminal trials. Violations, depending on their significance, may entail the invalidity of the proceedings and cancellation of the court decisions. Publicity also implies the accessibility of documents to the participants of the proceedings, the public judgment, notification of participants about claims, creation of a single database of court verdicts and decisions, and free access to them.

752. The limitations of the publicity of civil proceedings in Kazakhstan can be for the reasons of protection of the private, family, commercial or other protected by law secrets, and other circumstances, such as ensuring public order in the courtroom which hinders the publicity of civil proceedings and should be based on a motivated written decision of the court (Article 19 Civil Procedure Code). Overall, the publicity of trial in civil proceedings implies openness, transparency and accessibility of its procedures, i.e., public proclamation of a court judgment, acquaintance with the case claims of trial participants, getting information on time and place of proceedings also in higher instances, free access to the database of case decisions and to information about their realization.

753. The presumption of innocence as an element of the right to a fair trial implies that 'the burden of proof of the charge is on the prosecution and the accused has the benefit of doubt' and public authorities have a duty 'to refrain from prejudging the outcome of a trial'.[195] Kazakhstan's Constitution declares the principle of presumption of innocence in paragraph 3 of Article 77: 'A person shall be considered to be innocent of committing a crime until his guilt is established by a court's sentence that has come into force'; 'the accused shall not be obliged to prove his innocence'; 'any doubt of a person's guilt shall be interpreted in favour of the accused'. Article 19 of the Penal Procedure Code says that the insurmountable doubts arising from the application of the penal and penal-procedural law shall be interpreted in favour of the accused. A guilty verdict must not be based on assumptions and must be confirmed by a sufficient and reliable set of evidence.

194. Regulatory Decision of 6 Dec. 2002 No. 25 on Publicity of Criminal Proceedings of the Supreme Court of Kazakhstan. Available at: https://online.zakon.kz/Document/?doc_id=1035464#pos=9;-52 (accessed on 3 Aug. 2021).
195. UN Human Rights Committee (HRC), CCPR General Comment No. 13: Article 14 (Administration of Justice), Equality before the Courts and the Right to a Fair and Public Hearing by an Independent Court Established by Law, 13 Apr. 1984, available at: https://www.refworld.org/docid/453883f90.html (accessed 8 Apr. 2019), para. 7.

754. Another element of due process rights is the right to be informed promptly about the nature and charge against him. This is envisaged in Article 14(3)(a) of the ICCPR. The information about 'the nature' and 'the cause' must be sufficient for the preparation of a defence.[196] According to CCPR General Comment No. 13 on Article 14, this applies to all cases of criminal charges, including those of persons not in detention. As given in paragraph 8 of the General Comments No. 13, the requirement 'promptly' means 'that information is given in the manner described as soon as the charge is first made by a competent authority' and this right 'must arise when in the course of an investigation a court or an authority of the prosecution decides to take procedural steps against a person suspected of a crime or publicly names him as such'.

755. The issues of the indictment in Kazakhstan are regulated by the Penal Procedure Code. In line with Article 131 of the Code, an official, while arresting a suspected person, shall inform about committing of which criminal offence he is suspected, about the right of a suspected person to invite a lawyer, the right to remain silent in a court, to inform that anything said by a suspected person can be used against him. According to Articles 64–65, 298–300 of the Code, an official who conducted a pretrial investigation draws up the indictment and sends it for the consideration of a prosecutor. A written motivated indictment of the official who conducted a pretrial investigation must include all necessary detailed information, including the description of the offence and alleged facts.

756. The understanding of language is an important element of the right to defence. The language of the proceedings is regulated by Article 30 of the Penal Procedure Code. If participants of the case cannot sufficiently understand the language of the proceedings, they must be given the documents requested in the language of their choosing and provided with a free interpreter. Article 78(3) of the Penal Procedure Code provides the rights of a witness to testify in his/her native language or in the language that she/he understands and the right to have the free assistance of an interpreter.

757. Another element of the right to a fair trial is the right to defence and to have legal assistance and having enough time for preparation and access to documents of the case. Article 16 paragraph 3 of the Kazakh Constitution establishes that 'every person detained, arrested and accused of committing a crime shall have the right to the assistance of a defence lawyer (defender) from the moment of detention, arrest or accusation'.

758. Article 26 of the Penal Procedure Code provides defendants with a right to defence. Defendants can represent themselves or use a professional defender, a legal representative in procedures prescribed by law. The authority in charge of the criminal process is obliged to provide participation of the defender. Article 27 of the Code

---

196. *What Is a Fair Trial?* A Basic Guide to Legal Standards and Practice. Lawyers Committee for Human Rights, March 2000. Available at: https://tavaana.org/sites/default/files/fair_trial_0.pdf (accessed 30 Apr. 2020).

of Penal Procedure stipulates that everyone during the criminal process has a right to qualified legal assistance. In cases determined by law, legal assistance must be provided free of charge. Article 64(3) of the Penal Procedure Code asserts that a suspected person from the moment of detention and before the first interrogation has the right to confidential communication with the defender of his own choosing or appointed by the authority. The suspected person has a right to give explanations and testimonies only in the presence of the defender (Article 64(9(6))).

759. The legal status of the defender is given in Articles 66–70 of the Penal Procedure Code. According to it, the defender is obliged to use all legal measures and remedies of defence in order to identify circumstances for legal assistance of the defendant. The defender has a right to collect and submit objects, documents and information necessary for legal assistance; get the copies of procedural documents and be acquainted with the documents of the penal procedure, and other rights according to Article 70(2) of the Penal Procedure Code. After setting a date of the main trial, the judge must provide parties with an opportunity to familiarize themselves with the materials of the case which they have not seen at pretrial proceedings, and to write out the necessary information (Article 328).

760. The trial shall be carried out without undue delay is another requirement of the right to a fair trial. As a general rule, in accordance with Article 192 of the Penal Procedure Code, the pretrial investigation shall be carried out within a reasonable period of time. Decisions about dates for the main trial, shortened trial or preliminary hearings should be taken within five days from the date of receipt of the case by the court (Article 319(4)). As a general rule, the main trial should end within a reasonable time period (Article 322(4) of the Penal Procedure Code).

761. Another element of the right to a fair trial is that evidence shall be obtained without compulsion and 'the accused's silence may not be used as evidence of their guilt'.[197] The Constitution of Kazakhstan stipulates that no person shall be compelled to give testimony against oneself, one's spouse and close relatives whose circle is determined by law. The clergy shall not be obligated to testify against those who confided in them with some information at a confession (subparagraph 7, paragraph 3 of Article 77). As a general principle, according to Articles 26, 28, 71, 78 of the Penal Procedure Code, the suspect and the defendant must not be compelled to testify, and witnesses have a right to refuse to give testimony.

762. Taking into account the age, criminal trials against juvenile persons must be conducted differently than adult trials. This is also one of the requirements of the right to a fair trial. In practice, as mentioned in the report of UNICEF, the level of offences committed by juveniles in Kazakhstan is low because of social and economic factors, as well as cultural values and traditions. Kazakhstan addresses juvenile justice through specialized courts and special procedures regulated by the Penal

197. What Is a Fair Trial? *supra* n. 203, at 20.

Procedure Code and such other legislative and conceptual texts as the Juvenile Justice System Development Concept. In the beginning, juvenile courts were established on an experimental basis in Almaty and Astana (former name of the capital). From 2012 onwards, juvenile courts have been established all over the country. Certain judges are specialized in juvenile issues, and there are specialized interdistrict courts on juvenile justice.[198]

763. The Special Chapter 56 of the Penal Procedure Code is devoted to the procedures on criminal offences committed by juvenile persons. During the pretrial investigations and trial course, the authorities must reveal the age and date of birth, the conditions of life and upbringing of the juvenile, the level of intellectual, mental capacities, particularities of character and temperament, needs and interests and the influence of adults and other juveniles on misbehaviour (Article 531). Publicity in juvenile trials can be restricted (Article 532). The testimony of juveniles should be in the presence of the defender, the representative and in necessary cases in the presence of the pedagogue or the psychologist. The testimony must be given during the daytime and must not exceed in general more than four hours with a break (Article 535).

764. The peculiarities of testimony from juvenile persons as witnesses or victims are prescribed in Article 215 of the Penal Procedure Code. Juvenile persons are distinguished between persons under 14 years of age and persons from 14 up to 18 years of age. The testimony of persons under 14 years of age should be given in the presence of a pedagogue or/and psychologist; in the case of persons from 14 up to 18 years of age, the invitation of a pedagogue depends on the opinion of the investigator. Legal representatives of juvenile persons have a right to participate in the testimony. Juvenile persons up to 16 years of age, if they were witnesses or victims, are not warned about the responsibility for refusal from testimony and giving false evidence.

765. The participation of the defender in a criminal case of a juvenile is obligatory, and the authorities must provide the defender if the juvenile cannot afford it himself (Articles 67, 536). The participation of parents or legal representatives of juvenile defendants in the pretrial procedures is obligatory (Article 537). Arrested juveniles are kept separate from adults. Parents, legal representatives or close relatives are informed immediately about the arrest of a juvenile (Article 541). Further peculiarities of justice with juveniles are given in other articles of the Penal Procedure Code.

766. The right to a fair trial implies that everyone has the right to appeal and of being reviewed by an upper court. The national country should create conditions to provide access to an appeal and effective measures for it. In Kazakhstan, the revision of court judgment of the first instance can be by the appellate court and the

198. *Kak rabotayut yuvenal'nye sudy v. Kazakhstante/How the Juvenile Court Function in Kazakhstan.* Available at: https://www.zakon.kz/4879865-kak-rabotayut-yuvenalnye-sudy-v.html (accessed 9 Apr. 2019).

court of cassation. With regards to criminal cases, the right of a higher tribunal by appellate instance to revise court judgment is regulated by section 8 of the Penal Procedure Code (Chapters 48–49).

767. An appeal revises the validity of all facts and correct application of penal law, the observance of penal-procedural norms and the fairness, legality and validity of the judgment of the first instance on the grounds of materials of the case, as well as additionally presented, and their research (Article 424). An appellate court revises the decision of the first instance not only on the basis of the materials of the case but also takes into account materials submitted additionally. Appeals in Kazakhstan involve 'mainly new examination of a case'.[199] A higher court has a right to keep the judgment of the first instance as it is, to change or cancel the judgment of the first instance (Article 431). As a general rule, the case by the appeal authority should be examined within one month. Lodging on appeal should be within fifteen days from the day of the proclamation of a sentence, resolution; for convicted persons who are in custody – from the day of handing over a court sentence, resolution (Article 418).

768. The court of cassation revises the legality, justification and fairness of the judgment entered into force (Chapter 52 Penal Procedure Code). Article 485 of the Code stipulates that the reasons for cassation can be violations of the constitutional rights and freedoms of citizens or incorrect application of penal and penal-procedural laws that brought to consequences enumerated in the provisions of the article.

769. A right of compensation to a person who was punished due to a miscarriage of justice is a constitutive part of a right to a fair trial. The conditions for an application of this right is defined as the existence of 'a final conviction for a criminal offence; suffering punishment as a consequence of such conviction; a subsequent reversal or pardon on the grounds of a new or newly discovered fact showing conclusively that there has been a miscarriage of justice'.[200]

770. In legislative texts, issues of a right of compensation are regulated by Chapter 4 of the Penal Procedure Code. The practice of application of the provisions of the Code on Penal Procedure on compensation was generalized by the Normative Resolution of the Supreme Court of 9 July 1999 No. 7.[201]

---

199. Marat Koghamov, *Comments to General Procedure Code of the Republic of Kazakhstan. Common and Special Parts* 463 (2008).
200. *W.J.H. v. The Netherlands*, Communication No. 408/1990 (31 Jul. 1992) 6.3, CCPR/C/45/D/408/1990, available at: http://www1.umn.edu/humanrts/undocs/html/dec408.htm (accessed 8 Apr. 2019).
201. Normative Resolution of the Supreme Court of Kazakhstan of 9 Jul. 1999 No. 7 on the Practice of Application of Legislation on Compensation of Harms Inflicted by the Illegal Actions of State Bodies Responsible for Penal Procedures. Available at: Available at: http://hrlib.kz/wp-content/uploads/2016/05/1999Постановление-Пленума-ВС-РК-№7-О-практике-применения-законодательства-по-возмещению-вреда-с-изм.-от- -25.06.2010.pdf (accessed 9 Apr. 2019).

771. A right to a fair trial implies *ne bis in idem, or* res judicata or the prohibition against double jeopardy. A guarantee against this is provided in subparagraph 2, paragraph 3 of Article 77 of the Constitution: no one may be subject twice to criminal or administrative prosecution for one and the same offence.

772. So, here we can see that Kazakhstan has implemented in constitutional and legislative texts the requirements on due process. The establishment of juvenile courts and investigative judges, the institute of a jury and the institute of mediation for pretrial regulation of disputes, the simplification of pretrial proceedings are the new elements in the judicial system of Kazakhstan.

VI. Peaceful Enjoyment of Possessions

773. The Constitution of Kazakhstan contains two main articles – Articles 6 and 26 – that regulate issues of proprietorship and possessions. Article 6 envisages that state and private property are recognized by the Republic of Kazakhstan and are equally protected. The property shall impose obligations; its use shall be beneficial to society. Subjects and objects of ownership, their scope and limits of realization by owners of their rights, guarantees of their protection shall be defined by law. The land and subsoil, waters, flora and fauna, other natural resources are in state ownership. The land may also be privately owned on terms, conditions and limits established by law.

774. Pursuant to Article 26 of the Constitution, citizens of Kazakhstan may have in private property any legally acquired property. Property, including the right to inheritance, shall be guaranteed by law. No one may be deprived of property otherwise than the decision of the court. Forcible alienation of property for state needs may be done as exceptional cases on condition of equivalent compensation. Everyone has the right to freedom of entrepreneurial activity, free use of their own property for any legal entrepreneurial activity. Monopolistic activity shall be regulated and limited by law. Unfair competition shall be prohibited.

775. In line with Article 61(3) of the Constitution, the Parliament of Kazakhstan enacts laws regulating the regime of ownership and other propriety rights. As given in Article 66 of the Constitution, the Government organizes state property management. The local executive bodies manage the communal property.

776. Article 18 of the Penal Procedure Code guarantees the inviolability of property. No one may be deprived of his property otherwise than the decision of the court. An arrest of bank deposits and other property, as well as their seizure during legal proceedings, may be in cases and in a manner envisaged by the Code.

777. In line with Article 18 of the Penal Procedure Code, the proprietorship is guaranteed by law. No one may be deprived of his property otherwise than the decision of the court. An arrest of property to secure a claim may be made on the grounds and in a manner envisaged by the Code.

778. Part II of the Civil Code is devoted to the proprietorship and other property rights. According to Article 188 of the Civil Code, the proprietorship is the right of a person recognized and protected by legislative acts at his own discretion to possess, use and dispose of the property. The proprietorship can be transferred to another person with all the encumbrances existing at the time of the transaction. The owner exercises the right to possess, use and dispose of his own property. The owner at his own discretion has the right to exercise any actions with regard to property, including alienation this property to other people, transferring the right to possess, use and dispose of property, giving it as a pledge and encumber by other means, and dispose of it in any other way. The exercise by the owner of his powers shall not violate rights and be protected by law interests of other persons and the State. The owner must take measures that prevent the infliction of damage to the health of citizens and the environment that could be caused in the exercise of his rights. The proprietorship is not limited in time and can be terminated forcibly only on the grounds stipulated by the Code.

779. As envisaged in Article 189 of the Civil Code, the owner of property bears the burden of maintaining the property if other things are not stipulated in legislative acts and an agreement, and such burden cannot be unilaterally shifted to a third party.

§3. Social, Economic and Cultural Rights

I. Introduction

780. On 24 January 2006, Kazakhstan became a State Party to the ICESCR of 16 December 1966. On 23 September 2010, the country had signed but not yet ratified the OP to the Covenant of 10 December 2008 on recognition of the competence of the Committee.

781. As stated in the preamble to the ICESCR, the recognition and observance of social, economic and cultural rights stem from respect for the dignity of a human being that comprises the 'foundation of freedom, justice and peace in the world'. Full enjoyment of their social, economic and cultural rights is necessary for the development of a human being's capabilities which contributes to the well-being of society and national growth. In line with the ICESCR standards, the scope of such rights includes rights to work and to form trade unions, to have an adequate standard of living, to enjoy physical and mental health, to education, to marriage and family, to exercise his/her own culture, to social security, to participate in the development of science and culture, etc.

II. The Right to Work

782. In conformity with Article 6 of the ICESCR, *the right to work* should be freely chosen and accepted, implies having 'just and favourable' work conditions that safeguard 'fundamental political and economic freedoms of the individual' 'to achieve steady economic, social and cultural development and full productive employment'.

783. Pursuant to Article 24 of the Constitution, everyone shall have the right to freedom of labour, free choice of occupation and profession. Article 5 of the Labour Code says that everyone has the right to choose the work or freely give his/her consent to the work without any discrimination or force, freely dispose of their own capabilities to work, choose a profession and form of occupation. The Labour Code of Kazakhstan prohibits discrimination in the field of labour. According to the provisions of Article 6, everyone has equal opportunities in the realization of his/her rights and freedoms in the field of labour. No one can be restricted in his/her rights in the field of labour, except for circumstances and in a manner established by the Code and other laws of Kazakhstan. In the exercise of labour rights, no one can be discriminated against on the grounds of origin, social, official and property status, sex, race, nationality, language, attitude to religion, belief, place of residence, age or disability, as well as membership of public associations. Any other exceptions, preferences and restrictions which are in line with the laws of Kazakhstan are established for certain types of labour activities or conditioned by the special care of the State towards persons who need increased social and legal protection. People who consider that they are discriminated against in the field of labour have the right to go to court or other instances established by the laws of Kazakhstan.

784. In accordance with Article 24 of the Constitution, forced labour shall be allowed only on the grounds of a court sentence or in case of a state emergency and martial law. Article 7 of the Labour Code prohibits forced labour. 'Forced labour' means any work or service that is required from any other person under threat of punishment and for carrying out of which a person has not agreed voluntarily.

785. In line with Article 24 of the Constitution, everyone shall have the right to favourable labour conditions that respond to security requirements and hygiene, to remuneration for labour without any discrimination, as well as for social protection from unemployment.

786. The Constitution recognizes the right to individual or collective disputes with the use of methods of their resolving established by law, including the right to strike. Everyone has the right to rest. To people who are working under a labour contract, the length of working hours, weekends and holidays and paid annual leaves established by law shall be guaranteed (Article 24(3, 4) Constitution).

787. The Labour Code of Kazakhstan of 23 November 2015 regulates in detail such issues as the competence of state bodies in regulating labour relations, the legal grounds for labour relations, labour contracts, labour order and work discipline, working hours, resting time, norm-setting and remuneration of labour, professional training, retraining and advanced vocational training, the material responsibility of the parties to labour contracts, warranties and compensation payments, the peculiarities of labour regulations of workers of selected categories, social partnership and collective relations in the field of labour, collective agreement, consideration of individual labour disputes, consideration of collective labour disputes, safety and labour protection, state regulation in the field of safety and labour protection, rights and obligations of employees and employers in the field of safety and labour protection, organization of safety, investigation and accounting of accidents related to labour activities, monitoring the observance of labour legislation of the Republic, state and internal control over the observance of legislation.[202]

788. Article 4 of the Labour Code enumerates the following principles that underlie the labour legislation of Kazakhstan:

(1) inadmissibility of restrictions to human and citizens' rights in the field of labour;
(2) freedom of labour;
(3) prohibition of discrimination in the field of labour, prohibition of compulsory work and the worst forms of child labour;
(4) ensuring the right to labour conditions that respond to safety and hygiene requirements;
(5) priority of life and health of an employee;
(6) ensuring the right to remuneration for labour not lower than the minimum wage;
(7) ensuring the right to rest;
(8) equality of rights and opportunities of employees;
(9) ensuring the rights of employees and employers to assembly for protection of rights and interests;
(10) state assistance in strengthening and development of social partnership;
(11) state regulation of security issues and labour protection.

III. The Right to Form Trade Unions and Join Them, the Right to Strike

789. Article 8 of the ICESCR envisages the right of everyone to form trade unions and join the trade union of his choice. Freedom of association entails the right to form and join trade unions for the protection of common interests. Trade unions are associations of employees, which are created to represent the interests and undertake activities for its members for the protection of their rights.[203] The freedom of trade unions implies 'the rights to join an existing trade union of one's choice, to found a new trade union or to decide not to organize in a trade union'.[204] Protection of the interests of members of trade unions can be through organizing strikes. According to international human rights standards, the lawful activities of the trade unions must not be prevented.

202. On Labour Law in Kazakhstan, *see*: Nurghaliyeva, Ye.N. & Khassenov, M.Kh., *Labour Law in Kazakhstan* (2017).
203. Nowak, *supra* n. 142, at 501–502.
204. Nowak, *supra* n. 142, at 501.

790. According to Article 22(1(8)) of the Labour Code, the employee has a right to association, including the right to form trade unions and other associations, and of membership in them in order to protect his/her labour rights if other things are not envisaged by laws of Kazakhstan.[205] The trade unions can represent their members (employees) (Article 1(1(44)) and Article 20 Labour Code).

791. Along with the Labour Code, the legal status of trade unions is regulated by the special Law of Kazakhstan on Trade Unions.[206] The activities of trade unions (political parties as well) must not be financed by foreigners, foreign states and international organizations (Article 5 of the Law on public associations). In line with Article 8 of the Law on trade unions, the trade union is created upon the initiative of a group of at least ten Kazakhstani citizens, who are connected with common professional and industrial interests. They convene founding congress (congress, meeting) to approve the Charter and bodies of the union. Legal capacity of a trade union starts from the moment of state registration. All members of a trade union are equal; all trade unions are treated equally (Article 4 Law on Trade Unions).

792. The Labour Code of Kazakhstan recognizes the right to strike (Chapter 16). Participation in a strike is a voluntary action, and no one must be forced to take part in it (Article 171(4, 5)). Taking part in the strike cannot be treated as a breach of labour discipline; for the period of the strike, the employee is guaranteed to retain his position, the right to payment of social security benefits, and other labour rights (Article 175).

793. Article 176 of the Labour Code concerns the issue of unlawful strikes. Strikes during wartime and in a public emergency, or during the implementation of special measures in accordance with the national legislation, in the armed forces and other military formations and organizations responsible for ensuring state defence and security, emergency, search and rescue, fire safety measures, prevention or liquidation of emergency, or in the special state and law-enforcement bodies, at the emergency medical stations and organizations related to railway transport, civil aviation, health organizations and other organizations providing vital services to the population, are all recognized by the Code as unlawful. If the strike is convened neglecting the procedures prescribed by the Labour Code, or if it threatens the life and health of the people, or in other circumstances established by law, the strike will be found by a court as unlawful.

794. With regards to the application of the freedom of association, the scientists say that the Kazakh workers who participated in the strike at the *Karazhanbas* oil field in the *Mangistau* region in May 2011 were arrested. In the end, participants

205. Labour Code of the Republic of Kazakhstan of 23 Nov. 2015 No. 414-V ZRK. Available at: https://online.zakon.kz/document/?doc_id=38910832 (accessed 5 Apr. 2019).
206. Law on Trade Unions of 27 Jun. 2014 No. 211-V ZRK, available at: http://adilet.zan.kz/rus/docs/Z1400000211 (accessed 5 Apr. 2019).

were fired by the Chinese authorities of the company.[207] This strike of oil workers at the *Karazhanbas* oilfield was judged by the state court to be unlawful. The given reason was the infringement of procedural rules in conducting the strike. According to media reports, the strike in another oilfield *Ersay-Munay-Gaz* Oil Company in the *Mangistau* region in April–May 2011, was also deemed unlawful by the court, and the activists were fired from their jobs; some of them were arrested. The oil workers had demanded an improvement of working conditions and an increase in their salaries, the elimination of social inequality between citizens of the country and foreigners.[208] Oil is a hazardous industry, and the ecological conditions of poor and humiliated oil workers are really harsh. They work in an environment of strong winds and of heatwaves; in the summer at + 50°, and at – 50° in winter.

IV. Protection of Family and Marriage

795. Article 10 of the ICESCR envisages protection of family and assistance, free consent to marriage, protection of children from economic and social exploitation. According to the ICESCR, a family is 'the natural and fundamental group unit of society'. This corresponds to Article 23 of the ICCPR, which asserts that the family is the natural and fundamental unit of society and is entitled to protection by society and the State; the State Party shall recognize the right of men and women of marriageable age to marry and to found a family; no marriage shall be entered into without the free and full consent of the intending spouses.

796. According to Article 2(2) the Code on Marriage and Family, the national legislation regulating the matters of marriage and family is based on the principles of voluntariness of marriage between man and woman, equality of rights of spouses in family, the inadmissibility of arbitrary interference in family affairs, the priority of upbringing children within a family, care about the development and welfare of children, and other principles. The protection of marriage and family is guaranteed by the Code on Marriage and Family and other laws of Kazakhstan (Article 7 Code on Marriage).

797. In general, cultural traditions and values strongly influence the understanding of family in the country. The Code on Marriage recognizes 'family' as a group of persons connected with property and moral rights, contributing to the strengthening and development of relations arising from marriage (matrimony), kinship, relations through wedlock, adoption of children, and other forms of fostering (Article 1(29)). Family is protected by the Constitution of Kazakhstan (Article 27(1)) and the Code on Marriage (Article 2(1)).

207. Skvorzov, V & Silantyeva, E. *Protest Movements and Human Rights: Political, Social-Economic, Cultural Sources* 56 Legal Reform in Kazakhstan 67 (2011).

208. Igor' Kutzay, *Oil strikes*. Available at: http://www.caravan.kz/article/29638 (accessed 8 Nov. 2012).

798. Article 1 of the Code understands marriage as a union between man and woman based on equality and concluded on the free and full consent of the parties, established in accordance with the law of Kazakhstan, aiming at the creation of a family, with property and moral rights and duties between the spouses (paragraph 26). For the conclusion of a marriage, the Code demands two conditions: free and full consent and attainment of marriageable age (Article 9). The Code establishes 18 years of age for a person to be eligible to get married (Article 10). In circumstances of pregnancy and the birth of a child, the marriageable age may be reduced by two years. The marriage must be registered by state organs (Article 2(3)). Cohabitation is not accepted as marriage.

799. Article 30 of the Code mentions the general equality of rights and duties of spouses. Each spouse is free in choosing the activities, profession and religion. The issues of motherhood, fatherhood, parenting and education of children, place of residence and other matters of family are decided together. Spouses are obliged to build family relationships on the basis of mutual respect and assistance, to promote the welfare and strengthening of the family, to take care of the health, development and welfare of their children.

800. Among institutional achievements, the creation of the National Commission for Women's Affairs and Family can be mentioned as a positive practical measure. It is an advisory body to the President of Kazakhstan and works on different aspects of state policy on family matters and the equality of men and women.[209] The establishment of this National Commission was welcomed by international institutions and it helps to strengthen women's rights and the right to respect family life in the Republic. It is worth mentioning that the creation of the National Commission came after the signing of the ICCPR by Kazakhstan.

801. The Commission is entitled to demand that the heads of the responsible state bodies conduct the official investigations into alleged violations of the laws on the equality of sexes, family matters and demography (paragraph 4 subparagraph 3 Regulations on the National Commission for Women's Affairs and Family). It has a right to make proposals to the drafts of legislative acts of the President and the Government concerning gender issues, family and demography (paragraph 4 subparagraph 4). The Commission considers the complaints of citizens regarding the violations of their rights and is entitled to demand that the state offices responsible take necessary measures.

---

209. Regulations of the National Commission for Women, Family and Demographic Policy Under the President of the Republic of Kazakhstan, adopted by the Decree of the President of 1 Feb. 2006 No. 56. Available at: https://online.zakon.kz/DOCUMENT/?doc_id=30044669#pos=38;-28 (accessed 3 Aug. 2021).

V. The Right to Education

802. Article 13 of the ICESCR establishes the right of everyone to education. Education 'shall be directed to the full development of the human personality and the sense of its dignity, and shall strengthen the respect for human rights and fundamental freedoms'. According to the article under consideration, education 'shall enable all persons to participate effectively in a free society, promote understanding, tolerance and friendship among all nations and all racial, ethnic or religious groups, and further the activities of the United Nations for the maintenance of peace'.

803. According to the UN Human Development Reports of 2018, the literacy rate in Kazakhstan is 99.8%, that is higher than in many places in the world.[210] The right to education is envisaged in Article 30 of the Constitution of Kazakhstan, and citizens are guaranteed to receive free secondary education at public educational institutions. Secondary education is compulsory. Citizens have the right to get tertiary education at public educational institutions on competitive grounds. Obtaining for-profit education at private educational institutions is realized on the grounds and in a manner established by law. The State establishes uniform compulsory education. Activities of any educational institution should comply with these standards.

804. Issues of education in Kazakhstan are regulated by the Law of 27 July 2007 No. 319-III on Education.[211] In accordance with Article 3 of the Law, the state educational policy is based on the following principles:

(1) equality of all in receiving education of good quality;
(2) the priority of the development of the educational system;
(3) availability of all levels of education to the population that takes into consideration intellectual development, psycho-physiological and individual characteristics of the individual;
(4) secular, humanistic and evolving education, priority of civil and national values, human life and health, of free development of personality;
(5) respect for human rights and freedoms;
(6) stimulation of culture of education and the development of giftedness;
(7) continuity of educational process that ensures succession of its levels;
(8) unity of learning, bringing up and development;
(9) democratic character of education management, transparency of the education system;
(10) variety of educational institutions with different forms of property, forms of learning and bringing up, and directions.

---

210. Please *see* the Human Development Reports. Literacy rate, adult (% ages 15 and older). Available at: http://hdr.undp.org/en/countries/profiles/KAZ (accessed 3 Aug. 2021).

211. Law of Kazakhstan of 27 Jul. 2007 No. 319-III on Education. Available at: http://adilet.zan.kz/rus/docs/Z070000319_ (accessed 30 Apr. 2020).

805. Creation and operation of the political parties' and religious associations' structures at the educational organizations are prohibited in Kazakhstan (Article 3(2) Law on Education). In accordance with Article 4 of Law, the Government develops and realizes the state policy to develop education, approves the rules on awarding the grants for students, submits proposals to the President of the Republic on assigning special status to the tertiary or post-tertiary educational organizations and approves regulations on the special status of organizations of tertiary or post-tertiary education, creates, reorganizes and liquidates upon the proposals of the administrative body the state educational organizations financed by the national budget if other things are not stipulated by laws of the Republic, etc.

806. According to the Second Periodic Report of Kazakhstan on Implementation of the ICESCR, the Government of Kazakhstan pays significant attention to financing education, for instance, in 2010 – KZT 782.6 billion, in 2014 – KZT 1.4 trillion, in 2015 – KZT 1.5 billion.[212] Kazakhstan's educational policy pays considerable attention to the computerization of education, the development of multilingual and inclusive education. As mentioned in the State Report, the programme on inclusive education creates conditions for getting preschool and secondary education for all categories of children and is used for correction of children's developmental disability and for social adaptation of those children (paragraph 118).

807. Since November 1993, the State Programme on Awarding Scholarships to the Citizens of Kazakhstan to get Bachelor, Master and PhD degrees, scientific, language and other training abroad has been launched by the Government of Kazakhstan.[213]

212. Please *see* Second Periodic Report of the Republic of Kazakhstan on Implementation of the ICESCR, approved by the Resolution of the Government of Kazakhstan of 20 Jul. 2017 No. 435. Available at: https://tbinternet.ohchr.org/_layouts/15/treatybodyexternal/Download.aspx?symbolno=E%2fC.12%2fKAZ%2f2&Lang=en (accessed 3 Aug. 2021).
213. Please *see* the official website: https://www.bolashak.gov.kz/en/ (accessed 3 Apr. 2019).

Chapter 3. Constitutional Safeguards for Specific Groups and Minorities

§1. State and Official Languages: State Policy on the Use and Promotion of Languages

808. The nomadic culture of the Kazakhs during the Tsarist period was drastically changed as Kazakhs were forced to settle and to change their lifestyle. During the Soviet Union period, the status of the Kazakh language in society, state affairs and academia was diminished. After achieving independence, the revival of the Kazakh language was one of the important tasks of the state policy of Kazakhstan to preserve national identity in a globalized world.

809. According to Article 7 of the Constitution, the Kazakh language is a state language of the Republic. In the state and local self-governance bodies, the Russian language is officially used on an equal basis along with the Kazakh language. The State shall promote conditions for the study and development of the languages of the people of Kazakhstan

810. A special Law in Kazakhstan on the Languages in the Republic of Kazakhstan regulating the status of languages was adopted on 11 July 1997.[214] The Law on the Languages establishes that the Kazakh language is a language of the state administration, legislation, legal proceedings and the documentation that exists in all public relations within the whole territory of the State. In line with Article 4 of Law on the Languages, a state language consolidates the society of Kazakhstan. The Government, other state and local representative and executive bodies have duties to develop it, to strengthen its international image, and to create all necessary organizational, material and technical conditions for free use and free learning of a state language by all citizens of the Republic, to assist the Kazakh diaspora in the preservation and developing mother tongue.

811. The former nomadic lifestyle of the Kazakhs had a great influence on the openness of the society's consciousness to the surrounding world and on the depth of the spiritual culture of the steppe's inhabitants. This created a tolerance for other languages and cultures.[215] The State and society of Kazakhstan respect and promote other languages as well. In line with Article 5 of Law, the Russian language is officially used on an equal basis along with the Kazakh language at the state bodies and local self-governance bodies. In conformity with Article 6 of the Law under consideration, every citizen of Kazakhstan has the right to use his/her mother tongue, the right to choose freely their language of communication, bringing up, learning and creativity. As given in Article 7 of the Constitution and Article 6 of the Law on the Languages, the State shall promote conditions for the study and development of

214. Law of Kazakhstan of 11 Jul. 1997 No. 151-I on the Languages in the Republic of Kazakhstan. Available at: https://online.zakon.kz/Document/?doc_id=1008034 (accessed 3 Aug. 2021).

215. Saule Amandykova, *Sistemoobrazuyushie zennosti 'Mangilik El'/ Backbone Values of 'Mangilik El'*. Available at: http://www.enu.kz/ru/info/novosti-enu/32499/ (accessed 20 Jun. 2019).

the languages of the people of Kazakhstan. In the places where the minority groups are densely populated, the events there can be held in their native language. Apart from Kazakh and Russian schools, there are many public schools in Kazakhstan where individuals can receive education in Uzbek, Tajik, Uigur, German, Ukrainian and other languages.

812. In conformity with Article 14 of the Constitution, no one shall be discriminated against on the grounds of language or any other circumstances. Article 7 of Law on the Languages prohibits the infringement of the rights of citizens on the grounds of belonging to a language group. The actions of state officials that impede the functioning and studying of the state and other languages represented in Kazakhstan entails responsibility in accordance with the laws of the Republic.

813. On 31 December 2019, the Government of Kazakhstan approved the State Programme for the Implementation of Language Politics During 2020–2025.[216] The aim of the Programme is to maintain harmonious language policy and modernization of the Kazakh language on the ground of latinographic alphabet, further development of language culture and language capital, ensuring the full-fledged functioning of the Kazakh language as the state language.

814. The previous State Programme for 2011–2020 on the Development and Functioning of Languages had been adopted on 29 June 2011 by the Decree of the President of Kazakhstan.[217] According to that Programme, the Kazakh language as a state language was mentioned as a consolidating factor of national unity, and all measures envisaged in the Programme were aimed to satisfy the spiritual, cultural and linguistic needs of the citizens of the Republic. The main strategic goal of the document was the carrying out of harmonious language politics to ensure the full functioning of the state language as the most important factor in strengthening national unity while preserving the languages of other ethnic groups residing in Kazakhstan. The Language Programme asserted that the learning of English and other foreign languages by the people of Kazakhstan strengthens the human capital of the country. These foreign languages were placed as tools that give access to international business, communication and interactions.

815. Understanding that knowledge of foreign languages gives advantages to the new generation and access to world culture and advanced technology, Kazakhstan currently implements ‘A trinity of languages’ politics. This multilingual politics is aimed at integrating the country into the globalized world and making Kazakhstani

---

216. Resolution of the Government of Kazakhstan of 31 Dec. 2019 No. 1045 on Approval of the State Programme for the Implementation of Language Policy During 2020-2025. Available at: https://tengrinews.kz/zakon/pravitelstvo_respubliki_kazahstan_premer_ministr_rk/hozyaystvennaya_deyatelnost/id-P1900001045/ (accessed 30 Apr. 2020).
217. State Programme for 2011-2020 on the Development and Functioning of Languages approved by the Decree of the President of Kazakhstan of 29 Jun. 2011 No. 110, available at the official website of the Office of the Prime Minister of the Republic: http://adilet.zan.kz/rus/docs/U1100000110 (accessed 18 Apr. 2019). Ceased in force.

citizens more competitive on a global scale. The gradual transition to receiving education in English in the upper classes of high schools and at the institutions of tertiary education is the 79th step of the national programme 'The plan of nation – 100 steps for five institutional reforms'.[218] Enhancing the competitiveness of graduates and the development of the export potential of the educational sectors were mentioned as the main goals of the programme. The people of Kazakhstan are encouraged to know the Kazakh, Russian and English languages simultaneously. Learning these languages, learning school and university subjects in these three languages have been implemented in primary and secondary schools and in the tertiary education of the country.

816. Kazakhstan continues its modernization. The former President of Kazakhstan, Nursultan Nazarbayev, in April 2017 in his article 'The course towards the future: modernization of Kazakhstan's identity' announced measures to implement the smooth transition of the Kazakh alphabet from Cyrillic into Latin script by 2025.[219] In October 2017, the relevant Decree was adopted. The explanation for this transition was that the Latin script reflects the peculiarities of the Kazakh language and is more convenient in the use of information technology and the internet. In the history of the Kazakh language, the Latin alphabet was used from 1929 till 1940.

§2. Non-discrimination and the Prohibition of Racism, Gender Equality

I. Anti-discrimination and the Prohibition of Racism, Minorities' Rights

817. The preamble to the Constitution of Kazakhstan asserts that Kazakhstan is committed to the ideals of freedom, equality and concord and is conscious of responsibility before current and future generations. The constitutional provisions of Article 14 prohibiting discrimination were analysed in this writing several times: no one shall be discriminated on the grounds of origin, social, official or property status, sex, nationality, language, religious attitude, beliefs, a place of residence or any other circumstances. Additional guarantees on non-discrimination are envisaged in Article 19 of the Constitution where it is given that everyone has the right to define, mention or not to mention his/her ethnic, party and religious affiliation. Equality of individuals and entities and equal protection are mentioned several times in the Constitution of the Republic.

818. The Constitution prohibits the creation and activities of the public entities, which aims and actions are directed to undermine the security of the State and to

218. Article of the First President of Kazakhstan Nursultan Nazarbayev addressed to the people 'The plan of nation – 100 steps for five institutional reforms' of May 2015. Available at: https://online.zakon.kz/Document/?doc_id=31977084 (accessed 18 Apr. 2019).

219. Nursultan Nazarbayev, *The Course Towards the Future: Modernization of Kazakhstan's Identity* (12 Apr. 2017). Available at the official website of the Office of the President: http://www.akorda.kz/ru/events/akorda_news/press_conferences/statya-glavy-gosudarstva-vzglyad-v-budushchee-modernizaciya-obshchestvennogo-soznaniya (accessed 18 Apr. 2019).

incite social, racial, national, religious, class and tribal enmities (Article 5(3)). Propaganda or agitation for the forcible change of the constitutional system, violation of the integrity of the Republic, undermining the state security, advocating war, social, racial, national, religious, class or clannish superiority as well as the cult of cruelty and violence shall not be allowed (Article 20(3) Constitution).

819. In Kazakhstan, the individuals belonging to minority groups do enjoy their culture, practice their religion and use their language in community with other members of their group. All minorities in Kazakhstan are entitled to the protection of their rights.

820. There is no definition of the group constituting minority given by the Human Rights Committee or other international bodies. But its content implies a group of people with a shared culture, religion and/or language that is 'different from those of the rest of the population'.[220] According to the General Comment No. 23 of the Committee interpreting the rights of minorities, individuals belonging to minorities have the right in community with others to enjoy their own culture, to practice their religion and speak their language to preserve and promote their identity.[221]

821. Under Stalin in the 1930s and 1940s, diverse ethnic groups from different parts of the Soviet Union were forcibly deported to Kazakhstan to explore and settle its vast resources. These included Polish people from western Ukraine and western Belarus, Koreans from Primorye and Sakhalin, Germans from the Volga, Greeks from Krasnodar, Chechens and Ingush from the North Caucasus, Meskhetian Turks from Georgia, and Crimean Tatars from Crimea. Kazakhs helped them with food and shelters. In the 1950s, one million Russians moved to Kazakhstan, during the so-called Virgin Lands Campaign, to plough the land for the cultivation of grain. By the end of the 1960s, the indigenous people of Kazakhstan had become a minority group and constituted only 30% of the whole population.

822. As a consequence of these policies, according to the official information, now in contemporary Kazakhstan, there are 140 nationalities and 818 ethnic and cultural communities. Nowadays, Kazakhs are approximately 63.07% of the entire population. Russians are 23.7%. The Russian language is an official language of the country and remains dominant as an academic and intercultural language. Ethnic minorities have their own newspapers, magazines and even TV channels to promote their cultures. In 2010, Kazakhstan adopted a Doctrine of National Unity, introducing a 'Kazakhstani' identity that unites all people living in Kazakhstan.

---

220. United Nations Human Rights Office of the High Commissioner. Minority rights: international standards and guidance of implementation. New York and Geneva, 2010, at 2. Available at: http://www.ohchr.org/Documents/Publications/MinorityRights_en.pdf (accessed 19 Apr. 2019).
221. UN Human Rights Committee (HRC), ICCPR General Comment No. 23: Article 27 (Rights of Minorities), 8 Apr. 1994, CCPR/C/21/Rev.1/Add.5, available at: https://www.refworld.org/docid/453883fc0.html (accessed 19 Apr. 2019).

823. There is an Assembly of the People of Kazakhstan that is an advisory-consultative body to the President of Kazakhstan, which actively participates in the legislative power and the political decision-making process.[222] Nine members of the *Mazhilis* are elected by the Assembly of the People of Kazakhstan (Article 51 Constitution). The Assembly assists in the creation of favourable conditions for further strengthening of interethnic tolerance and mutual understanding for the prosperity of the country. The First President of the country, Nursultan Nazarbayev, is the lifetime Chair of the Assembly.

824. Sunni Islam of the Hanafi School and Russian Orthodox Christianity are two big religious confessions in Kazakhstan. Religious minorities, such as Catholics, Protestants, Baptists, Buddhists, Seventh-day Adventists, Jehovah's Witnesses, followers of Krishna's confession, Mormons, Shias and others peacefully coexist with each other in the country.[223] Once every four years, Kazakhstan hosts the Congress of World and Traditional Religions, promoting tolerance between different confessions in Kazakhstan.

825. Overall, the state policy of Kazakhstan towards minority rights encompasses providing secondary education in their native languages, the profession of their religious beliefs, and the opportunity to express themselves through mass media and publications and other tools. Kazakhstan takes appropriate measures to preserve the culture and social identity of individuals belonging to minority groups, allowing them to pursue and develop their own traditions and to be engaged in national politics.

II. Gender Equality

826. There are more than nine million women in Kazakhstan, i.e., 51.5 % of the whole population.[224] Former Kazakh nomadic liberal lifestyle that esteemed the dignity of a human being and valued the principle of meritocracy created the relevant cultural background to respect the role of girls and women in society. Kazakh women are highly educated, have grown to achieve a long life expectancy, and possess skills which are equal to men's in most aspects of the economy, civil society and leadership. Women in Kazakhstan are mainly involved in social service (education, public health and culture) and economically, they remain dependent on state support. But nevertheless, due to globalization and advanced technologies, the society of contemporary Kazakhstan is getting more modern, and women are becoming

---

222. Please *see* an official website of the Assembly: https://assembly.kz/ru/ (accessed 3 Aug. 2021).
223. UN Human Rights Council, Report of the Special Rapporteur on Freedom of Religion or Belief, Addendum: Mission to Kazakhstan, 23 Dec. 2014, A/HRC/28/66/Add.1, available at: https://www.refworld.org/docid/550822fe4.html (accessed 20 Apr. 2019).
224. *Supra*, n. 16. Please see as well: Statdannye: v Kazakhstane zhenshin bolshe, chem mujchin/ Statistics: there are more women than men in Kazakhstan. 15 Sep. 2018. Available at: https://otyrar.kz/2018/09/statdannye-v-kazaxstane-zhenshhin-bolshe-chem-muzhchin/ (accessed 23 Apr. 2019).

more independent, self-esteemed and self-sufficient in comparison with the previous generations. The new technology and support from the Government open to creative Kazakh women new perspectives and give access to online education and online business, breaking any mental and material borders. This makes it possible to create partnership relations in a family. Taking into account the economic potential and human capital of Kazakhstan, Kazakh women and their status will continue to grow and make important changes in society.

827. The Government of Kazakhstan adopts programme documents of strategic character and establishes special institutions for the promotion of gender equality in the country. For instance, the Decree of the President of 6 December 2016 No. 384 approved the Concept of Family and Gender Policy of the Republic of Kazakhstan until 2030.[225] This replaced the previous Gender Equality Strategy for the period 2006–2016. According to the actual Concept, the realization of gender politics of the country is based on principles for ensuring equality in using economic, social, cultural, civil and political rights regardless of gender; non-discrimination and gender asymmetry in state and public life; the formation of gender identity and the elimination of gender stereotypes in society.

828. As an advisory body to the President of the Republic, a National Commission on Women's Affairs and Family and Population Policy created in February 2006 defines priorities and develops recommendations to improve state policy on family, women and children affairs taking into account the peculiarities of the regional development; makes a comprehensive analysis of indicators of reproduction and health conditions of population, social and economic conditions of families; participates in drafting of concepts and programs of state policy on the issues; participates in preparation and consideration of draft laws and other normative legal acts aimed at improving conditions of family, women and children, etc.[226]

829. As mentioned in the previous sections of this writing on the protection of equality and non-discrimination, Kazakhstan, in 2009, for the first time in its history, adopted Law on State Guarantees For Equal Rights and Equal Opportunities For Men and Women. Law provides definitions of 'gender', 'gender equality', 'discrimination on the grounds of sex', 'equal rights' and 'equal opportunities' and contains overall guarantees of gender equality in the country.

830. Article 3 of Law on State Guarantees for Equal Rights enumerates the main tasks of the state policy in ensuring equal rights and opportunities:

(1) ensuring equal rights and equal opportunities for men and women in all fields of state and public life;

---

225. Concept of Family and Gender Policy of the Republic of Kazakhstan until 2030 approved by the Decree of the President of Kazakhstan of 6 Dec. 2016 No. 384. Available at: http://adilet.zan.kz/rus/docs/U1600000384 (accessed 23 Apr. 2019).

226. Please *see* the official website of the Office of the President: https://www.akorda.kz/ru/executive_office/presidential_commissions/commission_for_women (accessed 3 Aug. 2021).

(2) improvement and development of national legislation;
(3) bringing up and propaganda among the population of the country of culture of equality of men and women, non-discrimination on the grounds of sex;
(4) fulfilment of generally recognized principles and norms of international law and international obligations;
(5) increasing level of the legal and political culture of society to ensure equality of sexes in all areas of life, including politics, social-labour and family relations.

831. Article 4 of the Law concerns discrimination on the grounds of sex. So, the normative legal acts restricting or impairing equal rights and equal opportunities for men and women can be contested at the court in a manner envisaged by the laws of Kazakhstan. The following measures are not considered discriminatory on the grounds of sex if they are aimed:

(1) to protect motherhood, childhood and fatherhood;
(2) to protect women due to the fact of pregnancy and childbirth;
(3) to increase the life expectancy of men;
(4) to protect women by penal, penal-procedural and penal-enforcement legislation.

832. In line with the provisions of Article 4, differences, exceptions, preferences and restrictions which are required by the type of labour or conditioned by the special care of a state for people who need raised social and legal protection shall not be considered as discrimination.

833. From a legal point of view, national legislation does protect women in a particular way. The Penal Code of Kazakhstan forbids the application of the death penalty to women. The Code also contains punishments for violations of the rights of pregnant women and women with children under three years of age (Article 152(2)), for rape (Article 120), for the kidnapping of pregnant women (Article 125), for sexual intercourse with women under the age of 16 years (Article 122) and for illegal artificial termination of pregnancy (Article 319), etc.

834. The Labour Code of Kazakhstan of 23 November 2015 contains many provisions providing special care for women depending on their conditions. It envisages that there is a list in Kazakhstan adopted by the relevant authorities, which includes types of employment where the use of female labour is forbidden. On 8 December 2015, the Ministry of Healthcare and Social Development of Kazakhstan with its Order No. 944 approved such types of jobs.[227] They are jobs related to

227. Order of the Minister of Healthcare and Social Development of Kazakhstan of 8 Dec. 2015 No. 944 approved the list of jobs where the use of labour of employees under 18 years of age is prohibited, the limits for employees not reached 18 years of age in carrying and moving heavy goods, and the list of jobs where the use of women's labour is prohibited, limits for women in carrying and manually moving heavy goods. Available at: https://adilet.zan.kz/rus/docs/V1500012597 (accessed 3 Aug. 2021).

foundry and welding works, metal plating and painting, locksmithing and assembly work, etc. Overall, as mentioned in the Labour Code of Kazakhstan, heavy jobs, labour with harmful and (or) dangerous working conditions are prohibited for women (Article 26(2(4)) Labour Code).

835. The Labour Code takes care of pregnant women. So, in line with Article 44 of the Labour Code, on the grounds of a medical certificate, the employer is obliged to transfer a pregnant woman to another job that excludes harmful and (or) dangerous industrial factors with guaranteeing the average salary. There are some other advantages mentioned in Article 51(2) that concern prolongation of a contract for pregnant women or employees who have children under the age of 3 years. The contracts with pregnant women, women with children under the age of 3 years, single mothers bringing up children under the age of 14 years (a disabled child under the age of 18), or other persons who bring up such categories of children without a mother cannot be terminated at the initiative of the employer if the reasons for termination of a contract are the necessity to reduce the number of staff or decreased volume of production, performed work and services rendered, resulting in deterioration of economic conditions of the employer (Article 54(2) Labour Code).

836. Upon a written claim, an employer grants part-time work to a pregnant woman, one of the parents (adopter) who has a child under the age of 3 (Article 70(3) Labour Code). Article 76(2) of the Labour Code prohibits using the labour of pregnant women at night. The Labour Code protects women during pregnancy and maternity.

837. In December 2009, the Parliament of Kazakhstan adopted a special bill on Measures for Preventing Domestic Violence.[228] The adopted law is aimed at creating measures to help the victims of violence. There are around twenty-eight crisis centres in the Republic functioning in all regions that provide free medical, legal and psychological services to the victims of domestic abuse.[229]

838. On 29 June 1998, Kazakhstan ratified the CEDAW of 18 December 1979. In 2000, the country ratified the Convention on the Nationality of Married Women, the Convention on the Political Rights of Women, and the Convention of International Labour Organization concerning Equal Remuneration for Men and Women Workers for Work of Equal Value of 1951, and in 2001, the OP to CEDAW of 6 October 1999. Kazakhstan recognizes the competence of the Committee on the elimination of discrimination against women that accepts claims on violations of the

228. Law of Kazakhstan of 4 Dec. 2009 No. 214-IV ZRK on Measures for Preventing the Domestic Violence. Available at: https://online.zakon.kz/Document/?doc_id=30525680 (accessed on 3 Aug. 202 1).

229. Kazakhstan's non-state domestic violence crisis centres seek funding. Available at: https://eca.unwomen.org/en/news/stories/2016/10/kazakhstans-nonstate-domestic-violence-crisis-centres-seek-funding (accessed 3 Aug. 2021).

rights established by the CEDAW.[230] Up to now, the Committee considered a single case versus Kazakhstan in 2015, a case of *Anna Belousova* on sexual harassment in the workplace.[231]

839. Upon consideration of the state report under Article 40 of the ICCPR, the international observers, such as the UN Human Rights Committee advised Kazakhstan to 'strengthen its efforts to increase the participation of women in the public and private sectors', to 'take the necessary measures to eliminate the prevailing negative stereotypes against women' and also to 'ensure that female representation in both sectors reflects the progress made in improving their levels of education'.[232]

230. The status of ratification of the Optional Protocol to the Convention on the Elimination of All Forms of Discrimination against Women of 6 Oct. 1999. Available at: https://treaties.un.org/Pages/ViewDetails.aspx?src=TREATY&mtdsg_no=IV-8-b&chapter=4&clang=_en (accessed 23 Apr. 2019).

231. Committee on the Elimination of Discrimination Against Women. Communication No. 45/2012. *Anna Belousova v. Kazakhstan*. Views adopted by the Committee at its sixty-first session, 6–24 Jul. 2015. CEDAW/C/61/D/45/2012, available at: https://tbinternet.ohchr.org/_layouts/treatybodyexternal/Download.aspx?symbolno=CEDAW%2fC%2f61%2fD%2f45%2f2012&Lang=en (accessed 23 Apr. 2019).

232. UN Human Rights Committee (HRC), Consideration of Reports Submitted by States Parties Under Article 40 of the Covenant, Second Periodic Reports of States Parties Due in 2014: Kazakhstan, 12 Feb. 2015, CCPR/C/KAZ/2, available at: https://www.refworld.org/docid/5783a4934.html (accessed 22 Apr. 2019).

Chapter 4. Judicial Control of Administrative Action

840. In accordance with the national law of Kazakhstan, actions (inactions) of officials and acts (decisions) of state bodies are contested in accordance with the relevant laws of the Republic.

841. Previously, such complaints had been considered within the special claim proceedings of the civil procedural law. Subsection 3 of the Civil Procedure Code of Kazakhstan covered the special claim proceedings and Chapter 29 regulated proceedings on the cases challenging the decisions and actions (inactions) of state authorities, local government bodies, public associations, organizations, officials and civil servants.

842. Currently, section 4 of the Administrative Procedures Code regulates the issues of administrative legal proceedings. According to Article 102 of the Code, administrative legal proceedings is carried out by specialized district and equivalent to them administrative courts. Regional and equivalent to them courts consider appeals to the administrative cases (Article 104). As a general rule, in administrative cases, the Supreme Court acts as a cassation instance.

843. In line with Article 117 of the Code, the administrative legal proceedings consist of the following stages:

(1) registration of a claim by a court;
(2) actions of a court on the received administrative case and conducting a preliminary hearing;
(3) adoption of a decision by a court, its announcing and explanation;
(4) execution of a court decision and judicial control.

844. An administrative case shall be considered and resolved within a reasonable timeframe, but not longer than three months from the day of lodging of a claim. If a case is complex, the timeframe may be extended by a motivated court's decision but not more than for three months (Article 146(1)).

Chapter 5. Rights and Status of Foreigners

§1. Introduction

845. Kazakhstan is considered as a sending, transit and receiving country with strong migration processes. The problems of migration in Kazakhstan concern the high level of labour migration from Commonwealth of Independent States (CIS) and other countries, accepting ethnic Kazakhs from other countries, and internal migration from less developed regions to more developed urban areas. As is well known, Kazakhstan is attractive to migrant workers because of its economic conditions, geographical location, large territory and the low numbers of its population. Migrant workers are mainly from Central Asian countries (Kyrgyzstan, Uzbekistan and Tajikistan). As recognized in the Concept of Migration Policy, the country feels the pressure of low-skilled immigration flows.[233] International Organization for Migration (IOM) says that Central Asian countries also receive refugees and asylum seekers from Afghanistan and Eastern China as well.

§2. Constitutional Rights and Protections

I. Equal Protection

846. The status of foreigners and stateless persons in Kazakhstan is regulated by Article 12(4) of the Constitution of Kazakhstan. The legal status of foreigners in Kazakhstan is regulated by the Law of Kazakhstan on citizenship and the special Law on the Legal Status of Foreigners adopted on 19 June 1995.[234]

The Law on the Legal Status of Foreigners in Kazakhstan covers labour activity and recreation, health protection, social and pension benefits, the right to housing, other property and personal non-property rights, receiving education, use of cultural achievements, and participation in public associations, freedom of conscience, marital and family relations, and inviolability of housing, honour and dignity, movement within the territory of Kazakhstan and choice of a place of residence, taxes and fees, protection of the rights of foreigners, restrictions in electoral law, conscription issues. The Law also contains the procedures for their entry into and exit from Kazakhstan, their stay and movement within the territory of the Republic.

847. The Law distinguishes two categories of foreigners: those permanently residing and those temporarily residing in Kazakhstan. In accordance with Article 4 of the Law, permanently residing foreigners are those who have received permission for permanent residency in line with the procedures defined by the MIA of the

233. Concept on Migration Policy of Kazakhstan for 2017-2021, adopted by the Decree of the Resolution of the Government of the Republic of 29 Sep. 2017, No. 602. Available at: http://adilet.zan.kz/rus/docs/P1700000602 (accessed 27 Apr. 2019).
234. Law of Kazakhstan of 19 Jun. 1995 No. 2337 on the Legal Status of Foreigners. Available at: https://online.zakon.kz/document/?doc_id=1003764 (accessed 3 Aug. 2021).

Republic. The main mandatory condition for granting permanent residency is confirmation of his/her solvency. Ethnic Kazakhs, persons who were born in the territory of the Republic or previously had citizenship of Kazakhstan or of the Kazakh SSR, and members of their families are exempted from the condition to confirm solvency.

848. In conformity with Article 4(3) of Law on the Legal Status of Foreigners, foreigners staying in Kazakhstan on other legal grounds, as well as those recognized as victims, witnesses, suspects or accused persons in criminal cases, are considered as temporarily staying in Kazakhstan until entry into force of the court's sentence or adoption by the authorized bodies of other procedural decisions.

849. In line with the provisions of Article 12(4) of the Constitution, foreigners and stateless persons have equal rights and freedoms and bear equal responsibilities to those established for citizens of the Republic unless otherwise envisaged in the Constitution, the laws and international treaties. Such equal conditions are replicated in Article 6 of the Law of Kazakhstan on citizenship and in Article 3 of Law on the Legal Status of Foreigners. In particular, foreigners permanently staying in the Republic in employment contracts have the same rights and obligations as the citizens of Kazakhstan (Article 6 Law on the Legal Status of Foreigners).

850. According to Article 3 of the Law on the Legal Status of Foreigners, all foreigners are equal before the laws of Kazakhstan regardless of their origin, social and property status, race or ethnicity, sex, education, language, religion, type of occupation. In general, foreigners can undertake labour activity in the Republic of Kazakhstan on the grounds and in the way established by legislation and international treaties. Foreigners staying in Kazakhstan have the right to recreation under the same general conditions established for the citizens of Kazakhstan (Article 6 Law on the Legal Status of Foreigners). With regards to social and pension provisions, foreigners permanently staying in the Republic have the same rights and duties as the citizens of Kazakhstan; work experience of foreigners performed abroad may be counted on the grounds and in the way established by legislation and international treaties of Kazakhstan (Article 8 Law on the Legal Status of Foreigners).

851. As given in Article 9 of the Law on the legal status of foreigners, as regards housing relations, foreigners permanently staying in Kazakhstan have the same rights and bear the same responsibilities as the citizens of Kazakhstan unless otherwise established by the Constitution, laws and international treaties of Kazakhstan. They have property rights to housing and copyrights. Foreigners permanently staying in Kazakhstan use their property and personal non-property rights equally with the citizens of the Republic. In line with Article 14 of the Law on the legal status of foreigners, foreigners may conclude a marriage or divorce with citizens of Kazakhstan and other persons, use rights and bear responsibilities in marital and family relations equally with the citizens of Kazakhstan in accordance with the legislation and international treaties of the Republic.

852. The issues of migration in Kazakhstan are covered not only by legislation but also by political documents. The Concept of Migration Policy of the Republic of Kazakhstan for 2017–2021 of 29 September 2017, which replaced the previous one adopted for 2007–2015 by the Presidential Decree in August 2007, analyses the current situation of migration and its development, drawing conclusions and proposing further actions. According to the Concept, the state bodies should ensure and protect the rights and interests of migrants. Overall, the Concept supports the attraction of foreign migrant workers and takes into account that the younger generations of Kazakhstani people simply leave the country.

II. Restrictions

853. As stipulated in Article 3 of the Law on the legal status of foreigners, the enjoyment by foreigners of their rights and freedoms should not harm the interests of the Republic of Kazakhstan, the rights and legitimate interests of citizens and other persons and is inseparable from the carrying out of duties, as established by the national legislation. The legislative acts of Kazakhstan can establish restrictions in the realization by foreigners of labour activity in order to protect the constitutional right of citizens of Kazakhstan to freedom of labour. Foreigners cannot be appointed to certain positions or be engaged in certain labour activities in accordance with the national legislation. Foreigners temporarily staying in the Republic can do entrepreneurship only as legal entities (Article 6 Law on the Legal Status of Foreigners). Foreigners can neither elect nor be elected to a representative and other elected state bodies and positions, nor can they take part in the national referendum of Kazakhstan (Article 19 Law on the Legal Status of Foreigners). Conscription does not cover foreigners permanently residing in the territory of the Republic (Article 20 Law on the Legal Status of Foreigners).

§3. Immigration and Naturalization of Foreigners

I. Freedom of Movement of Foreigners

854. At the legislative level, this right is regulated by Law on the Legal Status of Foreigners of 19 June 1995 and Law on Population Migration of 22 July 2011.[235] According to Article 16 of Law on the Legal Status of Foreigners of 19 June 1995, foreigners can freely move within the territory of the Republic. Article 5(1(4,5)) of Law on Population Migration states that immigrants have the right to move freely within the territory of the Republic open to foreigners and to choose their place of residence freely in accordance with the national legislation. Kazakhstan is open for foreigners to visit and to choose their place of residence in accordance with the national legislation. This can be restricted if necessary for state security, protection

235. Law of Kazakhstan of 22 Jul. 2011 on Population Migration. Available at: https://online.zakon.kz/document/?doc_id=31038298 (accessed 3 Aug. 2021).

of public order, public health and morals, the rights and freedoms of citizens of Kazakhstan and others (Article 22 Law on the Legal Status of Foreigners).

855. Article 55 of the Law on Population Migration replicates the text of the Constitution concerning the right to leave the territory of the country and the right to freely return to the Republic. In line with Article 23 of the Law on the legal status of foreigners, the exit of foreigners can be restricted if there are grounds to bring him/her to justice or if he/she is convicted of a crime or if he/she refuses to perform obligations imposed by the court, and on other detailed grounds enumerated in the Article.

856. In general, the constitutional provisions and legislative acts of Kazakhstan on the freedom of movement satisfy the requirements of the ICCPR. Despite the fact that the Law on the legal status of foreigners was adopted ten years before the ratification of the ICCPR, most of its content is in compliance with the ICCPR provisions.

II. Immigration and Deportation

A. *Entry to the Territory of Kazakhstan*

857. According to Kazakhstan legislation, foreigners are obliged to be registered in their place of residence. Article 6 of the Law on population migration and Article 4 of the Law on the Legal Status of Foreigners require the registration of immigrants.

858. Article 22 of the Law on the legal status of foreigners stipulates the rules regulating issues of the entry of foreigners into the territory of Kazakhstan. As a general rule, foreigners are free to enter the country on the basis of valid passports (or other travel documents replacing the passport) and the entrance visa issued by the authorities of Kazakhstan, if other rules are not envisaged by agreement of the Republic. Entry to the territory for a foreigner is prohibited on the grounds enumerated in Article 22 of the Law on Legal Status of Foreigners. This includes the following and other grounds:

(1) in the interests of national security, protection of public order and health of the population;
(2) if his/her actions are aimed at forcible change of the current constitutional order;
(3) if he/she acts against the sovereignty and independence of the Republic or calls for the violation of the unity and integrity of its territory;
(4) if he/she instigates interethnic, interfaith and religious enmity;
(5) if it is necessary for the protection of the rights and legitimate interests of citizens of Kazakhstan and other persons;

(6) if the national security bodies have information about his involvement in extremist or terrorist activities, as well as in the case when a court recognizes a dangerous relapse in his/her actions;
(7) if he/she has not fully fulfilled any penalty for committing penal or administrative offences, previously imposed on him/her during a previous stay in Kazakhstan;
(8) if during his/her previous stay in Kazakhstan he/she had not presented a declaration on the individual income tax as envisaged by the legislation of the Republic;
(9) if he/she did not present a confirmation of the availability of funds necessary for staying or exiting from Kazakhstan in the manner determined by the Government, (with the exception of ethnic Kazakhs, and persons born or having previously acquired citizenship of Kazakhstan or the Kazakh SSR, along with members of their families;
(10) if, when applying for entry, he/she submitted false information about himself/herself or did not present necessary documents within the deadline established by the legislation of Kazakhstan;
(11) if he has any diseases that prevent entry to the territory of Kazakhstan;
(12) if he/she previously had lost the citizenship of Kazakhstan on the grounds envisaged by subparagraph 8 of Article 21 of the Law on the Citizenship of Kazakhstan (e.g., for participation in foreign armed conflicts and (or) terrorist activity on the territory of another country);
(13) if he/she was deprived of citizenship on the grounds envisaged by Article 20-1 of the Law on the Citizenship of Kazakhstan (deprivation of liberty is allowed only on the grounds of a court for terrorist crimes, as well as for crimes, envisaged by the relevant articles of the Special Part of the Penal Code of Kazakhstan, which might lead to other serious harm to the vital interests of the Republic).

859. Foreigners who have previously been expelled from the territory of Kazakhstan are prohibited from entering the territory of the Republic for at least five years from the date of the decision on expulsion. Entry visas and other relevant documents are issued by the diplomatic representatives or consular bodies of Kazakhstan and in certain cases the specially authorized representatives of the Republic. The grounds for issuing visas are the invitations from their hosts, or permission of the authorized state bodies of the Republic unless other things are envisaged by international treaties of Kazakhstan.

B. *Exclusion from the Territory of Kazakhstan and the Protection of Foreigners Against Arbitrary Expulsion*

860. Article 13 of the ICCPR guarantees that 'an alien lawfully in the territory of a State Party to the present Covenant may be expelled there from only in pursuance of a decision reached in accordance with the law and shall, except where compelling reasons of national security otherwise require, be allowed to submit the reasons against his expulsion and to have his case reviewed by, and be represented for the purpose before, the competent authority or a person or persons especially designated by the competent authority'. The legal position of aliens under the Covenant was examined in General Comment No. 15 of the Human Rights Committee.[236] The Committee was of the opinion that an alien who is allowed to enter the territory of a State Party is entitled to the rights set out in the Covenant (paragraph 6). The aim of that article is to prevent the arbitrary expulsion of aliens (paragraph 10 of General Comment No. 15). The term 'aliens' includes not only foreigners but also stateless persons and refugees. Article 13 concerns the rights of aliens who have legally entered the state and who lawfully reside within it; its provisions do not cover 'illegal entrants and aliens who have stayed longer than the law or their permits allow, in particular' (paragraph 9. of the General Comment No. 15). Issues of extradition are considered 'a matter outside the scope of application of the ICCPR', demanding their own specific procedures.[237]

861. The provisions of Article 13 apply to all obligatory expulsions and departures of an alien (paragraph 9 of the General Comment No. 15) and regulate the procedure. The decision on expulsion must be taken by a court or by an administrative authority.[238] The case of each alien should be considered individually. The article guarantees 'the right to submit reasons against expulsion and to have the decision reviewed by and to be represented before the competent authority or someone designated by it' (paragraph 10 of the General Comment No. 15). Thus, it establishes the procedural rights of a hearing, appeal, and the right to representation. The general requirement to a State Party to the Covenant, which stems from the General Comment, is that 'an alien must be given full facilities for pursuing his remedy against expulsion so that this right will in all the circumstances of his case be an effective one' (paragraph 10 of the General Comment No. 15).

862. The provisions of Article 14 of the Constitution of Kazakhstan guarantee the equality of everyone before the law and the courts, and no one must be discriminated against on the grounds of nationality or other circumstances. Equal conditions for foreigners imply that due process shall guarantee their rights and freedoms as defined in the Penal and Civil Procedures Codes and in the Code on Administrative Offences without any discrimination. These procedural guarantees include the right to a hearing, a right to appeal and a right to be represented, etc.

863. The decision to expel is regulated by Article 28 of the Law on Legal Status of Foreigners of 19 June 1995. That can be done on the following grounds:

(1) if the activities of a foreigner contradict the interests of state security or public order;

236. UN Human Rights Committee (HRC), CCPR General Comment No. 15: The Position of Aliens Under the Covenant, 11 Apr. 1986, available at: https://www.refworld.org/docid/45139acfc.html (accessed 26 Apr. 2019).
237. Alex Conte & Richard Burchill, *supra* n. 163, at 75.
238. Nowak, *supra* n. 142, at 294.

(2) if the expulsion is necessary for the protection of public health and morals, or the rights and legitimate interests of citizens of the Republic and of other people;
(3) if a foreigner has broken the laws of Kazakhstan;
(4) if the marriage of a foreigner with the citizen of the Republic has been recognized as invalid when the marriage had been the grounds for the permanent residency of that foreigner in Kazakhstan.

864. The application of administrative penalties towards foreigners is regulated by the Code on Administrative Offences of the Republic of Kazakhstan of 5 July 2014.[239] According to Articles 41(1(9)), 51 of the Code, expulsion from the country is an administrative penalty that is applied by a judge towards foreigners and stateless persons and should be done in the manner and on the grounds provided for in the Code. Violation by a foreigner of the rules of stay may bring the result in administrative expulsion (Article 517(7) Code on Administrative Offences). According to paragraph 3 of Article 19 of the Law on the National Safety of the Republic of Kazakhstan, if the foreigners and stateless persons residing in the territory of the Republic have infectious diseases that threaten public health, they shall be expelled from the country.[240]

865. The procedures of expulsion by a court are also regulated by Chapter 49 of the Civil Procedure Code. The decision on expulsion should be taken within ten days of the initiation of the case. The presence of the alien at the hearing is an obligatory condition (Article 384 Civil Procedure Code).

866. The foreigner is obliged to leave the Republic within the period defined by the decision of the authorities. If a foreigner does not leave the country by himself, he will be forced to depart from the country on the grounds of the prosecutor's sanction. The expelled person is handed over officially at the border to the representative of his/her foreign country (Article 28 Law on Legal Status of Foreigners, Articles 916–917 Code on Administrative Offences).

III. Extradition

867. Issues of extradition are regulated by Chapter 60 of the Penal Procedure Code. There are certain conditions for carrying out extradition enumerated in Article 579 of the Code. The request for extradition can be made if one of the crimes committed carries a sentence of at least a one-year imprisonment, or if the perpetrator has not less than six months of the unserved term of the sentence still to run. The

239. Code of Kazakhstan of 5 Jul. 2014 on the Administrative Offences. Available at: https://online.zakon.kz/document/?doc_id=31577399 (accessed 3 Aug. 2021).
240. Law of Kazakhstan of 6 Jan. 2012 No. 527-IV on the National Safety of the Republic of Kazakhstan. Available at: https://online.zakon.kz/document/?doc_id=31106860 (accessed 3 Aug. 2021).

Office of the General Prosecutor shall have the right to refuse the request of a competent body if there are circumstances envisaged in the Code on Penal Procedure or in international treaties of the Republic that may hinder that extradition.

868. In the cases and in the manner prescribed by the Penal Procedure Code and by international treaties of the Republic, the body which is responsible for the penal process sends a request to the Office of the General Prosecutor enclosing necessary documents on extradition of a person who has committed a crime on the territory of Kazakhstan and left its the territory (Article 580 Penal Procedure Code).

869. A person extradited from a foreign country cannot be prosecuted and punished for a crime that is not related to the reason for his extradition without the consent of the country that extradited him/her. A person extradited by a foreign State cannot be transferred to a third state without the consent of the country that extradited him/her. The prosecutor shall submit the results of the penal process to the Office of the General Prosecutor, who will further inform any other appropriate body (Articles 582–583 Penal Procedure Code).

870. Article 586 of the Penal Procedure Code states that a person whose extradition to a foreign country has been requested has the following rights:

(1) to know what kind of crime is a reason for extradition;
(2) to have a lawyer and to have a confidential appointment with him, and to have a lawyer during the process of interrogation;
(3) to inform his/her close relatives, members of the family or other persons about his arrest and place of stay;
(4) to take part in any consideration of questions related to his/her detention and extradition;
(5) to familiarize himself with the request for extradition;
(6) to appeal a decision on detention, on the application of an extradition warrant, and on the approval of the extradition request;
(7) to express an opinion at the court hearing that considers the extradition request;
(8) if a person is a foreigner and has been detained, he has the right to have a meeting with a representative of the diplomatic or consular mission of his/her state.

IV. Asylum

871. In line with Article 5 of the Law on the legal status of foreigners, Kazakhstan grants asylum to foreigners who are victims of human rights violations. The issue on political asylum shall be decided by the President of the Republic. The Commission on granting citizenship to the President of Kazakhstan also regulates issues of granting political asylum in the Republic.[241] The local executive bodies shall finance the expenses of the arrangement of persons who have been granted political asylum using the funds of the local budgets set aside for resettlement activities (paragraph 2 Decree).

872. In line with paragraph 5 of the Regulations, political asylum is granted to foreigners and stateless persons and members of their families who seek asylum and protection from persecution or real threat of falling victim to persecution in their country of citizenship and/or residence because of public and political activity, race or national identity, religious beliefs, as well as in cases of violation of human rights, envisaged in International Law provisions. As given in paragraph 38 of the Regulations, the MIA of Kazakhstan gives a certificate to a person who has been granted political asylum and members of his family above the age of 16.

873. In accordance with paragraph 40 of the Regulations, the right to political asylum may be lost in the following cases:

(1) voluntary refusal to get political asylum in Kazakhstan;
(2) acquisition of citizenship of Kazakhstan or another state;
(3) voluntary return to the country of his/her nationality or departure to a third country;
(4) loss of grounds established by these Regulations.

The President may deprive a person of political asylum if he/she engages in activities contrary to the interests of the national security of Kazakhstan and to the principles of the UN, or has committed a deliberate crime and the court's sentence regarding him has been enforced (paragraph 41 Regulations).

874. A decision on granting political asylum may be revised by the President of the Republic. Appeals may be made to a higher authority or court in cases of unjustified refusal of it, or of violations of the terms and procedures of consideration of the applications, as well as of other unlawful actions of the officials that violate these procedures and implementation of decisions on these issues (paragraphs 42–43 Regulations).

---

241. Regulations on the Commission on Granting Citizenship at the President of Kazakhstan approved by the Decree of the President of the Republic of Kazakhstan of 10 Oct. 2006 No. 198. Available at: https://adilet.zan.kz/rus/docs/U060000198_ (accessed 3 Aug. 2021).

Part V. Specific Issues

Chapter 1. War and Foreign Affairs Powers

§1. The Constitution About Wartime

875. As stated in the preamble to the Constitution, the people of Kazakhstan constitute themselves as a peace-loving civil society. In accordance with Article 53 of the Constitution of Kazakhstan, it is the Parliament in a joint session of the Chambers that makes a decision on war and peace. Similarly, it is the Parliament at a joint session of the Chambers which takes the decision on the use of the Armed Forces of Kazakhstan to fulfil international obligations for the maintenance of peace and security, acting on a proposal by the President of the Republic. In line with subparagraph 17 of Article 44 of the Constitution, in case of aggression against the Republic or a direct external threat to the security of the country, the President of Kazakhstan shall declare martial law in force throughout the entire territory, or in certain specified areas of Kazakhstan along with partial or full mobilization, and shall immediately inform the Parliament of the Republic. The President of Kazakhstan is the Supreme Commander-in-Chief of the Armed Forces of the Republic; he appoints and dismisses the military leaders of the Armed Forces (subparagraph 12 of Article 44 of the Constitution). Article 63(2) of the Constitution establishes that the Parliament and the *Mazhilis* of the Parliament cannot be dissolved during the period of a state of emergency or of martial war status.

§2. National Defence

876. Chapter 6 of the Law of 7 January 2005 on Defence and the Armed Forces of the Republic of Kazakhstan is devoted to issues of a state of war, martial law, mobilization, civil and territorial defence. A state of the law is proclaimed by the Parliament of the Republic in case of armed attack on Kazakhstan by another state (group or coalition of states), as well as in cases envisaged by international treaties ratified by Kazakhstan. Wartime starts from the declaration of a state of war or of the actual outbreak of armed action. It ends at the moment of the declaration on the cessation of the armed actions, but not earlier than their actual termination (Article 28 Law on Defence).

877. During martial law, the Armed Forces of Kazakhstan and other bodies conduct warfare and other actions to repel aggression regardless of a declaration of a state of war (Article 29 Law on Defence). Civil defence shall be organized for the protection of the population and the territory of Kazakhstan from damaging or destructive factors of contemporary means of attack, of natural or man-made emergencies (Article 30 Law on Defence).

878. Referring to Article 31 of Law on Defence, territorial defence shall be organized by the Government of the Republic. Within their competencies, other state bodies are involved in the planning and implementation of measures necessary for territorial defence. During the mobilization period, or martial law or wartime, the general leadership of territorial defence is carried out by the Supreme High Command General Headquarters via the General Staff of Armed Forces. The general tasks or the system of organization of territorial defence shall be defined by the President of Kazakhstan. Local executive bodies maintain territorial troops to fulfil the tasks of territorial defence. Special formations are created to ensure territorial defence by the state bodies and organizations regardless of ownership.

§3. The Police Services

879. Police services are carried out in Kazakhstan by the internal affairs bodies. The legal status and competence of the internal affairs bodies are regulated by the Law of Kazakhstan of 23 April 2014 No. 199-V ZRK on the Internal Affairs Bodies of the Republic of Kazakhstan.[242]

880. The internal affairs bodies of Kazakhstan are the law-enforcement bodies charged with protecting the life, rights and freedoms of the individual and citizen, the interests of society and state, from unlawful encroachments, to protect public order and ensure public safety. The activities of the law-enforcement bodies shall be carried out in line with the principles of civil service and special principles of the law-enforcement service of Kazakhstan (Articles 1, 3 Law on the Internal Affairs Bodies).

881. Article 4 of the Law on the Internal Affairs Bodies enumerates the tasks of internal affairs bodies that are necessary to provide public safety. These are:

(1) crime prevention;
(2) protection of public order;
(3) combating crime;
(4) enforcement of criminal penalties and other measures of penal pressure, as well as administrative sanctions.

Other tasks may be imposed on these bodies by the laws of Kazakhstan and the legal acts of the President of the Republic.

242. Law of Kazakhstan of 23 Apr. 2014 No. 199-V ZRK on the Internal Affairs Bodies of the Republic of Kazakhstan. Available at: https://online.zakon.kz/document/?doc_id=31538985 (accessed 3 Aug. 2021).

882. Article 5 of the Law covers the competence of internal affairs bodies. In accordance with the legislation of Kazakhstan, the internal affairs bodies have the following competence:

(1) to carry out measures aimed at revealing, studying, eliminating the causes and conditions of crime;
(2) to enforce measures for the protection of public order;
(3) to supervise road traffic and ensure its safety;
(4) to enforce state control over the turnover of civil and service weapons and their ammunition;
(5) to exercise control in the field of security guard activities;
(6) to protect individuals and objects that are subject to state protection;
(7) to control protection of the objects vulnerable to a terrorist attack;
(8) to carry out state policies in the field of citizenship, migration of population and refugees;
(9) to implement interdepartmental coordination in the field of population migration;
(10) to monitor, analyse and forecast migration processes;
(11) to develop a system of measures for the regulation of migration processes;
(12) to fulfil obligations of the Republic stemming from international treaties on readmission ratified by the country;
(13) to carry out the processing of identity documents, and maintain the National Register of individual identification numbers;
(14) to carry out licensing and permitting activities;
(15) to carry out proceedings in cases of administrative offences;
(16) to detect and investigate criminal offences;
(17) to carry out law-enforcement intelligence operations and secret investigative actions;
(18) to conduct research;
(19) to conduct a search;
(20) to implement state policy in the field of trafficking in narcotic drugs, psychotropic substances, precursors and prevent illicit trafficking and abuse;
(21) to carry out state protection of persons participating in the criminal process;
(22) to realize the state policy in the field of penal-penitentiary activities, conducts detention of people at the special institutions of the internal affairs bodies;
(23) to carry out state services;
(24) to conduct international cooperation;
(25) to carry out other functions envisaged by the laws of Kazakhstan, the legal acts of the President and the Government of Kazakhstan.

883. The system of internal affairs bodies is described in Article 7(1, 3) of the Law under consideration. The system of internal affairs bodies consists of the police, penal-penitentiary system, military investigative bodies, the National Guard of the Republic of Kazakhstan. The internal affairs bodies are composed of the MIA, departments, territorial units of police, as well as of other bodies subordinated to the MIA.

884. The police service is formed by the criminal police, the administrative police, and various subdivisions on investigation, inquiry and other units. Criminal police consist of the units for combating organized crime, extremism, illegal drug trafficking, psychotropic substances and precursors, and other units that carry out law-enforcement operations. Administrative police consist of the local police services in the field of turnover of civil and service weapons, migration police, escort service, special agencies and other units that are responsible for maintenance of public order. The territorial units of the police (departments of internal affairs bodies) are those units that in the regions, cities of national importance, the capital, at thc transport, cities, districts, cities in the districts, linear police bodies (bodies of internal affairs), military investigative bodies (Article 7(2, 3) Law on the Internal Affairs Bodies).

885. In line with Article 9-1 of the Law on the Internal Affairs Bodies, the local police service consists of the district police inspectors, units on juvenile affairs, for protection of women from violence, protection of nature, patrol police and other units that carry out activities in prevention of offences, protection of public order, and maintenance of traffic security. At least once a quarter, the district police inspector reports to the population residing in the relevant area of the administrative-territorial unit.

886. The MIA of the Republic develops the rules for organization and for reporting by heads of the police department of the region, a city of national importance and the capital, and the reports of the police bodies of a city, a district and a district in a city, and reports of district inspectors to the public, carries out many other functions enumerated in the Article (paragraph 24 Article 11 Law on the Internal Affairs Bodies). The Government of Kazakhstan approves these rules (Article 11 Law on the Internal Affairs Bodies).

§4. Foreign Relations and Representations of Kazakhstan Abroad

I. Introduction

887. Many issues concerning foreign policy, treaty-making power, conclusion of international treaties and their place in the national legal system have already been discussed in previous chapters. The President, the Parliament, the Government, and the MFA of Kazakhstan are the main state bodies that govern the foreign policy of the Republic. The President of Kazakhstan defines its main directions and represents the country in international relations; he conducts negotiations and signs international treaties of Kazakhstan; he also independently appoints the Minister of Foreign Affairs and the heads of diplomatic missions, etc. The Parliament of Kazakhstan gives its consent to international treaties that require its approval, adopts the laws that concern foreign policy of the Republic, and takes decisions on issues of war and peace, including issues of the participation of Kazakhstan in peacekeeping operations that stem from the Republic's international obligations, etc. The Government of Kazakhstan develops the main directions of social-economic policy, national defence capability and security of the State, formulates and develops measures for carrying out the external policy of the Republic, signs intergovernmental agreements, etc. As mentioned in Chapter 4 on 'The Executive' of this writing, the MFA of Kazakhstan develops the concept and the main directions of Kazakhstan's foreign policy and coordinates the international activity of other central state bodies to ensure the unified external political and economic investment policy of the Republic in relations with foreign States and international organizations.

888. Apart from legal documents already analysed, in fulfilling foreign policy of Kazakhstan plays such political guidance like the Concept of Foreign Policy of the Republic of Kazakhstan.

889. The previous Concept of Foreign Policy of the Republic of Kazakhstan for 2014–2020 was approved by the Decree of the President of Kazakhstan of 2014.[243] As was given in that Concept, Kazakhstan was interested in the politically stable, economically sustainable and secure development of Central Asia and making all-out efforts to ensure regional stability and security to counter new challenges and threats. The Concept enumerated eleven aims of the foreign policy of Kazakhstan, the first three of them concerned ensuring the national security, defence capacity, sovereignty and territorial integrity of the State, strengthening peace, regional and global security; ensuring stable positions and the formation of a positive image of the Republic in the world community, etc. Kazakhstan wished to see Central Asia as a single integrated actor in international politics and economy. As was given in the Concept, Kazakhstan was interested in strengthening the Customs Union and the Common Economic Space to create the Eurasian Economic Union (EAEU). The Concept established as its priority the finalization of an international legal framework in defining the status of the Caspian Sea, strengthening stable and friendly relations between its coastal countries based on principles and norms of international law. The state bodies of Kazakhstan were obligated to analyse, on a regular basis, the international treaties and obligations of the country, to develop strategic and tactical ways for the realization of foreign policy and to make relevant proposals, and to coordinate own actions with the MFA if they had had political consequences in external relations.

890. The current Concept of Foreign Policy of the Republic of Kazakhstan was adopted in May 2020 for 2020–2030 and approved by the Decree of the President of Kazakhstan.[244] The President's Administration is responsible for the control over the implementation of the Decree. The Concept contains an analysis of contemporary international relations, international experience of using foreign policy concepts in achieving national interests, the main principles of the foreign policy of Kazakhstan its aims and tasks, trends and vision of development of foreign policy

243. Concept of Foreign Policy of the Republic of Kazakhstan for 2014–2020, approved by the Decree of the President of Kazakhstan of 21 Jan. 2014 No. 741. Available at the official website of the MFA of Kazakhstan: https://adilet.zan.kz/rus/docs/U1400000741 (accessed 3 Aug. 2021).

244. Concept of Foreign Policy of the Republic of Kazakhstan for 2020-2030, approved by the Decree of the President of Kazakhstan of 6 Mar. 2020 No. 280. Available at: https://adilet.zan.kz/rus/docs/U2000000280 (accessed 3 Aug. 2021).

and the instruments of their realization, implementation phases and expected results, and the list of normative legal acts that will be used to implement foreign policy.

II. Mechanisms Ensuring the Coherence of Foreign Policy

891. The MFA is the central state body of the country that carries out foreign political activity. In line with the Regulations on the legal status of the MFA of Kazakhstan of 2004 that was discussed in the previous chapters, the MFA carries out the following and other functions:

(1) representation of Kazakhstan in relations with foreign States and international organizations;
(2) implementation of the foreign policy of the Republic;
(3) organization of negotiations and conclusion of international treaties of Kazakhstan;
(4) ensuring the participation of Kazakhstan in the activities of international organizations, conferences, meetings, forums, promoting the role of Kazakhstan as a member of the international community, in addressing global and regional problems;
(5) facilitation of interparliamentary relations of Kazakhstan with other countries;
(6) interaction on issues of its competence with the state bodies of Kazakhstan and other organizations;
(7) conducting relations with foreign countries or international organizations on issues of conclusion, entry into force, implementation, making amendments, suspension and termination of international treaties, etc.

892. Apart from the Regulations on the legal status of the MFA, the conduct of foreign policy in Kazakhstan is guided by the special Law on the diplomatic service of 7 March 2002.[245] According to Article 5 of the Law on the Diplomatic Service, the diplomatic service bodies carry out the following and other tasks:

(1) develop the concepts and main directions of foreign policy and submit relevant proposals to the President and the Government of Kazakhstan;
(2) develop for the attention of the President of Kazakhstan proposals on foreign political and foreign economic strategy of the Republic and realizes the international initiatives of the President;
(3) carry out the realization of foreign policy of the country, assistance in realization of foreign economic policy and strengthening of the international image of the Republic;
(4) ensuring, by diplomatic means and methods, the protection of the sovereignty, security, territorial integrity and inviolability of borders of the Republic, its political, trade-economic and other interests in relations with other States and in the international arena;

245. Law of Kazakhstan of 7 Mar. 2002 No. 299-II on the Diplomatic Service of the Republic of Kazakhstan. Available: https://online.zakon.kz/Document/?doc_id=1029703 (accessed 3 Aug. 2021).

(5) protection of the rights and interests of citizens and legal entities of Kazakhstan abroad;
(6) implementation by diplomatic means and methods of the efforts of Kazakhstan in ensuring international peace, global and regional security;
(7) realization of diplomatic and consular relations of Kazakhstan with foreign States and international organizations;
(8) coordinate international activity of other state bodies to ensure a unified foreign policy and economic course and investment policy of the Republic in relations with foreign States and international organizations, in line with procedures approved by the President;
(9) carry out the coordination of activities of state bodies and other organizations on official development assistance issues;
(10) maintain all official affairs with diplomatic representations, international organizations, as well as consular institutions, accredited to Kazakhstan;
(11) carry out analysis of political and social-economic situations in the world, the external and internal policies of foreign countries, the activity of international organizations and provide necessary information to the central state bodies.

III. Diplomatic Representation

A. *Diplomatic Representation and Representation of Kazakhstan in International Organizations*

893. The bodies of the diplomatic service are the state bodies that conduct the foreign policy activity of the Republic of Kazakhstan (Article 3 Law on the Diplomatic Service). A uniform system of the diplomatic service is led by the MFA and is composed of the MFA, its institutions, the Representation of the MFA in Almaty, its overseas agencies, as well as subordinate organizations created to ensure activities of the MFA, and the research and educational institutions under the jurisdiction of the Ministry (Article 4 Law on the Diplomatic Service).

894. The functions of the diplomatic service given in Article 6 of Law on the Diplomatic Service in many cases correspond to the previously discussed functions of the MFA. Article 6 enumerates many functions, including the following ones:

(1) the representation of Kazakhstan in relations with foreign States and international organizations;
(2) realization of the foreign policy of Kazakhstan;
(3) organization for conducting negotiations and conclusion of international treaties;
(4) preparation of proposals for the conclusion, execution, suspension and withdrawal from international treaties, their submission in a prescribed manner for consideration to the President or the Government;
(5) the submission in a prescribed manner to the President, the Parliament and the Government of Kazakhstan of proposals and recommendations on relations of Kazakhstan with foreign countries and international organizations;

(6) ensuring the participation of the Republic in the activities of international organizations, conferences, meetings, forums, promoting the role of the Republic as a member of the international community in the resolution of global and regional problems;
(7) ensuring the interests of Kazakhstan in the field of international protection and rational use of water resources and the environment, the development of resources of the world's ocean and of cosmic exploration;
(8) participation in the development of measures for the protection of the rights and freedoms of citizens of Kazakhstan, protection of public order, development and enlargement of trade-economic, financial, scientific and technological, cultural, and other relations of Kazakhstan with foreign States and international organizations;
(9) carrying out general monitoring and control over the implementation of international treaties to which Kazakhstan is a Party;
(10) the preparation of proposals for the improvement of national legislation in the field of international relations, bringing it into compliance with the international legal obligations of Kazakhstan;
(11) ensuring protocol and organizational support in carrying out domestic and international events organized by the country;
(12) control over observance of the state protocol by the state bodies of Kazakhstan in organizing domestic and international events that take place in Kazakhstan, etc.

895. Article 19 of the Law on the Diplomatic Service regulates the rights and duties of diplomatic personnel. In line with the Article, diplomatic personnel have the right:

(1) to make proposals on improving the activity of the bodies of diplomatic service;
(2) to enjoy the privileges and immunities abroad established by international law; and
(3) to enjoy the rights and freedoms guaranteed to citizens of Kazakhstan by the Constitution and the legislative acts of Kazakhstan.

896. Diplomatic service staff also has the right to make proposals on issues of the foreign policy of the State, on the improvement of national legislation in the field of international relations, and on making it coherent with the international legal obligations of the Republic. Diplomatic service staff of the rank of the Ambassador Extraordinary and Plenipotentiary and their spouses have the right to use a diplomatic passport of Kazakhstan for life.

897. The diplomatic personnel shall:

(1) fulfil in good faith the duties related to the performance of the diplomatic service;
(2) respect the legislation, traditions and customs of the host State;

(3) not disclose information concerning state secrets or other secrets protected by law even after the termination of diplomatic service;
(4) develop professional level, qualifications, general political training, and improve knowledge of state and foreign languages;
(5) perform other duties established by the legislative acts of the country.

898. The status of the diplomatic representation of Kazakhstan is regulated by the Regulations on the diplomatic representation and the representation equivalent to the diplomatic representation of Kazakhstan, approved by the Decree of the President of Kazakhstan of 4 February 2004 No. 1287.[246] In line with Article 1 of the Regulations, there are three representations of Kazakhstan abroad: an embassy, a diplomatic mission and a permanent representation of Kazakhstan at an international organization. An embassy is led by the Ambassador; a diplomatic mission is headed by a Charge d'Affaires; and a representation at the international organization by a Permanent Representative. A representation is established, reorganized and terminates its activity by Decree of the President of Kazakhstan.

899. In accordance with the Regulations, the main tasks of diplomatic representation are the following:

(1) the realization of foreign policy of Kazakhstan and assistance in the realization of foreign economic policy;
(2) representation of Kazakhstan in relations with a host country or international organization;
(3) ensuring by diplomatic means and methods protection of the sovereignty, security, territorial integrity and inviolability of the borders of Kazakhstan, its political, trade-economic and other interests in relations with a host country or international organization;
(4) protection of the rights and interests of the Republic, its citizens and legal entities in a host country.

900. The Regulations define the functions of a representative office of Kazakhstan abroad, among which are the following:

(1) contributes to the realization of a strategy of international policy of Kazakhstan;
(2) ensures conducting a single political line of Kazakhstan in a host country or an international organization;
(3) submits proposals to the Ministry on relations of Kazakhstan with a host country or an international organization;

246. Regulations on the Diplomatic Representation and the Representation Equivalent to the Diplomatic Representation of the Republic of Kazakhstan, approved by the Decree of the President of Kazakhstan of 4 Feb. 2004 No. 1287. Available at: https://adilet.zan.kz/rus/docs/U040001287_ (accessed 3 Aug. 2021).

(4) conducts negotiations and contributes to the support of official contacts with the state bodies of a host country or with an international organization within its framework;
(5) contributes to the realization of objectives and principles, as well as to the realization of decisions within the cooperation framework of the Republic with a host country or with an international organization;
(6) organizes negotiations and signing of international treaties of Kazakhstan with a host country or with an international organization;
(7) assists official delegations and representatives of the country in the realization of the tasks assigned;
(8) carries out protocol-organizational support of events with the participation of the President of Kazakhstan, Chairs of the Chambers of the Parliament and the Prime Minister of Kazakhstan and other officials of the Republic, etc.

B. Representation of Kazakhstan in Supranational Organizations: The EAEU

901. The Republic of Kazakhstan is actively engaged in regional cooperation and is a member of the EAEU. The treaty on the EAEU between Kazakhstan, the Russian Federation and the Republic of Belarus was signed on 29 May 2014.[247] In line with the provisions of the Treaty, the Eurasian Economic Commission is a permanent regulating body of the Union that consists of the Council and the Board. The headquarters of the Commission are in Moscow, Russian Federation. The status, tasks, composition, functions and procedure of work of the Commission are covered by the Regulations on the Eurasian Economic Commission of 29 May 2014.[248]

902. According to the Regulations, the main tasks of the Commission are ensuring conditions for the functioning and development of the Union, drawing up proposals in the field of economic integration within the Union. The main principles of the Commission are:

(1) ensuring mutual benefit and equality, taking into account the national interests of the State Parties;
(2) the economic feasibility of decisions;
(3) their openness, publicity and impartiality.

903. The Commission can be given a right by the Supreme Council to sign international treaties on issues of its competencies. Within its competencies, the Commission ensures realization of international treaties of the Union. Within its

247. Treaty on the Eurasian Economic Union of 29 May 2014. Available at: https://online.zakon.kz/document/?doc_id=31565247 (accessed 3 Aug. 2021).
248. Regulations of 29 May 2014 on the Eurasian Economic Commission. Available at: http://www.eurasiancommission.org/ru/act/chairman/ad/Documents/%D0%9F%D0%BE%D0%BB%D0%BE%D0%B6%D0%B5%D0%BD%D0%B8%D0%B5%20%D0%BE%20%D0%95%D0%AD%D0%9A.pdf (accessed 8 May 2019).

competencies, the Commission has the right to adopt decisions of a normative legal character that have a binding force on the Member States and shall be applied directly at the domestic level.

904. As given in the Regulations, the Council of the Commission carries out a general regulation of integration processes in the Union, as well as a general leadership by the Commission's activities. Each Member State nominates one representative, at the level of a deputy head of the government to the Council. In line with Article 8(4) of the Treaty on the EEU, the presidency of the Supreme Council, Intergovernmental Council and the Council of the Commission shall be rotated, using the Russian alphabetical order, by one Member State for one calendar year only. The meetings of the Council are carried out in accordance with the procedural rules. Any member of the Council can initiate a meeting and make proposals for the agenda.

905. The Board of the Commission is an executive body of the Commission. The Board consists of the members of the Commission, and one of them is a Chair. The Board is composed of the representatives of the Member States and based on the principle of equal representation of Member States. Strength of the Board and distribution of duties between members of the Board is defined by the Supreme Council. The Board of the Commission leads the Department of the Commission.

906. A member of the Board must be a citizen of a Member State whom he/she represents. He/she shall have a professional qualification that corresponds to duties of the job, as well as work experience relevant to the official functions of not less than seven years, that include at least one year in a managerial position in the state bodies of the Member States. The members of the Board are appointed by the Supreme Board for four years with possible prolongation of powers. The Chair of the Board is appointed by the Supreme Council for four years in rotation. The rotation is decided alternately by state names in accordance with the Russian alphabet.

907. The members of the Board work at the Commission on a regular basis. They are independent of the state bodies and officials of the Member States while carrying out their competencies and they cannot make inquiries or receive instructions from the state bodies and officials of Member States. The mechanism of interaction of members of the Board with state bodies on issues of international activities is defined in accordance with the Procedures of realization by the EAEU of international cooperation approved by the Supreme Council. While working at the Board, the members of the Board have no right to do other paid work, apart from teaching, scientific or any creative activity.

908. Every Member State proposes the candidatures for a position of a member of the Board to the Supreme Council. If the Supreme Council does not approve a candidature for the position of a member of the Board, a Member State must propose a new candidate within thirty calendar days.

IV. Proceedings Before Supranational Courts: The Court of the EAEU

909. The Statute of the Court of the EAEU regulates the proceedings at the Court.[249] In line with the Statute, the Court of the EAEU is a judicial body of the Union that is formed and works on a permanent basis in accordance with the Treaty on the EAEU and the Statute. The aim of the Court is to ensure the unified application of the Treaty, international treaties within the framework of the Union, international treaties of the Union with third parties, and of decisions of the Union's bodies by the Member States and bodies of the Union.

910. Chapter 2 of the Statute regulates the composition of the Court. The Court is composed of two members of each Member State. The term of a judge is nine years. A judge shall meet high moral standards, be a highly qualified specialist in the field of international and national law, and, as a general rule, satisfy the same requirements as for the judges of the highest judicial bodies of Member States. The judges are appointed by the Supreme Eurasian Economic Council upon the recommendation of the Member States. The judges are released by the Supreme Eurasian Economic Council. The Court is led by a Chair who has one deputy. A Chair and a deputy are elected by the judges among the judges in line with the Rules of Procedure of the Court, and the elected judges shall be approved by the Supreme Eurasian Economic Council. The term of a Chair and his deputy is three years, and they cannot be citizens of the same country.

911. The judges cannot represent the interests of the State and interstate bodies and organizations, commercial entities, political parties and movements, as well as territories, nations, nationalities, social and religious groups, and individuals. They cannot be engaged in activities related to earning income apart from scientific, creative and teaching activities. A judge cannot participate in consideration of a case where he/she previously participated as a representative, attorney or lawyer of one of the parties, as a member of the national or international court, commission of inquiry or in any other capacity. While rendering justice judges are equal and have the same status.

912. Chapter 4 of the Statute concerns the competence of the Court. In line with the provisions of the Chapter, the Court considers cases that arise on issues of realization of the Treaty on the Union, international treaties within the framework of the Union and (or) decisions of the bodies of the Union upon request of a Member State concerning:

(1) compliance with an international treaty concluded within the framework of the Union or its provisions to the Treaty on the Union;

249. Statute of the Court of the Eurasian Economic Union. Appendix No. 2 to the Treaty on the Eurasian Economic Union. Available at: http://courteurasian.org/upload/iblock/b30/2%200Статут%20Суда..pdf (accessed 3 Aug. 2021).

(2) observance by other Member State(s) of the Treaty on the Union, international treaties within the framework of the Union and (or) the decisions of the Union's bodies, as well as separate provisions of the mentioned international treaties and (or) decisions;
(3) compliance with the decision of the Commission or its separate provisions to the Treaty of the Union, to the international treaties within the Union and (or) decisions of the Union's bodies;
(4) contesting the action (inaction) of the Commission.

913. The Court considers cases upon request of an economic entity (a legal entity or an individual entrepreneur) concerning:

(1) compliance of the Commission's decision or its separate provisions, that directly concern the rights and legal interests of an economic entity in the field of entrepreneurial or any economic activity, to the Treaty of the Union and (or) international treaties within the Union, if such decision or its separate provisions result in a violation of the rights and legal interests of an economic entity envisaged in the Treaty of the Union and (or) international treaties within the Union;
(2) contesting the actions (inactions) of the Commission that directly concern the rights and legal interests of an economic entity in the field of entrepreneurial or any economic activity if such action (inaction) result in a violation of the rights and legal interests of an economic entity envisaged in the Treaty of the Union and (or) international treaties within the Union.

914. According to paragraph 40 of Chapter 4, Member States may refer to the competence of the Court other disputes the resolution of which are directly envisaged in the Treaty on the Union, international treaties within the Union, international treaties of the Union with the third party or other international treaties between the Member States. A dispute cannot be taken for consideration without the preliminary appeal of a claimant to a Member State or the Commission via a pre-judicial procedure of dispute settlement by way of the consultations, negotiations or other means envisaged in the Treaty on the Union or international treaties within the Union, apart from cases directly envisaged in the Treaty (paragraph 43).

915. As given in paragraph 46, the Court upon request of a Member State or the body of the Union clarifies the provisions of the Treaty on the Union, international treaties within the Union and decisions of the bodies of the Union, as well as upon the request of the employees and officials of the bodies of the Union and the Court to clarify the Treaty's provisions, international treaties within the Union and decisions of the bodies of the Union related to labour relations. Clarification carried out by the Court means consultative opinion and does not deprive the Member States of the right for joint interpretation of international treaties. The Court carries out a clarification of the provisions of an international treaty of the Union with the third party if it is stipulated by such an international treaty.

916. At the point of rendering justice, the Court applies:

- general principles and norms of international law;
- the Treaty on the Union, international treaties within the framework of the Union and other international treaties the participants of which are contesting parties;
- decisions and orders of the Union's bodies;
- international custom as evidence of a general practice recognized as legal norm (paragraph 50 Statute).

917. Chapter 5 of the Statute concerns proceedings. With regards to dispute resolution proceedings, the Court considers a case on the basis of the following principles, such as the independence of judges, the openness of the court hearing, publicity, equality of arms, competitiveness and collegiality. The Court may request the materials necessary for the consideration of cases from economic entities, authorized bodies and organizations, Member States, as well as from bodies of the Union that have submitted a claim. The proceeding at the Court takes place with the participation of the parties, a petitioner, their representatives, experts, including experts of specialized groups, specialists, witnesses and translators. The parties participating in consideration of a case enjoy procedural rights and bear procedural duties in line with the Rules of Procedure. At any stage of the consideration of a case, the dispute may be settled by concluding an amicable agreement, refusal by a petitioner of his claims or withdrawal of a claim. With regards to proceedings on giving clarification, the Court carries out proceedings following the principles of the independence of judges and collegiality.

918. In accordance with the Decision of the EAEU of 23 December 2014 No. 103 on the appointment of judges of the Court of the EAEU, *Bayishev Zholymbet* and *Seytimova Venera* were appointed as judges of the Court from Kazakhstan.[250]

V. The Interparliamentary Cooperation in Developing Law and Foreign Relations

A. *The Interparliamentary Assembly of Member Nations of the CIS*

919. The EAEU is a purely economic organization and does not contain interparliamentary cooperation. In comparison with the EAEU, the CIS does not have a supranational character. The Interparliamentary Assembly of Member Nations of the CIS, one of the eleven bodies of the CIS, makes a significant contribution to the development of regional law.[251] The Interparliamentary Assembly of Member Nations of the Commonwealth of Independent States (IPA CIS) was created on 27 March 1992 by the Agreement on the Interparliamentary Assembly of Member

250. Decision of the Eurasian Economic Union of 23 Dec. 2014 No. 103 on appointment of judges of the Court of the Eurasian Economic Union. Available at: http://adilet.zan.kz/rus/docs/H14B0000 103 (accessed 12 May 2019).

251. Please *see* more about IPA CIS at its official website: https://iacis.ru (accessed 12 May 2019).

Nations of the CIS.[252] Now the IPA CIS is an international organization according to the Convention on the IPA CIS of 23 October 1997.[253] The headquarters of the IPA CIS is located in St. Petersburg.

920. The Parliamentary delegations of State Parties, such as the Azerbaijan Republic, the Republic of Armenia, the Republic of Belarus, Kazakhstan, the Kyrghyz Republic, the Republic of Moldova, the Russian Federation, the Republic of Tajikistan, the Republic of Uzbekistan, and Ukraine comprise the IPA CIS. The National Assembly of the Islamic Republic of Afghanistan is an observer at the IPA CIS. The IPA CIS has its own bodies, such as the Council, Permanent Commissions, the Secretariat, the Young CIS Parliamentarians Assembly. The incumbent Chair of the IPA CIS is the Chair of the Federation Council of the Federal Assembly of the Russian Federation *Valentina Matviyenko*.

921. With regards to the role of the IPA CIS in developing the law, one of the main tasks of the IPA is the formation and approximation of the laws of the CIS countries. As given in its official website, the IPA CIS discusses issues of cooperation of Member States, adopts recommendations on the approximation of legislation of State Parties, adopts model legislative acts, adopts recommendations on the synchronization of procedures of approval by the parliaments of State Parties of agreements concluded within the CIS countries, adopts recommendations on bringing the legislation of State Parties into conformity with the provisions of international treaties concluded by these States within the CIS, carries out the exchange of legal information between the State Parties, etc. As mentioned on the website, the model laws recommended by the IPA CIS as samples for local legislation are the international and European standards adapted to the conditions of the CIS.

922. The IPA CIS is focused on developing legal regulation of the economic space of the CIS as well. In this regard, as given in the official website, the IPA CIS adopted three parts of the model Civil Code, the General Part of the Tax Code, the Regulations on the protection of investors' rights at the stock market, models laws on the free economic zone, on electronic digital signatures, on the stock market and others.

923. The Kazakhstani delegation at the IPA CIS is represented by the deputies of the Senate and the *Mazhilis* of the Parliament. The delegation is led by the Chairs of the Senate and the *Mazhilis* of the Parliament of Kazakhstan. There is also the Deputy Chair of the Senate (Deputy of the delegation), the Chair and members of the Committee of the Senate on Social-Cultural Development and Science, the Chair and a member of the Committee of the Senate on the Constitutional Legislation, Judicial System and Law-Enforcement Bodies, the Chair and a member of the Committee of the Senate on International Affairs, Defence and Security, the

252. Agreement on the Interparliamentary Assembly of Member Nations of the CIS of 27 Mar. 1992. Available at: http://docs.cntd.ru/document/901734628 (accessed 12 May 2019).
253. The Convention on the Interparliamentary Assembly of States Parties of the CIS of 23 Oct. 1997. Available at: http://docs.cntd.ru/document/1901958 (accessed 12 May 2019).

Chair and a Secretary of the Committee of the Senate on Finance and Budget, a Secretary of the Committee of the Senate on Agrarian Issues, Management of Natural Resources and Development of Rural Areas, the Chair of *the Mazhilis* of the Parliament of Kazakhstan and the members of its different committees.

B. *The Parliamentary Cooperation Committee Between Kazakhstan and the European Union*

924. On 21 December 2015, Kazakhstan and the European Union signed in Astana the Enhanced Partnership and Cooperation Agreement (EPCA) that covers twenty-nine areas of cooperation between the two parties.[254] In line with Article 270 of the EPCA, a Parliamentary Cooperation Committee had been established that consists of Members of the Parliament of Kazakhstan and of the European Parliament. It is a forum to meet and exchange views in order to develop mutually beneficial and effective parliamentary cooperation. In accordance with the provisions of Article 270, the Parliamentary Cooperation Committee may request information regarding the implementation of the EPCA from the Cooperation Council, which shall then supply the Committee with the requested information, and the Parliamentary Cooperation Committee may make recommendations to the Cooperation Council.

254. Enhanced Partnership and Cooperation Agreement between Kazakhstan and the European Union of 21 Dec. 2015. Available at: https://eeas.europa.eu/sites/eeas/files/enhanced_partnership_and_cooperation_agreement.pdf (accessed 12 May 2019).

Chapter 2. Taxing Power

§1. Introduction

925. The tax legislation of Kazakhstan is based on the Constitution of Kazakhstan, the Tax Code of 25 December 2017, as well as on other normative legal acts the adoption of which is envisaged by the Tax Code of Kazakhstan (Article 2 Tax Code).[255] For the purposes of taxation, in cases of discrepancies between the Code and the laws of Kazakhstan, the provisions of the Code shall be applied. If an international treaty ratified by Kazakhstan establishes other rules than those contained in the Code, the provisions of the international treaty shall be applied (Article 2 Tax Code). The tax legislation of Kazakhstan covers the entire territory of the Republic and applies to individuals, legal entities and their structural divisions.

926. According to Article 35 of the Constitution of Kazakhstan, the paying of taxes, fees and other obligatory payments established by law are the duty and obligation of everyone. In line with Article 2 of the Tax Code, the obligation to pay taxes and payments to the budget not envisaged in the Tax Code shall not be imposed on anyone. The Parliament of Kazakhstan establishes and abolishes state taxes and fees; it adopts laws on issues of taxation, setting fees and other obligatory payments (Articles 54, 61 Constitution).

927. As given in Article 11 of the Tax Code, the tax policy of Kazakhstan is a set of measures that establishes new and cancels existing taxes, changes rates, determines objects of taxation and objects related to taxation, the tax base for taxes and payments to the budget to meet the financial needs of the State and balances the economic interests of the State and taxpayers. The authorized body in the field of tax policy analyses the effectiveness of the use of tax incentives in accordance with the procedure determined by the Government of Kazakhstan. The Government of Kazakhstan may create the Tax Advisory Council to eliminate the obscurities, inaccuracies and contradictions that may arise in the course of performing tax obligations, as well as to suppress possible tax evasion schemes and evasion of payments to the budget (Article 12 Tax Code).

§2. The Principles of Taxation

928. The tax legislation of Kazakhstan is based on the principles of taxation established by the Tax Code. According to Article 4 of the Tax Code, the principles of taxation include the principle of obligatoriness, the fairness of taxation, definiteness (certainty) of taxation, a taxpayer's good faith, unity and accord of the tax system, and publicity of the tax legislation of the Republic.

255. Code of Kazakhstan of 25 Dec. 2017 No. 120-VI ZRK on Taxes and Other Obligatory Payments to the Budget (the Tax Code). Available at: https://online.zakon.kz/Document/?doc_id=36148637 (accessed 3 Aug. 2021).

929. The principle of obligatoriness means that a taxpayer is required to fulfil a tax obligation, and a tax agent is obliged to calculate, withhold and transfer taxes in accordance with the tax legislation of the Republic in full and on time (Article 4 Tax Code).

930. In line with Article 6 of the Tax Code, the taxes and payments to the budget of Kazakhstan must be definite (certain). Definiteness of taxation means that the tax legislation establishes all grounds and procedures for emergence, performance and termination of a taxpayer's obligation, and the obligation of a tax agent to calculate, withhold and transfer the taxes.

931. Article 7 of the Tax Code is about the principle of fair taxation. Taxation in the Republic of Kazakhstan is universal and mandatory. Any individual tax privileges are prohibited. No one must be taxed again by the same tax, by the same type of payment to the budget, and for the same taxable object occurring within the same time period.

932. Article 8 of the Tax Code sets out the principle of the taxpayer's good faith. It is assumed that a taxpayer (a tax agent) fulfils his/her tax obligation in good faith. A taxpayer should not receive benefits from his/her illegal actions that allow him/her to have tax savings and tax reductions. Violations of the legislation of the country committed by a taxpayer (a tax agent) must be reported during the tax audits. Justification of arguments and disclosure of the circumstances indicating the facts of violation of tax legislation of Kazakhstan is on the shoulders of the tax bodies. All uncertainties and unresolved issues of the tax legislation of Kazakhstan raised during consideration of a complaint on the reports of inspections are interpreted in favour of the taxpayer.

933. The principle of the unity of the tax system established by Article 9 of the Tax Code signifies that the tax system of Kazakhstan is uniform throughout the entire territory of Kazakhstan for all taxpayers (tax agents).

934. Publicity of the tax legislation of Kazakhstan implies that the normative legal acts on issues of taxation shall be published officially (Article 10 Tax Code).

§3. The Types of Taxes and Payments to the Budget

935. Article 189 of the Tax Code enumerates the following types of taxes:

- corporate income tax;
- individual income tax;
- value added tax;
- excise tax;
- rental tax on export;
- special payments and taxes of subsoil users;
- social tax;

– tax on vehicles;
– land tax;
– property tax;
– gambling tax;
– single land tax.

936. Article 189 of the Tax Code enumerates the following payments to the budget:

– public due;
– fees;
– payment for using the licenses to carry out certain types of activities;
– payment for the use of land;
– payment for the use of water resources from surface sources;
– payment for emissions to the environment;
– payment for the use of wildlife;
– payment for forest use;
– payment for the use of specially protected natural areas;
– payment for the use of the radio frequency spectrum;
– payment for the provision of long-distance and (or) international telephone communication, as well as cellular communication;
– payment for the placement of outdoor (visual) advertising.

§4. Rights and Obligations of the Taxpayer

937. The rights and obligations of the taxpayer are enumerated in Article 13(1) of the Tax Code of Kazakhstan. In line with the provisions of the Article, a taxpayer has the following rights:

(1) to receive from the tax authorities information about existing taxes and payments to the budget, about amendments to the tax legislation of Kazakhstan and explanations of the application of the tax legislation of Kazakhstan;
(2) to represent his/her own interests in relations covered by the tax legislation of Kazakhstan directly or via a legal or authorized representative in line with the Tax Code, or with the participation of a tax consultant;
(3) to conclude agreements for carrying out audits on taxes in accordance with the national legislation;
(4) to get the reports of tax control bodies in cases stipulated by the Tax Code;
(5) to get for free at tax bodies tax application forms and (or) the software necessary for the presenting of tax reports and the submission of applications in electronic forms;
(6) to appeal against the notifications on the results of the audit, the notifications on the results of consideration of a taxpayer's (tax agent's) complaint on the notification of the audit's results, as well as actions (inactions) of tax bodies' officials;

(7) not to provide information and documents not related to the taxable objects, apart from information and documents that shall be submitted according to the tax legislation, legislation on transfer pricing, on the issues of production and turnover certain types of excisable goods, aircraft fuel, biofuels and fuel oil.

938. A taxpayer has the right to submit to tax body information about telephone numbers and email addresses for the purposes of receiving information about existing tax obligations on transport vehicles, land tax and property tax for individuals.

939. In line with Article 13(3) of the Tax Code, a taxpayer bears the following obligations:

(1) to perform tax obligations in a timely fashion and in full;
(2) to present per request of tax bodies an agreement for carrying out a tax audit and the final report of a tax audit in case of signing such an agreement;
(3) to present information and documents envisaged by the tax legislation of Kazakhstan, the legislation of Kazakhstan on transfer pricing, as well as the legislation of Kazakhstan regulating the production and circulation of certain types of excisable goods, aviation fuel, biofuels and fuel oil;
(4) to comply with requirements in using cash register machines;
(5) to keep within five years from the day of printing out or fully filling out shift reports, the records of cash and sales receipts, the cancellation and returning of receipts, and to keep as well as the receipts of cash registers on which the operations of annulment and returning was fulfilled.

A taxpayer has other rights and performs other duties established by the tax legislation of Kazakhstan.

§5. Rights and Obligations of Tax Bodies

940. In accordance with Article 18 of the Tax Code of Kazakhstan, the tax bodies are bodies of state revenue and perform the following and other tasks:

(1) ensuring observance of the tax legislation of the Republic;
(2) ensuring the completeness and timeliness of revenues of taxes and payments to the budget;
(3) ensuring the completeness and timeliness of the calculation, withholding and transfer of social payments in accordance with the legislation of Kazakhstan and the Tax Code of Kazakhstan;
(4) participation in the realization of the tax policy of Kazakhstan;
(5) ensuring within its competence the economic security of the Republic;
(6) formation of, and ensuring the development of the information communication infrastructure and the availability of electronic services for taxpayers;
(7) carrying out other tasks envisaged by the legislation of Kazakhstan.

941. According to Article 19 of the Tax Code, the tax bodies have the following and other rights:

(1) within their competencies to draw up and approve normative legal acts, envisaged by the Tax Code;
(2) to carry out international cooperation on taxation issues, including the exchange of information with authorized bodies of foreign States;
(3) in the course of tax control to demand from taxpayers (tax agents), access to accounting and tax registers software and (or) information systems that contain data on primary accounting documents and registers, information about taxable objects and (or) the objects related to taxation, in cases where a taxpayer (tax agent) uses such software and (or) information systems. This is excepting access to the data of the second-tier banks and organizations that carry out certain bank operations containing bank secrecy in accordance with the laws of Kazakhstan;
(4) to demand from a taxpayer (a tax agent) submission of documents that confirm the correctness of calculation and timeliness of discharge (deduction and transfer) of taxes and payments to the budget, completeness and timeliness of calculation, deduction and transfer of social payments, etc.

942. In line with Article 19 of the Tax Code, the tax bodies have the following and other obligations:

(1) to respect the rights of a taxpayer (a tax agent);
(2) to protect the interests of the State;
(3) to provide a taxpayer with information on existing taxes and payments to the budget, amendments to the tax legislation of Kazakhstan, to explain issues on the application of the national tax legislation;
(4) within its competence to carry out interpretation and comment on emergence, performance and termination of tax obligation;
(5) to ensure during a limited period the keeping of information that confirms the fact of discharge of taxes and payments to the budget, etc.

§6. Legal Status of the Committee on the Tax Revenues of the Ministry of Finances of Kazakhstan

943. In accordance with the Regulations on the Committee on the Tax Revenues of the Ministry of Finances of Kazakhstan, the Committee is a responsible agency of the Ministry of Finances of the Republic of Kazakhstan that within the competence of the central executive body ensures the completeness and timeliness of tax revenues and other obligatory payments to the budget.[256] The state body participates in the realization of tax policy. The Committee has territorial representation in

256. Regulations on the Committee on the Tax Revenues of the Ministry of Finances of Kazakhstan approved by the Decree of the Minister of Finances on 14 Jun. 2016 No. 306. Available at: https://adilet.zan.kz/rus/docs/G16E0000306 (accessed 3 Aug. 2021).

the regions, the cities of national importance like *Nur-Sultan*, *Almaty* and *Shymkent*, districts, towns and districts in the towns, special economic zones.

944. Paragraph 16 of the Regulations enumerates the considerable number of the Committee's functions in the field of taxation, and there is mentioned that the Committee:

(1) carries out tax administration;
(2) in line with procedures established by the legislation of Kazakhstan provides information via the media about taxpayers (tax agents) who have tax arrears and about inactive legal entities and taxpayers;
(3) draws up and elaborates application forms and other documents stipulated by the tax legislation;
(4) develops the forms of notifications on the amounts of tax arrears and the paying off of the taxes;
(5) develops the rules relating to the application of the general ensuring of performance of tax duties;
(6) develops a structure, format and form of tax calculations;
(7) develops the rules for offsetting and (or) returning overpaid, overcharged or mistakenly paid taxes;
(8) submits information, including preliminary information, to the state bodies of the Republic if such information is necessary for these bodies to perform their tasks and functions assigned by the legislation of Kazakhstan, in a manner and in compliance with the requirements of the legislation of the Republic for the protection of state, commercial, banking, tax and other secrets protected by law, as well as other confidential information, international treaties of Kazakhstan;
(9) monitors the payment of taxes;
(10) adopts measures for collection of tax debts;
(11) carries out tax control;
(12) modernizes and carries out re-engineering of the business processes of tax administration;
(13) creates (forms) the state database of taxpayers;
(14) ensures the completeness of collection and timeliness of tax transfers to the budget;
(15) performs control over the change of timing for the fulfilment of tax obligations to pay taxes and (or) fees in accordance with the legislation of Kazakhstan;
(16) performs the international treaties' provisions in a manner established by the tax legislation of Kazakhstan and the relevant international treaty;
(17) carries out the offsetting and refund of tax and non-tax revenues within its competence established by the normative legal acts;
(18) interacts with central and local state bodies to monitor the implementation of tax legislation, etc.

Chapter 3. Emergency Laws

§1. Public Emergency and International Standards on Permissible Derogations in Time of Public Emergency

945. The Siracusa Principles on the Limitation and Derogation Provisions in the ICCPR adopted in 1984 by a number of non-governmental organizations (the International Commission of Jurists, the International Association of Penal Law, the American Association for the International Commission of Jurists, etc.) represented by leading experts in international law from different parts of the world elaborated certain international standards on emergency laws.[257] They provide useful interpretations of the limitation and derogation provisions of the ICCPR in general, and of Article 4 in particular. In comparison with the ICCPR, the Siracusa Principles contain the types of 'threats' that can be reasons for the imposition of a time of emergency.

946. As mentioned in paragraph 2 of Article 29 of the UDHR 'in the exercise of his rights and freedoms, everyone shall be subject only to such limitations as are determined by law solely for the purpose of securing due recognition and respect for the rights and freedoms of others and of meeting the just requirements of morality, public order and the general welfare in a democratic society'. The Paris Minimum Standards of Human Rights Norms in a State of Emergency (International Law Association, 1984) developed the human rights standards for 'emergency scenarios'.[258] Similar issues are covered by the European Convention on Human Rights (Article 15), the European Social Charter (Article 30) and the American Convention on Human Rights (Article 27).

947. Referring to the provisions of Article 4 of the ICCPR, in exceptional instances and for a limited time, a State party may derogate from some of the rights proclaimed in the ICCPR in the case of a public emergency threatening the life of the nation. In such cases, a State must guarantee the protection of non-derogable rights and the derogating measures must be 'strictly required by the exigencies of the situation'. They must not entail any discrimination solely on the grounds of race, colour, sex, language, religion, or social origin and they must not be inconsistent with other international obligations of the State; a derogating State must notify the other States parties to the instrument concerned.[259]

948. The derogation must be necessary, namely, one required by a situation which must have a character of 'actual or imminent danger' and which threatens the life of the nation. The effect of threats should be on the 'whole of the population

257. UN Commission on Human Rights, *The Siracusa Principles on the Limitation and Derogation Provisions in the International Covenant on Civil and Political Rights*, 28 Sep. 1984, E/CN.4/1985/4, available at: https://www.refworld.org/docid/4672bc122.html (accessed 29 Apr. 2019).
258. Richard B. Lillich, *The Paris Minimum Standards of Human Rights Norms in a State of Emergency*. 79 Am. J. Int'l L., 1072–1081 (1985).
259. Olivier De Schutter, *supra* n. 191, at 514.

and either the whole or part of the territory of the State'; threats to the physical integrity of the population, the political independence, or territorial integrity of the State or the existence or basic functioning of institutions indispensable to ensure and protect the rights recognized in the Covenant would be considered as causes for a public emergency.[260] A 'natural catastrophe, a mass demonstration, or a major industrial accident' if they threaten the life of people, could be sufficient reasons to announce a public emergency.[261] Economic difficulties cannot be a reason for the justification of derogation measures.

949. A situation of public emergency must be officially proclaimed by a state, and this must be done in writing. According to international law, the initiating declaration of a public emergency should be carefully justified, and a derogating State has the burden of proof to justify its actions to the international community. The derogation should be based on the principles of legality, legitimacy, proportionality, good faith, and the rule of law. Its measures should be proportionate and adequate to the nature and extent of the threat and 'may not go beyond what is required'.[262]

950. The derogating State must notify other State parties of the Covenant immediately about the nature, extent and the reasons of the derogations through the General Secretary of the UN (Article 4(3) ICCPR) so that the other States have the opportunity to monitor the derogating measures. The Human Rights Committee has a duty to assess whether the derogating measures were strictly required by the exigencies of the situation. In the reports submitted under Article 40 to the Human Rights Committee, State parties should provide 'sufficient and precise information' on the law and practice in the field of emergency powers (paragraph 3 General Comment No. 29).

§2. PUBLIC EMERGENCIES WHICH THREATEN THE LIFE OF THE NATION: INTERNATIONAL REQUIREMENTS AND KAZAKHSTAN'S LAW AND PRACTICE

951. In Kazakhstan, incidences of emergency are regulated by the Constitution of the Republic and the Law of Kazakhstan on a State of Emergency of 8 February 2003.[263] According to the Constitutional provisions, the concept of 'emergency' covers a serious and immediate threat to the democratic institutions of the Republic, its independence and territorial integrity, the political stability of the Republic, the security of its citizens and the functioning of the Constitutional bodies of the state (subparagraph 16, Article 44). Here, by 'constitutional bodies' has been understood only state bodies to which the titled chapters in the Constitution are devoted.

---

260. Siracusa Principles, *supra* n. 257, at 9.
261. UN Human Rights Committee (HRC), CCPR General Comment No. 29: Article 4: Derogations during a State of Emergency, 31 Aug. 2001, CCPR/C/21/Rev.1/Add.11. Available at: https://www.refworld.org/docid/453883fd1f.html (accessed 29 Apr. 2019).
262. Olivier De Schutter, *supra* n. 191, at 288.
263. Law of Kazakhstan of 8 Feb. 2003 No. 387-II on the State of Emergency. Available at: https://online.zakon.kz/document/?doc_id=1036912 (accessed 3 Aug. 2021).

These are the President, the Parliament, the Government, the Courts, the Constitutional Council, the local state governance and self-governance bodies.

952. In 2003, the Constitutional Council of Kazakhstan gave the official explanation to the term 'territorial integrity' along with 'its inviolability and non-alienation' in its Normative Resolution.[264] Territorial integrity cannot be changed, and it is a determining condition for national security (Article 91(2) Constitution). The term implies a non-separation of the territory, prohibition of a territorial concession to the detriment of national interests of the country and equality of states. It means that threats to the separation of Kazakhstan's territory are sufficient reasons for a proclamation of an emergency.

953. Article 4 of the Law of Kazakhstan on the State of Emergency elaborates the circumstances which can be reasons for the proclamation of an emergency. Among them are terrorist acts, mass disorders, conflicts between nations/communities and religious believers, the activity of illegal military units, and so on. An incidence of state emergency can extend over the whole territory or only a part of it. According to Article 17 of the Law, measures and restrictions adopted during a time of emergency may not contradict the international human rights treaties of Kazakhstan.

954. The constitutional bodies of Kazakhstan that take decisions on the declaration of a public emergency are the President of Kazakhstan, the Prime Minister and Chairs of the Parliamentary Chambers. After consultation with the Prime Minister and Chairs of the Parliamentary Chambers of the Republic, the President proclaims a state of emergency and takes measures required by it, including the adoption of a decree on a state of emergency. In the period of a state of emergency, the whole Parliament and the lower Chamber of the Parliament *Mazhilis* may not be dissolved (Article 63(1) Constitution).

955. In compliance with international human rights standards, there are core human rights, which are non-derogable and protected from derogation. The non-derogable rights mentioned in the ICCPR are the right to life (Article 6), the prohibition of torture or cruel, inhuman or degrading punishment, or of medical or scientific experimentation without consent (Article 7), the prohibition of slavery, the slave trade and servitude (Article 8), the prohibition of detention for debt (Article 11), the prohibition of retrospective criminal laws (Article 15), the right of recognition of legal personality (Article 16) and freedom of thought, conscience and religion (Article 18). These rights are fundamental, and some of them have a peremptory nature (e.g., Articles 6 and 7).

956. According to Article 39 of the Constitution, the following rights and freedoms shall not be restricted in any event: the protection of own citizens (Article 11); a right to the recognition of legal personality, to defence in law of one's rights and freedoms, to qualified legal assistance (Article 13); a right to equality before the law

264. *Supra* n. 11.

and courts and a guarantee of non-discrimination (Article 14); a right to life (Article 15); a right to personal freedom (Article 16(1)); a right to the inviolability of a person's dignity and prohibition of torture (Article 17); a right to determine and indicate (if any) a national, party and religious affiliation (Article 19); a right to freedom of conscience (Article 22) and to protection by law of property and right to inheritance (Article 26(2)). As a general rule, during the time of an emergency, an individual can be restricted in his freedom and can be forced to do involuntary labour (Article 24(1)).

957. Thus, in comparison with international standards, the Constitution has expanded the scope of rights which may not be restricted. These include the right to citizenship, the right to equality before the law and courts and the guarantee of non-discrimination, the right to personal freedom, the right to determine and indicate a national, party and religious affiliation, the right to protection by law of property and the right to inheritance.

958. On 16–17 December 2011, Kazakhstan proclaimed for the first time a public emergency because of the oil workers' strikes in the Zhanaozen district of the Mangistau region.[265] Zhanaozen is a geographically isolated and far-reaching place in the western part of Kazakhstan rich in oil resources. The Decree of the President on 17 December 2011 established a public emergency for twenty days, which was extended until 31 January by another Decree. According to the Decree of the President, the holding of meetings, rallies and demonstrations, marches and picketing and other mass events, strikes and other means of suspension or termination of activities of legal entities were not allowed. In Zhanaozen, since emergency actions were restricted to the people from one region, belonging to one religion and language, and doing similar jobs, there was no evidence in this scenario for discrimination.

With the Decree of the President of Kazakhstan dated 15 March 2020 No. 285, another state of emergency was introduced over the whole territory of Kazakhstan for the period from 16 March to 15 April 2020.[266] The reason was an announcement on 11 March 2020 by the World Health Organization defining the outbreak of a new coronavirus, COVID-19, as a pandemic. The purpose of introducing a state of emergency in Kazakhstan was to avoid the spreading of infection and to protect the life and health of citizens of the country.

During this state of emergency, the Government introduced such temporary measures as:

---

265. Decree of the President of Kazakhstan of 17 Dec. 2011 No. 197 on Introducing of a State of Emergency in Zhanaozen District of the Mangystau Region. Available at: https://adilet.zan.kz/rus/docs/U1100000197 (accessed 29 Apr. 2019).
266. Decree of the President of Kazakhstan of 15 Mar. 2020 No. 285 on Introducing of a State of Emergency in the Republic of Kazakhstan. Available at: https://online.zakon.kz/document/?doc_id=32648341 (accessed 30 Apr. 2020).

(1) strengthening public order, strengthening the protection of important state strategic objects, and other specially protected objects and those that ensure the vital activities of the population and the functioning of transport;
(2) limiting the functioning of large trade centres and suspending the activities of shopping and entertainment centres, cinemas, theatres and other venues which attract massive crowds of people;
(3) introducing quarantines, carrying out large-scale sanitary and epidemiological measures with the participation of subdivisions of the Ministry of Defence and of internal affairs bodies specialized in the sanitary and epidemiological well-being of the population;
(4) prohibiting entertainment, sports and other public events, as well as family and commemorative events; and
(5) establishing restrictions on the entry into and exit from the territory of the Republic affecting all means of transport, excluding the personnel of the diplomatic service of Kazakhstan and foreign States, and members of the delegations of international organizations invited by the MFA of Kazakhstan.

The State Commission for ensuring a state of emergency at the President's Office, the MIA, the Committee on National Security, the Ministry of Defence, the Ministry of Healthcare, the Ministry of Industry and Infrastructure Development of Kazakhstan, the Ministry of Finance, the mayors of Nur-Sultan, Almaty and Shymkent cities and of regions were defined as State bodies responsible for the implementation of temporary restrictive measures during a state of emergency. Observance of the rule of law during the implementation of the restrictive measures was on the shoulders of the Office of General Prosecutor.

The Government of Kazakhstan was instructed:

(1) to allocate funds from the Government reserves as necessary to ensure the state of emergency;
(2) to strengthen control over persons who evade medical examination and treatment, and over those who violate the quarantine regime, and hide information important for measuring the epidemiological situation, and the Government should define responsibility for violations of the measures;
(3) jointly with central and local state bodies to adopt other measures for realization of the Decree in order to avoid spreading coronavirus COVID-19 within the territory of the Republic.

To realize this Decree, the Minister of Trade and Integration and the Minister of Healthcare adopted a joint Order with recommendations for the functioning of the trade centres during the period of the state of emergency.[267] Later, the state of

267. Joint Order of the Minister of Trade and Integration of 17 Mar. 2020 No. 53 NK and the Minister of Healthcare of Kazakhstan of 18 Mar. 2020 No. 169 on Approval of Recommendations For the Functioning of the Trade Centres During the Period of the State of Emergency Introduced by the Decree of the President of the Republic of Kazakhstan of 15 Mar. 2020 No. 285. Available at: https://online.zakon.kz/Document/?doc_id=32299104 (accessed 30 Apr. 2020).

emergency in the country was extended by the Decrees of the President of Kazakhstan of 14 April 2020 No. 306 and of 29 April 2020 No. 310, respectively from 15 March to 1 May, and from 1 May to 11 May.[268]

268. Decree of the President of Kazakhstan of 14 Apr. 2020 No. 306 on Prolongation of the State of Emergency in the Republic of Kazakhstan. Available at: https://online.zakon.kz/document/?doc_id=32986543 (accessed 30 Apr. 2020); Decree of the President of Kazakhstan of 29 Apr. 2020 No. 310 on Prolongation of the State of Emergency in the Republic of Kazakhstan. Available at: https://online.zakon.kz/document/?doc_id=34412366 (accessed 30 Apr. 2020).

Chapter 4. The Constitutional Relationship Between Religion and State

§1. International Standards to Freedom of Religion

959. According to international human rights standards, freedom of religion is a non-derogable right and unconditional. This freedom includes the freedom to have or to adopt a religion of one's own choice and the freedom, either individually or in community with others, in public or private, to manifest one's religion in worship, observance, practice and teaching. This freedom concerns not only traditional but also newly established and minority religions.

960. The Human Rights Committee in its 48th session provided the official interpretation of Article 18 of the ICCPR (freedom of thought, conscience, religion and belief).[269] As was explained by the Committee, freedom to manifest implies ritual and ceremonial acts and following the customs. For example, 'the building of places of worship, the use of ritual formulae and objects, the display of symbols, and the observance of holidays and days of rest', 'the observance of dietary regulations, the wearing of distinctive clothing or head coverings', and so on. The practice of teaching includes 'the freedom to choose religious leaders, priests and teachers, the freedom to establish seminars or religious schools and the freedom to prepare and distribute texts or publications' (paragraph 4 General Comment on Freedom of Thought).

961. This right implies a freedom from coercion to adopt a religion. 'The prohibition of coercion was to ensure that one's decision to structure his or her life in accordance with a religion or non-religious belief, including a political conviction, was free from external coercion and could be reserved at any time.'[270]

962. Referring to Article 20 of the ICCPR, religion should not be used for propaganda, for war, or for advocacy of national, racial or religious hatred that constitutes incitement to discrimination, hostility or violence. The freedom to manifest one's religion may be subject only to such limitations as are prescribed by law and are necessary to protect public safety, order, health, or morals, or the fundamental rights and freedoms of others. Restrictions must not be used in a discriminatory manner (Article 18(3) ICCPR). Measures discriminating against religious minorities or non-believers shall not be exercised because all persons shall be equally treated.

963. Paragraph 4 demands that the States party to the Covenant undertake to have respect for the liberty of parents and, when applicable, legal guardians to ensure the religious and moral education of their children in conformity with their

269. UN Human Rights Committee (HRC), CCPR General Comment No. 22: Article 18 (Freedom of Thought, Conscience or Religion), 30 Jul. 1993, CCPR/C/21/Rev.1/Add.4. Available at: https://www.refworld.org/docid/453883fb22.html (accessed 29 Apr. 2019).
270. Nowak, *supra* n. 142, at 417.

own convictions. Parents have the right to make decisions on behalf of their children. In accordance with the interpretation given by the Committee, Article 18 allows instruction at schools in subjects such as the general history of religions and ethics in a neutral and objective way (paragraph 6 Comment).

§2. Freedom of Religion in Kazakhstan

964. Kazakhstan is a secular country, which comes from both nomadic (with strong secular social norms) and historical traditions (during the Soviet Union, the profession of religion was prohibited). There was and is no state or compulsory religion in Kazakhstan. For the first time, secularism was textually proclaimed in the Constitution of 1993 in Article 1(1). The contemporary Constitution of Kazakhstan replicated the provisions of the previous Constitution. The special Law on the religious activity and religious associations of 11 October 2011 developed the constitutional provisions on manifesting religion.[271]

965. Traditionally Kazakhs are Muslims of the Hanafi School, but there are many followers of other religions (Christians, Buddhists, Judaists, etc.) seeing as 130 ethnic groups exist. Kazakhstan is famous at the international level as a country which promotes religious tolerance by initiating and hosting the Congress of the World and Traditional Religions. The Congress is aimed at building a dialogue between civilizations and religions.

966. Education in the public schools of Kazakhstan has a secular character. Religious associations must not perform the functions of state bodies and have no right to support the activity of political parties. The creation of religious parties is prohibited (Article 5(4) of the Constitution). The Committee on religious matters of the Ministry of Culture was first responsible for the implementation and regulation of the freedom of religion. Later, the Agency on Religious Matters was created by the Government to fulfil that role, then, the Committee of public consent of the Ministry of Public Development of Kazakhstan. Currently, since March 2019, the Committee on religious affairs of the Ministry of Information and Public Development of Kazakhstan takes care of religious affairs in the country.[272] Regulation of religious issues in Kazakhstan is increasingly crucial because the profession of religion is becoming more important in the daily life of the people of Kazakhstan.

967. The Constitution guarantees the right to freedom of conscience, but the manifestation of this right must not limit universal and civil rights and obligations to the State (Article 22). In accordance with Article 39(3) of the Constitution of

271. Law of Kazakhstan of 11 Oct. 2011 No. 483-IV on the Religious Activity and Religious Associations. Available at: http://adilet.zan.kz/rus/docs/Z1100000483 (accessed 29 Apr. 2019).
272. Regulations on the Status of the Ministry of Information and Public Development of the Republic of Kazakhstan adopted by the Resolution of the Government of Kazakhstan of 26 Mar. 2019 No. 142. Available at: http://adilet.zan.kz/rus/docs/P1900000142 (accessed 3 Aug. 2021).

Kazakhstan, the provisions of Article 22 must not be limited at all. In regional post-Soviet Union traditions, the notion of 'conscience' can be understood as an attitude towards religion. For example, the interpretation of the freedom of conscience given in the Belarus legislation refers to the freedom of conviction to determine freely one's attitude towards religion, and to profess a religion or not.

968. The Law on religious activity establishes freedom from coercion (Article 3). The activity of religious associations is not allowed if they coerce individuals to become their members or impede them freely leaving the association (paragraph 13). The coercion of members to alienate their property in favour of religious associations is prohibited (paragraph 14).

969. The requirement of paragraph 4 of Article 18 of the ICCPR to have respect for the liberty of parents and, when applicable, legal guardians to ensure the religious and moral education of their children in conformity with their own convictions is reflected in the Law on religious activity. The head of a religious association is obligated to take measures to prevent the involvement of minors in the activity of their organization if one of the parents or the legal guardian objects. The provision of the ICCPR under consideration was reflected in the Law on the rights of the child of Kazakhstan. The religious views of the child are based on the religious convictions of the parents; coercive measures to involve children in the religion are prohibited (Article 35 of the Law on children's rights). Noteworthy is the fact that those legal provisions were adopted before the ratification of the ICCPR by Kazakhstan.

970. The Constitution of Kazakhstan prohibits the creation and activity of public associations aimed at advocating religious enmity (Article 5(3)) and religious superiority (Article 20(3)), thus establishing the principle of non-discrimination on the grounds of religion and beliefs (Article 14). The activities of foreign religious associations on the territory of Kazakhstan as well as the appointment of the heads of religious associations in the Republic by foreign religious centres shall be carried out in consultation with the relevant state institutions of the Republic (paragraphs 4–5) of Article 5 Constitution).

971. As a general constitutional rule, the formation and the activity of public associations must be prohibited if they act to change the constitutional system violently, to destroy the integrity of the Republic, to undermine the security of the state, to incite social, race, ethnic, religious, class and tribal enmity, or to create unauthorized paramilitary units (Article 5(3)). This provision implies the activity of religious organizations as well and in particular covers the limitations on their formation and functionality. As recognized by the Resolution of the Constitutional Council, the right to profess religion in an association can be limited by law in accordance with the Constitution.

972. Kazakhstan legislation accepts different varieties of religious activity. The Law on Religious Activity and Religious Associations allows individuals to practice as missionaries (citizens, foreigners, stateless persons) after official registration at state bodies (Article 8). Religious associations can be at the local, regional and national level (Article 12). The creation of religious associations needs official registration if the numbers of people initiating the creation and other factors satisfy the requirements prescribed by law. For example, the organization of a religious association at the local level needs fifty citizens initiating its creation within one region (*oblast*), a city of national importance, or the capital.

973. Conscientious objection is not allowed in the Republic. According to the provisions of Article 36 of the Constitution, the defence of the Republic shall be a sacred duty and the responsibility of every citizen. Citizens of the Republic shall perform military service according to the procedure and in the forms established by law. Additionally, the Law on religious activity and religious associations asserts that no one has the right to refuse to perform duties prescribed by the Constitution and laws of the Republic of Kazakhstan (Article 3(7)). It is generally accepted that Kazakhstan is one of the ten largest countries in the world yet with only a small population; its shortage of population for the protection of state security can justify the duty to perform military service.

974. By way of concluding remarks, Kazakhstan does not have any historical precedent for regulating religious matters; one reason for this being the prohibition of religion during the time of Soviet rule. Moreover, the nomadic background of Kazakhs allows for religious tolerance and the cultural and traditional basis for peace. A mosque is separated from power. As we have seen in the legislative practice of contemporary Kazakhstan, some matters, for example, the child's rights in religion, were regulated before the ratification of the ICCPR. Religion in Kazakhstan is becoming a new social force and a new movement in Kazakhstan; this requires a comprehensive dialogue with people, as well as identifying the problems in the enjoyment of this freedom.

Appendix I. List of National Institutions in Kazakhstan for the Protection of Human Rights Created[273]

No	*The Name of the Institution*	*Date of the Document Regulating the Current Legal Status*	*The Competence of the Institute*	*Embodied in the Structure Of*
1	The Commission on Citizenship	Decree of the President of the Republic of 10 October 2006 No. 198	The consultative-advisory body for preliminary consideration of materials on the granting, restoration and renunciation of citizenship, and the granting of political asylum	The Office of the President of Kazakhstan
2	The Commission on Amnesty	Decree of the President of the Republic of 5 July 2006 No. 140	The consultative-advisory body for preliminary consideration of materials on amnesty	The Office of the President of Kazakhstan

273. The institutions in the table are enumerated chronologically. The table does not pretend to cover all state commissions and institutions that exist in the Republic of Kazakhstan.

Appendix I

No	*The Name of the Institution*	*Date of the Document Regulating the Current Legal Status*	*The Competence of the Institute*	*Embodied in the Structure Of*
3	The Commissioner for Human Rights of Kazakhstan	Statute on Commissioner for Human Rights, approved by the Decree of the President of the Republic of 19 September 2002 No. 947	The official who supervises the observance of human rights and freedoms, within the competence takes measures to restore infringements.	Independent; complements existing state measures for the protection of human rights
4	The Commission on Human Rights	Decree of the President of the Republic of Kazakhstan of 19 March 2003 No. 1042	The consultative-advisory body that assists the President of Kazakhstan to realize the constitutional competence as a guarantor of human rights and freedoms recognized and guaranteed in accordance with the Constitution of the Republic.	The Office of the President of Kazakhstan

No	*The Name of the Institution*	*Date of the Document Regulating the Current Legal Status*	*The Competence of the Institute*	*Embodied in the Structure Of*
5	The National Commission For Women's Affairs And Family Demographic Policy	Decree of the President of Kazakhstan of 1 February 2006 No. 56	Different aspects of state policy on family matters, and the equality of men and women. Can demand official investigations into alleged violations of the laws on the equality of sexes, family matters and demography. Makes relevant legislative proposals. Considers the complaints of citizens and demands that the responsible state offices take necessary measures.	The Office of the President of Kazakhstan
6	The National Coordinating Council for the Elimination of the Worst Forms of Child Labour	Order of the Minister of Labour and Social Protection of Population of the Republic of 31 March 2006 No. 73-п	Coordinates the activities of state bodies regarding the elimination of the worst forms of child labour; dissemination of information; provides leadership and political support for the relevant state bodies and organizations	Ministry of Labour and Social Protection of the Population

Appendix I

No	*The Name of the Institution*	*Date of the Document Regulating the Current Legal Status*	*The Competence of the Institute*	*Embodied in the Structure Of*
7	The Interdepartmental Commission on Juvenile Affairs and the Protection of their Rights	Resolution of the Government of Kazakhstan of 24 May 2007 No. 415	The consultative-advisory body is aimed to develop proposals for the realization of state policy on prevention of offences, child neglect and homelessness among juveniles, for protection of rights and legal interests of juveniles and children	The Government of Kazakhstan
8	The Commission on Issues of Non-Proliferation of Weapons Of Mass Destruction	Decree of the President of the Republic of Kazakhstan of 11 January 2010 No. 915	The consultative-advisory bodies aimed at the realization of further strengthening the role of Kazakhstan in the field of non-proliferation and developing ideas on non-proliferation	The Office of the President of Kazakhstan
9	The Committee for the Protection of the Children's Rights	Order of the Minister of Education and Science of the Republic of Kazakhstan of 7 June 2016 No. 132-K	Realizes the state policy for ensuring the protection of children's rights and carries out regulation, implementation and control on the issues	The Ministry of Education and Science of the Republic of Kazakhstan

Appendix II. List of International Treaties on the Protection of Human Rights Ratified by the Republic of Kazakhstan

No	*Title of the International Treaty*	*Date of International Adoption of the Document*	*Signature by Kazakhstan*	*Accession, Succession, Ratification by Kazakhstan*
1	Convention on the Rights of the Child (CRC)	20 November 1989	16 February 1994	12 August 1994
2	Occupational Safety and Health Convention	22 June 1981		30 July 1996
3	Convention on the Prevention and Punishment of the Crime of Genocide	9 December 1948		26 August 1998
4	International Convention on the Elimination of All Forms of Racial Discrimination (ICERD)	7 March 1966		26 August 1998

Appendix II

No	*Title of the International Treaty*	*Date of International Adoption of the Document*	*Signature by Kazakhstan*	*Accession, Succession, Ratification by Kazakhstan*
5	Convention against Torture and Other Cruel, Inhuman or Degrading Treatment or Punishment (CAT)	10 December 1984		26 August 1998
6	Convention on the Elimination of All Forms of Discrimination against Women (CEDAW)	18 December 1979		26 August 1998
7	Discrimination (Employment and Occupation) Convention	25 June 1958		6 December 1999
8	Freedom of Association and Protection of the Right to Organise Convention	9 July 1948		13 December 2000
9	Tripartite Consultation (International Labour Standards) Convention	21 June 1976		13 December 2000
10	Convention on the Political Rights of Women	20 December 1952	31 March 1953	28 March 2000
11	Convention on the Nationality of Married Women	20 February 1957	11 August 1958	28 March 2000

No	Title of the International Treaty	Date of International Adoption of the Document	Signature by Kazakhstan	Accession, Succession, Ratification by Kazakhstan
12	The Forced Labour Convention	28 June 1930		18 May 2001
13	Right to Organise and Collective Bargaining Convention	1 July 1949		18 May 2001
14	Equal Remuneration Convention	29 June 1951		18 May 2001
15	Abolition of Forced Labour Convention	25 June 1957		18 May 2001
16	Minimum Age Convention	26 June 1973		18 May 2001
17	OP to The Convention on the Rights of the Child on the Sale of Children, Child Prostitution and Child Pornography (OP-CRC-SC)	25 May 2000	6 September 2000	24 Aug 2001
18	OP to Convention on the Elimination of All Forms of Discrimination against Women (OP – CEDAW)	6 October 1999	6 September 2000	24 Aug 2001
19	Worst Forms of Child Labour Convention	17 June 1999		26 February 2003

Appendix II

No	*Title of the International Treaty*	*Date of International Adoption of the Document*	*Signature by Kazakhstan*	*Accession, Succession, Ratification by Kazakhstan*
20	OP to The Convention on the Rights of the Child on the Involvement of Children in armed conflict (OP-CRC-AC)	25 May 2000	6 September 2000	10 April 2003
21	International Covenant on Civil and Political Rights (ICCPR)	16 December 1966	2 December 2003	24 January 2006
22	International Covenant on Economic, Social and Cultural Rights (ICESCR)	16 December 1966	2 December 2003	24 January 2006
23	Convention for the Suppression of the Traffic in Persons and of the Exploitation of the Prostitution of Others	21 March 1950	17 November 2004	24 January 2006
24	United Nations Convention against Transnational Organized Crime	15 November 2000	13 December 2000	31 July 2008

No	*Title of the International Treaty*	*Date of International Adoption of the Document*	*Signature by Kazakhstan*	*Accession, Succession, Ratification by Kazakhstan*
25	Protocol to Prevent, Suppress and Punish Trafficking in Persons, Especially Women and Children, supplementing the United Nations Convention Against Transnational Organized Crime	15 November 2000		31 July 2008
26	OP to Convention against Torture and Other Cruel, Inhuman or Degrading Treatment or Punishment (OP – CAT)	18 December 2002	25 September 2007	22 October 2008
27	The Slavery Convention signed at Geneva on 25 September 1926 and amended by the Protocol	7 September 1953		1 May 2008

Appendix II

No	*Title of the International Treaty*	*Date of International Adoption of the Document*	*Signature by Kazakhstan*	*Accession, Succession, Ratification by Kazakhstan*
28	Supplementary Convention on the Abolition of Slavery, the Slave Trade, and Institutions and Practices Similar to Slavery	7 September 1956		1 May 2008
29	International Convention for the Protection of All Persons from Enforced Disappearance (CED)	20 December 2006		27 February 2009
30	OP to the International Covenant on Civil and Political Rights (OP – ICCPR)	16 December 1966	25 September 2007	30 June 2009
31	OP to the International Covenant on Economic, Social and Cultural Rights (OP-ICESCR)	10 December 2008	23 September 2010	
32	Convention on the Rights of Persons with Disabilities (CPRD)	13 December 2006	11 December 2008	21 April 2015

No	*Title of the International Treaty*	*Date of International Adoption of the Document*	*Signature by Kazakhstan*	*Accession, Succession, Ratification by Kazakhstan*
33	OP to the Convention on the Rights of Persons with Disabilities (OP-CPRD)	13 December 2006	11 December 2008	
34	Second Optional Protocol to the International Covenant on Civil and Political Rights, Aiming at the Abolition of the Death Penalty	15 December 1989	23 September 2020	

Appendix II

Selected Bibliography

Amandykova, S. *Sistemoobrazuyushie zennosti 'Mangilik El'* (*Backbone values of 'Mangilik El'*). Available at: http://www.enu.kz/ru/info/novosti-enu/32499/ (accessed 20 June 2019).

Auanasova, A. & Ye. Nurpeisov. *Institut Prsidentstva – shag k demokratocheskim peremenam* (*The Institute of Presidency – Step Towards the Democratic Changes*), Newspaper *Kazakhstanskaya Pravda* of 30 November 2018.

Baymakhanov, M. *The Constitutional Reform: Searches and Finds*. In Selected Works on Theory of State and Law. Almaty: Adilet High Law School, 2003, 356–362.

Conte, A. & R. Burchill. *Defining Civil and Political Rights. The Jurisprudence of the United Nations Human Rights Committee*. 2nd edn. London: Ashgate Publishing Co., 2009, 85.

Kak rabotayut yuvenalnye sudy v. Kazakhstante (*How the Juvenile Court Function in Kazakhstan*), https://www.zakon.kz/4879865-kak-rabotayut-yuvenalnye-sudy-v.html (accessed 9 April 2019).

Koghamov, M.Ch. *Comments to General Procedure Code of the Republic of Kazakhstan. Common and Special Parts*. Almaty: Zhety Zhargy, 2008.

Konstituziya Respubliki Kazakhstan. Nauchno-pravovoy kommentaryi (*Constitution of the Republic of Kazakhstan. Scientific Legal Commentary*). Prepared by the Constitutional Council of the Republic of Kazakhstan, 10, Almaty, 2010.

Lillich, R. 'The Paris Minimum Standards of Human Rights Norms in a State of Emergency'. *The American Journal of International Law* 79, no. 4 (1985): 1072–1081.

Mathieu, B. *The Right to Life in European Constitutional and International Case-Law.* Council of Europe Publishing, France, April 2006, 44, 95.

Nazarbayev, N. *The Kazakhstan Way.* Karaganda: Arko, 2006.

Nazarbayev, N. *Era of Independence*. Astana, 2017.

Nazarbayev, N. *The Course Towards the Future: Modernization of Kazakhstan's Identity* of 12 April 2017, http://www.akorda.kz/ru/events/akorda_news/press_conferences/statya-glavy-gosudarstva-vzglyad-v-budushchee-modernizaciya-obshchestvennogo-soznaniya (accessed 18 April 2019).

Nowak, M. *UN Covenant on Civil and Political Rights. CCPR Commentary.* 2nd edn, Germany: N.P. Engel Publisher, 2005.

Nurghaliyeva, Ye.N. & M.Kh Khassenov. *Labour Law in Kazakhstan.* Alphen aan den Rijn: Wolters Kluwer, 2017.

Selected Bibliography

Sapargaliyev, G. 'Nekotorye konzeptualnye idei o gosudarstvennom ustroistve, o prinzipe razdeleniya gosudarstvennoy vlasti na vetvi' ('Some Conceptual Ideas about the State System, and the Principle of Separation of Power into Branches'). *The Bulletin of the Institute of Legislation of the Republic of Kazakhstan* 5, no. 1 (2007): 5–17, 5.

Sapargaliyev, G. *The Constitutional Law of the Republic of Kazakhstan. Academic Course.* Almaty: Zhety Zharghy, 2002.

Schutter, O. *International Human Rights Law. Cases, Materials, Commentary.* Cambridge, UK: Cambridge University Press, 2010.

Carlson, S.N & G. Gisvold. *Practical Guide to the International Covenant on Civil and Political Rights.* Ardsley, NY: Transnational Publishers, 2003.

Seydgaparov, K. *Modernizaziya ugolovnogo processa: pervye rezultaty* (*Modernization of the Penal Proceedings: The First Results*). Newspaper *Kazakhstanskaya pravda* of 27 September 2018.

Sen, A. *Normative Evaluation and Legal Analogues*. Public lecture at the School of Law of Washington University in St. Louis, at a conference on Norms and the Law, on 31 March 2011, https://www.cambridge.org/core/books/norms-and-the-law/AD942F5BFA60095DC909DFF7211207EC (accessed 20 March 2019).

Shangirbayeva, B. *Rol gosudarstva v mejdunarodnom pravotvorchestve* (*The Role of State in* International Lawmaking), Dissertation for the Candidate's Degree in Jurisprudence. Astana: Kazakh Law University of the Humanities, 2007.

Shangirbayeva, B. *Problemy sovershenstvovaniya nazionalnogo zakonodatelstva po voprosam uchastiya Respubliki Kazakhstan v mejdunarodnom pravotvorchestve* (*The Problems of Development of the National Legislation of Kazakhstan on Its Participation in International Lawmaking*, *Materials of International Scientific Conference 'National Legislation of the Republic of Kazakhstan: The Ways of Development'*), The Institute of legislation, The Ministry of Justice of Kazakhstan, 150–153. Astana, 2008.

Shangirbayeva, B. *The Impact of the Implementation of the International Covenant on Civil and Political Rights on the Protection of Human Rights in Kazakhstan.* PhD dissertation, Pisa: Sant'Anna School of Advanced Studies, July 2013.

Shangirbayeva, B. *Obychnoe pravo i institute byiev. Rol dlya implementazii prava na spravedlivoe razbiratelstvo v sovremennom Kazakhstane* (*Customary Law of Kazakhs and the Institute of Biys. Their Role in the Implementation of the Right to a Fair Trial in Contemporary Kazakhstan*). Amanach 'Via Evrasia', Eurasia Center of Sofia University (Bulgaria). Available at: http://www.viaevrasia.com/documents/37.%20BEIBIT%20SHANGIRBAYEVA,%20VIA%20EVRASIA,%202016,%205.pdf (2017).

Simmons, A. Beth. *Mobilizing for Human Rights: International Law in Domestic Politics.* Cambridge: Cambridge University Press, 2009.

Skvorzov, V. & E. Silantyeva. 'Protest Movements and Human Rights: Political, Social-Economic, Cultural Sources'. *Legal Reform in Kazakhstan* 56, no. 4 (2011): 67.

Tokayev, K.-J. *Svet i ten/Light and Shadow*, vol. 4. Almaty, 2017, 146–247.

Tokayev, K.-J. *He Makes History. Essays of Kazakhstani Diplomat*. Almaty: Foliant, 2018, 185–190.

Tokayev, K.-J. *V sisteme obrazovaniya nelzya provodit neobdumannye eksperimenty/Hasty Experiments in the System of Education Should Not Be Conducted*, http://www.parlam.kz/ru/senate/press-center/article/30315 (accessed 2 April 2018).

Zimanov, S. *The Parliament of the Republic of Kazakhstan in the Difficult Years of Proclamation of Independence.* Almaty: Alash Baspasy, 2011.

What Is a Fair Trial? A Basic Guide to Legal Standards and Practice. Lawyers Committee for Human Rights. March 2000, http://www.humanrightsfirst.org/wp-content/uploads/pdf/fair_trial.pdf (accessed 9 April 2019).

Internet Resources

'Bolashak' International Scholarship of the President Nazarbayev: https://www.bolashak.gov.kz/en/.

The Constitutional Council of the Republic of Kazakhstan: https://ksrk.gov.kz/en.

The Foreign Investors' Council: https://fic.kz/en.

The Interparliamentary Assembly of Member Nations of the CIS: https://iacis.ru/iacis-eng.

The *Mazhilis* of the Parliament of the Republic of Kazakhstan: https://www.parlam.kz/en/mazhilis.

The National Center of Legal Information: http://www.zqai.kz/ru/node/4172.

The Office of the Prime Minister: https://primeminister.kz/en.

The President of the Republic of Kazakhstan: https://www.akorda.kz/en.

The Senate of the Parliament of the Republic of Kazakhstan: http://senate.parlam.kz/en-US.

The Standard Control Bank of the Normative Legal Acts: http://zan.gov.kz/client/#.

Index

The numbers here refer to paragraph numbers.

Index

Printed in the USA
CPSIA information can be obtained
at www.ICGtesting.com
LVHW020600170924
791293LV00001B/73

9 789403 546612